The
Greatest
War Stories
Ever Told

The Greatest War Stories Ever Told

Twenty-four Incredible War Tales

EDITED AND WITH AN INTRODUCTION BY
LAMAR UNDERWOOD

THE LYONS PRESS
Guilford, Connecticut
An imprint of The Globe Pequot Press

The Lyons Press is an imprint of The Globe Pequot Press.

10 9 8 7 6 5 4 3

Printed in the United States of America

Designed by Compset, Inc.

ISBN 1-59228-560-0 (paperback)
ISBN 1-58574-239-2 (hardcover)

Library of Congress Cataloging-in-Publication Data is available on file.

To the Fallen

The tumult and the shouting dies;
The captains and the kings depart;
Still stands Thine ancient sacrifice,
An humble and contrite heart.
Lord God of Hosts, be with us yet,
Lest we forget–lest we forget!
                    –Rudyard Kipling,
                    Recessional

Acknowledgments

The Editor's deepest thanks and appreciation goes out to the following people who made this book possible: to Tony Lyons, for coming up with the idea and trusting me to bring it to fruition. To Mark Weinstein, the Lyons Press editor who nursed the book through every stage of production. To Fred Courtright, for his coordination with the many fine publishers represented to obtain permissions. And to my wife Debbie for the stacks of pages she copied from innumerable works to give our readers the great selections that make up our contents.

                                        –Lamar Underwood

Contents

Introduction

High and dangerous action teaches us to believe as right beyond dispute things for which our doubting minds are slow to find words of proof; out of heroism grows faith in the worth of heroism.

—Justice Oliver Wendell Holmes

BOOTS. THEY TREAD heavily upon my soul. I am haunted by the images of boots.

The boots that flicker through my mind's eye are frozen there from the pages of books, newspapers, and magazines. Sometimes they are remembered from segments of film, shown on television, when the camera paused in its relentless searching and held on a scene about which the photographer's eye was clearly saying, "Don't miss this. Don't forget this."

To me, photographs and film of the boots of fallen soldiers seem to instantly create a deeper sense of sadness and empathy than any full picture of their savaged bodies could convey. Often, the boots are all one sees, protruding with numbing stillness from tarps, ponchos, discarded blankets and clothing, piles of battlefield junk—anything that was handy to hide the full view of the horror that has recently occurred there. Sometimes too, from Mathew Brady's Civil War photos to today's newsreels, the boots seem to be emphatic survivors, untouched on limbs torn asunder, the boots muddy perhaps but bloodless on the fringes of blood-soaked ground or pavement. And then there are the occasions—we've all seen them—when the boots lie waiting in neat, almost-ceremonial rows where the bodies have been gathered.

I stare at the boots and wonder: How many hours had gone by since those boots had been pulled on? Were the fingers that tied them nervous and expectant, knowing the battle was near? Or was it just another day, the kind where you'll be going where you have to go and doing what you have to do like every day before? What paths had those boots traveled to reach the realms where explosions and death mingled with fear and courage?

As an avid reader of military history, I have become well aware that I am not alone with my melancholy over boots. In this book's excerpt from the chapter "Breathing In" from his superb book *Dispatches,* noted writer Michael Herr describes a ceremony in Vietnam in which boots of the fallen made an interesting centerpiece:

> When the 173rd held services for their dead from Dak To, the boots of the dead men were arranged in formation on the ground. It was an old paratrooper tradition, but knowing that didn't reduce it or make it any less spooky, a company's worth of jump boots standing empty in the dust taking benediction, while the real substance of the ceremony was being bagged and tagged and shipped back home through what they called the KIA Travel Bureau. A lot of people there that day accepted the boots as solemn symbols and went into deep prayer. Others stood around watching with grudging respect, others photographed it and some just thought it was a lot of bitter bullshit.

Whether they are "bullshit" as symbols or not, the boots I find so fascinating are like the universal "walls" we all refer to from time to time: "If they could speak . . ."

I find myself wanting to know the stories the boots could tell us. I want to follow their prints back down the forgotten trails through the distant battlefields of the past, over the beaches and plains, jungles and deserts where battles were won and lost. And, because I find the subject endlessly fascinating, I also wish to follow the wakes of great ships and the contrails of airplanes— back, back to events that helped shape history and our very lives.

I am quite certain that I am not alone with my insatiable appetite for reading about military history and the experience of combat, as depicted in both nonfiction and fiction. Hence the mission of this book: to share with others, in one place, some of the greatest writing I have ever been privileged to read on the subject of war. My standard for "greatest" goes beyond the kind of literary merit that earns high praise from the critical hallways of literary academia. I have sought to find the "greatest" of prose that is both engaging and illuminating; prose that jolts my sensibilities loose from their comfortable moorings and demands that I pay heed; prose that thereby becomes something of a tribute to all those who lived through the real thing, including those who made it home and those who did not.

One of my favorite authors of military history has always been the late S.L.A. Marshall (Brig. Gen., U.S. Army Reserve, Ret.), whose numerous books and articles detailing events of small-unit action during World War Two, Korea, and Vietnam are rightly considered classics. As an army historian actually in the field, interviewing troops and participants sometimes literally before the smoke had cleared from the battlefields, Marshall gave his accounts a sense of realism that only great detail can provide. His prose conveys unsparingly the events of battle as confusion and uncertainty, where random forces collide, recoil, collide again with chance and circumstances more in control than any battle plan or orders being given.

In one of his Vietnam books, *Ambush: The Battle of Dau Tieng,* Marshall put into words what he sees as the most common characteristic shared by all battles, throughout time—the randomness and unpredictability of events. His words seem so on target and important to me that I have obtained permission from his publisher to quote them here:

> As I have written many times, most battles are more like a schoolyard in a rough neighborhood at recess time than a clash between football giants in the Rose Bowl. They are messy, inorganic, and uncoordinated. It is only much later, after the clerks have tidied up their reports and the generals have published their memoirs, that the historian with his orderly mind professes to discern an understandable pattern in what was essentially catch-as-catch-can, if not chaotic, at the time.
>
> Although the clash may be widespread and immediate, what happens in any one sector is all too often almost unrelated to the action of any other. From the firing of the first bullet or shell, units tend to become fractionalized and to fight much for themselves, not simply to survive, but to vindicate that which they too little understand. Within a given company, each platoon may have its own fight virtually in isolation, and within one battalion, each company may get the feeling that it is standing at Armageddon and battling pretty much alone for the Lord.
>
> In this respect, conventional war and irregular operations are far more alike than unalike. Nor does the resemblance end there. I am well aware that the average American who has not been to Vietnam believes that the war there has nothing in common with operations against the North Koreans and Communist Chinese, against the Japanese in World War II, or the Germans in 1918. The military analyst who has worked all these fields is far more impressed by the identicalness of features, the similarity of problems, the grinding repetition of historical incident.

As your editor, it is my strong hunch that in reading the stories of this collection, including a powerful excerpt from one of Marshall's books, you will be struck more than once by accounts of action that seem to confirm his views. Perhaps Tacitus had it right long before Marshall, back in A.D. 54: "Valor

is of no service, chance rules all, and the bravest often fall by the hands of cowards." From Waterloo to Dau Tieng, the similarity between battles seems to be
the randomness—the heavy hand of fate. Even so, events time and again reveal
that men and women who were prepared to fight and did their duty could be
victorious—over their enemies and their fears. As Damon Runyon joked,
"The race is not always to the swift, nor the battle to the strong, but that's the
way to bet."

—Lamar Underwood
March, 2001

The Cornfield

From *The Army of the Potomac: Mr. Lincoln's Army*

BY BRUCE CATTON

BRUCE CATTON'S (1899–1978) Civil War trilogy, *The Army of the Potomac,* including *Mr. Lincoln's Army, Glory Road,* and the Pulitzer Prize–winning *A Stillness at Appomattox* (1953), is a towering achievement of great prose and illuminating history. Catton's words literally hurl the reader back through the years in a sort of literary time capsule. Reading Catton, you are *there,* on the battlefields, in the commanders' tents, alongside the marching men.

This excerpt from *Mr. Lincoln's Army* is but a portion of Catton's moving and detailed account of the bloodiest single day of fighting on American soil, alternately called "The Battle of Antietam," or sometimes, simply "Sharpsburg." On September 16, 1862, the outskirts of this small Maryland town and nearby Antietam Creek were the scene of a one-day battle of staggering casualties in which a profoundly important opportunity for the Union Army to cripple the Confederate forces and shorten the war was lost.

On September 12, in the vicinity of Frederick, Maryland, Union General George McClellan's troops had discovered a paper, wrapped around three cigars, that had been inadvertently dropped or misplaced by some Confederate officer. The paper was dated September 9 and provided a stunning testament of the disposition of Robert E. Lee's armies along the Potomac River.

McClellan maneuvered his forces—too slowly, some critics claim— toward the area where he hoped to attack Lee's strung-out divisions and cut them to shreds. On September 15, McClellan was in position near the town of Sharpsburg, not far from the Potomac River, where Lee's main body of troops was located.

Bruce Catton describes the setting:

As one comes up the hill on the road from Boonsboro, after crossing the creek and just before entering the town, there is the National Cemetery, green and well kept, white headstones marking the places where many dead men lie in orderly military formations, with pleasant trees casting broken shadows on the lawn. It is a large cemetery, and it was not there at all on the morning of September 16, 1862; there was nothing there then but the broad crest and the peaceful grove with the spires and roofs of Sharpsburg half hidden beyond. If a man stood in this grove and looked to the north he could see the white block of the little Dunker church, a mile away, beside the Hagerstown Pike. And on that September morning in 1862, anyone who looked at the church would have seen two bits of woodland lying near it—one west of the Hagerstown road, surrounding the church on three sides and stretching northward for half a mile or more, and the other east of the road, separated from it by open fields, several hundred yards wide. Two quieter bits of woodland could not have been found in North America, and no one outside the immediate neighborhood had ever heard of them; no one had ever taken human life in either of them. But ever since then, because of what was about to take place there, the two wood lots have had a grim, specialized fame and have been known in innumerable books and official records as the West Wood and the East Wood—as if, in all that countryside, there were not other bits of wood that lay just east and west of a country road. In the same way, there was a forty-acre cornfield lying on the east side of the road, between the two plots of trees, which ever since has simply been *the* cornfield, as if there had never been any other.

The woods have been cut down since then, and where the cornfield used to be there is a macadamized roadway flanked by gleaming, archaic-looking monuments and statues, with little markers here and there unobtrusively beckoning for attention. But in the fall of 1862 no one was dreaming of statues, and because they had had good growing weather the corn was in fine shape—more than head-high, strong, richly green, the tall stalks waving in the last winds of summer.

Mr. Catton has set the scene for us. Now it is the evening of September 15, and we are with the Union troops, expecting battle on the morrow, but hoping to get some sleep. And so to begin:

★   ★   ★   ★   ★

It wasn't a very good night for sleeping. It began to rain after the sun went down, and there were intermittent spells of what one veteran recalled as "dismal, drizzling rain" all through the night; and out in front the pickets were nervous, opening up now and then with a blaze of firing that occasionally stirred some of the batteries and caused them to join in, although it was too dark for the gunners to hit much of anything. The gunfire rose to such a pitch, once, that an aide roused Hooker and called him out of his tent, fearing that the Rebels might be beginning a night attack. Hooker stood in the farmyard and listened, the raindrops glistening on his florid, handsome face, and looked at the spurts of flame off in the dark, estimating the direction of the fire. Then he shook his head. "The Rebels must be firing into their own men—we haven't any troops off that way," he said. Then he went back to bed.

There was a tension in the atmosphere for the whole army that night. Survivors wrote long afterward that there seemed to be something mysteriously ominous in the very air—stealthy, muffled tramp of marching men who could not be seen but were sensed dimly as moving shadows in the dark; outbursts of rifle fire up and down the invisible picket lines, with flames lighting the sky now and then when gunners in the advanced batteries opened fire; taut and nervous anxiety of those alert sentinels communicating itself through all the bivouacs, where men tried to sleep away the knowledge that the morrow would bring the biggest battle the army had ever had, a ceaseless, restless sense of movement, as if the army stirred blindly in its sleep, with the clop-clop of belated couriers riding down the inky-dark lanes heard at intervals, sounding very lonely and far off. The 16th Connecticut, a new and almost completely untrained regiment, which was lying along the Antietam near the downstream bridge, fell into a panic and sprang wildly to arms once when some clumsy rookie accidentally discharged his musket. Veteran regiments nearby cursed them wearily, cursed the high command for banning all campfires—the Rebels had had all day to spot the Union positions, but the top brass had ruled out fires that night for security reasons—and glumly munched the handfuls of ground coffee they couldn't boil. In Richardson's division the men were marched to the ammunition wagons in the darkness to draw eighty rounds per man, twice the usual allotment; they accepted the grim omen in expressionless silence.

Not far from the Pry house Mansfield's corps had turned in for the night. The men had been there since the afternoon of the day before, and they had their pup tents up and were feeling snug; but along toward midnight Mansfield came riding up from the Pry house to corps headquarters and the outfit was summoned to move—no drums and no bugles, just officers going down the regimental streets from tent to tent, quietly rousing the men and telling them to pack up. The sleepy soldiers made up their blanket rolls, took their muskets, and went off in the darkness, crossing the Antietam where Hooker had crossed in the afternoon, and following the guides he had sent back, old Mansfield riding at the head. They stumbled along, blind as moles in the drizzling night, holding their canteens and bayonets as they went, to keep them from jingling, following the obscure roads while the sky to the left was periodically lit by the mock lightning of the fitful cannonade.

They tramped for several miles and finally were halted on somebody's farm to the north and east of where Hooker's men were posted. General Mansfield spread a blanket for himself on the grass in a fence corner next to a field where the 10th Maine had turned in. The Maine boys were wakeful and did a lot of chattering—the march in the rain had roused them, and the thought of what was coming in the morning made it hard to go back to sleep—and the old general got up once and went over to shush them. They recalled that he was nice about it and not at all like a major general: just told them that if they had to talk they might as well do it in a whisper so that their comrades could get a little rest. And at last, long after midnight, there was quiet and the army slept a little.

How far they had marched, those soldiers—down the lanes and crosslots over the cornfields to get into position, and from the distant corners of the country before that; they were marching, really, out of one era and into another, leaving much behind them, going ahead to much that they did not know about. For some of them there were just a few steps left: from the rumpled grass of a bed in a pasture down to a fence or a thicket where there would be an appointment with a flying bullet or shell fragment, the miraculous and infinitely complicated trajectory of the man meeting the flat, whining trajectory of the bullet without fail. And while they slept the lazy, rainy breeze drifted through the East Wood and the West Wood and the cornfield, and riffled over the copings of the stone bridge to the south, touching them for the last time before dead men made them famous. The flags were all furled and the bugles stilled, and the hot metal of the guns on the ridges had cooled, and the army was asleep—tenting tonight on the old camp ground, with never a song to cheer because the voices that might sing it were all stilled on this most crowded and most lonely of fields. And whatever it may be that nerves men to die for a flag or a phrase or a man or an inexpressible dream was drowsing with them, ready to wake with the dawn.

The morning came in like the beginning of the Last Day, gray and dark and tensely expectant. Mist lay on the ground, heavy as a fog in the hollow places, and the groves and valleys were drenched in immense shadows. For a brief time there was an ominous hush on the rolling fields, where the rival pickets crouched behind bushes and fence corners, peering watchfully forward under damp hatbrims. Little by little things began to be visible. The outlines of trees and farm buildings slowly came into focus against blurred backgrounds; the pickets grew more wary and alert, and when one of them saw movement in the half-light he raised his musket and fired. The two armies, lying so close in the rainy night, had been no more than half asleep; once aroused, they began to fight instinctively, as if knowing that the very moment of waking must lead to the fatal embrace of battle.

The random picket-firing increased as the light grew, and the advanced batteries were drawn into it. On the high ground around the Dunker church Stonewall Jackson had massed his artillery, and the gunners were astir early. As soon as they could see any details on the ridges to the north they sprang to their places and fired, and the men who were still in bivouac could feel the earth beneath them tremble faintly with the jar of the firing. Farther west, half a mile from the dusty line of the Hagerstown road, Jeb Stuart's horse artillery was drawn up on a wooded hill. When Jackson's guns opened, these guns began firing, too, and to the north and east the Yankee gunners returned the fire. Long before six o'clock the air shook with the rolling, rocking crash of gunfire.

Joe Hooker was up promptly, riding to the front before the light came. The men of his army corps had slept in a sheltered valley which ran eastward from the Hagerstown road, a mile or more north of the Dunker church, and Hooker went south through the bivouac, coming out on a wooded ridge and studying the landscape in the misty twilight. In front of him there was a broad field, sloping gently down to a hollow where there were an orchard, a patchwork of kitchen gardens and fences, and a big stone house, the home of a prosperous farmer named Miller. On the far side of the hollow, where the ground began to rise again, Mr. Miller had built a stout post-and-rail fence, going due east from the Hagerstown road to the edge of that pleasant grove which the generals were noting on their maps as the East Wood; and south of the fence, filling all of the ground between the road and the wood, was Mr. Miller's thriving cornfield—*the* cornfield, forever, after that morning. Beyond the cornfield and a little less than a mile from his present position Hooker could just see the white block of the Dunker church, framed by the dark growth of the West Wood. The high ground marked by that church was his objective; if it could be seized and held, Lee's whole army would have to retreat.

Hooker was an army politician and a devious man, approaching his ultimate goal—command of the Army of the Potomac—by round-about ways which he discussed with nobody; but as a fighter he was direct and straightforward, and it was direct, straightforward fighting that was called for this morning. His army corps was camped due north of the Dunker church plateau; it would get there in the obvious way—by marching straight south, with Doubleday's division going along the Hagerstown road, Ricketts's division going through the East Wood, and Meade's Pennsylvanians going in between them. Each division would be massed so that reinforcements from the rear ranks could be hurried up to the front line quickly. Mansfield's corps was not far away and could be called on if Hooker's men needed help. Neither Hooker nor anyone else knew how many Rebels might be waiting in the cornfield and the wood. This was one of the things the advancing battle lines would have to find out for themselves. Meanwhile, it was time to get moving.

It was still early, and the gray light of the dawn was still dim. The army was awake, the men coming reluctantly out of sleep to the sound of the guns, knowing that this fight was going to be worse than anything they had ever been in before. Aroused by the cannon, the men reacted in their different ways. The 1st Minnesota, still safely behind the lines near McClellan's headquarters, noted the mist and the cloudy sky and profanely gave thanks that they would at least be fighting in the shade this day. (They were wrong, as it turned out; in another hour or two the mist would vanish and there would be a scorching sun all day.) Abner Doubleday found the men of his division hard to rouse; they took up their muskets and fell into ranks sluggishly, and they did not even grumble when they were marched off without time to boil coffee. Over in Mansfield's corps there was less of a rush and the men cooked sketchy breakfasts. There were many new regiments in this corps, and the veterans—quietly handing valuables and trinkets to members of the ambulance corps and other non-combat details for safekeeping—noticed with grim amusement that most of the straw-feet were too nervous to eat. In the 27th Indiana men stood up by · their campfires to jeer and curse at one desperate soldier whose nerves had given way, out on the picket line, and who was running madly for the rear, oblivious of the taunts and laughter—a man whose legs had simply taken control of him. From one end of the army to the other, bivouacs were littered with discarded decks of cards. Card games were held sinful in that generation, and most men who were about to fight preferred not to have these tangible evidences of evil on their persons when they went out to face death.

The men of Hooker's army corps left their bivouac and in heavy columns made their way through the timber to the ridge which was to be their jumping-off point. Some of the columns could be seen by the distant Confederate gunners, and the shells came over faster—the men had hardly started when one of Stuart's guns put a shell right in the middle of the 6th Wisconsin, knocking out thirteen men and bringing the column to a halt while stretcher-bearers ran in to carry off the wounded. The 90th and 107th Pennsylvania, moving up toward the outer fringe of the East Wood, also came within Stuart's range and had losses; and men were maimed for life who saw no more of the battle than a peaceful field and a sandy lane in the wood in the early light of dawn. As they reached the ridge the leading elements of the divisional columns sent out skirmish lines, and in the broad hollow of the Miller farm the sporadic pop-pop of picket firing became much heavier while the skirmish lines went down the slope—each man in the line separated from his fellows by half a dozen paces, holding his musket as if he were a quail hunter with a shotgun, moving ahead step by step, dropping to one knee to shoot when he found a target, pausing to reload, and then moving on again, feeling the army's way into the danger zone.

Rebel skirmishers held the Miller farm in some strength, and there were many more along the fence by the cornfield. The sound of the musket fire suddenly rose to a long, echoing crash that ran from the highway to the East Wood and back again. The Confederate batteries to the south and off to the right stepped up the pace, and the shells came over faster. Beyond the hollow ground the green cornfield swayed and moved, although there was no wind. The glint of bayonets could be seen here and there amid the leafage, and long, tearing volleys came out of the corn, while wreaths of yellowish-white smoke drifted up above it as if the whole field were steaming. More men were hurt, and the Yankee skirmishers halted and took cover.

There was a pause, while the battle lines waited under fire. Then there was a great rush and a pounding of hoofs as Hooker's corps artillery dashed up into line—six batteries coming up at a mad gallop, gun carriages bouncing wildly with spinning wheels, drivers lashing the six-horse teams, officers riding on ahead and turning to signal with flashing swords when they reached the chosen firing line. In some of these batteries orders for field maneuvers were given by bugle, and the high thin notes could be heard above all the racket, the teams wheeling in a spatter of rising dust—veteran artillery horses knew what the bugle calls meant as well as the men did, and would obey without waiting to be told. In a few minutes three dozen guns were lined up on the slope, limbers a dozen yards to the rear, teamsters taking the horses back into the wood, gun crews busy with ramrod and handspike. The guns began to plaster the cornfield unmercifully, and the air above the field was filled with clods of dirt and flying cornstalks and knapsacks and broken muskets as the canister ripped the standing grain.

Far off to the left, beyond the Antietam, McClellan's long-range rifles came into action, hammering hard at the Rebel guns by the Dunker church and reaching out to plow the cornfield with a terrible cross fire of shell and solid shot; and the waiting Federal infantry hugged the ground, half dazed by the tremendous waves of noise. Hooker exaggerated a little, but only a little, when he wrote afterward that "every stalk in the northern and greater part of the field was cut as closely as could have been done with a knife"; and he exaggerated not at all when he wrote that in all the war he never looked upon "a more bloody, dismal battlefield." The Confederates in the northern part of the cornfield went down in rows, scores at a time. Then after a while the great thunder of the guns died down a little and the Yankee infantry went forward.

It all looks very simple and orderly on the map, where the advance of the I Corps is represented by a straight line following neat little arrows, three divisions moving snugly abreast and everyone present presumably knowing at all times just what was going on and what the score was. But in reality there was nothing simple or orderly about any part of it. Instead there was an appalling confusion of shattering sound, an unending chaos of violence and heat and intense combat, with fields and thickets wrapped in shifting layers of blinding smoke so that no man could know and understand any more of what was happening than the part he could see immediately around him. There was no solid connected battle line neatly ranked in clear light; there was a whole series of battle lines swaying haphazardly in an infernal choking fog, with brigades and regiments standing by themselves and fighting their enemies where they found them, attack and counterattack taking place in every conceivable direction and in no recognizable time sequence, Northerners and Southerners wrestling back and forth in the cornfield in one tremendous free-for-all. The black powder used in those days left heavy masses of smoke which stayed on the ground or hung at waist level in long tattered sheets until the wind blew it away, and this smoke deposited a black, greasy film on sweaty skins, so that men who had been fighting hard looked grotesque, as if they had been ineptly made up for a minstrel show.

The fighting surged back and forth from the East Wood to the highway and beyond, and the most any general could do was push new troops in from the rear where they seemed to be needed—or, at times, rally soldiers who were coming disorganized out of action and send them back in again: what was happening up front was beyond anyone's control and depended entirely on the men themselves. And a wild, primitive madness seemed to descend on the men who fought in the cornfield: they went beyond the limits of sanity and endurance at times, Northerners and Southerners alike, until it seems that they tore at each other for the sheer sake of fighting. The men who fought there are all dead now, and it may be that we misinterpret the sketchy accounts which they left of the combat; yet from the diaries and the reports and the histories we get glimpses of what might well have been the most savage and consuming fighting American soldiers ever engaged in.

General Ricketts sent his men in through the East Wood—New York regiments, mostly, with a few from Pennsylvania and Massachusetts—and they fought step by step through the thickets and over the rocky ledges and fallen trees in the misty light of early morning, slowly driving the tenacious Confederates out and swinging around unconsciously until they faced toward the west, so that as they came out of the wood they went into the cornfield, with Stuart's cannon hitting them hard from the western hills. They pulled themselves together on the edge of the cornfield, getting an enfilade fire on a Confederate brigade there and sending it flying; then they advanced again, and as they moved the regiments were separated, each one automatically adjusting its lines to face whatever formation of Rebels might be in front of it. When they got deeper into the field the opposition became heavier, until at last whole brigades were shaken by the deadly, racking volleys—the most terrible fire, one veteran wrote, that they ever had to endure. Rifles were splintered and broken in men's hands, canteens and haversacks were riddled, platoons and companies seemed to dissolve. They closed ranks as well as they could amid the cornstalks, sweating officers gesturing with swords and yelling orders no one could hear in the overpowering racket, and they kept pushing on. They attacked and they were counterattacked; they drove certain Rebels and were themselves driven in turn; at times they exchanged stand-up volleys at incredibly close ranges, wrecking their enemies and seeing their own lines wrecked, while the smoke settled thicker and thicker and they fought in utter blindness.

At last they went back, straggling through the East Wood to reform in the rear—a full third of the division shot down and half of the survivors hopelessly scattered. The 12th Massachusetts—the kid-glove boys from Boston who had brought a great song to the war and carried a noble flag of white and blue and gold presented by the ladies of Beacon Hill—took 334 men into action and lost 220 of them, and when it tried to rally behind the wood fewer than three dozen men were still with the colors. Duryée's brigade of four regiments found hardly a hundred men to form a line when it finished its retreat. For the time being, except for a few valiant fragments which hung on at the edge of the wood, the entire division was out of the fight.

Meade's Pennsylvanians had gone into the cornfield at the center of the line, and their story is just about the same: advance and retreat, charge and countercharge, victory and retreat all blended. Once the center brigade broke under a driving Rebel charge and went streaming toward the rear. Meade came thundering up with the battle fury on him, yanked the 8th Reserve Regiment back into line, hurried it off to a vantage point by Mr. Miller's fence. A Georgia regiment, lying unseen in the corn, let fly with a volley from a distance of thirty feet, knocking out half the regiment at one sweep. The Pennsylvania color-bearer went down with a foot shot off, struggled to his knees, jabbing his flagstaff into the ground, and struck wildly at a comrade who tried to take the colors away from him. A charging Georgian shot him dead and was himself killed by a Pennsylvania lieutenant; and there were wild tumult and heavy smoke and crazy shouting all around, with the entire war narrowed to the focus of this single combat between Pennsylvanians and Georgians. Then the Pennsylvanians broke and ran again—to be stopped, incomprehensibly, a few yards in the rear by a boyish private who stood on a little hillock and kept swinging his hat, shouting: "Rally, boys, rally! Die like men, don't run like dogs!"

Strangely, on that desperate field where men were madly heroic and full of abject panic by turns, this lone private stopped the retreat. What was left of the regiment fell in beside him. Fugitives from other regiments in the shattered brigade fell in with them, and Meade—who had gone galloping away to bring up a battery to plug the gap—came back and got the uncertain line straightened out, while canister from the new battery uprooted green cornstalks and tore the bodies of Rebels who crouched low on the powdery ground. Then presently the brigade went forward again.

Over by the turnpike the Black Hat Brigade charged around the Miller farm buildings, driving out the Confederate skirmishers but breaking apart somewhat as the men surged past dwelling and outhouses under heavy fire. There is a glimpse of a young Wisconsin officer standing by a gap in a fence, waving his sword and crying: "Company E! On the right, by file, into line!" Then a bullet hit him in his open mouth and he toppled over dead in mid-shout; and the brigade got by the obstructions and went into the cornfield near the highway. Here it seemed to be every man for himself. There was Rebel infantry west of the road, pouring in a tremendous fire; some of the men formed a new line facing west, lying down behind the turnpike fence to fight back. Gibbon sent a couple of regiments across the road to deal with this flank attack, and a moment later Doubleday sent four New York regiments over there to help; part of his division was going south through the cornfield and part of it was struggling desperately in the fields and woods to the west, and shells and bullets were coming in from all directions at once. Men said afterward that the bullets seemed to be as thick as hail in a great storm. Formations were lost, regiments and brigades were jumbled up together, and as the men advanced they bent their heads as if they were walking into a driving rain. And under all the deafening tumult there was a soft, unceasing clip-snip-clip of bullets shearing off the leaves and stalks of corn. Near the highway some officer was yelling the obvious—"This fire is murderous!"—and then, at last, the sweating mob of soldiers came out by a fence at the southern edge of the cornfield, and as they did so a long line of Confederates arose from the plowed ground in front of them and the high sound of rifle fire rose to a new intensity.

A terrible frenzy of battle descended on the fighting line. Men were possessed by a hysterical excitement, shouting furiously, bursting out in shrill insane laughter, crowding up to the fence to fire at the Rebel line. A survivor of this attack, recalling the merciless fire that greeted the men at the line of the fence, wrote: "Men, I cannot say fell—they were knocked out of ranks by the dozen." Cartridges were torn with nervous haste. Muskets became foul from much firing, so that men took stones to hammer their ramrods down. Wanting to fire faster than ever before, they found they could not—a nightmare slowness was upon them as the black powder caked in hot rifle barrels. Some soldiers threw their pieces away and took up the rifles of dead men.

All along the fence the men were jostling together, with soldiers in the rear ranks passing loaded rifles forward to the men in front; battle flags waved in sweeping, smoke-fringed arcs, color-bearers swinging the flag staffs frantically, as if the mere fluttering of the colors would help bring victory. Brigades and regiments were all helter-skelter—Pennsylvanians and New Yorkers were jammed in with men from Wisconsin and Massachusetts, everyone was cheering hoarsely, new elements were coming up from the rear to add to the crush along the fence, the noise of battle was one great unending roar louder than anything the men had ever heard before. And at last, as if by common impulse, the whole crowd swarmed forward over the fence and started up the open field toward the Dunker church—very near now, its whitewashed walls all splotched and patchy from flying bullets. The Confederate line, terribly thinned by rifle fire, broke in wild flight. Some of the Southerners tried to escape over the turnpike fences and were left spread-eagled on the rails as the Federals shot them; others fell back into the wood around the church. The Northerners raised a great new shout and went ahead on the run, with victory in sight.

Then, dramatically, from the wood around the church a new Confederate battle line emerged, trotting forward with the shrill yip-yip-yip of the

Rebel yell—John B. Hood's division, swinging into action with an irresistible counterattack.

Hood's men had been pulled out of the front lines late the night before, after their brush with the Pennsylvanians in the East Wood. They had been on short rations for days, and early this morning the commissary department finally caught up with them, delivering ample supplies of bread and meat. The division had been in the act of cooking the first solid meal in a week when word came back that they were needed up front without a moment's delay—the Yankees had broken the line and would have the battle won unless somebody did something about it. So the Texans and Mississippians left their half-cooked breakfasts, grabbed their rifles, and came storming out into the open, mad clean through: and here, within easy range, were the Yankees who were the cause of it all, the Yankees on whom the overmastering anger of hungry men could be vented.

Hood's men drew up and delivered a volley which, said a Federal survivor, "was like a scythe running through our line." It hit the Federals head-on and stopped them. There was a brief pause, and then the Northern soldiers turned and made for the rear on the run, back over the fence and into the raddled cornfield and down the long slope, Hood's men following them with triumphant, jeering shouts, while three brigades from D. H. Hill's command came in from below the East Wood and added their own weight to the pursuit.

Down in the open ground by the Miller house the flight was checked. General Gibbon had brought up old Battery B, and its six brass smoothbores were drawn up in a barnyard west of the road. The Rebels were advancing on both sides of the pike, converging on the barnyard—the Federals west of the road had had to retire when the cornfield was lost—and the guns became a strong point where the beaten soldiers could make a stand again. Some of the fugitives fell in behind the battery, kneeling and firing out between the guns. Gibbon got two of his regiments drawn up farther west, a little ahead of the guns and facing east; General Patrick brought his four New York regiments up amid the crush; and the charging Confederates came out of the corn from the south and east, smashing straight at the battery, firing as they came.

Battery B was pounding away furiously, but Gibbon, looking on with the eye of a gunner, noticed that in the mad excitement the gun crews had let the elevating screws run down so that the guns were pointing up for extreme long range, blasting their charges into the empty air. He shouted and gestured from the saddle, but no one could hear anything in that unearthly din, so he threw himself to the ground, ran to the nearest gun, shouldered the gun crew aside, and spun the little wheel under the breech so that the muzzle slowly sank until it seemed almost to be pointing at the ground. Gibbon stepped aside, the gunner jerked the lanyard, and the gun smashed a section of rail fence, sending the splintered pieces flying in the faces of Hood's men. The other gunners hastily corrected their elevation and fired double-shotted rounds of canister at the range of fifty feet, while the Northern infantry cracked in with volleys of musket fire. In all its history the battery never fired so fast; its haste was so feverish that a veteran regular-army sergeant forgot to step away from his gun when it was discharged, and as it bounded backward in recoil a wheel knocked him down and crushed him.

The front of the Confederate column was blown away, and the survivors withdrew sullenly into what was left of the cornfield. Some of the Federals west of the road raised a yell and went into the cornfield after them, were struck in the flank by unseen Confederates farther south, and came streaming back across the pike again to take shelter among the rocky ledges west of the guns. The Rebels re-formed behind a low ridge, then came on again. A soldier in the 80th New York, helping to defend the battery, called this assault "one of the finest exhibitions of pluck and manhood ever seen on any battlefield." But the heroism served only to swell the casualty lists. There were too many Yankees there and the guns were firing too fast, the charging Rebel line simply melted away under the fire, the men who were not hit ran back into the cornfield again, and for a moment there was something like a breathing spell, while the rival armies lay, as one soldier wrote, "like burnt-out slag" on the battlefield.

Two hours of fighting in one forty-acre field, with the drumming guns never silent for a moment; Northerners and Southerners had fought themselves out, and the fields and woods for miles to the rear were filled with fugitives. A steady leakage had been taking place from each army as all but the stoutest found themselves carried beyond the limit of endurance. The skulkers and the unabashed cowards, who always ran in every battle at the first chance they could get—and there was hardly a regiment, North or South, which did not have a few of them—had drifted away at the first shock. Later others had gone: the men who could stand something but not everything, men who had stood fast in all previous fights but found this one too terrible to be borne; the men who helped wounded comrades to the rear and then either honestly got lost (which was easy to do, in that smoking madness) or found that they could not quite make themselves go back into it. All of these had faded out, leaving the fighting lines dreadfully thin, so that the loss of strength on each side was far greater, just then, than the casualty lists would show. Hooker's corps had lost nearly twenty-five hundred men killed and wounded—a fearful loss, considering that he had sent hardly more than nine thousand into action—but for the moment the story was much worse than that. The number of uninjured men who left the ranks was probably fully as great as the number of casualties. The proud I Corps of the Army of the Potomac was wrecked.

On the Confederate side the story was about the same. The troops who had held the cornfield and East Wood when the fight began had been splintered and smashed and driven to the rear. Their dazed remnants were painfully trying to regroup themselves far behind the Dunker church, fugitives were trailed out all the way back to the Potomac, and field and wood were held now by the reinforcements, Hood's men and D. H. Hill's. There was still fight left in these men, but they had been ground down unmercifully. At the height of his counterattack Hood had sent back word that unless he could be reinforced he would have to withdraw, but that meanwhile he would go on as far as he could. He had gone to the northern limit of the cornfield, had seen the striking spearhead of his division broken by the Yankee guns and rifles around Miller's barnyard, and he was holding on now in grim expectancy of a new Federal attack. The cornfield itself was a hideous spectacle—broken stalks lying every which way, green leaves spattered with blood, ground all torn and broken, littered everywhere with discarded weapons. Inconceivable numbers of dead and wounded lay in all parts of the field, whole ranks of them at the northern border where Hooker's first blasts of cannon fire had caught them— after the battle Massachusetts soldiers said they had found 146 bodies from one Rebel brigade lying in a neat, soldierly line. Hood wrote afterward that on no other field in the whole war was he so constantly troubled by the fear that his horse would step on some helpless wounded man. The Rebel brigades that were in the field when the fighting began had lost about 50 per cent of their numbers.

But there could be no lull. Hooker had Mansfield's corps at his disposal, and when the Rebels drove his men back through the cornfield he sent for it. Old General Mansfield went galloping up to his troops, his hat in his hand, long white hair and beard streaming in the wind. The men in Gordon's brigade jumped up and ran for their rifles as soon as they saw him coming, falling in without waiting for orders, cheering loudly. Something about the old soldier, with his air of competence and his unexpected mixture of stiff military dignity and youthful fire and vigor, had aroused their enthusiasm during the two days he had been with them. Mansfield reined up in front of them, calling: "That's right, boys, cheer—we're going to whip them today!" He rode down the line from regiment to regiment, waving his hat and repeating: "Boys, we're going to lick them today!"

They were a mile and more from the battlefield, and the uproar beat upon their ears as they moved forward. The noise seemed to be coming in great, swinging pulsations, as if whole brigades or divisions were firing successive volleys. The booming of the cannon was continuous, so steady that no individual shots could be heard; and before the field could be seen the men could make out great billowing clouds of smoke drifting up in the windless air. As they got nearer they met wounded men going to the rear—chipper enough, most of them, all things considered, calling out that they "had the Johnnies on the run." Gordon's brigade came out on the ridge near the Miller farm, with the northern border of the cornfield in view. Federal regiments were withdrawing across the hollow, stepping backward, loading and firing as they retreated. One pitiful skeleton of a beaten regiment saw the fresh 27th Indiana coming up behind it. Heedless that they were still under fire, the men shouted with joy, threw caps, knapsacks, and canteens in the air, waving jubilant welcome to the reinforcements; and when the Indiana soldiers came abreast of them the retreating soldiers halted, re-formed ranks, and started back into battle again without orders.

Mansfield went in at the head of his first brigade, heading straight for the northern part of the East Wood. The situation was not at all clear to him, and he halted the column briefly while he tried to make out what was in front of him. Hooker came cantering up, crying: "The enemy are breaking through my lines—you must hold this wood!" Then Hooker rode away and Mansfield started putting his leading regiments, 10th Maine and 128th Pennsylvania, into line of battle. The East Wood presented almost as ghastly a sight as the cornfield, by now—dead and living bodies everywhere, little groups of men trying to help wounded comrades to the rear, shattered limbs of trees lying on the ground in a tangle, wreckage of artillery equipment strewn about, with unseen Rebels keeping the air alive with bullets, and streaky sheets of acrid smoke lying in the air. Nobody knew whether there were Union troops in front or not. The ground was uneven, crossed with rocky ledges and ridges. Organized bodies of troops could be seen in the distance now and then, but the light was bad and the skirmishers, shooting at everything that moved, did not know whether they were firing at friends or enemies.

Brigadier General Samuel Crawford made his way through the wood, trying to get his brigade into line: an unusual man, doctor turned soldier, who had taken an unusual route to his general's commission. He had been a regular-army surgeon before the war and was in the Fort Sumter garrison. Back at the beginning of 1861, when Major Anderson moved the garrison from Moultrie to Sumter, all the line officers being busy, the doctor was posted at a loaded columbiad to sink the Confederate guard boat if it tried to interfere. He didn't have to shoot just then, but either that experience or the later bombardment itself apparently inspired him to give up medicine for line command, and when the garrison came north he got a brigadier's star. His brigade had been badly cut to pieces at Cedar Mountain early this summer, when Pope's advance guard had its first meeting with Stonewall Jackson. Since then Crawford had been vainly writing applications to have the brigade withdrawn for reorganization and recruitment, pointing out that his four regiments numbered only 629 men altogether, with so many officers gone that three of the regiments were in command of inexperienced captains. His 28th New York had been consolidated into four companies and was going into action today with sixty-five men. Crawford had got nowhere with his applications, but a couple of days before this battle the high command had given him three brand-new regiments of Pennsylvania recruits, and with this lopsided command—four understrength regiments of veterans and three big, half-trained regiments of rookies—he was now going into action against Hood and D. H. Hill. Understandably, he was nervous about it.

Most of the enemy fire seemed to be coming from the cornfield at the western edge of the wood, so Crawford wheeled his regiments in that direction. The Rebel skirmishers were playing Indian again, dodging back from tree to tree and ledge to ledge and firing from behind the piles of cordwood that some thrifty farmer had stacked here and there; but the Maine regiment, the veteran 46th Pennsylvania, and the tiny 28th New York finally got to the edge of the wood, with two of the greenhorn regiments struggling up on their right, and began to fire at moving figures among the shattered cornstalks. Mansfield rode up, worried; he still didn't know where the enemy was, and Hooker had given him the impression that Meade's Pennsylvanians were still in the field. He made the Maine regiment cease firing—"You are firing into our own men"—then put his horse over the fence and rode on ahead to get a better look. Some soldier called out, "Those are Rebels, General!" Mansfield took a last look, said: "Yes—you're right"—and then a volley came out of the cornfield. Mansfield's horse was hit, and when the old man dismounted to clamber over the fence he himself got a bullet in the stomach.

Some of the rookies from the 125th Pennsylvania picked him up, made a crude litter of muskets, and got him back into the wood, where they laid him down, uncertain what to do next. They had been soldiers for only a month, this was their first battle, and what did one do with a badly wounded major general, anyhow? Three boys from the 10th Maine took over—as veterans, one gathers, they knew a good excuse to get away from the firing line when they saw it—the Pennsylvanians went back to the fence, and the down-Easters tried to lug the general back to the rear. And they found, in the wood, a bewildered contraband who was company cook in one of Hooker's regiments and who, with a clumsy incompetence rare even among company cooks, had chosen this time and place to lose, and then to hunt for, a prized frying pan. The Maine boys seized him that he might make a fourth at carrying the general, who was heavy and helpless. The contraband demurred—he had to find the captain's frying pan, and nothing else mattered—but the soldiers pounded him with their fists, the whine of ricocheting bullets cutting the air all around, shells crashing through the branches overhead, and he gave in at last and poor General Mansfield somehow was got back to a dressing station. There a flurried surgeon pressed a flask of whisky to his mouth, almost strangling him; and, what with the wound and the clumsy handling, the old man presently died. He had had the corps only two days, but he had already made the soldiers like and respect him; it seems likely that he might have made quite a name if he had been spared.

But there was no holding up the fight because a general had been killed. Crawford went down, too, with a bad wound, and a colonel took over the brigade, and the veterans and the rookies got into a tremendous fire fight with some of D. H. Hill's men along the east side of the cornfield. Farther west General Gordon drove his brigade in past the Miller farm buildings and over the pitiful human wreckage that littered the ground in front of Battery B. The Rebels in the corner of the cornfield and along the fence on the northern side were not disposed to go away, and the 3rd Wisconsin took a beating when it got up to the fence; but Gordon worked the 2nd Massachusetts around on the right and got an enfilade on the Texans, and the 27th Indiana came up on the other side, and the Confederate line gave way.

So once more there was a bitter fight in the cornfield, with the Federals coming in from the north and the east; and Hood, as he had foreseen, was compelled to withdraw, with half of his men shot down. As Gordon's lines went in Hooker got a bullet in the foot and rode to the rear, dripping blood, and command of this part of the battle passed temporarily to Mansfield's senior division commander, General Alpheus S. Williams, who rode about the field with the unlighted stub of a cigar gripped in his teeth and who was called "Pop" by his troops—sure sign that they liked him. The retreating Rebels made a desperate fight of it. One of Crawford's men asserted that "on all other fields, from the beginning to the end of our long service, we never had to face their equals," and the 27th Indiana came to a halt in the middle of the smoky field, standing erect in close order and firing as fast as it could handle its muskets, which finally became too hot to be used. One Hoosier, badly wounded, laid down his rifle and went a few yards to the rear, where he sat down, opened his clothing, and examined his wound. After studying it, he mused aloud: "Well, I guess I'm hurt about as bad as I can be. I believe I'll go back and give 'em some more." So he picked up a discarded musket and returned to the firing line.

The regiment shot up all its ammunition, a hundred rounds per man, and sent details around the field to loot the cartridge boxes of the dead and wounded. In this fight the 27th lost a good non-com—Corporal Barton W. Mitchell, who had caused the battle in the first place by finding Lee's lost order; he went down with a wound that kept him out of action for months. His company commander, Captain Kopp, to whom he had first taken the lost order, was killed.

At last the 2nd Massachusetts came in on the right, its colonel jubilantly waving a captured Texas battle flag, and the Confederate defense began to crumble. Crawford's men came out of the East Wood at last, rookies and veterans all yelling and firing as they came, and the Rebels gave way and went back, running south and west across the turnpike and into the West Wood. Once more the cornfield, for whatever it was worth, belonged to the Union. Gordon's and Crawford's men tried to get across the turnpike and pursue, but nobody had ever yet cleaned up on the Rebel strength to the west of this highway—Mansfield had sent a brigade over there when he first took his corps into action, but the regiments had been put in clumsily and had been driven off—and the Federal advance was halted along the rail fence, and that dusty country highway once more became a lane of death.

Half a mile farther east things were going better. General George Sears Greene, a relative of Revolutionary War hero Nathanael Greene, had the rest of Mansfield's troops—a battle-worn division of some seventeen hundred men— and these had cut through the eastern fringe of the East Wood and had gone driving straight for the Dunker church. Some of the Confederates who had been driven out of the cornfield rallied and hit them in the flank as they got past the timber, some of Hill's men gouged at their other flank, and Lee brought reinforcements over from the right of his line to make a stand in front of the church. The Northerners had a hard time of it for a while, coming under fire from three directions, and when the Confederates came in with a counterattack the outlook was bad; but just in time a Rhode Island battery came galloping up, the infantry broke ranks to let the guns through, and the counterattack was smashed with canister and rifle fire. Then one of Crawford's rookie regiments—125th Pennsylvania, seven hundred strong, a giant of a regiment for that field—came up, separated from its brigade and slightly lost but anxious to get into the nearest fight; and Greene's division ran on past the guns and got into the West Wood around the Dunker church, forming a solid line on the far side of that battle-scarred building. Here was victory, if someone could just bring up reinforcements.

But the reinforcements didn't show up. This spearhead had got clear through the Confederate line. The high ground around the church, objective of all the morning's fighting, had been seized at last. But Greene had lost a third of his men, more than two hundred of the Pennsylvania straw-feet were down, and the survivors could do no more than hang on where they were, the Rebels keeping them under a steady fire. Completely wrecked, Hooker's army corps was trying to round up its stragglers and reassemble on the hills a mile to the north. The rest of Mansfield's corps was in position around the Miller barnyard and along the western edge of the cornfield, solidly posted but too busy to send any help. Greene's boys had reached the goal, but they couldn't do anything with it now that they had it. The fire that was being played upon their lines was not strong enough to drive them out, but it was too strong to advance against; and off to the southeast they could make out the movement of marching bodies of men, as if heavy Confederate reinforcements were coming up. The right wing of McClellan's army was beaten out, with this one advanced detachment huddling under the trees to mark high tide.

It may be that life is not man's most precious possession, after all. Certainly men can be induced to give it away very freely at times, and the terms hardly seem to make sense unless there is something about the whole business that we don't understand. Lives are spent for very insignificant things which benefit the dead not at all—a few rods of ground in a cornfield, for instance, or temporary ownership of a little hill or a piece of windy pasture; and now and then they are simply wasted outright, with nobody gaining anything at all. And we talk glibly about the accidents of battle and the mistakes of generalship without figuring out just which end of the stick the man who died was holding. As, for instance:

By seven-thirty in the morning a dim sense that something had gone wrong had reached McClellan's headquarters. The signal flags had been wig-wagging ever since it was light enough to see them, and at one time McClellan came out of his tent, smiling and saying, "All goes well—Hooker is driving them." But all had not gone well thereafter, and presently white-haired old General Sumner was ordered to take his corps across the creek and get into action. Sumner moved promptly, and before long, from Mr. Pry's yard, McClellan could see the three parallel lines of John Sedgwick's division threading their way up the farther hillsides, heading for the East Wood.

Sumner rode with Sedgwick, letting the two remaining divisions of his corps follow as best they could. He was strictly the Indian fighter of the Western plains this morning, putting himself in the front rank of the column of attack, ready for a straight cut-and-thrust onslaught on the Rebel lines. He knew almost nothing about what had happened so far—had the impression, even, that the right wing of the army had gained a victory and that he was being sent in to make it complete. But when he got to the East Wood the omens under the shattered trees were sinister. The place was packed with wounded men, and there were far too many able-bodied soldiers wandering around trying to help them. (One of Sedgwick's colonels wrote sagely: "When good Samaritans so abound it is a strong indication that the discipline of the troops in front is not good and that the battle is not going so as to encourage the half-hearted.")[1] And when the division came out on the far side of the wood, facing west, the picture looked even worse. Sumner could see smoke and hear gunfire off to the right, where tenacious Rebels and Northerners still disputed possession of the Miller barnyard and adjacent pastures, and some firing seemed to be going on to the south by the Dunker church; but in front, as far as Sumner could see, there was nothing at all except for the ghastly debris that filled the cornfield. From the sketchy evidence he had, Sumner concluded that two whole army corps had ceased to exist: the right wing of the army was gone, except for scattered fragments, and he had this end of the battle all to himself.

The plan of attack which he decided on was very simple. If he was now beyond the Federal flank, then he must be beyond the Rebel flank as well: so he would move straight west, at right angles to the earlier lines of attack, advancing until he was in rear of Lee's left. Then he would wheel to his own left and sweep down the ridge behind Lee's line, crumpling the Army of Northern Virginia into McClellan's net. He had Sedgwick form his division in three lines, a brigade to each line, five thousand men altogether, and he started out across the cornfield full of confidence: if Sedgwick's men got into any trouble they could cut their way out, and besides, to other divisions were following.

Sumner supposed they were following, at any rate. They had been told to do so. But he was the cavalry colonel, riding in the front line as he led his men to the charge, not the corps commander staying back to make sure that everybody understood what he was to do and did it; and his second division was even now going astray, swinging about for an attack on the high ground southeast of the Dunker church, half a mile or more away from Sumner's target. The third division had not even started, staff work having been fouled up. Worst of all, Sedgwick's division was formed for a head-on attack and nothing else. The three brigade lines were so close together that maneuvering would be almost impossible, and if the division should be hit in the flanks there would be great trouble.

The five thousand enlisted men who would have to foot the bill if anything went wrong were not thinking of possible errors in tactics as they moved forward. They were veterans and they were rated with the best troops in the army, but the march so far had been rather unnerving. They had come up through all the backwash of battle, seeing many wounded, hearing many discouraging remarks by demoralized stragglers; they had seen ambulances jolting to the rear from advanced operating stations, carrying men who held the stumps of their amputated limbs erect in a desperate effort to ease the pain of the rough ride. When they formed line at the edge of the wood, even the veteran 19th Massachusetts had been so visibly nervous that its colonel had put the men through the manual of arms for a few minutes to steady their nerves. (This was another of the old fancy-Dan regiments; in the beginning it had elected not merely its officers but its enlisted men as well, just like a club, and when it left Boston in 1861 it had two complete baggage wagons for each company, four for regimental headquarters and four for the commissary— enough, as one member said, for an army corps, by later standards. It had learned much since those days.)

The division went west across the cornfield, the lines wavering as the men stepped carefully to avoid the dead and wounded, and it came under artillery fire. Stuart's horse artillery had moved south to a hill behind the West Wood, firing over the treetops, and the division was so wide and solid that the gunners could not miss—a shot that carried over the first battle line was sure to hit the second or the third. (One veteran wrote disgustedly afterward: "We were as easy to hit as the town of Sharpsburg.") The men could see the shells coming, but they had learned by now that it was useless to duck and dodge, and they went straight ahead, bending their heads a little as if they were walking into a high wind. From the rear they made a handsome sight—long lines carefully aligned, battle flags fluttering, little white smoke clouds breaking out overhead here and there as shells exploded, green wood ahead of them: very nice to look at, so long as you could look from a distance. Far away, near McClellan's headquarters, staff officers swung their telescopes on the moving lines and remarked to one another that this was going to do it—that division could not be stopped.

Out of the cornfield and over the turnpike they went, past narrow fields and into the West Wood, that long belt of trees which ran north and south from below the Dunker church to a spot opposite Mr. Miller's barnyard. The trees gave protection from the shells, and the only Rebels in sight were skirmishers who faded back and disappeared as the division came on. The wood was open enough so that the brigade lines were maintained without much difficulty, and in a few minutes the leading brigade came out on the far side, facing open fields that rose slowly to an irregular ridge several hundred yards off. Stuart's guns were up there, and a few thin lines of infantry, but nothing very solid. The division was halted, with nobody able to see anything much except the men in the leading brigade. Sumner's idea might be right: he was on the flank, and all he had to do now was get his cumbersome battle lines out into the open, chase the last Rebels off that ridge, perform a left wheel, and march down toward Sharpsburg.

But it wasn't going to be that way. The left of Lee's line had been mangled quite as badly as the right of McClellan's, but in the precise nick of time Lee had sent up strong reinforcements—McLaws's division and Walker's, with Jackson's indomitable lieutenant, Jubal Early, bringing in his own brigade and such other stray elements as he could collect. And all of these, totaling more men than Sumner had with him, were now poised to attack just where it would hurt most—from the left.

The blow came with demoralizing suddenness, and for most of the men it was completely invisible, and there was nothing whatever they could do about it. One minute Sumner was sitting his horse amid the leading brigade, watching the firing that was coming from the Rebels on the ridge, sizing up the situation; the next minute there was a great uproar of musketry and screaming men in the wood to the left, the air was full of bullets, an unexpected host of new Rebels was going into line on the ridge in front, guns were appearing from nowhere and going into battery there, and there was complete and unmerciful hell to pay.

It hit the rear ranks first. One-armed General Howard had four Pennsylvania regiments in the third brigade—all the men came from Philadelphia, and the outfit was known as the "Philadelphia Brigade"—and these men, who had been standing at ease in the wood, abruptly found themselves under a deadly fire from behind. Regiments broke, men scrambled for cover, officers shouted frantically; the enemy was out of sight, dense smoke was seeping in through the trees, the air was alive with bullets, fugitives were running every which way. Howard—never an inspirational leader, but a solid citizen who was never scared, either—went riding along the line trying to get the men realigned, which was hard because nobody knew which way the men ought to be faced in order to fight effectively. Sumner galloped up, shouted something, and galloped off again. In the unceasing racket Howard could not hear a word he said; an aide yelled in his ear that Sumner had been shouting: "My God, Howard! You must get out of here!"—an idea which by now had seized every man in the brigade. The 72nd Pennsylvania, at the far left, gave way completely, its frantic stragglers adding to the confusion. Some detachments were faced by the rear rank and started off, but that didn't seem to work—more often than not the men found themselves marching straight into a consuming fire; and presently the whole brigade simply dissolved and the men ran back out of the wood and into an open field, a disordered mob rather than a brigade of troops. In the field they were caught by artillery, the Rebels having wheeled up guns to sweep the open ground, and the rout of the brigade became complete. In something less than ten minutes the brigade had lost more than five hundred men and had hardly been able to fire a shot in reply.

Up front it was a little better, but not much. A savage Rebel charge came in from the open field, and the 15th Massachusetts took it head-on, exchanging volleys at a scant fifteen yards. One soldier in this regiment later wrote that "the loss of life was fearful; we had never seen anything like it." The 34th New York, which was at the left end of the front line, tried to move over to help and somehow got squarely in between two Confederate lines and took a horrible fire from front and rear at the same time, losing half of its men in a few minutes. General Sedgwick hurried back to his second brigade, trying to get a regiment or two wheeled around for flank protection, but it was simply impossible—there just was no room to maneuver in all that crush even if the Rebel fire had permitted it, which it didn't. Sedgwick got a wound in the arm and an aide urged him to go to the rear. He refused, saying that the wound was a nuisance and nothing more; then another bullet lifted him out of the saddle with a wound that kept him in hospital for five months. (He made a bad patient, it seems. Impatient with hospital routine, he jokingly said that if he ever got hit again he hoped the bullet would finish him off—anything was better than a hospital. Cracks like that are bad luck for soldiers: Uncle John got his wish at Spotsylvania Courthouse in 1864, when a Rebel sharpshooter hit him under the eye and killed him.)

Minutes seemed like hours in the uproar under the smoky trees. The sound of rifle fire rose higher and higher as more Rebel brigades got into action. Over and over, in official reports and in regimental histories, one finds Federals giving the same account of it—the heaviest, deadliest fire they ever saw in the entire war. The rear brigade was gone and the second brigade was going. General Dana, commanding the second brigade, managed to get parts of the 42nd New York and the 7th Michigan swung around to meet the fire from the left, but they couldn't hold on. When Howard's brigade went to pieces the Rebels came in from the rear and the two regiments were overwhelmed, with a few platoons managing to keep some sort of formation as they backed off to the north.

The colonel of the 59th New York rode back and forth with a flag, bawling: "Rally on the colors!" His men grouped themselves around him and tried to return a heavy fire that came out of the wood in front; and in the smoke and the confusion they volleyed into the backs of the 15th Massachusetts, and there was a terrible shouting and cursing amid all the din. Then a Confederate regiment worked its way around and fired into the 59th from the rear, and the New Yorkers lost nearly two thirds of their numbers. Young Captain Oliver Wendell Holmes of the 20th Massachusetts went down with his second wound of the war; and somehow, amazingly, that wandering rookie regiment from General Samuel Crawford's brigade, the greenhorn 125th Pennsylvania, showed up and fell into line beside the battered 34th New York, where it fought manfully. (Nobody ever knew quite how it got there; it had been fighting with Greene's boys south of the Dunker church, and in some incomprehensible manner it had got detached and in all the fury of this infighting had managed to get into the middle of Sedgwick's front line. Those rookies seemed to have a genius for wandering into fights, and they were packing a whole year's experience into one desperate morning.)

If the time seemed endless, it was really very short. Just fifteen minutes after the first shot had been fired, the last of the division retreated. From first to last, the division had not had a chance; it was attacked from three sides at once—front, left, and rear—and the collapse ran from rear rank to front rank. It left more than twenty-one hundred men dead or wounded in the West Wood, and a good half of its units had never been able to fire a shot; some of those that did fought facing by the rear rank. Confederate losses in this fight had been negligible; the sacrifice of Sedgwick's division had accomplished nothing whatever.

A few regiments got out in good order. The 20th Massachusetts proudly recorded that it left the West Wood at a walk, in column of fours, muskets at right shoulder; and the 1st Minnesota, which had been lucky—it had lost only a fourth of its men—went out beside it, similarly formed. These and a few other unbroken units were lined up perpendicular to the Hagerstown pike, a few hundred yards north of the spot where the division had crossed the

road on its way in, and they laid down a strong fire when the triumphant
Rebels came out of the wood to finish the rout. The Rebel lines swept into the
cornfield—one more charge across that cornfield!—where wounded men
cursed wearily and pressed their faces against the dirt, hoping that pounding
feet and bursting shells and low-flying bullets would not hurt them further as
they lay there helpless—and for a few minutes it looked as if this counterattack
might destroy the whole right wing of McClellan's army and end the battle
then and there. But the remnant of Sedgwick's division gave ground stubbornly and at a price, Gordon's tired brigade from Mansfield's corps came in to
help, a good deal of rifle fire was still coming out of the East Wood, and an
enormous line of fieldpieces was waiting on the slope north of the cornfield.
For the last time that day the cornfield was swept by murderous fire, and the
Confederates slowed down, halted, and went back to the shelter of the West
Wood, while the beaten Federals withdrew to the ridge in rear of the guns,
leaving a fringe of pickets and skirmishers behind.

And while this area north of the Dunker church was smoldering and
fitfully exploding all the rest of the day with long-range rifle and artillery fire,
there was no more real fighting here. There had been enough, in all conscience. In a square of ground measuring very little more than one thousand
yards on a side—cornfield, barnyard, orchard, East and West Woods, and the
fields by the turnpike—nearly twelve thousand men were lying on the ground,
dead or wounded. It had not taken long to put them there, either. The fighting
began with daylight—around five-thirty or six o'clock. It was now nine-thirty;
four hours, at the most, from the time Hooker's batteries began to rake the
cornfield to the end of the last Rebel countercharge. They fought with muz-
zle-loaders in those days, the men who got off two shots a minute were doing
well, and it took, as one might say, a real effort to kill a man then. But considering their handicaps, they did pretty well.

★   ★   ★   ★   ★

Editor's Postscript: At this point in the battle, the killing was far from ended. In
fact, only the first of three distinct phases was over. Still to come was the fighting in the West Wood and along the sunken road, where bodies would be
stacked like cordwood. Even later, in the vicinity of what would come to be
called "Burnside's Bridge," over Antietam Creek itself, the waters would flow
red with blood when the day finally ended. Historians who call this the bloodiest single day on American soil are probably correct, according to Bruce

Catton. You can visit the battlefield today, walk over the actual ground where all this happened—the site of the cornfield, the sunken road ("Bloody Lane") and the original, still standing, "Burnside's Bridge." It is an experience as stirring as visiting Gettysburg. The Park Service people will take good care of you. Tell them Mr. Bruce Catton sent you.

The Morning They Shot the Spies

BY W. C. HEINZ

FOR A MAGAZINE MAN like myself, the demise of the old *True* magazine was painful to watch. During the late 1940s and through the 1950s, *True* could be counted on for strong male-oriented nonfiction on subjects ranging from cars to fishing. The rise of *Playboy* and other so-called "girlie" or "skin" magazines doomed such traditional stalwarts as *True* and *Argosy.*

A fine collection of *True* articles was *A Treasury of True,* edited by Charles Barnard. Long out of print, the book contains stories, cartoons, illustrations, and covers. In it, Barnard points out that whenever and wherever the old *True* editors got together, "The Morning They Shot the Spies" always came up in conversation as one of the most respected pieces. The author, W. C. Heinz, went on to write the outstanding boxing novel, *The Professional.*

The setting here is the Ardennes in the Battle of the Bulge in the winter of 1944–45. Part of the German plan to smash through the Allied forces in the region included using German soldiers wearing U.S. uniforms to wreak havoc behind the lines.

Some of them didn't make it!

★   ★   ★   ★   ★

We skirted Liege and turned east on the road that leads past the Belgian forts dug into the ground. It was cold. It was two days to Christmas. It was still early and the mist hung over the fields and, in some places, over the road. I remembered when we went through here with the tanks in September. The sun shone every day and it was warm then, and the Germans were running for the Rhine. It was hard to find Germans then, and when the Americans found them the Germans quit easy and it seemed that the war would be over by Christmas and maybe we would be home.

27

"Stay on here," I said to the driver. "After we go through Henri Chapelle I'll tell you. I remember it's on the left-hand side of the road."

When we went through Henri Chapelle the people were just starting the day. There were a few of them on the street—a woman in a shawl pouring a pail of steaming, cloudy water into the cobblestone gutter, and a couple of workers walking along the sidewalk, their breaths showing, the collars of their old jackets turned up and their hands in their pants pockets. They paid no attention to us.

"That's the place up on the left," I said to the driver. "I can remember it."

I could remember the wall along the road, and the opening in it. I could remember the low stucco barracks on the other three sides of the dirt quadrangle, and we drove past the guard at the gate and across the frozen yard. The driver put the jeep in with some others at the far end, and we got out, stiff from the cold, and walked back across the dry, hard dirt to what looked like the office.

There were some M.P. personnel working in there at desks behind a guard rail. There was a pot-bellied stove at the back, and we walked over to it, standing around it and taking the heat and talking about it until a young lieutenant came over and asked us if he could help us.

"We're here for this spy thing," I said.

"Oh," he said. "Then you go across there to the messhall."

He pointed and you could see through the glass in the far door the building that he meant.

"What time is it coming off?"

"I'm afraid I don't know," the lieutenant said. "This place is in a mess. Just go over there, I'm sure that someone will tell you in plenty of time for you to see it."

We went out and walked across the quadrangle toward the building. The side showing on the quadrangle was made up almost entirely of wide sliding doors. One of them was open and, looking in, I could see some people who had driven down from the Ninth Army at Maastricht.

I judged this place had been a stable when the Germans had used it. Now the Americans were using it as a messhall, and a couple of the people from Ninth Army were sitting on the benches, their backs to the long tables, while the others moved around, stamping their feet, their hands in their pockets. There was no heat in the place.

The Ninth Army people didn't know anything. I could tell from the way they talked that they didn't know the censors had put a stop on this, that you couldn't write about it, but I wasn't going to tell them.

In a few minutes a captain came in. He was quite young and freshly shaven, and he looked cleaner than anything else around the place. He was smiling and he went around introducing himself and shaking hands. He seemed to be trying to be the perfect host, and his enthusiasm and his friendliness made me a little annoyed with him.

"I suppose," he said, "that you gentlemen understand about the censorship of all pictures."

"We know about it," one of the photographers said. "You don't have to worry about it."

"And I suppose you also understand," the captain said, "that nothing is to be written about this."

I felt a little sorry for the writers who had come down from Maastricht. It came to them as a surprise. They started to put up a real kick, but they must have known it was a waste of time to argue.

"But I thought they wanted a lot of publicity about it," one of them said. "I thought they wanted it to get back to the Germans so they'd stop this sneaking guys into our lines."

"I don't know anything about that," the captain said.

"Then why didn't they tell us?" somebody else said. "Why didn't they tell us before we wasted our time driving way down here in this cold?"

"I'm sorry," the captain said. "You know as much about it as I do."

Several of them said they would leave, talking about it among themselves, but they all stayed. To put an end to the argument someone asked the captain what he knew about the prisoners.

"All I know," he said, and you could see him thinking about what he had rehearsed, "is that they were picked up at night inside our lines in an American jeep. They were wearing American uniforms, and had a radio. They hadn't accomplished anything, as they had just entered our lines when they were picked up.

"One of them is an out-and-out Nazi. He's the short one. The other two, I believe, are innocent of any original intent of spying. One of them is a farm boy from Westphalia.

"He's quite simple and, I think, quite honest.

"The story he tells—and I'm inclined to believe it—is that several weeks ago, before this German counteroffensive started, a call went out for men who speak English. He volunteered, he said, because he thought it would be a soft job back at headquarters on propaganda or prisoner interrogation or something like that. The next thing he knew, he was in an American uniform and in an American jeep and heading for our lines. He said there was nothing he could do, and I don't suppose there was, because they always put one Nazi in with the weak ones to see that they keep in line."

We stood around the captain listening, and some of the Ninth Army people were taking notes. I thought the captain was very efficient. He was telling us all that he could.

"We've never done anything like this before," he said. "It's rather a messy thing, and we'll be glad to get it over."

"Then what are we waiting for? We were notified this thing would be at nine-thirty."

"I don't know," the captain said. "I imagine they may be waiting to see if there's any other word from Shaef. I suppose they want to be sure Shaef hasn't had a change of mind about it."

"Then how long do we have to wait?"

"I haven't found out," the captain said, "but it should be within a half hour."

"How about the prisoners? Can you tell us how they're taking it?"

"All right," the captain said. "The chaplain has been seeing two of them, but the Nazi wants nothing to do with him. We have some Wehrmacht nurses in the next cell, and last night the three asked that the nurses be allowed to sing some Christmas carols for them."

"Then they know they're going to be shot this morning?"

"Yes. The chaplain informed them last night."

"Was the request for the carols granted?"

"Of course."

"What carols did the nurses sing?"

"I don't remember exactly," the captain said, "because the only one I recognized was Silent Night. We had to stop them after a while."

"Why?"

"Because they were disturbing our troops."

I wondered if the captain knew that Silent Night is a German carol that the rest of us borrowed.

"We can go now," he said. "Keep together and follow me.

"When you get there, keep about twenty-five or thirty feet back. There will be an M.P. stationed there, and you are to keep behind that line. That goes for the photographers, too. Also, once you get there you will have to stay because no one will be allowed to leave."

"In other words," one of the Ninth Army people said, "if we want to back out, we have to back out now."

"That's right," the captain said, smiling.

I thought about backing out and I wished no one had mentioned it. I was starting to be afraid, and we followed the captain out and across the quadrangle. We walked in a straggling group past the place where the jeeps were parked, and we took a path that ran along, on the left, the sidewall of a low, gray stucco building. On the right there was a field, gray with frost, and the path was rough with frozen footprints. I wondered if the prisoners knew now how close they were to it.

The path we took led down into a field behind the stucco building. The field sloped a little away from the building, running down to a barbed-wire fence. Beyond that the ground dropped rather suddenly, and you could see into a valley, filled now with the mist. We walked maybe fifty feet into the field, the captain taking us around several M.P.s standing at ease in the field, and then we turned and faced the back wall of the building.

The wall was about ten feet high. About three feet out from it and spaced about twenty feet apart were three squared posts painted black. The post holes were new.

We stood there in a group, an M.P. to our left, looking at the posts. I looked at the ground, frost-white, the grass tufts frozen, the soil hard and uneven. I wondered if it is better to die on a warm, bright day among friends, or on a day when even the weather is your enemy. I turned around and looked down into the valley. The mist still hung in the valley, but it was starting to take on a brassy tint from the sun trying to work through it. I could make out three white farm buildings on the valley floor—a little yellowed now from the weak sunlight—and I could envision this, in the spring, a pleasant valley.

This view I see now, I said to myself, will be the last thing their eyes will ever see. I looked at it intently for that reason. I thought of the human eye and of its complexity and its marvelous efficiency. I found myself thinking only of the farm boy, the Westphalian, for whom this would be the last room, the last view, and I turned back to the others.

That was when we heard the sound of marching feet. I turned and I saw them coming around the corner of the building, along the path we had taken.

There was, first, an M.P. officer. Behind him came the first prisoner and I knew at once that he was the one the captain had described as the farm boy from Westphalia. Behind him, in twos, marched eight M.P.s, then another prisoner, eight M.P.s, the third prisoner and eight more M.P.s. The boots of the M.P.s shone with polish and on their helmets the letting and bands were a fresh, new white. The prisoners wore American fatigue jumpers like those that garage mechanics sometimes wear—more green than khaki—and there was a band of blue paint on each leg and each arm.

So that technically they won't be shot in American uniforms, I thought. They had to give them something to wear.

It was difficult to march well over the rough, frozen ground. You could tell this by the way the tips of the rifles wavered in the lines. I watched them, thinking that these were among the last steps these prisoners would ever take, thinking of the wonders of the walking process, of the countless steps we give away so cheaply for needless reasons until there are no more. Now the column seemed to be marching so quickly.

They had turned off the path and now moved across in front of us, between us and the wall. When they reached a point where the Westphalian was opposite the last post, the officer at the head shouted and the column stopped, the men marking time, the feet of the prisoners a part of the rhythm. Then he shouted again and the feet stopped and the column stood at attention. Both times that he shouted I noticed that the Westphalian looked down and back nervously at the feet of the M.P.s behind him as he obeyed the orders.

He is a good soldier, I thought. At a time like this he is worrying about being in step, and he is afraid that he is not catching the commands. You have to give him something for that, I thought, and I looked at him carefully. He was the one all right—tall, big-boned, long-faced, with long arms and large, homely red hands that hung below the sleeves of the American fatigues. The fatigues were too small for him and made him seem all the more pathetic.

There was no doubt about the second one either. He was the one the captain had described as the Nazi. He was short, about 5 feet 4, and he had a high, bulging forehead and flat, black hair and he wore black-rimmed glasses. He stood very erect, his face set as stiffly as his body.

The third one did not impress me. He was well built—by far the best looking of the three—and he had black, curly hair. In my mind he was something between the farm boy and the Nazi, and he was not, for my purposes, important.

I saw these things quickly, for the officer was shouting again and the M.P.s, the prisoners a split second behind them, were facing left. They were facing the wall and the three posts in front of it, and then two M.P.s were leading each prisoner to a post, and the column was turning and marching back toward us, then turning back again to the wall and standing in two rows, twelve men to a row.

The prisoners standing in front of the posts looked very pale now. I looked at their thin fatigues and their bare hands. I wondered if the Westphalian felt the cold. I should have liked to have asked him.

Now, while the squad and the rest of us waited, two M.P.s walked to the post where the Westphalian stood, and there were strands of yellow, braided rope in their hands. You could see how new and clean the rope was, and when one of the M.P.s took a strand of rope and bent down at the post the other took the Westphalian by the shoulders and moved him back an inch or two. The first M.P. wrapped the rope around the Westphalian's ankles and around the post, and as he started to do this the Westphalian looked down, his hair falling forward, and he shuffled his feet back, watching until the M.P. was done. After that the second M.P. took the Westphalian's arms and put them back, one on each side, behind the post. Then the first M.P. tied them there, and the Westphalian, turning first to one side and then the other, watched intently.

He is trying to help them, I said to myself. Even now he is trying to do the right thing. I wondered how he could do this, and I knew he was brave because he was very afraid. I wondered how a man could be that brave, and then I saw a photographer, disobeying what the captain had told us, kneeling a few feet in front of the Westphalian, focusing his camera on him. I saw the Westphalian staring right back at the photographer, his eyes wide, his whole face questioning, and for that moment he seemed about to cry.

They left the Westphalian and went to the one in the middle, the one the captain had described as the Nazi. He already stood very stiffly against the post, and he did not move when they tied his feet. When they tied his arms behind his post he thrust them back there for them, and he squared his head and shoulders against the post. He was looking over the heads of all of us, and his face was very stern.

They went, then, to tie the third prisoner, the unimportant one. I looked at the other two, tied to the posts, looking out over the heads of the firing squad. I remembered the view of the valley behind my back. That is the last thing, I thought again, that the Westphalian will ever see. I looked at his long, pale face and I wondered if he was seeing anything. I knew that somewhere someone would think of him presently, as they might be thinking of him now, wondering what he was doing. I thought of a farmhouse, like so many we had passed in this war, the whitened stone cottage, the flat fields, an old woman, a turnip heap and, somewhere in the yard, a dung pile.

They had finished tying the third prisoner. The three stood rigid against the posts like woodcuts of men facing execution. There were M.P. officers, clean and erect and efficient, moving between them, inspecting knots and saluting one another and then a chaplain—a full colonel, helmeted, wearing a trench coat but with a black-satin stole around his neck and hanging down his front—stepped out from beside the squad and walked slowly, a small black book held in his hands in front of him, to the post where the Westphalian was tied.

I saw him say something to the Westphalian and I saw the Westphalian look to him and stare into his face and nod his head. I saw the chaplain reading from the book, and once I saw the Westphalian's lips moving, his head nodding a little, and then the chaplain was finished and the Westphalian was staring into his face as he moved away.

The chaplain stopped beside the one in the middle, the one described as the Nazi. The prisoner shook his head without looking at the chaplain, but the chaplain was saying something anyway, and then he moved on to the prisoner at the end who listened as the chaplain spoke.

When the chaplain had finished he walked back to a point behind the firing squad. Then two M.P.s stepped forward and walked to the Westphalian and one of them had in his hand a band of black cloth. He stood in back of the post and he reached around the head of the Westphalian to fix the cloth across his eyes.

This now, I said to myself, is that last moment that he will see anything on this earth. I wondered if the Westphalian was thinking that thought.

They fixed the bands over the eyes of the others. Then two M.P.s stepped forward and, starting with the prisoner on the left, pinned over the hearts of each prisoner white paper circles. The circles were about the size of a large orange. So they won't miss, I thought.

I was very cold, now, in these few gray seconds in this field. There was some saluting among the M.P. officers, and there were the three prisoners, each alone, their eyes bound with black and the white circles over their hearts, waiting.

I will not look, I was saying to myself. I think I am afraid to look. It is so easy to turn away, I thought, and then I said that I had come to see this when I did not have to because I had wanted to study myself.

I heard then the M.P. officer at the right of the firing squad give a command, and I saw the first row of twelve men drop to one knee. I heard another command and saw the rifles come up and I heard the sound of the stocks rustling against the clothing, and then I heard the Nazi in the middle shouting, guttural and loud in the morning, and I caught the end of his sentence.

"—Unser Fuehrer Adolf Hitler!"

At that moment—with the Nazi shouting—I heard the command to fire and I heard the explosion of the rifles, not quite all together and almost like a short burst from a machine gun. I was watching the Nazi, whose cry had drawn me at the last second, and I saw him stiffen in the noise and I saw the wall behind him chip and the dust come off it, and the Nazi stood flattened and rigid still against the post.

He's dead, I said to myself. They're all dead.

I looked, then, to the Westphalian, and as I looked I saw the blood on his front and I saw his head fall forward and then his shoulders and chest move out from the pole. I saw the Nazi standing rigid and the other prisoner beginning to sag out, and I was conscious again of the photographers. I remembered, now, seeing the one moving up to take pictures as they had prepared the prisoners, and now again he was kneeling in front of the Westphalian and shooting his camera at him and the others were moving about rapidly and shooting quickly, and I envied them their occupation.

I watched the weird dance, then, of the prisoners, dead but still dying. The Nazi stood firm against the post, only his head bent forward, but the one on the left sagged forward slowly, and then I saw the Westphalian go, first to his left and then, pausing, to his right, swaying. I saw him hang there for a moment, and then I saw him pitch forward, hung by his wrists, bent in the middle, his head down to his knees, his long hair hanging, the whole of him straining at the ropes around his wrists.

He's not alive, I said to myself. He's really dead.

Two medics walked up to him then and the one, bending down, looked into his eyes and, with his fingers, closed the lids. Then the second, bending down, slid his hands under the Westphalian's armpits, lifting him so that the first could put a stethoscope to his chest. In a moment they dropped him, leaving him sagging and swaying a little, and they moved on to the Nazi in the middle.

The Nazi strained a little at the ropes but his body was still rigid. I saw them pausing longer at the Nazi, the two of them looking at him more carefully. I was wondering if they were really finding the Nazi harder to kill. They stood there, talking to each other, putting the stethoscope on him for the second time, and then they finally moved on. They found the other prisoner dead and they walked back to the group beside the firing squad. They saluted the officer in charge and I heard the officer's command to the squad and saw the squad, facing about, march back across the field and up the path.

"What he said," one of the Ninth Army men was saying, "means: 'Long live our Fuehrer, Adolph Hitler.' "

We waited for the photographers to finish taking their pictures of the prisoners in their positions of death and of the two M.P.s cutting them from the poles. They cut the Westphalian down first and put him on a stretcher, and then two others came with a white mattress cover and they slid him, feet first, off the stretcher and into the mattress cover. They left the mattress cover in front of the post and they went on to the Nazi.

When the M.P.s were finished and we were ready to leave I looked for the last time at what was left. There was the wall, chipped behind each post, and among the marks the bullets had made were small splashes of blood. There were the three posts, spattered, and before each post a white mattress cover, filled with a body. There was the stretcher, blood-spattered, and on the frozen ground were strewn the things typically American—the black paper ends from the film packs, the flash bulbs, milky-white and expended, and an empty, crumpled Lucky Strike cigaret package. An M.P., a rifle on his shoulder, walked up and down.

We went back to the small office near the gate. Our fingers and hands were stiff and ached from the cold, and we stood near the pot-bellied stove. There was a G.I. working at a filing cabinet near the stove and he started to talk to us.

"I'm glad it's over," he said.

"I am, too," I said.

"Not as much as us," he said. "For three days this place has been on end. We haven't been able to get anything else done."

The captain who had led us to the field came in. I thanked him and told him I thought it had all gone very well.

"We should have used combat troops," he said. "This bunch was so nervous that—just between us—there were only three bullets in one of the bull's-eyes, only three out of eight."

"Maybe one had the blank," I said. "That would be three out of seven."

"I don't know," the captain said. "I don't know if they used one blank."

The chaplain who had pronounced the last rites came in. He stood talking with another officer who was, I judged, the chaplain attached to the M.P. battalion.

"Well," he said, sticking out his hand, "I think it was conducted very well."

"Thank you," the other said, taking his hand. "Come and see us again. We hope next time it will be under more pleasant circumstances."

We went out and found our driver and he wanted to know how it was. We said it was all right, and we drove back. By afternoon the weather had cleared and the Germans came over. They came in so low that I could see the swastikas on the first plane and they bombed hell out of us. They killed Jack Frankish and three Belgians, and Col. Andrews died later in the hospital.

Damn, I said to myself, I wish this war were over and I wish I were home. For such a long time in September we had all thought we might be home for Christmas.

The Fight at the Bridge

From *For Whom the Bell Tolls*

BY ERNEST HEMINGWAY

H e lay flat on the brown, pine-needled floor of the forest, his chin on his folded arms, and high overhead the wind blew in the tops of the pine trees. The mountainside sloped gently where he lay; but below it was steep and he could see the dark of the oiled road winding through the pass."

With those words, Ernest Hemingway began one of his most ambitious and ultimately successful novels. Four hundred and seventy pages later, in a masterful stroke of story-telling, Hemingway would end his tale of the Spanish Civil War with his leading character—a guerrilla bridge dynamiter named Robert Jordan—lying once again on the same pine needles where the story began. Only this time, Jordan would be in the most desperate situation imaginable.

Although it is safe to say that *For Whom the Bell Tolls* does not enjoy the critical acclaim of Hemingway's novels *A Farewell to Arms* and *The Sun Also Rises,* as well as short stories such as "The Snows of Kilimanjaro," the book is a powerhouse of a story and has deservedly earned a huge reading audience over the decades.

This excerpt contains the climatic pages of the book. In the scenes depicted Robert Jordan, after great difficulty, has just completed his task of blowing up the bridge in conjunction with an attack by the Loyalist forces he supports. Now he and his other guerrilla comrades are about to try their escape by horseback. His companions include the band's leader, the enigmatic Pablo, and Pablo's stalwart wife, Pilar. The other most important character is the young girl Maria, living with the band since rescued by Pablo and Pilar from wartime atrocities, and now Robert Jordan's lover.

The drama that follows is prime, bonded Hemingway.

★   ★   ★   ★   ★

Just then Pablo dug both his spurs into the big bay and he plunged down the last pine-needled slope and crossed the road in a pounding, sparking of shod hooves. The others came behind him and Robert Jordan saw them crossing the road and slamming on up the green slope and heard the machine gun hammer at the bridge. Then he heard a noise come sweeeish-crack-boom! The boom was a sharp crack that widened in the cracking and on the hillside he saw a small fountain of earth rise with a plume of gray smoke. Sweeeish-crack-boom! It came again, the swishing like the noise of a rocket and there was another up-pulsing of dirt and smoke farther up the hillside.

Ahead of him the gypsy was stopped beside the road in the shelter of the last trees. He looked ahead at the slope and then he looked back toward Robert Jordan.

"Go ahead, Rafael," Robert Jordan said, "Gallop, man!"

The gypsy was holding the lead rope with the pack-horse pulling his head taut behind him.

"Drop the pack-horse and gallop!" Robert Jordan said.

He saw the gypsy's hand extended behind him, rising higher and higher, seeming to take forever as his heels kicked into the horse he was riding and the rope came taut, then dropped, and he was across the road and Robert Jordan was knee-ing against a frightened pack-horse that bumped back into him as the gypsy crossed the hard, dark road and he heard his horse's hooves clumping as he galloped up the slope.

Wheeeeeeish-ca-rack! The flat trajectory of the shell came and he saw the gypsy jink like a running boar as the earth spouted the little black and gray geyser ahead of him. He watched him galloping, slow and reaching now, up the long green slope and the gun threw behind him and ahead of him and he was under the fold of the hill with the others.

I can't take the damned pack-horse, Robert Jordan thought. Though I wish I could keep the son of a bitch on my off side. I'd like to have him between me and that 47 mm. they're throwing with. By God, I'll try to get him up there anyway.

He rode up to the pack-horse, caught hold of the hackamore, and then, holding the rope, the horse trotting behind him, rode fifty yards up through the trees. At the edge of the trees he looked down the road past the truck to the bridge. He could see men out on the bridge and behind it looked like a traffic jam on the road. Robert Jordan looked around, saw what he wanted finally and reached up and broke a dead limb from a pine tree. He dropped the hackamore, edged the pack-horse up to the slope that slanted down to the road and then hit him hard across the rump with the tree branch. "Go on, you son of a bitch," he said, and threw the dead branch after him as the pack-horse crossed the road and started across the slope. The branch hit him and the horse broke from a run into a gallop.

Robert Jordan rode thirty yards farther up the road; beyond that the bank was too steep. The gun was firing now with the rocket whish and the cracking, dirt-spouting boom. "Come on, you big gray fascist bastard," Robert Jordan said to the horse and put him down the slope in a sliding plunge. Then he was out in the open, over the road that was so hard under the hooves he felt the pound of it come up all the way to his shoulders, his neck and his teeth, onto the smooth of the slope, the hooves finding it, cutting it, pounding it, reaching, throwing, going, and he looked down across the slope to where the bridge showed now at a new angle he had never seen. It crossed in profile now without foreshortening and in the center was the broken place and behind it on the road was the little tank and behind the little tank was a big tank with a gun that flashed now yellow-bright as a mirror and the screech as the air ripped apart seemed almost over the gray neck that stretched ahead of him, and he turned his head as the dirt fountained up the hillside. The pack-horse was ahead of him swinging too far to the right and slowing down and Robert Jordan, galloping, his head turned a little toward the bridge, saw the line of trucks halted behind the turn that showed now clearly as he was gaining height, and he saw the bright yellow flash that signalled the instant whish and boom, and the shell fell short, but he heard the metal sailing from where the dirt rose.

He saw them all ahead in the edge of the timber watching him and he said, "*Arre caballo!* Go on, horse!" and felt his big horse's chest surging with the steepening of the slope and saw the gray neck stretching and the gray ears ahead and he reached and patted the wet gray neck, and he looked back at the bridge and saw the bright flash from the heavy, squat, mud-colored tank there on the road and then he did not hear any whish but only a banging acrid smelling clang like a boiler being ripped apart and he was under the gray horse and the gray horse was kicking and he was trying to pull out from under the weight.

He could move all right. He could move toward the right. But his left leg stayed perfectly flat under the horse as he moved to the right. It was as though there was a new joint in it; not the hip joint but another one that went sideways like a hinge. Then he knew what it was all right and just then the gray horse knee-ed himself up and Robert Jordan's right leg, that had kicked the stirrup loose just as it should, slipped clear over the saddle and came down beside him and he felt with his two hands of his thigh bone where the left leg lay flat against the ground and his hands both felt the sharp bone and where it pressed against the skin.

The gray horse was standing almost over him and he could see his ribs heaving. The grass was green where he sat and there were meadow flowers in it and he looked down the slope across to the road and the bridge and the gorge and the road and saw the tank and waited for the next flash. It came almost at once with again no whish and in the burst of it, with the smell of the high explosive, the dirt clods scattering and the steel whirring off, he saw the big gray horse sit quietly down beside him as though it were a horse in a circus. And then, looking at the horse sitting there, he heard the sound the horse was making.

Then Primitivo and Agustín had him under the arm-pits and were dragging him up the last of the slope and the new joint in his leg let it swing any way the ground swung it. Once a shell whished close over them and they dropped him and fell flat, but the dirt scattered over them and the metal sung off and they picked him up again. And then they had him up to the shelter of the long draw in the timber where the horses were, and Maria, Pilar and Pablo were standing over him.

Maria was kneeling by him and saying, "Roberto, what hast thou?"

He said, sweating heavily, "The left leg is broken, *guapa.*"

"We will bind it up," Pilar said. "Thou canst ride that." She pointed to one of the horses that was packed. "Cut off the load."

Robert Jordan saw Pablo shake his head and he nodded at him.

"Get along," he said. Then he said, "Listen, Pablo. Come here."

The sweat-streaked, bristly face bent down by him and Robert Jordan smelt the full smell of Pablo.

"Let us speak," he said to Pilar and Maria. "I have to speak to Pablo."

"Does it hurt much?" Pablo asked. He was bending close over Robert Jordan.

"No. I think the nerve is crushed. Listen. Get along. I am mucked, see? I will talk to the girl for a moment. When I say to take her, take her. She will want to stay. I will only speak to her for a moment."

"Clearly, there is not much time," Pablo said.

"Clearly."

"I think you would do better in the Republic," Robert Jordan said.

"Nay. I am for Gredos."

"Use thy head."

"Talk to her now," Pablo said. "There is little time. I am sorry thou hast this, *Inglés.*"

"Since I have it—" Robert Jordan said. "Let us not speak of it. But use thy head. Thou has much head. Use it."

"Why would I not?" said Pablo. "Talk now fast, *Inglés.* There is no time."

Pablo went over to the nearest tree and watched down the slope, across the slope and up the road across the gorge. Pablo was looking at the gray horse on the slope with true regret on his face and Pilar and Maria were with Robert Jordan where he sat against the tree trunk.

"Slit the trouser, will thee?" he said to Pilar. Maria crouched by him and did not speak. The sun was on her hair and her face was twisted as a child's contorts before it cries. But she was not crying.

Pilar took her knife and slit his trouser leg down below the left-hand pocket. Robert Jordan spread the cloth with his hands and looked at the stretch of his thigh. Ten inches below the hip joint there was a pointed, purple swelling like a sharp-peaked little tent and as he touched it with his fingers he could feel the snapped-off thigh bone tight against the skin. His leg was lying at an odd angle. He looked up at Pilar. Her face had the same expression as Maria's.

"*Anda,*" he said to her. "Go."

She went away with her head down without saying anything nor looking back and Robert Jordan could see her shoulders shaking.

"*Guapa,*" he said to Maria and took hold of her two hands. "Listen. We will not be going to Madrid—"

Then she started to cry.

"No, *guapa,* don't," he said. "Listen. We will not go to Madrid now but I go always with thee wherever thou goest. Understand?"

She said nothing and pushed her head against his cheek with her arms around him.

"Listen to this well, rabbit," he said. He knew there was a great hurry and he was sweating very much, but this had to be said and understood. "Thou wilt go now, rabbit. But I go with thee. As long as there is one of us there is both of us. Do you understand?"

"Nay, I stay with thee."

"Nay, rabbit. What I do now I do alone. I could not do it well with thee. If thou goest then I go, too. Do you not see how it is? Whichever one there is, is both."

"I will stay with thee."

"Nay, rabbit. Listen. That people cannot do together. Each one must do it alone. But if thou goest then I go with thee. It is in that way that I go too. Thou wilt go now, I know. For thou art good and kind. Thou wilt go now for us both."

"But it is easier if I stay with thee," she said. "It is better for me."

"Yes. Therefore go for a favor. Do it for me since it is what thou canst do."

"But you don't understand, Roberto. What about *me?* It is worse for me to go."

"Surely," he said. "It is harder for thee. But I am thee also now."

She said nothing.

He looked at her and he was sweating heavily and he spoke now, trying harder to do something than he had ever tried in all his life.

"Now you will go for us both," he said. "You must not be selfish, rabbit. You must do your duty now."

She shook her head.

"You are me now," he said. "Surely thou must feel it, rabbit.

"Rabbit, listen," he said. "Truly thus I go too. I swear it to thee."

She said nothing.

"Now you see it," he said. "Now I see it is clear. Now thou wilt go. Good. Now you are going. Now you have said you will go."

She had said nothing.

"Now I thank thee for it. Now you are going well and fast and far and we both go in thee. Now put thy hand here. Now put thy head down. Nay, put it down. That is right. Now I put my hand there. Good. Thou art so good. Now do not think more. Now art thou doing what thou should. Now thou art obeying. Not me but us both. The me in thee. Now you go for us both. Truly. We both go in thee now. This I have promised thee. Thou art very good to go and very kind."

He jerked his head at Pablo, who was half-looking at him from the tree and Pablo started over. He motioned with his thumb to Pilar.

"We will go to Madrid another time, rabbit," he said. "Truly. Now stand up and go and we both go. Stand up. See?"

"No," she said and held him tight around the neck.

He spoke now still calmly and reasonably but with great authority.

"Stand up," he said. "Thou art me too now. Thou art all there will be of me. Stand up."

She stood up slowly, crying, and with her head down. Then she dropped quickly beside him and then stood up again, slowly and tiredly, as he said, "Stand up, *guapa.*"

Pilar was holding her by the arm and she was standing there.

"*Vamonos,*" Pilar said. "Dost lack anything, *Inglés?*" She looked at him and shook her head.

"No," he said and went on talking to Maria.

"There is no good-by, *guapa,* because we are not apart. That it should be good in the Gredos. Go now. Go good. Nay," he spoke now still calmly and reasonably as Pilar walked the girl along. "Do not turn around. Put thy foot in. Yes. Thy foot in. Help her up," he said to Pilar. "Get her in the saddle. Swing up now."

He turned his head, sweating, and looked down the slope, then back toward where the girl was in the saddle with Pilar by her and Pablo just behind. "Now go," he said. "Go."

She started to look around. "Don't look around," Robert Jordan said. "Go." And Pablo hit the horse across the crupper with a hobbling strap and it looked as though Maria tried to slip from the saddle but Pilar and Pablo were riding close up against her and Pilar was holding her and the three horses were going up the draw.

"Roberto," Maria turned and shouted. "Let me stay! Let me stay!"

"I am with thee," Robert Jordan shouted. "I am with thee now. We are both there. Go!" Then they were out of sight around the corner of the draw and he was soaking wet with sweat and looking at nothing.

Agustín was standing by him.

"Do you want me to shoot thee, *Inglés?*" he asked, leaning down close. "*Quieres?* It is nothing."

"*No hace falta,*" Robert Jordan said. "Get along. I am very well here."

"*Me cago en la leche que me han dado!*" Agustín said. He was crying so he could not see Robert Jordan clearly. "*Salud, Inglés.*"

"*Salud,* old one," Robert Jordan said. He was looking down the slope now. "Look well after the cropped head, wilt thou?"

"There is no problem," Agustín said. "Thou hast what thou needest?"

"There are very few shells for this *máquina,* so I will keep it," Robert Jordan said. "Thou canst not get more. For that other and the one of Pablo, yes."

"I cleaned out the barrel," Agustín said. "Where thou plugged it in the dirt with the fall."

"What became of the pack-horse?"

"The gypsy caught it."

Agustín was on the horse now but he did not want to go. He leaned far over toward the tree where Robert Jordan lay.

"Go on, *viejo,*" Robert Jordan said to him. "In war there are many things like this."

"*Qué puta es la guerra,*" Agustíain said. "War is a bitchery."

"Yes man, yes. But get on with thee."

"*Salud, Inglés,*" Agustín said, clenching his right fist.

"*Salud,*" Robert Jordan said. "But get along, man."

Agustín wheeled his horse and brought his right fist down as though he cursed again with the motion of it and rode up the draw. All the others had been out of sight long before. He looked back where the draw turned in the timber and waved his fist. Robert Jordan waved and then Agustín, too, was out of sight. . . . Robert Jordan looked down the green slope of the hillside to the road and the bridge. I'm as well this way as any, he thought. It wouldn't be worth risking getting over on my belly yet, not as close as that thing was to the surface, and I can see better this way.

He felt empty and drained and exhausted from all of it and from them going and his mouth tasted of bile. Now, finally and at last, there was no problem. However all of it had been and however all of it would ever be now, for him, no longer was there any problem.

They were all gone now and he was alone with his back against a tree. He looked down across the green slope, seeing the gray horse where Agustín had shot him, and on down the slope to the road with the timber-covered country behind it. Then he looked at the bridge and across the bridge and watched the activity on the bridge and the road. He could see the trucks now, all down the lower road. The gray of the trucks showed through the trees. Then he looked back up the road to where it came down over the hill. They will be coming soon now, he thought.

Pilar will take care of her as well as any one can. You know that. Pablo must have a sound plan or he would not have tried it. You do not have to worry about Pablo. It does no good to think about Maria. Try to believe what you told her. That is the best. And who says it is not true? Not you. You don't say it, any more than you would say the things did not happen that happened. Stay with what you believe now. Don't get cynical. The time is too short and you have just sent her away. Each one does what he can. You can do nothing for yourself but perhaps you can do something for another. Well, we had all our luck in four days. Not four days. It was afternoon when I first got there and it will not be noon today. That makes not quite three days and three nights. Keep it accurate, he said. Quite accurate.

I think you better get down now, he thought. You better get fixed around some way where you will be useful instead of leaning against this tree like a tramp. You have had much luck. There are many worse things than this. Every one has to do this, one day or another. You are not afraid of it once you know you have to do it, are you? No, he said, truly. It was lucky the nerve was crushed, though. I cannot even feel that there is anything below the break. He touched the lower part of his leg and it was as though it were not part of his body.

He looked down the hill slope again and he thought. I hate to leave it, is all. I hate to leave it very much and I hope I have done some good in it. I have tried to with what talent I had. *Have, you mean. All right, have.*

I have fought for what I believed in for a year now. If we win here we will win everywhere. The world is a fine place and worth the fighting for and I hate very much to leave it. And you had a lot of luck, he told himself, to have had such a good life. You've had just as good a life as grandfather's though not as long. You've had as good a life as any one because of these last days. You do not want to complain when you have been so lucky. I wish there was some way to pass on what I've learned, though. Christ, I was learning fast there at the end. I'd like to talk to Karkov. That is in Madrid. Just over the hills there, and down across the plain. Down out of the gray rocks and the pines, the heather and the gorse, across the yellow high plateau you see it rising white and beautiful. That part is just as true as Pilar's old women drinking the blood down at the slaughterhouse. There's no *one* thing that's true. It's all true. The way the planes are beautiful whether they are ours or theirs. The hell they are, he thought.

You take it easy, now, he said. Get turned over now while you still have time. Listen, one thing. Do you remember? Pilar and the hand? Do you believe that crap? No, he said. Not with everything that's happened? No, I don't believe it. She was nice about it early this morning before the show started. She was afraid maybe I believed it. I don't, though. But she does. They see something. Or they feel something. Like a bird dog. What about extra-sensory perception? What about obscenity? he said. She wouldn't say good-by, he thought, because she knew if she did Maria would never go. That Pilar. Get yourself turned over, Jordan. But he was reluctant to try it.

Then he remembered that he had the small flask in his hip pocket and he thought, I'll take a good spot of the giant killer and then I'll try it. But the flask was not there when he felt for it. Then he felt that much more alone because he knew there was not going to be even that. I guess I'd counted on that, he said.

Do you suppose Pablo took it? Don't be silly. You must have lost it at the bridge. "Come on now, Jordan," he said. "Over you go."

Then he took hold of his left leg with both hands and pulled on it hard, pulling toward the foot while he lay down beside the tree he had been resting his back against. Then lying flat and pulling hard on the leg, so the broken end of the bone would not come up and cut through the thigh, he turned slowly around on his rump until the back of his head was facing downhill. Then with his broken leg, held by both hands, uphill, he put the sole of his right foot against the instep of his left foot and pressed hard while he rolled, sweating, over onto his face and chest. He got onto his elbows, stretched the left leg well behind him with both hands and a far, sweating, push with the right foot and there he was. He felt with his fingers on the left thigh and it was all right. The bone end had not punctured the skin and the broken end was well into the muscle now.

The big nerve must have been truly smashed when that damned horse rolled on it, he thought. It truly doesn't hurt at all. Except now in certain changes of positions. That's when the bone pinches something else. You see? he said. You see what luck is? You didn't need the giant killer at all.

He reached over for the submachine gun, took the clip out that was in the magazine, felt in his pocket for clips, opened the action and looked through the barrel, put the clip back into the groove of the magazine until it clicked, and then looked down the hill slope. Maybe half an hour, he thought. Now take it easy.

Then he looked at the hillside and he looked at the pines and he tried not to think at all.

He looked at the stream and he remembered how it had been under the bridge in the cool of the shadow. I wish they would come, he thought. I do not want to get in any sort of mixed-up state before they come.

Who do you suppose has it easier? Ones with religion or just taking it straight? It comforts them very much but we know there is no thing to fear. It is only missing it that's bad. Dying is only bad when it takes a long time and hurts so much that it humiliates you. That is where you have all the luck, see? You don't have any of that.

It's wonderful they've got away. I don't mind this at all now they are away. It *is* sort of the way I said. It is really very much that way. Look how different it would be if they were all scattered out across that hill where that gray horse is. Or if we were all cooped up here waiting for it. No. They're gone. They're away. Now if the attack were only a success. What do you want? Everything. I want everything and I will take whatever I get. If this attack is no good another one will be. I never noticed when the planes came back. *God, that was lucky I could make her go.*

I'd like to tell grandfather about this one. I'll bet he never had to go over and find his people and do a show like this. How do you know? He may have done fifty. No, he said. Be accurate. Nobody did any fifty like this one. Nobody did five. Nobody did one maybe not just like this. Sure. They must have.

I wish they would come now, he said. I wish they would come right now because the leg is starting to hurt now. It must be the swelling.

We were going awfully good when that thing hit us, he thought. But it was only luck it didn't come while I was under the bridge. When a thing is wrong something's bound to happen. You were bitched when they gave Golz those orders. That was what you knew and it was probably that which Pilar felt. But later on we will have these things much better organized. We ought to have portable short wave transmitters. *Yes, there's a lot of things we ought to have.* I ought to carry a spare leg, too.

He grinned at that sweatily because the leg, where the big nerve had been bruised by the fall, was hurting badly now. Oh, let them come, he said. I don't want to do that business that my father did. I will do it all right but I'd much prefer not to have to. I'm against that. Don't think about that. Don't think at all. I wish the bastards would come, he said. I wish so very much they'd come.

His leg was hurting very badly now. The pain had started suddenly with the swelling after he had moved and he said, Maybe I'll just do it now. I guess I'm not awfully good at pain. Listen, if I do that now you wouldn't mis-understand, would you? *Who are you talking to?* Nobody, he said. Grandfather, I guess. No. Nobody. Oh bloody it, I wish that they would come.

Listen, I may have to do that because if I pass out or anything that I am no good at all and if they bring me to they will ask me a lot of questions and do things and all and that is no good. It's much best not to have them do those things. So why wouldn't it be all right to just do it now and then the whole thing would be over with? Because oh, listen, yes, listen, *let them come now.*

You're not so good at this, Jordan, he said. Not so good at this. And who is so good at this? I don't know and I don't really care right now. But you are not. That's right. You're not at all. Oh not at all, at all. I think it would be all right to do it now? Don't you?

No, it isn't. Because there is something you can do yet. As long as you know what it is you have to do it. As long as you remember what it is you have to wait for that. *Come on. Let them come. Let them come. Let them come!*

Think about them being away, he said. Think about them going through the timber. Think about them crossing a creek. Think about them riding through the heather. Think about them going up the slope. Think about them O. K. tonight. Think about them travelling, all night. Think about them hiding up tomorrow. Think about them. God damn it, think about them. *That's just as far as I can think about them,* he said.

Think about Montana. *I can't.* Think about Madrid. *I can't.* Think about a cool drink of water. *All right.* That's what it will be like. Like a cool drink of water. *You're a liar.* It will just be nothing. That's all it will be. Just nothing. Then do it. *Do it.* Do it now. It's all right to do it now. Go on and do it now. *No, you have to wait.* What for? You know all right. *Then wait.*

I can't wait any longer now, he said. If I wait any longer I'll pass out. I know because I've felt it starting to go three times now and I've held it. I held it all right. But I don't know about any more. What I think is you've got an internal hemorrhage there from where that thigh bone's cut around inside. Especially on that turning business. That makes the swelling and that's what weakens you and makes you start to pass. It would be all right to do it now. Really, I'm telling you that it would be all right.

And if you wait and hold them up even a little while or just get the officer that may make all the difference. One thing well done can make—

All right, he said. And he lay very quietly and tried to hold on to himself that he felt slipping away from himself as you feel snow starting to slip sometimes on a mountain slope, and he said, now quietly, then let me last until they come.

Robert Jordan's luck held very good because he saw, just then, the cavalry ride out of the timber and cross the road. He watched them coming riding up the slope. He saw the trooper who stopped by the gray horse and shouted to the officer who rode over to him. He watched them both looking down at the gray horse. They recognized him of course. He and his rider had been missing since the early morning of the day before.

Robert Jordan saw them there on the slope, close to him now, and below he saw the road and the bridge and the long lines of vehicles below it. He was completely integrated now and he took a good long look at everything. Then he looked up at the sky. There were big white clouds in it. He touched the palm of his hand against the pine needles where he lay and he touched the bark of the pine trunk that he lay behind.

Then he rested as easily as he could with his two elbows in the pine needles and the muzzle of the submachine gun resting against the trunk of the pine tree.

As the officer came trotting now on the trail of the horses of the band he would pass twenty yards below where Robert Jordan lay. At that distance there would be no problem. The officer was Lieutenant Berrendo. He had come up from La Granja when they had been ordered up after the first report of the attack on the lower post. They had ridden hard and had then had to swing back, because the bridge had been blown, to cross the gorge high above and come around through the timber. Their horses were wet and blown and they had to be urged into the trot.

Lieutenant Berrendo, watching the trail, came riding up, his thin face serious and grave. His submachine gun lay across his saddle in the crook of his left arm. Robert Jordan lay behind the tree, holding onto himself very carefully and delicately to keep his hands steady. He was waiting until the officer reached the sunlit place where the first trees of the pine forest joined the green slope of the meadow. He could feel his heart beating against the pine needle floor of the forest.

Frozen Chosin

From *Breakout*

BY MARTIN RUSS

ONE OF THE FINEST chronicles of combat to appear in recent years was Martin Russ's *Breakout,* published in 1999. *Breakout* is the detailed story of the Marines fighting their way back to the coast after being surrounded and cut off by six Chinese divisions (60,000 men) in the Chosin Reservoir area in late 1950. During their "breakout," the Marines killed over 25,000 Chinese while wounding about 12,500 between October 15 and December 15. Marine casualties were 700 dead, 200 missing, 2,500 wounded, and 6,200 frostbite cases.

When the action was called a "retreat," a "Retreat Hell!" remark came into legend. The phrase has been attributed to various officers over the years, but finally Martin Russ has chased it to earth.

The phrase originally came during World War I when Marine Capt. Lloyd Williams answered a messenger from the French commander as the U.S. troops were arriving at Belleau Wood in 1918. "Retreat, hell. We just got here!"

In the Chosin Reservoir action, the closest phrases to the remark came from comments by Marine Major General Oliver P. Smith speaking to a British reporter at Hagaru, North Korea. "There can be no retreat when there's no rear. You can't retreat, or even withdraw, when you're surrounded. The only thing you can do is to break out, and in order to do that you have to attack, and that is what we're about to do. Heck, all we're doing is attacking in a different direction."

One last comment about the "retreat" question. Here is Lieutenant Joseph Owen, reported by Martin Russ: "We kicked the shit out of the Chinese the first time we met them, which was at Sudong, and we were still kicking the shit out of them when we crossed the Tredway Bridge. They were surrendering to us, not the other way around. Retreat, you say?"

★ ★ ★ ★ ★

Back in September there had been some resentment in Easy Company over the sudden influx of Reservists, and when the veterans of the First Platoon learned that their new officer was a "weekend warrior," they expected the worst. Lt. Yancey, getting wind of this, gathered his thirty-five men on the grass of a soccer field outside Uijongbu and delivered a short address. "I know what's on your mind, you Regulars. Yes, I'm a Reserve officer, but I earned this commission the hard way, and I'm not going to stand for any foolishness about Regulars versus Reservists. When the fighting begins you won't be able to tell one from the other. We're all United States Marines."

Yancey let them find out for themselves that he had won a battlefield commission by leading a squad against a crowd of Japanese, accounting for thirty dead himself, including the commanding officer "who attempted with great vigor to decapitate me with a samurai sword." Yancey had joined the Reserves after the war, got married, and opened a business called Yancey's Liquors in Little Rock.

Corpsman James Claypool: "Yancey and I were wondering how Private Stanley Robinson was doing back at Regiment as Litzenberg's bodyguard. I was worried that outside the umbrella of Yancey's supervision this youngster might be unable to restrain the wild streak in him. This was the kid who was considered such a badass he had to be brought aboard ship under guard. . . . Well, guess who came toiling up the hill late that afternoon? We were glad to see him and his BAR; but I noticed he was limping and got him to sit down and take off his boots even before he reported to Mr. Yancey.

"I was always fanatical about foot care. During the march to Yudam-ni, whenever we took a break I was all over those kids: 'I want those shoe-pacs off and I want those felt liners out and I want those socks changed.' I made them dry their feet and rub them. I made them keep their wet socks inside their clothing to dry out. I wouldn't let anybody keep their shoe-pacs on when they crawled into their bags. I wouldn't let them wear dirty socks because the dirt in the cloth was like fine sandpaper and led to abrasions. As soon as we occupied 1282 I went right to work on their feet, making them clean them with snow, applying boric-acid ointment after they were dry.

"Robinson of course tried to give me a hard time. I looked him in the eye and said, 'Are you going to argue with me?' He thought it over and finally unlaced his boot. I was shocked by what I saw. The skin between his toes was raw, and the skin on his ankles too. There was infection. He had the equivalent of second- and third-degree burns. He was virtually crippled with frostbite. 'You're going back down the hill,' I told him.

" 'The hell I am.'

" 'Robinson . . .'

" 'Don't fuck with me, swabbie.'

"In the end I had to go tell Yancey; it was like a teacher reporting a defiant student to the principal. I told Yancey that Robinson's feet were beyond my resources to treat, that he would probably have to be evacuated. He didn't ask to look at Robinson's feet; he just accepted my word for it. 'Robbie, I'm glad to see you,' he told him, 'but you're going to have to go back down the hill and turn yourself in to Battalion Aid.' Robinson was so angry he didn't even say good-bye. We watched him limp down the back trail. We were *all* disappointed.

"After Robinson departed, Yancey got into a tense discussion with PFC James Gallagher. Gallagher was a blatant racist from Philadelphia. You might think the jarheads of that day were racist in general, so many of them hailing from the poor white South, but that wasn't the case; a fellow like Gallagher really stood out. His Irish father and Italian mother lived in a neighborhood that black folks were beginning to move into and Gallagher didn't like it. Yancey, though a Southerner, wouldn't tolerate racism in his platoon.

"He was a daring young man, that Gallagher. Short, powerful, tough. Face like an Italian leprechaun. At Sudong he was as much a hero as Robinson, running half a mile up 698 with a machine gun and two boxes of ammo to keep Robinson company on the crest. Frankly, I didn't like the kid much, but I was glad he was on our side. Anyway, Yancey was trying to set him straight when someone on watch interrupted to call our attention to a man in white on the skyline a few hundred yards to the left front. He had a pair of binoculars trained on us. We let him look. We didn't have anything to hide."

Captain Walter Phillips had placed Yancey's and 1st Lt. Leonard Clements's platoons in a semicircle on the crest. The usual fifty percent watch was in effect. Phillips and Captain Milton Hull on Hill 1240 had arranged to send out a patrol from each company every half hour, to meet halfway along the saddle connecting the two hills. The night's password: *Lua lua lei.* The countersign: *Hawaii.* Shortly before dusk, Yancey sent Corporal Lee Phillips and his squad about three hundred yards out and told him to dig in. This was to be Easy Company's listening post for the night. Phillips had barely reached the spot when two F4U Corsairs came roaring in over 1282; both cut loose with a burst that plowed long furrows in the snow, barely missing Phillips and his men. 1st Lt. Neal E. Heffernan, the forward air controller, got on the radio and called them off: "Secure the mission, Blueberry!"

Yancey: "I brought Phillips in after that because I didn't trust those airdales."

("When the Chosin Few get together at these reunions, you know," says Yancey, "they always pay tribute to the Corsair pilots and their close air support; but some of us recall the times when the pilots were too eager or got their signals crossed and instead of threatening the shambos they threatened the Marines. That's the reality of it.")

The moon came up over the southern skyline at a little past six. Yancey: "It rose behind us, and that worried me, because we were silhouetted on the skyline. In front of us was this desolate landscape with the lake off to the right, with open spaces of black ice where wind had blown away the snow."

Some of the Marines thought they heard music in the distance; when the wind changed, they realized it was the sound of Chinese bugles, faint and eerie.

At 9:45 p.m. Easy Company's radio operator picked up an odd warning from Dog Company on 1240: "Heads up, over there! One of our guys just got bayoneted in his bag." While the radio operator was trying to confirm this, word was quietly passed along the crest of 1282 that "Mr. Yancey wants to see bayonets on the end of those rifles and carbines."

Corporal Earl Pickens, machine gunner: "Sergeant Cruz was the first to detect movement out front. As he was reaching for the sound-power phone, a Chinese soldier jumped up about ten feet in front of us and charged. I saw Cruz thrust out his .45 and shoot him in the face before I realized what was going on. When Gallagher opened up with the machine gun, it was music to my ears, because I had been worried about the gun freezing up. Because of their white uniforms, all you could see were their shadows and the muzzle blasts of their burp guns. There were only a handful of them, though. It was another probe, aimed at drawing our fire so they could tell where our automatic weapons were."

After the Chinese were driven off, Captains Phillips and Hull, conferring by radio, decided to cancel the hourly patrols along the connecting saddle. It remained quiet on 1282 and 120 for two hours.

"Something you gotta see, Lieutenant."

"Later, I'm busy."

But Gallagher persisted and Yancey went over. Yancey: "You get to see some strange sights in war. Here's Gallagher with this grin on his face, and what he's grinning about is this string of bodies stretching right up to the gun, with the elbow of the last one actually touching the forward leg of the tripod. 'Pretty good, huh, Lieutenant?' I told him to drag in two or three of the bodies and use them like sandbags in front of his position. He thought that was a great idea."

Yancey went back to making his rounds. Some of the young Marines needed calming down. "Sure, they'll be back," he told them, "but we're ready for them, understand? Just do what I tell you."

A shot rang out at long range and the spent bullet grazed Yancey's right cheek and lodged in his nose. Calmly he removed one glove and plucked it out. Yancey: "Blood was oozing down my cheek into my mouth, but then it froze up. I didn't say anything about this to anyone."

Knots of Chinese had now slipped across the saddle between the two hills and were beginning to fire directly down on the 5th Marines headquarters in the valley below.

2nd Lt. Thomas Gibson, a 4.2-inch mortar officer on phone watch, began getting inquiries about green tracers flying across the sky. The roar of the Coleman lantern masked the start of the battle; Gibson hadn't heard any gunfire at all. After the third inquiry he stepped outside for a look, and there they were. Gibson: "Americans don't use green tracers. I went back inside and woke up the operations officer and told him about it. He wasn't impressed; he went back to sleep. After making the appropriate notations in the logbook, I started checking around by phone. I couldn't find anyone who was stirred up about it. When the tempo of the firing began to pick up, I shook the ops officer awake again. Squinting one eye open, he cocked an ear and was just telling me there was nothing to worry about when a long burst of automatic fire came ripping through the tent, rattling the tin spark-arrestor on top. I think the ops officer was shod and armed and outside before the burst ended."

Everybody was flying out of their tents now, taking up defensive positions in the roadside ditch. Lt. Col. Raymond Murray: "We had been subjected to night attacks throughout our operations in Korea, so at first I considered this just another local action. But all of a sudden the command post came under fire and that's when I began to pay attention. I turned to my exec and said, 'We better get our asses out of here.' I recalled a mound of earth next to the road and thought that if we could get a phone line put in over there we could operate with a bit of cover. I was able to stay in touch with all three battalions without any of them knowing I had opened shop in the middle of an empty field. When I called Taplett and asked what was happening in his neighborhood, he said the enemy was attacking his command post at that very moment and could he call me back later. We heard lots of gunfire over in his sector and a good deal of shouting. At first I assumed it was the Chinese doing the shouting and thought he was being overrun. I was on the point of bringing Jack Stevens's battalion [1/5] into counterattacking position, but then Tap called back to say that two of his platoons were counterattacking and I realized it was our guys who were doing all the yelling."

Murray, on learning that Roise's flanks were in the air, decided it was time to pull 2/5 back and have Roise tie in with William Harris's 3/7 on the left and Taplett's 3/5 on the right.

At 5:45 a.m. on the twenty-eighth the regimental commander alerted Roise to the probability that his battalion would be retracted. Rearward was not a direction Marines liked to go; Roise's immediate reaction, when he found the coordinates Murray had given him on the map, was that there had been a map-reading error at regiment. He asked for confirmation of the coordinates and was surprised when they were confirmed.

Thus Lt. Col. Harold Roise learned that the forward momentum of the 1st Marine Division had been brought to a halt, perhaps permanently as far as this particular campaign was concerned. Years later he told an interviewer, "I had a hard time accepting it. When an entire battalion is geared up for a sustained attack, it's hard to cancel out. I felt frustrated, frankly. I think we all did."

Yancey: "It had been quiet for an hour or two, then we began hearing these odd noises down at the bottom of the slope, like hundreds of feet walking slowly across a big carpet of cornflakes." Yancey cranked the handle on the field phone. The response was a whisper from the company exec, 1st Lt. Raymond Ball.

"That you, Ray?"

"Go ahead, John."

"They're coming up the hill."

"You sure?"

"I can hear the fuckers crunching through the snow. How about some illumination?"

"Hold on."

1st Lt. William Schreier, mortar officer: "The cold weather affected the burning rate of the fuses. The first rounds hit the ground before they flashed. We increased the charges to maximum and finally got them to illuminate overhead. We only had about thirty rounds of illum and less than a hundred of high explosive. This wasn't nearby enough, as we were soon to discover."

By then the crunching noise had stopped and the Marines of the First Platoon heard the shrill voice of an officer shouting in English: "Thank God nobody lives forever!"

Yancey: "I don't need to tell you that's not the kind of thing you expect to hear on an Asian battlefield; but it's what the man said and we all heard it. I had a violent reaction: I decided he must have learned his English at a Christian missionary school. The son of a bitch had been fed and sheltered and given a good education by Americans—and here he was leading Red troops against us. That annoyed me."

The first flare popped overhead, and Yancey spotted the officer in front of the first rank of troops, holding a machine-pistol in one hand. The Marines were shocked to see several ranks of Chinese arrayed behind him, spaced ten or fifteen yards apart, the whole formation ascending the slope. The battle of 1282 began in earnest when Yancey yelled, "You're damn right nobody lives forever, you renegade bastard!" and brought him down with a burst from his carbine. The ranks continued to ascend, the soldiers now wailing in a minor key: 'Son of a bitch Marine we kill. Son of a bitch Marine you die.'

Yancey: "It was altogether most eerie."

Corpsman Claypool: "Gallagher, firing short bursts with his machine gun, was taking incoming in return; but he never flinched. The company mortars were in pits just behind us, and every time they fired there were sparks and fireworks as a round left the tube. I heard someone yelling for a corpsman and that meant I had to leave the protection of my hole. Then a star round burst overhead and everything in that wilderness of snow below us was brilliantly illuminated. I saw men in white writhing on the ground while others stepped over or around them. The Marines fired methodically, spanged empty, reloaded, fired again. Sergeant Allen Madden, Yancey's platoon sergeant, saw me and beckoned and pointed to two downed Marines. Together we carried the first one out of the line of fire, and when I came back for the second I had a shelter half to use as a sled; but there were more wounded Marines now and I didn't have time to lay the cloth down and load each man aboard, so I began dragging them backward by their parka hoods."

Captain Walter Phillips, already wounded in the arm and leg, was hobbling about offering encouragement. "You're doing fine," he told his troops.

The Chinese were hurling their grenades in clusters. ("They looked like flights of blackbirds," said Yancey.) Some of the survivors said they saw Chinese carrying *baskets* of grenades. Yancey was moving from hole to hole, passing out bandoliers of M-1 ammunition, when an explosion blew him off his feet, a piece of shrapnel piercing the roof of his mouth. "After that, blood kept trickling down my throat and I kept spitting it out."

Captain Phillips's voice broke through the din again and again: "You're doing well, Marines. . . . Stay loose, Marines. . . . You're doing fine, Marines."

Corporal Earl Pickens: "The Chinese were charging us continually, wave after wave. They wanted that hill."

Staff Sergeant Robert Kennemore, a machine-gun section leader, was making himself useful by crawling among the wounded and dead, collecting ammunition and distributing it to those who needed it. The Chinese were so close that he could hear them tapping the handles of their potato-masher grenades on the frozen ground to arm them. In the gloom below, Kennemore thought he saw a group of Chinese dragging a machine gunner from a foxhole by the legs, clubbing him, bayoneting him. Kennemore maneuvered down the slope, looking for a shooting position.

"Where are you going?" It was Captain Phillips, white-faced and wobbly.

"One of my gunners, sir—"

"Don't go down there, you damn fool." The officer resumed his painful progress along the lines while Kennemore dragged a load of ammo to the other gun in his section, still in action with a crew of three despite the hail of fire. A Chinese grenade plopped in the snow beside the assistant gunner; Kennemore scooped it up and sidearmed it down the slope before it exploded. Another landed nearby and there was only time for Kennemore to put his foot on it, driving it into the snow, as a third grenade landed beside it. Kennemore, willing to die to save his fellow Marines, dropped his knee on it and absorbed the force of both explosions. The three crewmen were temporarily deafened but otherwise unhurt.

Yancey: "Sometime during the night I caught a glimpse of Ray Ball firing his carbine from a sitting position. The Chinese were coming over the ridge on the right flank and he was calmly picking them off, one by one. He continued to do this until a burp gunner blindsided him, catching him in the side with a burst. I thought he was dead but he wasn't."

Easy Company's machine gun platoon leader, a second lieutenant, had been sent down the reverse slope earlier to report to the battalion command post, where he was to link up with ammo-bearers and reinforcements and guide them back to 1282. Yancey: "I heard Ray Ball talking with him on the radio, telling him to get his ass back to 1282. The lieutenant said he would try, and Ray said, 'Try? That's not good enough.' " The lieutenant, for reasons of his own, could not bring himself to return to that hilltop scene of concentrated, deadly chaos, where it seemed a company of United States Marines was in the process of being wiped out.

Private Stanley Robinson lay disgruntled and foot-sore on a stretcher in the battalion aid station, listening to the sound of distant firefights, wondering how Easy Company was doing. An ambulance jeep pulled up outside; litter-bearers brought in a stretcher and put a wounded man down beside him.

"What outfit you with?"

"Easy Company, 7th."

"They got hit pretty good?"

"Clobbered. The captain and Mr. Ball are down. Mr. Yancey's been hit but he's still going."

Robinson sat up. In the darkness of the tent he began to pull on his boots, grunting with pain as he stuffed his swollen feet into the stiff shoe-pacs. It took several minutes to do the job. At last he stood up, pulled on his dirty parka, and went stumbling through the tent flaps. Outside he snatched up a rifle and cartridge belt from the pile of discards. A corpsman appeared. "Where do you think you're going, Robinson?"

"What does it look like, Doc?"

"Go back inside."

"Get the fuck outta my way."

The scrawny youngster slung the rifle and tottered toward the big hill like a crippled old man. An hour later, having been forced to crawl up the steeper portions of the path, he was asking directions to the First Platoon.

"Top of the hill, straight over."

"Seen Mr. Yancey?"

"He's been hit twice, but he's still at it."

Yancey was hunched beside a machine gunner, directing his fire, when he felt a sharp slap on the bottom of his boot. "I looked down and there he was, with his off-kilter grin, looking sloppier and dirtier than ever. 'What the hell are *you* doing here?'

" 'I heard you candyassed pogues needed help.'

" 'I'll be damned.'

" 'So,' said Robinson, 'you got any work for a BAR man?'

"I pointed over the right. 'See those kids over there? Go over and get 'em squared away. They need a little encouragement.' Robbie was younger than any of them, but I knew he would get results."

Claypool: "Robinson had returned to his true home."

Yancey's platoon was running out of men. He went over to talk to 1st Lt. Leonard Clements about it. "Clem, can you spare a squad? I got to get these shambos off my flank." As we were talking, a bullet caught him dead center in the forehead and down he went. He had just called the squad leader over. 'The lieutenant's dead,' I told him. 'Get your kids in hand and follow me.' I scooped up some other Marines and ended up with about twenty altogether, including Robbie and his four or five."

PFC Wilmer Swett: "He shouted, 'Here we go,' and him and Robinson took off, but when he looked back there was nobody following him. This pissed him off royally. 'Gung ho, you miserable cowardly bastards! I said *Follow me.*' He stood there waiting, and one by one the rest of us moved up, and pretty soon we had something like a skirmish line in motion."

Yancey: "Once we got going, two or three of the kids actually moved ahead of me. I recognize how hard it is to get your ass in gear in a situation like that, where chances are you're going to get killed or at least hurt pretty bad; but that's what Marines are supposed to do. Marines don't get any slack."

The battle atop 1282 began tapering off around 2 a.m., as the Chinese, responding to the signal from a bugle, began to pull back down the slope. Soon it was quiet except for the moans of the wounded and dying.

The next assault began around 3 a.m. Yancey turned to his runner, PFC Marshall McCann. "I don't need you right now, McCann. Get up there in the hole with Rick, and make every shot count." Soon after the attack began, Yancey heard a Marine yell, "I'm hit."

"Where're you hit?"

"In the balls."

Yancey crawled across open ground and took a look. "You ain't shot in the balls, you're grazed in the hams. Pick up that rifle and earn your pay!"

Corpsman Claypool: "When you get hit, your first thought is that you're dying. This one Marine was knocked down by a burst from a burp gun, but I found that his skin wasn't even broken. His parka and field jacket and wool sweater and vest and wool shirt and utility jacket and long johns had saved him. He was convinced he was dying of multiple wounds.

" 'I tell ya, I'm on the way out, Doc.'

" 'Uh-huh.'

" 'Doc, listen to me—I been hit all over!'

" 'Son, you're not even wounded.'

"That really offended him. He called me an old bastard."

(Dr. Henry Litvin: "Somewhere in your book I hope you'll tell the reader about the role of the Navy corpsman. He was the guy who stopped the bleeding and made it possible for a wounded Marine either to stay in action or at least stay alive until he could be sent back to the surgical team. The up-front Navy corpsman was the most important link in the whole chain of evacuation.")

Claypool: "Whenever a Marine would die on me I would just move over to the next man. At the start of the battle I would write 'KIA' [killed in action] on each tag along with the approximate time of death and attach it to the top button of his jacket. But soon we had so many casualties I didn't have time to tag them. Several times that night the thought crossed my mind that I wasn't going to get off that hill alive. With so many dead and dying Marines around me, it was obvious my chances were slender. There were so many grenades going off that I stopped paying attention to them. I spent a lot of time bent over, and sometimes when I stood up, the tail of my parka wouldn't drop down because it was pinned against my pants by slivers of shrapnel; every so often I'd reach back and yank the tail down and pull the slivers out of the cloth."

Claypool kept seeing Yancey stalk back and forth, yelling and spitting blood, shouting through a blood-clogged throat: "Gung ho, Marines!" By the light of the flares he made a perfect target.

"Gung ho," said Gallagher.

"Gung ho," said Robinson."

Yancey: "It was as close to Custer's Last Stand as you can get outside of the movies. I kept asking myself, 'Where did all these shambos come from?' "

Claypool: "A couple of times I tried to stop him and treat his wounds but he was too busy moving 'the kids' to the best spots to keep the Chinese from overwhelming us. No one wanted to argue with Yancey, and none of us wanted to stay on that damn hill without him being there too."

The Marine line was faltering, about to break. Captain Phillips appeared behind them holding an M-1 rifle tipped with a bayonet. Turning it upside down, he rammed it into the hard earth with all his diminishing strength. "This is Easy Company," he shouted hoarsely, "and this is where we stand!"

Shortly afterward, a burst of fire cut him down. Lt. Ball, nearly immobilized with multiple wounds, took command, yelling instructions and occasionally firing his carbine from a sitting position.

Claypool: "The other company corpsman was a guy named George Fisher. He was a good-natured fellow much younger than me—I was twenty-six at the time—and much smaller. George was sort of insignificant looking, peering out at the world through a pair of government-issue glasses. We worked pretty well together. Because I was so much bigger, I was the one who dragged the wounded Marines off the line if they couldn't negotiate under their own power, while George stayed busy at the aid tent."

Yancey: "Yes, I remember George Fisher very well—for two reasons. First of all, he cried a lot. The suffering of the Marines really tore him up, and he couldn't hide it. Second, he had no aptitude for the work at all: he was not only physically clumsy, he was sort of delicate, and he seemed to have to force himself to keep going. But he did his duty. Marines have a lot of respect for their Navy corpsmen, as you know."

Claypool:"We put as many of the wounded as we could in sleeping bags to keep them warm so that shock wouldn't kill them. We tried to save our morphine for Marines hit in the chest or gut. (You had to hold the syrettes in your mouth to keep them thawed out.) Often we had to inject a wounded man on the little-finger side of the wrist. Not a very sterile situation: everyone's wrist was black with dirt and soot from the campfires. We had too little morphine, too few bandages, too little time, and we had to make decisions that were extremely unpleasant. On the spot we had to decide which Marines were worth working on and which to ignore since they were going to die shortly, and sometimes you didn't even have time to stop and hold a kid's hand. Most of them asked for their mother. I was accustomed to all that from World War Two. George wasn't."

A Chinese soldier about twenty yards away fired a burst in Yancey's direction, and one of the rounds hit him under the right eye, jarring the eyeball loose from its socket and knocking him over. With his left eye Yancey saw the soldier crouch down and jam another magazine into his weapon. Yancey groped around for the carbine and, not finding it, took the .45 from under his armpit and pumped two rounds into the soldier. Then, as carefully as he could, Yancey removed his gloves and pushed the eye back where it belonged. "It was like pushing a hard-boiled egg into a knothole, but it went in and stayed there."

It was clear by now that unless the companies on 1282 and 1240 were reinforced, the northern defense line was going to fold. Phillips's Easy Company was barely hanging on; Hull's Dog Company had been shoved off 1240 but was presently fighting its way back to the top. During the lull after midnight, Phillips called Lt. Col. Davis and, in the understated Marine style of the day, asked for assistance. "We've taken too many casualties. We're holding, but we can use some help."

With the luckless Randolph Lockwood stuck in Hagaru, Raymond Davis, as we have seen, was burdened with five rifle companies, at least two of which were now in serious trouble. After Davis discussed the situation with Murray at the combined regimental headquarters, reinforcements from First Battalion, 5th Marines, were placed on full alert. A platoon of Captain Jack Jones's Charlie Company/5 was assigned to support Hull's counterattack on 1240; the other two were sent to rescue Phillips's remnant on 1282.

Lt. Col. John W. Stevens, 1/5's commanding officer, recalls that the confusion of the moment was compounded by a frantic call from the C.O. of the Third Battalion, 7th, Lt. Col. William Harris, begging Stevens to send his entire battalion to extricate him from entrapment. "I more or less put him on hold—told him I'd call back. After that I went out to brief the troops [elements of Jones's and Heater's companies] who were about to climb the back of the two northern hills in the dark. The briefing didn't have a great deal of substance. All I could tell them was that when they got to the top of their respective hills they could expect a terrific fight."

Captain Jack Jones recalls the resentment he felt at having his company split up; it was against doctrine. On the other hand, he recognized it was an emergency and what was needed on the hilltop were warm bodies, armed.

PFC Ray Walker, Able Company, 5th: "We were bedded down close to the village and feeling pretty secure. I had just stretched out on a pile of straw and saw a stream of green tracers come scooting over the crest of a hill north of us. It was quite a show: The tracers raced like comets, bouncing off slopes, zooming straight up toward the stars—and every once in awhile you could see the yellowish light from Chinese flares. My enjoyment of the show was interrupted by the appearance of Gunnery Sergeant Stanley Millar.

" 'All right, drop your cocks and grab your socks! We're going up that hill.'

" 'What's going on, Gunny?'

" 'The 7th Marines need help, as usual. Saddle up!'

"Right away we started bitching about the pitiful Reservists who couldn't handle a few stragglers and were now whining for the Regulars to come get them out of a fix." About half of the 7th Regiment was made up of Reservists.

2nd Lt. Nicholas Trapnell, Able/5, recalls that things got quiet when the reinforcements began climbing the slope, and that the point man kept calling out: "Easy Company . . . Where you at, Easy Company? . . . Hey, Easy Company!"

Lt. John Yancey: "We didn't know reinforcements were on the way, because our phone lines were cut and the radio had been smashed in the fight. During this second lull, one of things we found time for was wrapping the dead Marines in ponchos and carrying them to the top of the back trail so the ammo carriers could drag them off the hill."

When the moon went down behind the mountain, Yancey had a reaction to the sudden darkness: he thought he saw "all sorts of boogymen." The Chinese corpses down below came to life: wriggling, rolling over, crawling, sitting up, getting to their feet—turning into nightmare monsters.

Corpsman Claypool: "There were bodies everywhere, especially in front of Gallagher's and Robinson's positions. I watched Robinson search through a dead soldier's pack and pockets. He found a lump of rice mixed with some other grain cooked into a ball about the size of a grapefruit, wrapped in a brown handkerchief. He showed it to me: 'Look at this, Doc!' "

Lt. Robert Bey and his men were watching the Chinese on the crest as Staff Sergeant Daniel Murphy approached him. Bey: "The only thing I could hear up there was the Chinese language being spoken. There was no question they had the top of the hill."

"If you let me counterattack," said Murphy, "I think we can push them back from the command post."

Bey turned his Third Squad over to Murphy. Corpsman Claypool volunteered to go along. He was warmly welcomed. Claypool: " 'Volunteer' might not be the right word. I was coming down from Yancey's command post when I spotted several Chinese soldiers. They didn't see me, and I hugged the ground until they passed by. When Sergeant Murphy was getting his group together, I figured that maybe being with them was the safest place on the hill, so I tagged along. In terms of numbers we didn't amount to much: Murphy and Sergeant Keith's squad plus five stragglers from Lieutenant Clements's platoon; but we clawed our way upslope and chased the Chinese off the crest. I saw a Chinese officer up close: he was wearing a dark sweater under his coat and the coat was open. What I remember best about him, though, is that he didn't shoot me with the revolver he was carrying."

As he started tending to the wounded, Claypool could hear Murphy asking questions. "Where's everybody?"

"The Skipper's dead. Mr. Ball's dying."

"How about Lieutenant Clements?"

"Dead."

A voice sounded out of the darkness. "The hell I am!" Lt. Leonard Clements had been struck in the forehead by a burp gun bullet and lived to tell about it. Clements: "It felt like someone had hauled off with a sledgehammer. I didn't dare touch the spot with my hand because I was afraid part of my head was gone. When I asked after Lieutenant Yancey, someone said he had been shot several times and had bled to death. Funny, John thought I was dead and I thought John was dead."

Clements then spotted what he later called "this squared-away gent" climbing toward him, followed by a column of fresh-looking Marines. "I'm Jack Jones," said the squared-away gent. "I've got part of a company with me."

"Let me show you where my people are," said Clements.

By the light of a flare, the dying Lt. Ball greeted Captain Jones with a smile and a feeble wave.

Lt. William Schreier: "We were all wounded." Schreier himself was having difficulty walking, surprised that a simple wound in the wrist could affect him so strongly. What he didn't know was that a piece of shrapnel was lodged in his chest, that one of his lungs had collapsed and the other was filling with fluid. Try as he might, he couldn't function, and he was soon headed downhill on a stretcher. Schreier: "I felt bad because there was lots of fighting left to be done and I wanted to do my share. But I just couldn't hack it."

The lull in the battle came to an end with a bugle call, followed by "the most amazing pyrotechnical display I've ever seen," according to Lieutenant Trapnell. "Roman candles, Vesuvius fountains, pinwheels, skyrockets, and an infinite number of firecrackers. When that was over, the enemy started to climb toward us once again. The slopes of the saddle were quite steep, and the enemy got close before the shooting started up again. We smelled them before we saw them. Some folks are skeptical about this business of the garlic. It wasn't only garlic on the breath, it was in the clothing too. When you eat garlic over a period of time, it exudes from your pores and, believe me, it carries.

"Soon we were engaged across our entire front and hard pressed to keep them from spilling over into the draw behind us. When it got light enough, you could see that the whole top of the hill had been ground to pumice by grenades, mortars, and artillery shells."

PFC Ray Walker's BAR had stopped working; he couldn't get the bolt to slide forward. A group of enemy soldiers went by on his left; they saw the young Marine but didn't do anything about it. Walker was busy dismantling his weapon: he removed the trigger group, threw it one way, took out the firing pin, threw that another way. There were weapons all around, and he picked up an M-1 and fired one round with it before it malfunctioned too. Down the hill he saw a Chinese soldier walk up behind a Marine gunner ("very casually, as if he were a barber about to give a customer a haircut"), put a pistol to his head, pull the trigger, and walk on down the slope. Walker: "By this time I was frantically trying to find a weapon that worked and feeling nakeder and nakeder. Then a small Marine with curly black hair appeared and said, 'I know where we can get some grenades.' We dragged a whole case back to the spot, opened it with a K-Bar, and began tossing grenades down the slope. There was so much lead flying that there was no sense trying to find a safe place to throw from. By this time it looked like the whole hill was crawling with big white worms."

Walker never understood how it happened, but when he reached for the next grenade it was already sputtering, the spoon gone. He threw up his right arm and was backing away when it went off. Shrapnel from the explosion broke his right ulna, penetrated his left chest, and cut his lip, forehead, and fingers. A corpsman named Parker took an ampule of morphine out of his mouth and gave Walker a shot. A few minutes later, just at daybreak, he was heading down the backside of the hill with a group of wounded Marines that included John Yancey.

Corpsman Claypool was stepping around some brush and rocks looking for wounded Marines when he saw a Chinese soldier sitting with his body facing the corpsman but with his head twisted around and his weapon aimed toward a line of wounded descending the reverse slope. When Claypool shot him—from about ten yards away—his head hit his knees and the quilted hat with earflaps flew off. "He didn't know what hit him, didn't have time to experience the dread of death."

It was light enough now for air strikes, and the first one of the day was so close that the Marines on 1282 saw the upended wing of a Corsair flash by on the other side of the ridge, going from left to right—so close it seemed as though the pilot was scraping off his payload only a few yards in front of them.

Lt. Yancey's jaw was dislocated—he was never sure how it happened—and he had bound it up with a strip of blanket. Spotting Captain Jones, he went up to him and tried to give him an informal briefing on the situation on 1282. His face was covered with crusted blood, one eye was closed, and he was groggy from all the concussion grenades. Captain Jones took one look and told him to join the walking wounded being escorted down the hill.

Yancey: "A sergeant yelled at me, 'This way down!' and reached toward me with a long stick. I grabbed hold of it and he led me down the trail. By the time we got to Battalion Aid, I was bleeding again, so one of the corpsmen tied me sitting up to a tent pole to keep me from choking in my own blood."

Claypool: "None of us would have survived the night if Yancey hadn't been there. No one else could have bullied his troops into standing and facing almost certain death the way he did. Sometimes I wonder if maybe Yancey single-handedly saved the Marines at Yudam-ni, not just the Marines on 1282; because if the Chinese had taken 1282, they would have poured through the breach and overrun the 5th and 7th Marines command posts. All I know for sure is that the Chinese would have overrun 1282 if Yancey hadn't been there.

"I have one more thing to say about him. If a son or grandson of mine had to serve in combat, I wouldn't want him to serve in John Yancey's platoon.

His troops took twice as much ground and killed twice as many Chinese, but he also lost twice as many men. Then again, that's the way Marines do business. . . . But not with *my* kids."

The official history sums up the action on 1282 as follows: "[It was] basically the story of the suicide of the 1st Battalion, 235th CCF [Chinese Communist Forces] Regiment." There is no official tally of Chinese dead in the battle for 1282, but there were hundreds of corpses piled up on the forward slope and on the crest. As for the Marines, Easy/7 suffered 120 dead and wounded, out of the original 176. (Stanley Robinson and James Gallagher walked off the hill unscathed.) Jones's Charlie/5 had ten dead, thirty wounded. Heater's Able/5: five dead, thirty-seven wounded.

The second lieutenant who was sent down the hill for ammunition never did return. Such military cowards are in a peculiar way immortalized along with the heroes; they are often mentioned in discussions, the veterans still shaking their heads over a former comrade's moment of weakness on the field of battle. His privacy is always protected; the name is never mentioned in the presence of outsiders. Contempt or disgust are hardly ever expressed toward him. If any emotion is manifest it is likely to be pity, for everyone understands that the coward has to live with his shame for the rest of his life. In the case of this particular officer, his transgression was major: he could not bring himself to return at a moment when his unit desperately needed the ammunition and reinforcements he had been sent for.

Ignoring his own wounds, PFC Ray Walker spent part of that morning helping men who couldn't stand up to urinate into cans, "so they wouldn't wet themselves." He came across his assistant BAR man, PFC Middlekauf, on a stretcher; Middlekauf's jaw was badly swollen from a shrapnel wound. "I made some hot cocoa and helped him sit up and drink it." (Thirty-four years later, a portly, bald gentleman introduced himself at a Chosin Few reunion and thanked Walker for the companionship and comfort he had provided at a lonely moment.)

A Marine he didn't recognize came through the tent flaps.

"Hey, Walker—aren't you a friend of Reuben Fields? I got him outside in the truck."

"What's wrong with him?"

"He's had the course."

"You mean he's dead?"

"Not quite."

Walker: "Reuben Fields was a moonshiner's boy from Harlan County, Kentucky. I helped carry him in, busted ulna notwithstanding. He was unconscious and moaning. The doctors wouldn't treat him. I was indignant, then outraged—until someone explained that he was brain-injured and beyond help. We carried him back outside and put him down on some hay. He died in my arms. I cried. At least he wasn't alone."

Claypool: "Later that morning I found Mr. Ball down in the battalion aid station. He was just conscious enough to recognize me. 'What about the company?' he asked.

" 'Still holding on, sir.'

"He was gray from lack of blood. What plasma we had was frozen and unusable. The sun hadn't hit the valley floor yet and it was awfully cold in that tent. I took the sleeping bags off two dead Marines—not an easy job, what with rigor mortis—and put them around the lieutenant, stuffing the edges under the stretcher, tucking him in for the long journey. I was holding his hand when he passed. It was around 0830.

"I was going to miss Lieutenant Ball, and Captain Phillips too. They were close friends, by the way, and they complemented each other. Lieutenant Ball was quiet and studious and thorough. Captain Phillips was outgoing and dashing, a natural troop commander. Both of them had dedicated their adult lives to the Marine Corps, and they made being a Marine something special. I admired them. But then I admired the whole damn outfit. Easy Company, 7th Marines—they were the most exceptional group of people I've ever encountered."

Two Soldiers

BY WILLIAM FAULKNER

HERE IS AN EXCERPT from one of the most gripping and poignant war stories ever written, and in it not a shot is fired. There are no bombs, artillery, or hand grenades. And yet, it reads with the stunning feel of the impact of war. Considering that it was written by a Nobel Prize winner and one of the most remarkable writers in history, I suppose one should feel no surprise over its literary merit. Only appreciation.

In reflecting on the vastness and scope of William Faulkner's novels and short stories, I often return to an impression I have that some of his simpler and more straightforward works are better than some of the more critically acclaimed examples of literary pyrotechnics. Say, *The Bear* compared to *As I Lay Dying* or *The Sound and the Fury.* Say, the short stories "Turn About," "Delta Autumn" and "That Evening Sun" as compared to the novel *A Fable.* Oh well, I'm just a reader, not a critic or scholar, and I'm sure I have a lot to learn in those areas. But for my personal reading pleasure—call me old-fashioned or whatever you want—give me a story like "Two Soldiers." A story with feeling—about the possibilities of commitment, the shock of loss, and the enduring strength of hope.

The fictional events in this tale, told through the voice and eyes of a young boy, were no doubt actually lived in different ways countless times throughout America during World War II. Mr. William Faulkner of Oxford, Mississippi, was the messenger sent to spread the word about what was going on in the deep south in 1941, when poverty and lack of education—yes, ignorance!—were roommates in almost every rural household. Where even electricity was rare.

Despite sending troops to Europe to fight for a short time in World War I, Americans were essentially of an isolationist nature. "Not our boys!" was a common chant.

Pearl Harbor changed all that. The world would never be the same.

Here is a heart-wrenching glimpse back at those days when, for most Americans, the call for service could not be ignored.

★   ★   ★   ★   ★

Me and Pete would go down to Old Man Killegrew's and listen to his radio. We would wait until after supper, after dark, and we would stand outside Old Man Killegrew's parlor window, and we could hear it because Old Man Killegrew's wife was deaf, and so he run the radio as loud as it would run, and so me and Pete could hear it plain as Old Man Killegrew's wife could, I reckon, even standing outside with the window closed.

And that night I said, "What? Japanese? What's a pearl harbor?" and Pete said, "Hush."

And so we stood there, it was cold, listening to the fellow in the radio talking, only I couldn't make no heads nor tails neither out of it. Then the fellow said that would be all for a while, and me and Pete walked back up the road to home, and Pete told me what it was. Because he was nigh twenty and he had done finished the Consolidated last June and he knowed a heap: about them Japanese dropping bombs on Pearl Harbor and that Pearl Harbor was across the water.

"Across what water?" I said. "Across that Government reservoy up at Oxford?"

"Naw," Pete said. "Across the big water. The Pacific Ocean."

We went home. Maw and pap was already asleep, and me and Pete laid in the bed, and I still couldn't understand where it was, and Pete told me again—the Pacific Ocean.

"What's the matter with you?" Pete said. "You're going on nine years old. You been in school now ever since September. Ain't you learned nothing yet?"

"I reckon we ain't got as fer as the Pacific Ocean yet," I said.

We was still sowing the vetch then that ought to been all finished by the fifteenth of November, because pap was still behind, just like he had been ever since me and Pete had knowed him. And we had firewood to git in, too, but every night me and Pete would go down to Old Man Killegrew's and stand outside his parlor window in the cold and listen to his radio; then we would come back home and lay in the bed and Pete would tell me what it was. That is, he would tell me for a while. Then he wouldn't tell me. It was like he didn't want to talk about it no more. He would tell me to shut up because he wanted to go to sleep, but he never wanted to go to sleep.

He would lay there, a heap stiller than if he was asleep, and it would be something, I could feel it coming out of him, like he was mad at me even, only I knowed he wasn't thinking about me, or like he was worried about something, and it wasn't that neither, because he never had nothing to worry about. He never got behind like pap, let alone stayed behind. Pap give him ten acres when he graduated from the Consolidated, and me and Pete both reckoned pap was durn glad to get shut of at least ten acres, less to have to worry with himself; and Pete had them ten acres all sowed to vetch and busted out and bedded for the winter, and so it wasn't that. But it was something. And still we would go down to Old Man Killegrew's every night and listen to his radio, and they was at it in the Philippines now, but General MacArthur was holding um. Then we would come back home and lay in the bed, and Pete wouldn't tell me nothing or talk at all. He would just lay there still as a ambush and when I would touch him, his side or his leg would feel hard and still as iron, until after a while I would go to sleep.

Then one night—it was the first time he had said nothing to me except to jump on me about not chopping enough wood at the wood tree where we was cutting—he said, "I got to go."

"Go where?" I said.

"To that war," Pete said.

"Before we even finish gittin' in the firewood?"

"Firewood, hell," Pete said.

"All right," I said. "When we going to start?"

But he wasn't even listening. He laid there, hard and still as iron in the dark. "I got to go," he said. "I jest ain't going to put up with no folks treating the Unity States that way."

"Yes," I said. "Firewood or no firewood, I reckon we got to go."

This time he heard me. He laid still again, but it was a different kind of still.

"You?" he said. "To a war?"

"You'll whup the big uns and I'll whup the little uns," I said.

Then he told me I couldn't go. At first I thought he just never wanted me tagging after him, like he wouldn't leave me go with him when he went sparking them girls of Tull's. Then he told me the Army wouldn't leave me go because I was too little, and then I knowed he really meant it and that I couldn't go nohow noways. And somehow I hadn't believed until then that he was going himself, but now I knowed he was and that he wasn't going to leave me go with him a-tall.

"I'll chop the wood and tote the water for you-all then!" I said. "You got to have wood and water!"

Anyway, he was listening to me now. He wasn't like iron now.

He turned onto his side and put his hand on my chest because it was me that was laying straight and hard on my back now.

"No," he said. "You got to stay here and help pap."

"Help him what?" I said. "He ain't never caught up nohow. He can't get no further behind. He can sholy take care of this little shirttail of a farm while me and you are whupping them Japanese. I got to go too. If you got to go, then so have I."

"No," Pete said. "Hush now. Hush." And he meant it, and I knowed he did. Only I made sho from his own mouth. I quit.

"So I just can't go then," I said.

"No," Pete said. "You just can't go. You're too little, in the first place, and in the second place—"

"All right," I said. "Then shut up and leave me go to sleep."

So he hushed then and laid back. And I laid there like I was already asleep, and pretty soon he was asleep and I knowed it was the wanting to go to the war that had worried him and kept him awake, and now that he had decided to go, he wasn't worried any more.

The next morning he told maw and pap. Maw was all right. She cried.

"No," she said, crying, "I don't want him to go. I would rather go myself in his place, if I could. I don't want to save the country. Them Japanese could take it and keep it, so long as they left me and my family and my children alone. But I remember my brother Marsh in that other war. He had to go to that one when he wasn't but nineteen, and our mother couldn't understand it then any more than I can now. But she told Marsh if he had to go, he had to go. And so, if Pete's got to go to this one, he's got to go to it. Jest don't ask me to understand why."

But pap was the one. He was the feller. "To the war?" he said. "Why, I just don't see a bit of use in that. You ain't old enough for the draft, and the country ain't being invaded. Our President in Washington, D.C., is watching the conditions and he will notify us. Besides, in that other war your ma just mentioned, I was drafted and sent clean to Texas and was held there nigh eight months until they finally quit fighting. It seems to me that that, along with your Uncle Marsh who received a actual wound on the battlefields of France, is enough for me and mine to have to do to protect the country, at least in my lifetime. Besides, what'll I do for help on the farm with you gone? It seems to me I'll get mighty far behind."

"You been behind as long as I can remember," Pete said. "Anyway, I'm going. I got to."

"Of course he's got to go," I said. "Them Japanese—"

"You hush your mouth!" maw said, crying. "Nobody's talking to you! Go and get me a armful of wood! That's what you can do!"

So I got the wood. And all the next day, while me and Pete and pap was getting in as much wood as we could in that time because Pete said how pap's idea of plenty of wood was one more stick laying against the wall that maw ain't put on the fire yet, Maw was getting Pete ready to go. She washed and mended his clothes and cooked him a shoe box of vittles. And that night me and Pete laid in the bed and listened to her packing his grip and crying, until after a while Pete got up in his nightshirt and went back there, and I could hear them talking, until at last maw said, "You got to go, and so I want you to go. But I don't understand it, and I won't never, and so don't expect me to." And Pete come back and got into the bed again and laid again still and hard as iron on his back, and then he said, and he wasn't talking to me, he wasn't talking to nobody: "I got to go. I just got to."

"Sho you got to," I said. "Them Japanese—" He turned over hard, he kind of surged over onto his side, looking at me in the dark.

"Anyway, you're all right," he said. "I expected to have more trouble with you than with all the rest of them put together."

"I reckon I can't help it neither," I said. "But maybe it will run a few years longer and I can get there. Maybe someday I will jest walk in on you."

"I hope not," Pete said. "Folks don't go to wars for fun. A man don't leave his maw crying just for fun."

"Then why are you going?" I said.

"I got to," he said. "I just got to. Now you go on to sleep. I got to ketch that early bus in the morning."

"All right," I said. "I hear tell Memphis is a big place. How will you find where the Army's at?"

"I'll ask somebody where to go to join it," Pete said. "Go on to sleep now."

"Is that what you'll ask for? Where to join the Army?" I said.

"Yes," Pete said. He turned onto his back again. "Shut up and go to sleep."

We went to sleep. The next morning we et breakfast by lamplight because the bus would pass at six o'clock. Maw wasn't crying now. She jest looked grim and busy, putting breakfast on the table while we et it. Then she finished packing Pete's grip, except he never wanted to take no grip to the war, but maw said decent folks never went nowhere, not even to a war, without a change of clothes and something to tote them in. She put in the shoe box of fried chicken and biscuits and she put the Bible in, too, and then it was time to go. We didn't know until then that maw wasn't going to the bus. She jest brought Pete's cap and overcoat, and still she didn't cry no more, she jest stood with her hands on Pete's shoulders and she didn't move, but somehow, and just holding Pete's shoulders, she looked as hard and fierce as when Pete had turned toward me in the bed last night and tole me that anyway I was all right.

"They could take the country and keep the country, so long as they never bothered me and mine," she said. Then she said, "Don't never forget who you are. You ain't rich and the rest of the world outside of Frenchman's Bend never heard of you. But your blood is good as any blood anywhere, and don't you never forget it."

Then she kissed him, and then we was out of the house, with pap toting Pete's grip whether Pete wanted him to or not. There wasn't no dawn even yet, not even after we had stood on the highway by the mailbox, a while. Then we seen the lights of the bus coming and I was watching the bus until it come up and Pete flagged it, and then, sho enough, there was daylight—it had started while I wasn't watching. And now me and Pete expected pap to say something else foolish, like he done before, about how Uncle Marsh getting wounded in France and that trip to Texas pap taken in 1918 ought to be enough to save the Unity States in 1942, but he never. He done all right too. He jest said, "Goodby, son. Always remember what your ma told you and write her whenever you find the time." Then he shaken Pete's hand, and Pete looked at me a minute and put his hand on my head and rubbed my head durn nigh hard enough to wring my neck off and jumped into the bus, and the feller wound the door shut and the bus begun to hum; then it was moving, humming and grinding and whining louder and louder; it was going fast, with two little red lights behind it that never seemed to get no littler, but jest seemed to be running together until pretty soon they would touch and jest be one light. But they never did, and then the bus was gone, and even like it was, I could have pretty nigh busted out crying, nigh to nine years old and all.

The Leipzig Mission

From *Serenade to the Big Bird*

BY BERT STILES

MANY OF THE great battles of World War II were fought in the skies, over places with names like Schweinfurt and Regensburg. After Dunkirk, in the years and months leading up to D-Day, June 6, 1944, the U.S. Army Air Corps and the British Air Forces were the only allies taking the battle to the Germans.

While the British bombed at night, the Americans took on the daunting task of trying to prove that daylight precision bombing was feasible. Despite the fighting qualities of the B-17 bombers and their crews, losses were heavy.

Bert Stiles' account of his experiences as a B-17 copilot flying out of England can arguably be called the most gripping ever written concerning the air campaign against Germany. Stiles writes in vivid bursts of prose that seem to hit like physical blows, as indeed they were intended. His style is so intense that it seems to me as if I am listening to a survivor who can barely speak and is out of breath. The frequent use of ellipses are Stiles' own, used for dramatic effect, and do not represent omissions. Nothing has been deleted from this chapter of Bert Stiles' unforgettable book.

★   ★   ★   ★   ★

Leipzig

The crews scheduled for that haul were waked up around 0300 hours. There was plenty of bitching about that.

I was so tired I felt drunk.

They told us there'd be eggs for breakfast, but there was just bacon without eggs. There was plenty of bitching about that too.

In the equipment hut I heard somebody say, 'Today I'm catching up on my sack time.'

Some other gunner said, 'I slept most of the way to Augsburg yesterday.'

Nobody said anything about the Luftwaffe. Leipzig is in there deep, but plenty of gunners bitched about taking extra ammunition. Plenty of gunners didn't take any.

Beach was flying his last mission with Langford's crew.

'We're the last of Lieutenant Newton's gang,' he said wanly.

'And I'll be the very last,' I said. 'Take it easy today.'

We had an easy ride in. I didn't feel sleepy. I just felt dazed.

There was soft fuzz over a thin solid overcast going in, but inside Germany the clouds broke up. There was haze under the cumulus and the ground showed pale green through the holes.

'We're way back,' Green said.

The group was tucked in nicely, the low squadron was up close, and Langford was doing a pretty job of flying high.

The lead and high groups of our wing looked nice too. But our group, the low, was way back and below. Our wing was the rail end, with most of the 8th up ahead.

The wing had S-ed out and called our group leader to catch up. He didn't.

If I didn't listen to the engine roar it was quiet up there. The sky was a soft sterile blue. Somehow we didn't belong there.

There was death all over the sky, the quiet threat of death, the anesthesia of cold sunlight filled the cockpit.

The lady named Death is a whore . . . Luck is a lady . . . and so is Death. . . . I don't know why. And there's no telling who they'll go for. Sometimes it's a quiet, gentle, intelligent guy. The Lady Luck strings along with him for a while, and then she hands him over to the lady named Death. Sometimes a guy comes along who can laugh in their faces. The hell with luck, and the hell with death. . . . And maybe they go for it . . . and maybe they don't.

There's no way to tell. If you could become part of the sky you might know . . . because they're always out there. The lady of Luck has a lovely face you can never quite see, and her eyes are the night itself, and her hair is probably dark and very lovely . . . but she doesn't give a damn.

And the lady named Death is sometimes lovely too, and sometimes she's a screaming horrible bitch . . . and sometimes she's a quiet one, with soft hands that rest gently on top of yours on the throttles.

The wing leader called up, 'We're starting our climb now.' We only had a half hour or so until target time.

He hadn't listened. The lead and high groups were already far above us. We were back there alone.

We never caught up after that.

'I don't like this,' Green said.

'Tuck it in,' somebody said over VHF. 'Bandits in the target area.'

I was tense and drawn taut. The sky was cold and beautifully aloof.

Green was on interphone and I was on VHF, listening for anything from the lead ship.

I heard a gun open up.

Testing, I decided.

I saw some black puffs and a couple of bright bursts.

Jesus, we're in the flak already, I thought.

Then the guns opened up. Every gun on the ship opened up. A black Focke-Wulf slid under our wing, and rolled over low.

I flipped over on interphone and fear was hot in my throat and cold in my stomach.

'Here they come.' It was Mock, I think, cool and easy, like in a church. Then his guns fired steadily.

The air was nothing but black polka dots and firecrackers from the 20-millimeters.

'Keep you eye on 'em. Keep 'em out there. . . .' It was Mock and Bossert.

'Got the one at seven . . .' Bossert or Mock. Steady.

They came through again, coming through from the tail.

I saw two Forts blow up out at four o'clock. Some other group.

A trio of gray ones whipped past under the wing and rolled away at two o'clock. Black crosses on gray wings . . 109s.

A night-fighter Focke-Wulf moved up almost in formation with us, right outside the window, throwing shells into somebody up ahead. Somebody powdered him.

One came around at ten o'clock . . . and the nose guns opened up on him. He rolled over and fell away . . . maybe there was smoke. . . .

The instruments were fine. Green looked okay. My breath was in short gasps.

'Better give me everything,' Green said. Steady voice.

I jacked-up the RPM up to the hilt.

They were queuing up again back at four and six and eight. A hundred of them . . . maybe two hundred . . . getting set to come through again . . . fifteen or twenty abreast. . . .

. . . I looked up at the other wing-ship. The whole stabilizer was gone. I could see blue sky through there . . . but the rudder still worked . . . still flapped . . . then his wing flared up . . . he fell off to the right.

We were flying off Langford, but he was gone . . . sagging off low at three o'clock. Green slid us in under the lead squadron. Langford was in a dive . . . four or five planes were after him . . . coming in . . . letting them have it . . . swinging out . . . and coming in again. . . . Beach was in that ball . . . poor goddamn Beach. . . .

'Here they come!'

'Four o'clock level.'

'Take that one at six.'

All the guns were going again.

There wasn't any hope at all . . . just waiting for it . . . just sitting there hunched up . . . jerking around to check the right side . . . jerking back to check the instruments . . . everything okay . . . just waiting for it. . . .

They came through six times, I guess . . . maybe five . . . maybe seven . . . queuing up back there . . . coming in . . . throwing those 20s in there.

. . . we were hit . . .

. . . the whole law squadron was gone . . . blown up . . . burned up . . . shot to hell . . . one guy got out of that.

. . . we were the only ones left in the high . . . tucked in under the lead. The lead squadron was okay . . . we snuggled up almost under the tail guns. They were firing steadily . . the shell cases were dropping down and going through the cowling . . . smashing against the plexiglass . . . chipping away at the windshields . . . coming steady . . . coming all the time . . . then his guns must have burned out . . .

. . . there were a few 51s back there . . . four against a hundred . . . maybe eight. . . .

'Don't shoot that 51,' Mock again, cool as hell . . .

I punched the wheel forward. A burning plane was nosing over us.

Green nodded, kept on flying. . . .

The guns were going . . . not all of them any more . . . some of them were out . . . burned out . . . maybe.

And then it was over. They went away.

We closed up and dropped our bombs.

Six out of twelve gone.

We turned off the target, waiting for them . . . knowing they'd be back . . . cold . . . waiting for them. . . .

There was a flow to it . . . we were moving . . . we were always moving . . . sliding along through the dead sky. . . .

I flicked back to VHF.

No bandits called off.

Then, I heard, '. . . is my wing on fire? . . . will you check to see if my wing is on fire? . . .'

He gave his call sign. It was the lead ship.

We were right underneath. We pulled up even closer.

'You're okay,' I broke the safety wire on the transmitter. 'You're okay . . . baby . . . your wing is okay. No smoke . . . no flame . . . stay in there, baby.'

It was more of a prayer.

'. . . I'm bailing out my crew. . . .'

I couldn't see any flame. I wasn't sure it was the same plane. But they were pulling out to the side.

All my buddies. Maurie . . . Uggie . . .

I told Green. 'We better get back to the main group . . . we better get back there fast . . .'

We banked over. I saw the rear door come off and flip away end over end in the slipstream. Then the front door, then something else . . . maybe a guy doing a delayed jump. It didn't look like a guy very much.

It must have been set up on automatic pilot. It flew along out there for half an hour. If they jumped they were delayed jumps.

Maybe they made it.

We found a place under the wing lead.

I reached over and touched Green. What a guy. Then I felt the control column. Good airplane . . . still flying . . . still living. . . .

Everybody was talking.

Nobody knew what anybody said.

There was a sort of beautiful dazed wonder in the air . . .

. . . still here. . . . Still living . . . still breathing.

And then it came through . . . the thought of all those guys . . . those good guys . . . cooked and smashed and down there somewhere, dead or chopped up or headed for some Stalag.

We were never in that formation. We were all alone, trailing low.

From the day you first get in a 17 they say formation flying is the secret.

They tell you over and over. Keep those planes tucked in and you'll come home.

The ride home was easy. They never came back.

The sky was a soft unbelievable blue. The land was green, never so green.

When we got away from the Continent we began to come apart. Green took off his mask.

There weren't any words, but we tried to say them.

'Jesus, you're here,' I said.

'I'm awfully proud of them,' he said quietly.

Bradley came down out of the turret. His face was nothing but teeth. I mussed up his hair, and he beat on me.

The interphone was jammed.

'. . . all I could do was pray . . . and keep praying.' McAvoy had to stay in the radio room the whole time, seeing nothing, doing nothing. . . .

'You can be the chaplain,' Mock said. His voice just the same, only he was laughing a little now.

'. . . if they say go tomorrow . . . I'll hand in my wings. . . . I'll hand in every other goddamn thing . . . but I won't fly tomorrow . . .' Tolbert was positive.

. . . if Langford went down . . . that meant Fletch . . . Fletch and Johnny O'Leary and Beach . . .

. . . and all the others . . . Maurie had long black eyelashes, and sort of Persian's eyes . . . sort of the walking symbol of sex . . . and what a guy . . . maybe he made it . . . maybe he got out. . . .

It was low tide. The clouds were under us again, almost solid, and then I saw a beach through a hole . . . white sand and England.

There was never anywhere as beautiful as that.

We were home.

Green made a sweet landing. We opened up the side windows and looked around. Everything looked different. There was too much light, too much green . . . just too much . . .

We were home. . . .

They sent us out to get knocked off and we came home.

And then we taxied past E-East.

'Jesus, that's Langford,' I grabbed Green.

It was. Even from there we could see they were shot to hell. Their tail was all shot up . . . one wing was ripped and chopped away.

Green swung around into place, and I cut the engines.

. . . we were home . . .

There were empty spaces where ships were supposed to be, where they'd be again in a day, as soon as ATC could fly them down.

We started to talk to people. There were all kinds of people. Jerry, a crew chief, came up and asked us about the guys on the other wing. We told him. Blown up.

. . . honest to God . . . we were really home. . . .

The 20-millimeter hit our wing . . . blew up inside . . . blew away part of the top of number two gas tank . . . blew hell out of everything inside there . . . puffed out the leading edge . . . blew out an inspection panel.

We didn't even lose any gas.

We didn't even blow up.

I stood back by the tail and looked at the hole. I could feel the ground, and I wanted to take my shoes off. Every time I breathed, I knew it.

I could look out into the sky over the hangar and say thank you to the lady of the luck. She stayed.

I was all ripped apart. Part of me was dead, and part of me was wild, ready to take off, and part of me was just shaky and twisted and useless.

Maybe I told it a thousand times.

I could listen to myself. I could talk, and start my voice going, and step back and listen to it.

I went down to Thompson's room, and he listened. He listened a couple of times.

It was a pretty quiet place. Eight ships out of a group is a quiet day at any base.

Colonel Terry just got married. Thompson didn't know about it. I went back to my room and sat across the room from Langford and kept telling myself it was him.

'When I saw you there were at least eight of them,' I said. 'Just coming in, and pulling out, and coming in.' I showed him with my hands.

Then Fletch came in.

Then I thought about Beach.

Beach got three at least. He shot up every shell he had, and got three.

He came over after interrogation.

'I guess they can't kill us Denver guys,' he said. He didn't believe it either. He was all through.

'Jesus,' I said, 'I sure thought they had you.'

Green came in with O'Leary.

'I knew you were down,' O'Leary said. 'I told everyone.'

Green smiled. He looked okay, 'We're on pass,' he said quietly. 'Let's get out of here.'

I wanted to touch him again. I wanted to tell him I was glad I was on his crew, and it was the best goddamn crew I'd ever heard of, but I didn't say anything, and he didn't either.

I got out my typewriter and started a letter to my folks.

And then it came in again . . . all those guys . . . all those good guys . . . shot to hell . . . or captured . . . or hiding there waiting for it.

. . . waiting for it. . . .

Then I came all apart, and cried like a little kid. . . . I could watch myself, and hear myself, and I couldn't do a goddamn thing.

. . . just pieces of a guy . . . pieces of bertstiles all over the room . . . maybe some of the pieces were still over there.

And then it was all right. I went in and washed my face. Green was calling up about trains, standing there in his shorts.

'I think the boys need a rest,' he said. 'You going in?'

'I'll meet you in London at high noon,' I said. 'Lobby of the Regent Palace.'

'Okay,' he said. 'Get a good night's sleep.'

'Meet you there,' I said.

But I didn't.

They sent me to the Flak House. There was an opening, and the squadron sent me.

★   ★   ★   ★   ★

Editor's Postscript: After thirty-five missions completing his tour of duty as a copilot in B-17s, Bert Stiles volunteered to stay in Europe and fly fighters. He was shot down and killed in a P-51 Mustang escorting bombers over Hanover in November, 1944. He was twenty-three years old.

Breathing In

From *Dispatches*

BY MICHAEL HERR

THERE HAVE BEEN many excellent books written about America's bitterest and longest war, but one of the best was also one of the first to come to national prominence—Michael Herr's *Dispatches.* While some of its pieces were originally published in magazines while the Vietnam War raged in the 1960s, the book was first published by Knopf in 1977. *Dispatches* immediately established Herr as one of Vietnam's varsity correspondents. His prose on the jungle fighting in Vietnam jolted the sugarcoated consciousness of naive and indifferent Americans who had turned their backs on the crossfire being endured by our men and women in uniform in the field—the guerrillas and North Vietnamese fighting them on one side, while behind their backs many Americans wanted to (and did!) give aid and comfort to the enemy.

Dispatches is a down-and-dirty, no-holds-barred look into the hell of Vietnam combat, and this piece—which is excerpted from the first chapter of the book—is but a portion of the totally gripping reading experience.

The names of 58,209 Americans inscribed on the Vietnam Veterans Memorial Wall on the peaceful banks of the Potomac River in our nation's capital form a powerful reminder of the fact that American servicemen and women fought bravely in Vietnam. Other reminders are books like Michael Herr's.

Long after the war, in 1989, Michael Herr was quoted in *The London Observer:* "All the wrong people remember Vietnam. I think all those who remember it should forget it, and all the people who forgot it should remember it."

For many Americans, that's far easier said than done.

★　★　★　★　★

Airmobility, dig it, you weren't going anywhere. It made you feel safe, it made you feel Omni, but it was only a stunt, technology. Mobility was just mobility, it saved lives or took them all the time (saved mine I don't know how many times, maybe dozens, maybe none), what you really needed was a flexibility far greater than anything the technology could provide, some generous, spontaneous gift for accepting surprises, and I didn't have it. I got to hate surprises, control freak at the crossroads, if you were one of those people who always thought they had to know what was coming next, the war could cream you. It was the same with your ongoing attempts at getting used to the jungle or the blow-you-out climate or the saturating strangeness of the place which didn't lessen with exposure so often as it fattened and darkened in accumulating alienation. It was great if you could adapt, you had to try, but it wasn't the same as making a discipline, going into your own reserves and developing a real war metabolism, slow yourself down when your heart tried to punch its way through your chest, get swift when everything went to stop and all you could feel of your whole life was the entropy whipping through it. Unlovable terms.

The ground was always in play, always being swept. Under the ground was his, above it was ours. We had the air, we could get up in it but not disappear in *to* it, we could run but we couldn't hide, and he could do each so well that sometimes it looked like he was doing them both at once, while our finder just went limp. All the same, one place or another it was always going on, rock around the clock, we had the days and he had the nights. You could be in the most protected space in Vietnam and still know that your safety was provisional, that early death, blindness, loss of legs, arms or balls, major and lasting disfigurement—the whole rotten deal—could come in on the freakyfluky as easily as in the so-called expected ways, you heard so many of those stories it was a wonder anyone was left alive to die in firefights and mortar-rocket attacks. After a few weeks, when the nickel had jarred loose and dropped and I saw that everyone around me was carrying a gun, I also saw that any one of them could go off at any time, putting you where it wouldn't matter whether it had been an accident or not. The roads were mined, the trails booby-trapped, satchel charges and grenades blew up jeeps and movie theaters, the VC got work inside all the camps as shoeshine boys and laundresses and honey-dippers, they'd starch your fatigues and burn your shit and then go home and mortar your area. Saigon and Cholon and Danang held such hostile vibes that you felt you were being dry-sniped every time someone looked at you, and choppers fell out of the sky like fat poisoned birds a hundred times a day. After a while I couldn't get on one without thinking that I must be out of my fucking mind.

Fear and motion, fear and standstill, no preferred cut there, no way even to be clear about which was really worse, the wait or the delivery. Combat spared far more men than it wasted, but everyone suffered the time between contact, especially when they were going out every day looking for it; bad going on foot, terrible in trucks and APC's, awful in helicopters, the worst, traveling so fast toward something so frightening. I can remember times when I went half dead with my fear of the motion, the speed and direction already fixed and pointed one way. It was painful enough just flying "safe" hops between firebases and lz's; if you were ever on a helicopter that had been hit by ground fire your deep, perpetual chopper anxiety was guaranteed. At least actual contact when it was happening would draw long raggedy strands of energy out of you, it was juicy, fast and refining, and traveling toward it was hollow, dry, cold and steady, it never let you alone. All you could do was look around at the other people on board and see if they were as scared and numbed out as you were. If it looked like they weren't you thought they were insane, if it looked like they were it made you feel a lot worse.

I went through that thing a number of times and only got a fast return on my fear once, a too classic hot landing with the heat coming from the trees about 300 yards away, sweeping machine-gun fire that sent men head down into swampy water, running on their hands and knees toward the grass where it wasn't blown flat by the rotor blades, not much to be running for but better than nothing. The helicopter pulled up before we'd all gotten out, leaving the last few men to jump twenty feet down between the guns across the paddy and the gun on the chopper door. When we'd all reached the cover of the wall and the captain had made a check, we were amazed to see that no one had even been hurt, except for one man who'd sprained both his ankles jumping. Afterward, I remembered that I'd been down in the muck worrying about leeches. I guess you could say that I was refusing to accept the situation.

"Boy, you sure get offered some shitty choices," a Marine once said to me, and I couldn't help but feel that what he really meant was that you didn't get offered any at all. Specifically, he was just talking about a couple of C-ration cans, "dinner," but considering his young life you couldn't blame him for thinking that if he knew one thing for sure, it was that there was no one anywhere who cared less about what *he* wanted. There wasn't anybody he wanted to thank for his food, but he was grateful that he was still alive to eat it, that the motherfucker hadn't scarfed him up first. He hadn't been anything but tired and scared for six months and he'd lost a lot, mostly people, and seen far too much, but he was breathing in and breathing out, some kind of choice all by itself.

He had one of those faces, I saw that face at least a thousand times at a hundred bases and camps, all the youth sucked out of the eyes, the color drawn from the skin, cold white lips, you knew he wouldn't wait for any of it to come back. Life had made him old, he'd live it out old. All those faces, sometimes it was like looking into faces at a rock concert, locked in, the event had them; or like students who were very heavily advanced, serious beyond what you'd call their years if you didn't know for yourself what the minutes and hours of those years were made up of. Not just like all the ones you saw who looked like they couldn't drag their asses through another day of it. (How do you feel when a nineteen-year-old kid tells you from the bottom of his heart that he's gotten too old for this kind of shit?) Not like the faces of the dead or wounded either, they could look more released than overtaken. These were the faces of boys whose whole lives seemed to have backed up on them, they'd be a few feet away but they'd be looking back at you over a distance you knew you'd never really cross. We'd talk, sometimes fly together, guys going out on R&R, guys escorting bodies, guys who'd flipped over into extremes of peace or violence. Once I flew with a kid who was going home, he looked back down once at the ground where he'd spent the year and spilled his whole load of tears. Sometimes you even flew with the dead.

Once I jumped on a chopper that was full of them. The kid in the op shack had said that there would be a body on board, but he'd been given some wrong information. "How bad do you want to get to Danang?" he'd asked me, and I'd said, "Bad."

When I saw what was happening I didn't want to get on, but they'd made a divert and a special landing for me, I had to go with the chopper I'd drawn, I was afraid of looking squeamish. (I remember, too, thinking that a chopper full of dead men was far less likely to get shot down than one full of living.) They weren't even in bags. They'd been on a truck near one of the fire-bases in the DMZ that was firing support for Khe Sanh, and the truck had hit a Command-detonated mine, then they'd been rocketed. The Marines were always running out of things, even food, ammo and medicine, it wasn't so strange that they'd run out of bags too. The men had been wrapped around in ponchos, some of them carelessly fastened with plastic straps, and loaded on board. There was a small space cleared for me between one of them and the door gunner, who looked pale and so tremendously furious that I thought he was angry with me and I couldn't look at him for a while. When we went up the wind blew through the ship and made the ponchos shake and tremble until the one next to me blew back in a fast brutal flap, uncovering the face. They hadn't even closed his eyes for him.

The gunner started hollering as loud as he could, "Fix it! Fix it!," maybe he thought the eyes were looking at him, but there wasn't anything I could do. My hand went there a couple of times and I couldn't, and then I did. I pulled the poncho tight, lifted his head carefully and tucked the poncho under it, and then I couldn't believe that I'd done it. All during the ride the gunner kept trying to smile, and when we landed at Dong Ha he thanked me and ran off to get a detail. The pilots jumped down and walked away without looking back once, like they'd never seen that chopper before in their lives. I flew the rest of the way to Danang in a general's plane.

You know how it is, you want to look and you don't want to look. I can remember the strange feelings I had when I was a kid looking at war photographs in *Life,* the ones that showed dead people or a lot of dead people lying close together in a field or a street, often touching, seeming to hold each other. Even when the picture was sharp and cleanly defined, something wasn't clear at all, something repressed that monitored the images and withheld their essential information. It may have legitimized my fascination, letting me look for as long as I wanted; I didn't have a language for it then, but I remember now the shame I felt, like looking at first porn, all the porn in the world. I could have looked until my lamps went out and I still wouldn't have accepted the connection between a detached leg and the rest of a body, or the poses and positions that always happened (one day I'd hear it called "response-to-impact"), bodies wrenched too fast and violently into unbelievable contortion. Or the total impersonality of group death, making them lie anywhere and any way it left them, hanging over barbed wire or thrown promiscuously on top of other dead, or up into the trees like terminal acrobats, *Look what I can do.*

Supposedly, you weren't going to have that kind of obscuration when you finally started seeing them on real ground in front of you, but you tended to manufacture it anyway because of how often and how badly you needed protection from what you were seeing, had actually come 30,000 miles to see. Once I looked at them strung from the perimeter to the treeline, most of them clumped together nearest the wire, then in smaller numbers but tighter groups midway, fanning out into lots of scattered points nearer the treeline, with one all by himself half into the bush and half out. "Close but no cigar," the captain said, and then a few of his men went out there and kicked them all in the head, thirty-seven of them. Then I heard an M-16 on full automatic starting to go through clips, a second to fire, three to plug in a fresh clip, and I saw a man out there, doing it. Every round was like a tiny concentration of high-velocity wind, making the bodies wince and shiver. When he finished he walked by us on the way back to his hootch, and I knew I hadn't seen anything until I saw his face. It was flushed and mottled and twisted like he had his face skin on inside out, a patch of green that was too dark, a streak of red running into bruise purple, a lot of sick gray white in between, he looked like he'd had a heart attack out there. His eyes were rolled up half into his head, his mouth was sprung open and his tongue was out, but he was smiling. Really a dude who'd shot his wad. The captain wasn't too pleased about my having seen that.

There wasn't a day when someone didn't ask me what I was doing there. Sometimes an especially smart grunt or another correspondent would even ask me what I was *really* doing there, as though I could say anything honest about it except "Blah blah blah cover the war" or "Blah blah blah write a book." Maybe we accepted each other's stories about why we were there at face value: the grunts who "had" to be there, the spooks and civilians whose corporate faith had led them there, the correspondents whose curiosity or ambition drew them over. But somewhere all the mythic tracks intersected, from the lowest John Wayne wetdream to the most aggravated soldier-poet fantasy, and where they did I believe that everyone knew everything about everyone else, every one of us there a true volunteer. Not that you didn't hear some overripe bullshit about it: Hearts and Minds, Peoples of the Republic, tumbling dominoes, maintaining the equilibrium of the Dingdong by containing the ever encroaching Doodah; you could also hear the other, some young soldier speaking in all bloody innocence, saying, "All that's just a *load, man.* We're here to kill gooks. Period." Which wasn't at all true of me. I was there to watch.

Talk about impersonating an identity, about locking into a role, about irony: I went to cover the war and the war covered me; an old story, unless of course you've never heard it. I went there behind the crude but serious belief that you had to be able to look at anything, serious because I acted on it and went, crude because I didn't know, it took the war to teach it, that you were as responsible for everything you saw as you were for everything you did. The problem was that you didn't always know what you were seeing until later, maybe years later, that a lot of it never made it in at all, it just stayed stored there in your eyes. Time and information, rock and roll, life itself, the information isn't frozen, you are.

Sometimes I didn't know if an action took a second or an hour or if I dreamed it or what. In war more than in other life you don't really know what you're doing most of the time, you're just behaving, and afterward you can make up any kind of bullshit you want to about it, say you felt good or bad, loved it or hated it, did this or that, the right thing or the wrong thing; still, what happened happened.

Coming back, telling stories, I'd say, "Oh man I was scared," and, "Oh God I thought it was all over," a long time before I knew how scared I was really supposed to be, or how clear and closed and beyond my control "all over" could become. I wasn't dumb but I sure was raw, certain connections are hard to make when you come from a place where they go around with war in their heads all the time.

"If you get hit," a medic told me, "we can chopper you back to base-camp hospital in like twenty minutes."

"If you get hit real bad," a corpsman said, "they'll get your case to Japan in twelve hours."

"If you get killed," a spec 4 from Graves promised, "we'll have you home in a week."

Time is on my side, already written there across the first helmet I ever wore there. And underneath it, in smaller lettering that read more like a whispered prayer than an assertion, *No lie, GI*. The rear-hatch gunner on a Chinook threw it to me that first morning at the Kontum airstrip, a few hours after the Dak To fighting had ended, screaming at me through the rotor wind, "You *keep* that, we got *plenty*, good *luck!*" and then flying off. I was so glad to have the equipment that I didn't stop to think where it had to have come from. The sweatband inside was seasoned up black and greasy, it was more alive now than the man who'd worn it, when I got rid of it ten minutes later I didn't just leave it on the ground, I snuck away from it furtive and ashamed, afraid that someone would see it and call after me, "Hey numbnuts, you forgot something. . . ."

That morning when I tried to go out they sent me down the line from a colonel to a major to a captain to a sergeant, who took one look, called me Freshmeat, and told me to go find some other outfit to get myself killed with. I didn't know what was going on, I was so nervous I started to laugh. I told him that nothing was going to happen to me and he gave my shoulder a tender, menacing pat and said, "This ain't the fucking movies over here, you know." I laughed again and said that I knew, but he knew that I didn't.

Day one, if anything could have penetrated that first innocence I might have taken the next plane out. Out absolutely. It was like a walk through a colony of stroke victims, a thousand men on a cold rainy airfield after too much of something I'd never really know, "a way you'll never be," dirt and blood and torn fatigues, eyes that poured out a steady charge of wasted horror. I'd just missed the biggest battle of the war so far, I was telling myself that I was sorry, but it was right there all around me and I didn't even know it. I couldn't look at anyone for more than a second, I didn't want to be caught listening, some war correspondent, I didn't know what to say or do, I didn't like it already. When the rain stopped and the ponchos came off there was a smell that I thought was going to make me sick: rot, sump, tannery, open grave, dumpfire—awful, you'd walk into pockets of Old Spice that made it even worse. I wanted badly to find some place to sit alone and smoke a cigarette, to find a face that would cover my face the way my poncho covered my new fatigues. I'd worn them once before, yesterday morning in Saigon, bringing them out of the black market and back to the hotel, dressing up in front of the mirror, making faces and moves I'd never make again. And loving it. Now, nearby on the ground, there was a man sleeping with a poncho over his head and a radio in his arms, I heard Sam the Sham singing, "Lil' Red Riding Hood, I don't think little big girls should, Go walking in these spooky old woods alone. . . ."

I turned to walk some other way and there was a man standing in front of me. He didn't exactly block me, but he didn't move either. He tottered a little and blinked, he looked at me and through me, no one had ever looked at me like that before. I felt a cold fat drop of sweat start down the middle of my back like a spider, it seemed to take an hour to finish its run. The man lit a cigarette and then sort of slobbered it out, I couldn't imagine what I was seeing. He tried again with a fresh cigarette. I gave him the light for that one, there was a flicker of focus, acknowledgment, but after a few puffs it went out too, and he let it drop to the ground. "I couldn't spit for a week up there," he said, "and now I can't fucking stop."

When the 173rd held services for their dead from Dak To the boots of the dead men were arranged in formation on the ground. It was an old paratrooper tradition, but knowing that didn't reduce it or make it any less spooky, a company's worth of jump boots standing empty in the dust taking benediction, while the real substance of the ceremony was being bagged and tagged and shipped back home through what they called the KIA Travel Bureau. A lot of the people there that day accepted the boots as solemn symbols and went into deep prayer. Others stood around watching with grudging respect, others photographed it and some just thought it was a lot of bitter bullshit. All they saw out there was one more set of spare parts, and they wouldn't have looked around for holy ghosts if some of those boots filled up again and walked.

Dak To itself had only been the command point for a combat without focus that tore a thirty-mile arc over the hills running northeast to southwest of the small base and airfield there from early November through Thanksgiving 1967, fighting that grew in size and fame while it grew more vicious and out of control. In October the small Dak To Special Forces compound had taken some mortar and rocket fire, patrols went out, patrols collided, companies splintered the action and spread it across the hills in a sequence of small, isolated firefights that afterward were described as strategy; battalions were sucked into it, then divisions, then reinforced divisions. Anyway, we knew for sure that we had a reinforced division in it, the 4th plus, and we said that they had one in it too, although a lot of people believed that a couple of light flexible regiments could have done what the NVA did up and down those hills for three weeks, leaving us to claim that we'd driven him up 1338, up 943, up 875 and 876, while the opposing claims remained mostly unspoken and probably unnecessary. And then instead of really ending, the battle vanished. The North Vietnamese collected up their gear and most of their dead and "disappeared" during the night, leaving a few bodies behind for our troops to kick and count.

"Just like goin' in against the Japs," one kid called it; the heaviest fighting in Vietnam since the Ia Drang Valley two years before, and one of the only times after Ia Drang when ground fire was so intense that the medevacs couldn't land through it. Wounded backed up for hours and sometimes days, and a lot of men died who might have been saved. Resupply couldn't make it in either, and the early worry about running out of ammunition grew into a panic and beyond, it became real. At the worst, a battalion of Airborne assaulting 875 got caught in an ambush sprung from behind, where no NVA had been reported, and its three companies were pinned and cut off in the raking fire of that trap for two days. Afterward, when a correspondent asked one of the survivors what had happened he was told, "What the fuck do you think happened? We got shot to pieces." The correspondent started to write that down and the paratrooper said, "Make that 'little pieces.' We were still shaking the trees for dog tags when we pulled back out of there."

Even after the North had gone away, logistics and transport remained a problem. A big battle had to be dismantled piece by piece and man by man. It was raining hard every day now, the small strip at Dak To became overloaded and unworkable, and a lot of troops were shuttled down to the larger strip at Kontum. Some even ended up as far out of their way as Pleiku, fifty miles to the south, for sorting and transport back to their units around 11 Corps. The living, the wounded and the dead flew together in crowded Chinooks, and it was nothing for guys to walk on top of the half-covered corpses packed in the aisles to get to a seat, or to make jokes among themselves about how funny they all looked, the dumb dead fuckers.

There were men sitting in loose groups all around the strip at Kontum, hundreds of them arranged by unit waiting to be picked up again and flown out. Except for a small sandbagged ops shack and a medical tent, there was no shelter anywhere from the rain. Some of the men had rigged up mostly useless tents with their ponchos, a lot lay out sleeping in the rain with helmets or packs for pillows, most just sat or stood around waiting. Their faces were hidden deep inside the cover of their poncho hoods, white eye movement and silence, walking among them made you feel like you were being watched from hundreds of isolated caves. Every twenty minutes or so a helicopter would land, men would come out or be carried out, others would get on and the chopper would rear up on the strip and fly away, some toward Pleiku and the hospital, others back to the Dak To area and the mop-up operations there. The rotors of the Chinooks cut twin spaces out of the rain, forcing the spray in slanting jets for fifty yards around. Just knowing what was in those choppers gave the spray a bad taste, strong and briny. You didn't want to leave it on your face long enough to dry.

Back from the strip a fat, middle-aged man was screaming at some troops who were pissing on the ground. His poncho was pulled back away from the front of his helmet enough to show captain's bars, but nobody even turned around to look at him. He groped under his poncho and came up with a .45, pointed it into the rain and fired off a shot that made an empty faraway pop, like it had gone off under wet sand. The men finished, buttoned up and walked away laughing, leaving the captain alone shouting orders to police up the filth; thousands of empty and half-eaten ration cans, soggy clots of Stars and Strips, an M-16 that someone had just left lying there and, worse, evidence of a carelessness unimaginable to the captain, it stank even in the cold rain, but it would police itself in an hour or two if the rain kept up.

The ground action had been over for nearly twenty-four hours now, but it was still going on in compulsive replay among the men who'd been there:

"A dead buddy is some tough shit, but bringing your own ass out alive can sure help you to get over it."

"We had this lieutenant, honest to Christ he was about the biggest dipshit fool of all time, all time. We called him Lieutenant Gladly 'cause he was always going like, 'Men . . . Men, I won't never ask you to do nothing I wouldn't do myself gladly,' what an asshole. We was on 1338 and he goes to me, 'Take a little run up to the ridge and report to me,' and I goes like, 'Never happen, Sir.' So he does, he goes up there himself and damned if the fucker didn't get zapped. He said we was gonna have a real serious talk when he come back, too. Sorry 'bout that."

"Kid here [not really here, "here" just a figure of speech] gets blown away ten feet in back of us. I swear to God, I thought I was looking at ten different guys when I turned around. . . ."

"You guys are so full of shit it's coming out of your fucking ears!" one man was saying. Pray for war was written on the side of his helmet, and he was talking mostly to a man whose helmet name was swinging dick. "You were pissing up every-

thing but your fucking toenails, Scudo, don't you tell me you weren't scared man, don't you fucking dare, 'cause I was right fucking there man, and I was scared shit! I was scared every fucking minute, and I'm no different from any body else!"

"Well big deal, candy ass," Swinging Dick said. "You were scared."

"Damn straight! Damn straight! You're damn fucking straight I was scared! You're about the dumbest motherfucker I ever met, Scudo, but you're not that dumb. The Marines aren't even that dumb man, I don't care, all that bullshit they've got in the Marine Corps about how Marines aren't ever afraid, oh wow, I'll fucking bet. . . . I'll bet the Marines are just as scared!"

He started to get up but his knees gave under him. He made a quick grasping spasm out of control, like a misfire in the nervous system, and when he fell back he brought a stack of M-16's with him. They made a sharp clatter and everyone jerked and twitched out of the way, looking at each other as though they couldn't remember for a minute whether they needed to find cover or not.

"Hey baby, hey, watch where you're goin' there," a paratrooper said, but he was laughing, they were all laughing, and Pray For War was laughing harder than any of them, so hard that it filled suddenly with air and cracked over into high giggles. When he lifted his face again it was all tracked with tears.

"You gonna stand there, asshole?" he said to Swinging Dick. "Or are you gonna help me up on my fucking feet?"

Swinging Dick reached down and grabbed his wrists, locking them and pulling him up slowly until their faces were a couple of inches apart. For a second it looked like they were going to kiss.

"Looking good," Pray For War said. "Mmmm, Scudo, you are really looking good, man. It don't look to me like you were scared at all up there. You only look like about ten thousand miles of bad road."

What they say is totally true, it's funny the things you remember. Like a black paratrooper with the 101st who glided by and said, "I been *scaled* man, I'm *smooth* now," and went on, into my past and I hope his future, leaving me to wonder not what he meant (that was easy), but where he'd been to get his language. On a cold wet day in Hue our jeep turned into the soccer stadium where hundreds of North Vietnamese bodies had been collected, I saw them, but they don't have the force in my memory that a dog and a duck have who died together in a small terrorist explosion in Saigon. Once I ran into a soldier standing by himself in the middle of a small jungle clearing where I'd wandered off to take a leak. We said hello, but he seemed very uptight about my being there. He told me that the guys were all sick of sitting around waiting and that he'd come out to see if he could draw a little fire. What a look we gave each other. I backed out of there fast, I didn't want to bother him while he was working.

This is already a long time ago, I can remember the feelings but I can't still have them. A common prayer for the overattached: You'll let it go sooner or later, why not do it now? Memory print, voices and faces, stories like filament through a piece of time, so attached to the experience that nothing moved and nothing went away.

"First letter I got from my old man was all about how proud he was that I'm here and how we have this *duty* to, you know, *I* don't fucking know, whatever . . . and it really made me feel great. Shit, my father hardly said good morning to me before. Well, I been here eight months now, and when I get home I'm gonna have all I can do to keep from killing that cocksucker. . . ."

Everywhere you went people said, "Well, I hope you get a story," and everywhere you went you did.

"Oh, it ain't so bad. My last tour was better though, not so much mickeymouse. Command gettin' in your way so you can't even do your job. Shit, last three patrols I was on we had fucking *orders* not to return fire going through the villages, that's what a fucked-up war it's gettin' to be anymore. My *last* tour we'd go through and that was it, we'd rip out the hedges and burn the hootches and blow all the wells and kill every chicken, pig and cow in the whole fucking ville. I mean, if we can't shoot these people, what the fuck are we doing here?"

Some journalists talked about no-story operations, but I never went on one. Even when an operation never got off the ground, there was always the strip. Those were the same journalists who would ask us what the fuck we ever found to talk to grunts about, who said they never heard a grunt talk about anything except cars, football and chone. But they all had a story, and in the war they were driven to tell it.

"We was getting killed and the Dinks was panicking, and when the choppers come in to get us out, there wasn't enough room for everybody. The Dinks was screaming and carrying on, grabbing hold of the treads and grabbing hold of our legs till we couldn't get the choppers up. So we just said smack it, let these people get their own fucking choppers, and we started shooting them. And even then they kept on coming, oh man it was wild. I mean they could sure as shit believe that Charlie was shooting them, but they couldn't believe that we was doing it too. . . ."

That was a story from the A Shau Valley years before my time there, an old story with the hair still growing on it. Sometimes the stories were so fresh that the teller was in shock, sometimes they were long and complex, sometimes the whole thing was contained in a few words on a helmet or a wall, and sometimes they were hardly stories at all but sounds and gestures packed with so much urgency that they became more dramatic than a novel, men talking in short violent bursts as though they were afraid they might not get to finish, or saying it almost out of a dream, innocent, offhand and mighty direct, "Oh you know, it was just a firefight, we killed some of them and they killed some of us." A lot of what you heard, you heard all the time, men on tape, deceitful and counterarticulate, and some of it was low enough, guys whose range seemed to stop at "Git some, git some, harharhar!" But once in a while you'd hear something fresh, and a couple of times you'd even hear something high, like the corpsman at Khe Sanh who said, "If it ain't the fucking incoming it's the fucking outgoing. Only difference is who gets the fucking grease, and that ain't no fucking difference at all."

The mix was so amazing; incipient saints and realized homicidals, unconscious lyric poets and mean dumb motherfuckers with their brains all down in their necks; and even though by the time I left I knew where all the stories came from and where they were going, I was never bored, never even unsurprised. Obviously, what they really wanted to tell you was how tired they were and how sick of it, how moved they'd been and how afraid. But maybe that was me, by then my posture was shot: "reporter." ("Must be pretty hard to stay detached," a man on the plane to San Francisco said, and I said, "Impossible.") After a year I felt so plugged in to all the stories and the images and the fear that even the dead started telling me stories, you'd hear them out of a remote but accessible space where there were no ideas, no emotions, no facts, no proper language, only clean information. However many times it happened, whether I'd known them or not, no matter what I'd felt about them or the way they'd died, their story was always there and it was always the same: it went, "Put yourself in my place."

The Sword of the Lord and of Gideon

BY COLONEL THEODORE ROOSEVELT

A MERICAN TROOPS WERE not in the actual fighting in World War I for very long—only five months in 1918—but that was long enough for many acts of gallantry, including one massive display of fortitude that made the name Alvin York a legend.

The husky redhead from the remote Tennessee valley called "Three Forks of the Wolf"—one of eleven children raised with scant "book l'arnin'"—killed twenty German soldiers and captured one hundred thirty-two, including a battalion commander and thirty-five guns, virtually single-handedly.

Colonel Roosevelt's account of the action is my favorite. It first appeared in *Rank and File,* published by Scribners in 1928, and was later collected in the anthology edited by Ernest Hemingway, *Men at War,* published by Crown.

★　★　★　★　★

A scant hundred and fifty years ago the United States was but a fringe of settlements that clung to the skirts of the Atlantic. A few miles inland from the seaboard the "backwoods" stretched unbroken from north to south. The restless pioneer spirit that built our country was astir, and hardy men and brave women were pushing westward, ever westward. The rush was starting over trackless mountain and tangled forest, turbulent river and wide, shimmering plain, which never faltered until the covered wagons jolted over a crest and the broad Pacific stretched horizon-far.

To the north the stream westward flowed along the lake-shore by the Wilderness Trail. By the wagons walked the men. When there was a halt for the night children tumbled out over the tail-board like mud-turtles from a log in a pond. The families carried their scant household goods. At Oyster Bay, we have in our library a Windsor rocking-chair that went with my wife's great-great-grandparents over this trail from Vermont to the settlement of Ohio.

To the south the pioneers struck the Appalachian Mountains as the first great barrier to their advance. These ranges stretch like a bulwark down the mid-eastern part of our country. Though not high, they are rugged and very beautiful. In spring they are cloaked in green, save where some gray shoulder of rock has thrust through. In autumn they are painted by the purple pomp of changing foliage gorgeous as a columbine.

Into these mountains tramped the wilderness hunters. They were lean, silent men, clad in coonskin caps and homespun. Around their necks were slung powder-horns. They carried the heavy, smooth-bore flint-lock guns. Such men were Daniel Boone and Simon Kenton.

These lone hunters carried more than their rifles over their shoulders; they carried the destiny of a nation. They were stout fighting men. Under Braddock they were all that stood between the British regulars and massacre. During the Revolutionary War they fought notably for the colonies and independence. Morgan's rifles were composed of them. Under General Clarke they beat the Indians time and again, and won Kentucky and Ohio for the colonists.

In the closing years of the eighteenth century one of these wilderness hunters worked his way over the Cumberland Mountains. He wandered south along the western slope until he came to the lovely little valley now known as the "Three Forks of the Wolf." The country looked so friendly and fertile that he settled there, cleared his fields, and travelled no more. His name was Conrad Pile.

The land attracted other settlers, and soon a little community was nestling between the rugged slopes of the mountains. It was christened Pall Mall, though no one knows why. After many years of uncertainty it was assigned to the State of Tennessee.

Like most of the other settlements in these hills the people were isolated, and had but little contact with the men and women of the lowlands. They were poor, for the valley yielded a scanty living. Most of them left but rarely the mountains that surrounded their log and board cabins. Schools were almost unknown. Children worked, not as training for life, but because it was necessary to work to live. The fiery spirit still flamed, and it was from the men of the Tennessee and Kentucky Mountains that "Old Hickory" drew the raw levees that beat the pick of the veteran British regulars at New Orleans.

Perhaps the strongest force in shaping these men and women was their religion. Their faith was of the deep-rooted, zealous type that carried the Roundheads to victory under Cromwell. Their ministers were circuit-riders, who travelled weary miles to carry the gospel to their widely scattered flocks. It was the religion of the Bible, hard and narrow at times but living, and was brought into the occurrences of every-day life, not kept as a thing apart. It was not merely for Sunday consumption in a padded pew. The citizens were the spiritual as well as probably the physical descendants of the Covenanters. For their general, when forming them for battle, to ride down their lines with a sword in one hand and a Bible in the other, would not have struck them as strange but as natural.

Next to their religion they were perhaps most influenced by the wilds. Hunting or trapping in the wooded hills was the recreation of the men. The youth of the mountains were learned in woodcraft. They could shoot rapidly and accurately and were toughened by life in the open.

During the Civil War these mountains formed an isolated island of loyalty to the Union in a sea of secession. Though the majority of the people were Federals some were Confederate sympathizers, and bitter bloody feuds tore the little hill settlements.

At the dawn of the twentieth century more than a hundred years had passed since old Conrad Pile halted from his wandering in the valley of the Three Forks of the Wolf, but Pall Mall was not greatly changed. The men wore homespun, the women calico. The houses were but little improved. Indeed, the log cabin Conrad built was still in use. The people spoke a language which was not, as many believe, a corruption of English, but an old form. They used "hit" for "it," which is the old neuter form of he or him. They spoke of "you'uns," which is an old colloquial plural of you. Over their sewing the girls sang early English ballads, long forgotten by the rest of the world. Their recreations were husking-bees and log-rolling parties. This little valley in the mountains seemed a changeless back-eddy in the march of progress. The Reverend Rosier Pile, the great-great-grandson of Conrad, was preacher. Full 80 per cent of the people were descendants of the first half-dozen settlers.

Among these were William York and his wife. They had eleven children, one of whom was a strapping, red-headed young mountaineer named Alvin. The family lived in a little two-room board cabin. William York was a blacksmith by profession, but loved hunting and spent much of his time wandering over the hills.

Alvin was much like the boys of his acquaintance. His education was scant. The little mountain school he attended was open only for three months during the summer. For the rest of the year it was closed, because the children had to work, or were winter-bound in their scattered homes on the hillsides. All young York got of "book-larnin' " was a foundation in the "three Rs." There was other training, however, that stood him in good stead. When he was not working on the farm or at the school, he was hunting. At an early age he had been given a rifle and it was his most valued possession.

The men of Pall Mall had cleared a rough rifle-range for themselves and had competitions on Saturdays. They used the old muzzle-loading, ball-powder-and-patch rifles handed down by their forefathers. Such rifles are very accurate for perhaps seventy-five yards. Turkeys and beeves were the usual prizes. In a turkey contest they did not use a target, but the turkey itself. In one competition the turkey was tethered by its foot to a stake some hundred and forty yards from the competitors. In another it was tied behind a log forty yards distant in such fashion that only its head showed. In both instances the turkey was given freedom of action, so that the target was constantly on the move. A turkey's head is not large, and a man who can hit it when it is bobbing about is a real marksman.

John Sowders, young York's principal rival at these matches, used to "limber up" by sticking carpet-tacks in a board and driving them home with his bullets at a range of twenty-five yards.

When Alvin York and two of his brothers were well grown, their father died. The mother, however, with their aid and the small farm, managed to keep the family together. There was no money for trimmings, but everyone had enough to eat. Her tall, red-headed son for a time had a mild "fling"—drank his corn whiskey and went on parties with his contemporaries among the boys. In the mid-twenties his stern religion gripped him and he stopped drinking. He took a deeper interest in church affairs and became an elder.

Early in the spring of 1917, word came to the little mountain community that the United States had declared war on Germany. They were such a back-eddy of the country that they had heard very little of the cumulative causes. Indeed, I have been told that the men who came to enlist in the army from some of the more isolated spots in these mountains believed that we were again at war with England, and were deeply suspicious when told we were her ally. At the Three Forks of the Wolf the War was not popular. Memories of the Civil War, with its bitter interfamily feuds, were still alive in the community. Few of the young fellows volunteered. At last the draft came.

Alvin York was a husky six-footer nearly thirty years old. He did not believe in war. He felt that the New Testament definitely stood against the killing of man by man. "For all they that take the sword shall perish with the sword." He was engaged to be married and was the principal support of his mother. Pastor Pile, of whose church he was a member, firmly believed that the tenets of his church forbade war. All York had to do was to state his case. He had clear grounds on which to claim exemption, but he was made of sterner stuff. Though he believed it wrong to kill, he believed it necessary to serve his country. He refused to claim exemption or let any one make such application in his behalf.

Down to Jamestown, the county-seat, he rode on one of his two mules. He registered, was examined and passed. Back at Pall Mall he told his womenfolk the news. They grieved bitterly, but they knew that a man must seek his happiness by following what he believes to be right.

His blue card reached him in November. In a few hours he said good-by and drove in a buggy to Jamestown. He was sent to Camp Gordon near Atlanta, Ga. It was the first time he had ever been out of sight of his beloved mountains. In his diary he wrote: "I was the homesickest boy you ever seen."

After nearly three months' training he was assigned in February, 1918, to Company G, 328th Infantry, 82nd Division. This division was really a cross-section of the country. Its men were drawn from every State of the Union. They were of every racial stock that goes to make up our nation, from the descendants of colonial English to the children of lately arrived Italian immigrants. Every trade and occupation was represented among its personnel.

Now began his battle with himself as to what course it was right for him to follow. His mother had weakened at the thought that he might be killed, and together with Pastor Pile had written to the officers stating that York's religion forbade war. York himself was deeply troubled, for Pastor Pile in letters pleaded with him not to jeopardize his eternal salvation by killing man.

He turned, in his distress, to his immediate superiors, Major G. E. Buxton and Captain E. C. B. Danforth, Jr. Fortunately both were men of high principle and broad vision. They realized at once that here was no yellow-streaked malingerer but a sincere man seeking guidance.

Late one evening the three men met in the little tar-paper shack that served Buxton for quarters. There, in the hard light of the single unshaded electric bulb that dangled from the ceiling, the officers reasoned with the lanky, red-headed private. The causes that led to the War were explained in detail. Then they turned to the Bible, and by text and teaching showed that while peace was desirable it must not be a peace at any price. Though we are in the world to strive for righteousness, justice, and peace, if one of these has to be sacrificed in order to obtain the other two, it must be peace.

They read him the thirty-third chapter of Ezekiel, and told him that he and all Americans were as "the watchman" in the Bible. On them was laid the charge of guarding humanity. To fail in the task would be traitorous.

York was absolutely honest. He strove for light. Gradually he became convinced, as had his spiritual ancestors the Covenanters, that right and war were bedfellows in this instance. Once his mind was clear, there was no faltering or hesitation. If it was right to fight at all, then it was right to fight with all your might. He flung himself into the drill and training with every ounce of energy he possessed. He soon showed that his days of shooting at the Three Forks of the Wolf were not ill spent. The Enfield rifle with which the division was equipped was the best firearm he had ever used. In rapid firing at moving targets he easily outdistanced the other men.

Some months passed. The American troops had reached Europe. Instead of a division or two scattered through the line that stretched like a dike across the north of France, the Americans now had over two million men. The United States had an army in the field and was prepared to carry her share of the battle. The tide had turned, and the Allies were crushing the gray lines back. The Germans had lost the initiative.

Our army was attacking as a unit. The battle of the Argonne was raging. Through the shell-torn woods and fields, over hills and valleys, the American troops were fighting their way forward. Then came a check. The 1st Division had gone through, but the divisions on its right and left had encountered severe resistance. As a result the Regulars were thrust out in the enemies' lines, and were swept with fire from three sides. It was imperative that the lines on the right and left be advanced. The 82nd Division was selected for this mission. On October 6th they were assigned a position on the left of the 1st Division, with orders to attack on Chatel Chehery Hills.

All day on October 7th the 328th Infantry lay in shell-holes and ditches on the slopes of Hill 223, and along the road that stretched to its rear. All day long the German shrapnel and high explosive burst along their lines. Behind them and in front were the wooded slopes of the rough Argonne hills. The ground was heavy with rain, the soldiers were mud-caked and sodden with wet.

Beyond Hill 223, the farthest point of their advance, was an open valley about five hundred yards wide. On the other side of this valley rose three hills, the central one steep and rugged, the other two gently sloping. The crest of the ridge formed by these was held by a division of veteran German troops, hard-schooled by years of war.

The position was of great importance, for behind these hills lay the narrow-gauge railroad, which supplied the Germans in the forest where they had checked the advance of the American battle line.

Late in the afternoon of October 8th York's battalion, the 2nd, received its orders. It was to relieve the 1st which had seized the hill, and then to thrust due west into the German flank. The attack was to start at six next morning from Hill 223, and the final objective was the railroad.

Through the black of the night the troops stumbled up the wooded slopes and took their position. Dawn came with gray reluctance; a heavy mist drifted through the tree-tops and choked the valley below. Gradually it lifted and shredded off. Zero hour had come.

The Americans started down through the tangled undergrowth. The sun rose and swallowed the last remnants of mist, giving the Germans a fair view of the attacking troops. Immediately from all sides the hostile fire burst. High explosives shrieked through the trees, filling the air with scraps of iron and flying splinters. Shrapnel exploded in puffs of smoke and rained down its bullets on the advancing men. Through it all machine-guns spattered our advance with a rattling hurricane of lead.

When they had descended the long wooded slope they started across the open country. The flanking fire was so ferocious that the American lines melted like snow in a spring thaw. To advance was impossible. The companies lay frozen to the ground while bullets whipped over them like sleet in a northeaster.

Lieutenant Stewart, a splendid young giant from Florida, commanded a platoon in York's company. He jumped to his feet and called to his men to follow. So great was their confidence in him that they struggled up and started ahead, though it looked certain death. He had not gone ten yards before a bullet struck him shattering his right thigh, and he crashed to the ground. Though his leg was shattered his manhood was not. By a supreme effort he shoved himself erect on the one leg left, and started to hop forward. A couple of yards farther he pitched on his face. A bullet had struck him in the head and his gallant spirit had joined the hero-dead of the nation.

The platoon dropped to the ground again and lay flat. It was clear that no advance could be attempted until the guns that were sweeping the plain with flanking fire were silenced. Captain Danforth decided to send a detachment from York's platoon on this mission.

Raising his head from the ground he turned to the platoon. Sergeant Harry Parsons, an ex-vaudeville actor from New York, was commanding it. Like a well-trained soldier he was watching his company commander for orders.

The roar of the artillery drowned all sound of his voice, so Danforth pointed to the hill on the left and motioned in its direction. Parsons understood at once. Quietly but quickly he chose three squads of his platoon. The German fire had taken its toll, a third of the men were wounded or dead. Of the twenty-four who had composed these squads when they left the hill-crest half an hour ago, only sixteen remained.

The make-up of this detachment was in itself a mute comment on our country and our army. Of the sixteen soldiers, eight had English names; the other eight were men whose parents had come from Ireland, Italy, Poland, Germany, and Sweden. One of the members of this patrol was Alvin York of Tennessee, lately promoted corporal.

Sergeant Early was placed in command. He was told to outflank in any fashion possible the machine-guns that were causing the damage, and beat down their fire or destroy them.

On their bellies the men wormed their way to the woods, hitching themselves along below the bullets that swept scythelike across the field.

When they reached the cover of the trees they rose and, crouching, threaded their way to the left. Stealing from stump to stump, taking cover wherever possible, they reached the far end of the valley without casualties. Here fortune favored them, for they found a thicket that concealed them until they were nearly half-way across.

Suddenly bullets began to rattle around them, passing with the crack of a whip. They were under fire from the right flank. They must either retreat and abandon their mission or quickly pass on. Sergeant Early's decision was made without hesitation. They moved forward. In a few seconds they were clambering up the steep hillside beyond the valley. The boldness of this move protected them. The Germans were watching the hills opposite and the valley, but not the slopes on which their own guns rested. For a moment the Americans were sheltered. The soul-satisfying relief that comes to a soldier when he finds himself defiladed from fire is like waking after a severe illness to find the pain gone.

Stumbling through the brush and dead leaves they came to a wood path that led in rear of the crest. Here they halted for a moment to get their bearings and decide on the next move. To their left stretched unbroken woodlands from which no sound of firing came. To their right crackled the machine-guns they were to silence. They had succeeded in reaching a position in rear of the Germans.

While they were standing breathless, listening for any sound that might give a further clew, they caught faintly the guttural sound of Germans talking in the valley on the reverse slope of the hill. Just at this moment a twig snapped, and right ahead of them they saw two German stretcher-bearers. There was no time to be lost, for these men might give the alarm to the machine-guns, and the Americans opened fire at once. Both Germans escaped into the woods, though one was wounded. The time for discussion had passed. It was now or never. Quick as a flash Early called: "As skirmishers, forward!"

Down the bank of a small stream they plunged, and up the other side. Here the woods were thinner. Suddenly they saw just above them about fifty Germans gathered near a small board hut. The surprise of the Americans was nothing to that of the Germans, who knew themselves to be well in rear of their own lines. They had been getting their orders for a counterattack when out of the bush had burst the Americans, ragged, unshaven, with fierce eyes and gleaming bayonets.

A couple of Boches tried to reach for their rifles, but the crack of the Enfields halted them. Up went their hands, and "Kamerad!" echoed through the grove.

It was the battalion headquarters of the machine-guns. Among the group were a major and two junior officers. The Americans formed a crescent and moved toward their prisoners, who were on high ground just above them. On the left flank was Alvin York. As he approached the group the bushes became sparser. Right above him, not forty yards away, he saw German machine-guns. The Boche gunners had got the alarm. They were trying frantically to turn their guns to the rear. A few of them picked up rifles and fired at York, who stood in plain sight. The bullets burnt his face.

A command in German was shouted. At once the prisoners dropped flat on their faces. York and six of his comrades, who were now close to the Germans, did the same. Sergeant Early, with the other Americans, did not understand what was happening and remained standing. A burst of fire swept the grove.

Six of our patrol fell dead and three were wounded, including the sergeant. The surviving Americans were now among their prisoners. Probably on this account the hail of bullets was held two or three feet above the ground. There were no more casualties.

York was a comparatively green soldier. He was fighting not for the love of fighting, but for a firm conviction of the righteousness and justice of our cause. The shadows of the men who fought at Naseby and Marston Moor stood at his elbow. The spirit that inspired Cromwell and Ireton, Hampden and Vane, stirred in him. He saw "enfranchised insult" in the persons of the German soldiers, and, like the Covenanters, with a cold fury he "smote them hip and thigh."

He was in the open. Calling to his comrades, who were cloaked by the bushes and could neither see nor be seen, to stay where they were and guard the prisoners, he prepared to take the offensive. Crawling to the left through some weeds, he reached a point from which he got a clear view of the German emplacements. Just as the got there the German fire ceased. Several rose and started down the slope in the direction of the Americans to investigate. Quick as a flash York's rifle spoke. One pitched forward on his face and the rest scuttled back. Again a hail of bullets swept through the grove.

In a few minutes it slackened. York sat up and took the position used by hunters since rifles were first invented. The range to the gun-pits was that at which he had so often shot in those seemingly distant days, in his far-off home in the Tennessee mountains. This time, however, he was not shooting for sport but "battling for the Lord." He saw several German heads peering cautiously over the emplacements. He swung his rifle toward one and fired; the helmet flew up and the head disappeared. Four times more he fired before the Germans realized what was happening and ducked back.

Bullets spattered around him, splintering the tree at his elbow and covering him with slivers of wood and dust. Heedless of the danger, he watched the ridge until another head appeared. Again his rifle cracked and again the head disappeared. Hitting German heads at forty yards was easy for a man who had hit turkey heads at the same range, and whose nerves were of iron because of his belief in his cause.

The battle rested entirely on his shoulders, for the rest of the Americans were so screened by the brush that they were only able to fire a few scattered shots.

The Germans could not aim at this lone rifleman, for whenever a head appeared it was met with a bullet from the mountaineer. York was not fighting from a passion for slaughter. He would kill any one without compunction who stood in the way of victory; but it was not killing but victory for which he strove. He began calling: "Come down, you-all, and give up."

The battle went on.

At times the Boche riflemen would creep out of their emplacements, take cover behind some tree, and try to get the American. The hunter from the Cumberland Mountains was trained to note the slightest movement. The man who could see a squirrel in the tree-top could not fail to observe a German when he moved. Every time he found them and fired before they found him. That ended the story.

The Germans by this time knew that the brunt of the battle was being borne by one American. They realized they were not quick enough to kill him by frontal attack, so they sent an officer and seven men around his left flank to rush him. These crawled carefully through the brush until they were within twenty yards of him. Then with a yell they sprang up and came at him on a dead run, their fixed bayonets flashing in the sun.

The clip of cartridges in York's rifle was nearly exhausted and he had no time to reload. Dropping his Enfield he seized his automatic pistol. As they came lunging forward through the undergrowth he fired. One after another the Germans pitched forward and lay where they fell, huddled gray heaps in the tangled woods. Not only had York killed them all, but each time he had shot at the man in rear in order that the others might not halt and fire a volley on seeing their comrade fall. The machine-gun fire had slackened during the charge. Again it burst forth and again York stilled it with his rifle.

The grim, red-headed mountaineer was invincible. Almost unaided he had already killed some twenty of his opponents. The German major's nerve was shaken. He could speak English. Slowly he wriggled on his stomach to where the American sat and offered to tell the machine-gunners to surrender. "Do it and I'll treat ye white," said York.

At this moment a lone German crawled close, jumped to his feet, and hurled a grenade. It went wide, but when the Enfield spoke its bullet did not. The German pitched forward on his face, groaning. The Boche major then rose to his knees and blew his whistle shrilly. All firing ceased. He called an order to his men. Instantly they began scrambling to their feet, throwing down belts and side-arms.

The American was alert for treachery. When they were half-way down the hill, with their hands held high over their heads, he halted them. With the eyes of a backwoodsman he scanned each for weapons. There were none. The surrender was genuine.

Corporal York stood up and called to his comrades. They answered him from where they had been guarding their first prisoners. The thick grove had prevented them from taking an active part in the fighting, but they had protected York from attacks by the prisoners who would otherwise have taken him from the rear.

Sergeant Early, the leader of the patrol, was lying in the brush desperately wounded in the abdomen. York called: "Early, are you alive?"

"I am all through," groaned the sergeant. "You take command. You'll need a compass. Turn me over. You'll find mine in my pocket. Get our men back as soon as you can, and leave me here."

York had well over a hundred prisoners, as sixty had come from the machine-gun emplacements. Some of the Americans doubted the possibility of getting them back to the lines. York paid no attention to this. He formed the Germans in column of twos, placing our wounded at the rear, with prisoners to carry Sergeant Early, who could not walk. Along the flanks he stationed his surviving comrades, with instructions to keep the column closed up and to watch for treachery. He himself led, with the German major in front of him and a German officer on each side.

Before they started York had had the major explain to the men that at any sign of hostility he would shoot to kill, and the major would be the first to die. They had seen enough of the deadly prowess of the mountaineer. Not one made the attempt. He marched his column around the hill to a point from which he could probably have taken them back safely, but his mission was to clear the hill of machine-guns. He knew that some still remained on the front slope.

Turning the column to the left, he advanced on the Boche garrisons. As he approached he had the German major call to each in turn to surrender. When they did he disarmed them and added them to his train of prisoners. In only one instance did a man attempt to resist. He went to join the long roll of German dead.

York's troubles were not over. Though he had cleaned up and de-stroyed the machine-guns, he still had to get back to our lines with the men he had captured. To do this he had to be very careful, for so large a body of Ger-mans marching toward our lines might well be taken for a counter-attack and mowed down with rifle-fire. Bringing all his woodcraft into play he led his long column of gray-clad prisoners over the ridge and down through the brush, until he reached the foot of the slope up which his patrol had climbed earlier in the day.

Suddenly from the brush on the other side the command "Halt!" rang out. York jumped to the front to show his uniform, and called out that he was bringing in prisoners. He was just in time to prevent casualties. The lines of our infantry opened to let the party through. As the doughboys from left and right looked between the tree-trunks they saw gray form after gray form pass. A yell of approval rang out. Some one shouted: "Are you bringing in the whole Ger-man Army?" The lines closed behind the column. Corporal York had fulfilled his mission.

In a few minutes he reported at battalion headquarters. The prisoners were counted. There were one hundred and thirty-two, including three offi-cers, one a major. With less than a year's military training a red-headed mountaineer, practically single-handed, had fought a veteran battalion of German troops, taken thirty-five guns, killed twenty men, captured one hundred and thirty-two and the battalion commander.

For three weeks more the Division hammered its way forward. The stubborn German defense was beaten back, the Allies drove on to Sedan. Even among the fighting troops rumors of peace became more persistent. One morning word came to the front lines where the tired men stood, ankle-deep in mud—an armistice had been signed.

York had become a sergeant. He was with his company. His feat, as he saw it, was merely a part of the day's work. The officers and men of the 82nd Division, however, were very proud of him. They had reported the facts to General Headquarters. The story had spread like wild-fire, and Alvin York was famous.

During his simple country life York had never met any of the great of the world. His nearest approach to a general had been when he stood stiffly at attention while the general inspected the ranks. Now he found himself honored of all, because physical courage, especially when backed by moral worth, commands universal admiration. General Headquarters ordered him from place to place in France. A brigade review was held in his honor. He was decorated not only by the United States but also by the Allies. At Paris Poincaré, the president of the French Republic, pinned the highest decorations to his coat.

In May, 1919, he came back with his regiment to our country. Here enthusiasm ran even higher. The streets of New York were jammed with people who cheered themselves hoarse. He went to see the Stock Exchange, where no visitors are allowed on the floor. Not only was he permitted to visit the floor but business was suspended and the stockbrokers carried him around on their shoulders.

In Washington, when he went to the gallery of the House of Representatives, the congressmen stopped debate and cheered him to the echo. Great banquets were given for him, which were attended by the highest ranking civil, military, and naval officials.

In his olive-drab uniform, with his medals and shock of red hair, he was a marked man. When he walked the streets enthusiastic crowds gathered. There were men and women to greet him at the railroad-stations as he travelled back to Tennessee to be mustered out.

He was offered a contract for $75,000 to appear in a moving-picture play on the War. He was approached by vaudeville firms, who suggested tours on which they agreed to give him a salary of $1,000 a week. Newspapers were willing to pay fabulous sums for articles by him.

He was taken up on a mountain and shown the kingdoms of the world. Ninety-nine men out of a hundred would have cracked under the adulation. Ninety-nine men out of a hundred who can bear the famine worthily will lose their heads at the feast. York did not. Though his twelve months in the army had greatly broadened him, his character was still as strong and unshaken as the rock of his own hills. He refused the offers of money or position, saying rightly that these were made him only because of his feat in the Argonne. To sell his war record would be putting a price on patriotism.

As soon as he could he made his way back to his home in the mountains, his family, and his friends. There he was met by his mother in her calico bonnet, his sisters and brothers, and Grace Williams, the mountain girl to whom he was betrothed.

In a few days there was an open-air wedding at Pall Mall. It was held on the hillside. A gray ledge of rock served as altar. The new leaves of spring danced in the sunlight, casting flickering shadows on the white starched "Sunday-go-to-meeting" dresses and blue serge "store clothes" of the mountain folk, who had driven in from the surrounding country. The governor of the State officiated, assisted by Pastor Pile. The bride and groom were Grace Williams and Sergeant Alvin York, late of the United States Army.

Though York refused to sell his service record, he knew his Bible far too well to have forgotten the parable of the talents. That which it would be wrong to use for his own benefit, it would be wrong not to use for the benefit of others. His experience in the world had made him bitterly conscious of his scanty education. He realized that "wisdom excelleth folly as far as light excelleth darkness." He decided to bend his efforts toward establishing proper schools for the children of the hills.

The people of Tennessee had been collecting an Alvin York Fund. He asked them to turn it into a foundation for building schools in the mountains. All he would accept for himself was a small farm.

Waterloo

From *Les Miserables*

BY VICTOR HUGO

Was it possible for Napoleon to win that battle? We answer No. Why? Because of Wellington? Because of Blucher? No. Because of God. . . . It was time that this vast man should fall."

Napoleon against the Duke of Wellington, with a supporting cast of thousands. One of the greatest novelists who ever lived recreates this amazing battle with the vividness of a widescreen movie.

★   ★   ★   ★   ★

Let us go back,—that is one of the story-teller's privileges,—and put ourselves once more in the year 1815, and even a little prior to the period when the action narrated in the first part of this book took place.

If it had not rained in the night between the 17th and the 18th of June, 1815, the fate of Europe would have been different. A few drops of water, more or less, made Napoleon waver. All that Providence required in order to make Waterloo the end of Austerlitz was a little more rain, and a cloud crossing the sky out of season sufficed to overthrow the world.

The battle of Waterloo could not be begun until half-past eleven o'-clock, and that gave Blücher time to come up. Why? Because the ground was moist. The artillery had to wait until it became a little firmer before they could manoeuvre.

Napoleon was an artillery officer, and felt the effects of one. All his plans of battle were arranged for projectiles. The key to his victory was to make the artillery converge on one point. He treated the strategy of the hostile general like a citadel, and made a breach in it. He crushed the weak point with grape-shot; he joined and dissolved battles with artillery. There was something of the sharpshooter in his genius. To beat in squares, to pulverize regiments, to break lines, to destroy and disperse masses,—for him everything lay in this, to strike, strike, strike incessantly,—and he entrusted this task to the cannon-ball. It was a formidable method, and one which, united with genius, rendered this gloomy athlete of the pugilism of war invincible for the space of fifteen years.

On the 18th of June, 1815, he relied all the more on his artillery, because he had numbers on his side. Wellington had only one hundred and fifty-nine guns; Napoleon had two hundred and forty.

Suppose the soil dry, and the artillery capable of moving, the action would have begun at six o'clock in the morning. The battle would have been won and ended at two o'clock, three hours before the change of fortune in favour of the Prussians. How much blame attaches to Napoleon for the loss of this battle? Is the shipwreck due to the pilot?

Was it the evident physical decline of Napoleon that complicated this epoch by an inward diminution of force? Had the twenty years of war worn out the blade as it had worn the scabbard, the soul as well as the body? Did the veteran make himself disastrously felt in the leader? In a word, was this genius, as many historians of note have thought, eclipsed? Did he go into a frenzy in order to disguise his weakened powers from himself? Did he begin to waver under the delusion of a breath of adventure? Had he become—a grave matter in a general—unconscious of peril? Is there an age, in this class of material great men, who may be called the giants of action, when genius becomes short-sighted? Old age has no hold on ideal genius; for the Dantes and Michael Angelos to grow old is to grow in greatness; is it declension for the Hannibals and the Bonapartes? Had Napoleon lost the direct sense of victory? Had he reached the point where he could no longer recognize the rock, could no longer divine the snare, no longer discern the crumbling edge of the abyss? Had he lost his power of scenting out catastrophes? He who had in former days known all the roads to victory, and who, from the summit of his chariot of lightning, pointed them out with a sovereign finger, had he now reached that state of sinister amazement when he could lead his tumultuous legions harnessed to it, to the precipice? Was he seized at the age of forty-six with a supreme madness? Was that titanic charioteer of destiny now only a Phaëton?

We do not believe it.

His plan of battle was, by the confession of all, a masterpiece. To go straight to the centre of the Allies' lines, to make a breach in the enemy, to cut them in two, to drive the British half back on Halle, and the Prussian half on Tingres, to make two shattered fragments of Wellington and Blücher, to carry Mont-Saint-Jean, to seize Brussels, to hurl the German into the Rhine, and the

Englishman into the sea. All this was contained in that battle, for Napoleon. Afterwards people would see.

Of course, we do not here pretend to furnish a history of the battle of Waterloo; one of the scenes of the foundation of the drama which we are relating is connected with this battle, but this history is not our subject; this history, moreover, has been finished, and finished in a masterly manner, from one point of view by Napoleon, from another by Charras.

For our part, we leave the historians to contend; we are but a distant witness, a passer-by along the plain, a seeker bending over that soil all made of human flesh, perhaps taking appearances for realities; we have no right to oppose, in the name of science, a collection of facts which contain illusions, no doubt; we possess neither military practice nor strategic ability which authorize a system; in our opinion, a chain of accidents dominated the two captains at Waterloo; and when it becomes a question of destiny, that mysterious culprit, we judge like the people.

Those who wish to gain a clear idea of the battle of Waterloo have only to place, mentally, on the ground, a capital A. The left leg of the A is the road to Nivelles, the right one is the road to Genappe, the tie of the A is the hollow road to Ohain from Braine-l'Alleud. The top of the A is Mont-Saint-Jean, where Wellington is; the lower left tip is Hougomont, where Reille is stationed with Jérôme Bonaparte; the right tip is the Belle-Alliance, where Napoleon is. At the centre of this point is the precise point where the final word of the battle was pronounced. It was there that the lion has been placed, the involuntary symbol of the supreme heroism of the Imperial Guard.

The triangle comprised in the top of the A, between the two limbs and the tie, is the plateau of Mont-Saint-Jean. The dispute over this plateau was the whole battle. The wings of the two armies extended to the right and left of the two roads to Genappe and Nivelles; d'Erlon facing Picton, Reille facing Hill.

Behind the point of the A, behind the plateau of Mont-Saint-Jean, is the forest of Soignes.

As for the plain itself, imagine a vast undulating sweep of ground; each ascent commands the next rise, and all the undulations mount towards Mont-Saint-Jean, and there end in the forest.

Two hostile troops on a field of battle are two wrestlers. It is a question of seizing the opponent round the waist. The one tries to throw the other. They cling at everything; a bush is a point of support; an angle of the wall offers them a rest to the shoulder; for the lack of a hovel under whose cover they can draw up, a regiment yields its ground; an unevenness in the ground, a chance turn in the landscape, a cross-path encountered at the right moment, a grove, a ravine, can stay the heel of that colossus which is called an army, and prevent its retreat. He who leaves the field is beaten; hence the necessity devolving on the responsible leader of examining the smallest clump of trees and of studying deeply the slightest rise in the ground.

The two generals had attentively studied the plain of Mont-Saint-Jean, which is known as the plain of Waterloo. In the preceding year, Wellington, with the sagacity of foresight, had examined it as the future seat of a great battle. Upon this spot, and for this duel, on the 18th of June, Wellington had the good post, Napoleon the bad post. The English army was above, the French army below.

On the morning of Waterloo, then, Napoleon was content.

He was right; the plan of battle drawn up by him was, as we have seen, really admirable.

The battle once begun, its various incidents,—the resistance of Hougomont; the tenacity of La Haie-Sainte; the killing of Dauduin; the disabling of Foy; the unexpected wall against which Soye's brigade was broken; Guilleminot's fatal heedlessness when he had neither petard nor powder sacks; the sticking of the batteries in the mud; the fifteen unescorted pieces overwhelmed in a hollow way by Uxbridge; the small effect of the shells falling in the English lines, and there embedding themselves in the rain soaked soil, and only succeeding in producing volcanoes of mud, so that the canister was turned into a splash; the inutility of Piré's demonstration on Braine-l'Alleud; all that cavalry, fifteen squadrons almost annihilated; the right wing of the English badly alarmed, the left wing poorly attacked; Ney's strange mistake in massing, instead of echelonning the four divisions of the first corps; men delivered over to grape-shot, arranged in ranks twenty-seven deep and with a frontage of two hundred; the terrible gaps made in these masses by the cannon-balls; attacking columns disorganized; the side-battery suddenly unmasked on their flank; Bourgeois, Donzelot, and Durutte compromised; Quiot repulsed; Lieutenant Vieux, that Hercules graduated at the Polytechnic School, wounded at the moment when he was beating in which an axe the door of La Haie-Sainte under the downright fire of the English barricade which barred the angle on the Genappe road; Marcognet's division caught between the infantry and the cavalry, shot down at the very muzzle of the guns amid the grain by Best and Pack, put to the sword by Ponsonby; his battery of seven pieces spiked; the Prince of Saxe-Weimar holding and guarding, in spite of the Comte d'Erlon, both Frischemont and Smohain; the flags of the 105th taken, the flags of the 45th captured; that black Prussian hussar stopped by the flying column of three hundred light cavalry on the scout between Wavre and Plancenoit; the alarming things that had been said by prisoners; Grouchy's delay; fifteen hundred men killed in the orchard of Hougomont in less than an hour; eighteen hundred men overthrown in a still shorter time about La Haie-Sainte,—all these stormy incidents passing like the clouds of battle before Napoleon, had hardly troubled his gaze and had not overshadowed his imperial face. Napoleon was accustomed to gaze steadily at war; he never added up the poignant details. He cared little for figures, provided that they furnished the total, victory; he was not alarmed if the beginnings did go astray, since he thought himself the master and the possessor at the end; he knew how to wait, supposing himself to be out of the question, and he treated destiny as his equal: he seemed to say to fate, You would not dare.

Composed half of light and half of shadow, Napoleon felt himself protected in good and tolerated in evil. He had, or thought that he had, a connivance, one might almost say a complicity, of events in his favour, which was equivalent to the invulnerability of antiquity.

Nevertheless, when one has Bérésina, Leipzig, and Fontainebleau behind one, it seems as though one might defy Waterloo. A mysterious frown becomes perceptible on the face of the heavens.

At the moment when Wellington retreated, Napoleon quivered. He suddenly beheld the plateau of Mont-Saint-Jean deserted, and the van of the English army disappear. It was rallying, but hiding itself. The Emperor half rose in his stirrups. Victory flashed from his eyes.

Wellington, driven into a corner at the forest of Soignes and destroyed—that was the definite conquest of England by France; it would be Crécy, Poitiers, Malplaquet, and Ramillies avenged. The man of Marengo was wiping out Agincourt.

So the Emperor, meditating on this terrible turn of fortune, swept his glass for the last time over all the points of the field of battle. His guard, standing behind him with grounded arms, watched him from below with a sort of religious awe. He pondered; he examined the slopes, noted the declivities, scrutinized the clumps of trees, the patches of rye, the path; he seemed to be counting each bush. He gazed with some intentness at the English barricades of the two highways,—two large masses of felled trees, the one on the road to Genappe above La Haie-Sainte, defended with two cannon, the only ones out of all the English artillery which commanded the extremity of the field of battle, and that on the road to Nivelles where gleamed the Dutch bayonets of Chassé's brigade. Near this barricade he observed the old chapel of Saint

Nicholas, which stands at the angle of the cross-road near Braine-l'Alleud; he bent down and spoke in a low voice to the guide Lacoste. The guide made a negative sign with his head, which was probably perfidious.

The Emperor straightened himself up and reflected.

Wellington had withdrawn.

All that remained to do was to complete this retreat by crushing him.

Napoleon turning round abruptly, dispatched an express at full speed to Paris to announce that the battle was won.

Napoleon was one of those geniuses from whom thunder issues.

He had just found his thunder-stroke.

He gave orders to Milhaud's cuirassiers to carry the plateau of Mont-Saint-Jean.

There were three thousand five hundred of them. They formed a front a quarter of a league in length. They were giants, on colossal horses. There were six and twenty squadrons of them; and they had behind them to support them Lefebvre-Desnouettes's division,—the one hundred and six picked gendarmes, the light cavalry of the Guard, eleven hundred and ninety-seven men, and the lancers of the guard of eight hundred and eighty lances. They wore casques without plumes, and cuirasses of beaten iron, with horse-pistols in their holsters, and long sabre-swords. That morning the whole army had admired them, when, at nine o'clock, with blare of trumpets and all the music playing "Let us watch o'er the Safety of the Empire," they had come in a solid column, with one of their batteries on their flank, another in their centre, and deployed in two ranks between the roads to Genappe and Frischemont, and taken up their position for battle in that powerful second line, so cleverly arranged by Napoleon, which, having on its extreme left Kellermann's cuirassiers and on its extreme right Milhaud's cuirassiers, had, so to speak, two wings of iron.

The aide-de-camp Bernard carried them the Emperor's orders. Ney drew his sword and placed himself at their head. The enormous squadrons were set in motion.

Then a formidable spectacle was seen.

The whole of the cavalry, with upraised swords, standards and trumpets flung to the breeze, formed in columns by divisions, descended, by a si-multaneous movement and like one man, with the precision of a brazen bat-tering-ram which is affecting a breach, the hill of La Belle-Alliance. They plunged into the terrible depths in which so many men had already fallen, dis-appeared there in the smoke, then emerging from that shadow, reappeared on the other side of the valley, still compact and in close ranks, mounting at a full trot, through a storm of grape-shot which burst upon them, the terrible muddy slope of the plateau of Mont-Saint-Jean. They ascended, grave, threatening, imperturbable; in the intervals between the musketry and the artillery, their colossal trampling was audible. Being two divisions, there were two columns of them; Wathier's division held the right, Delort's division was on the left. It seemed as though two immense steel lizards were to be seen crawling towards the crest of the plateau. They traversed the battle like a flash.

Nothing like it had been seen since the taking of the great redoubt of the Moskowa by the heavy cavalry; Murat was missing, but Ney was again present. It seemed as though that mass had become a monster and had but one soul. Each column undulated and swelled like the rings of a polyp. They could be seen through a vast cloud of smoke which was rent at intervals. A confusion of helmets, of cries, of sabres, a stormy heaving of horses amid the cannons and the flourish of trumpets, a terrible and disciplined tumult; over all, the cuirasses like the scales on the dragon.

These narrations seemed to belong to another age. Something parallel to this vision appeared, no doubt, in the ancient Orphic epics, which told of the centaurs, the old hippanthropes, those Titans with human heads and equestrian chests who scaled Olympus at a gallop, horrible, invulnerable, sublime—gods and brutes.

It was a curious numerical coincidence that twenty-six battalions rode to meet twenty-six battalions. Behind the crest of the plateau, in the shadow of the masked battery, the English infantry, formed into thirteen squares, two battalions to the square, in two lines, with seven in the first line, six in the second, the stocks of their guns to their shoulders, taking aim at that which was on the point of appearing, waited, calm, mute, motionless. They did not see the cuirassiers, and the cuirassiers did not see them. They listened to the rise of this tide of men. They heard the swelling sound of three thousand horse, the alternate and symmetrical tramp of their hoofs at full trot, the jingling of the cuirasses, the clang of the sabres, and a sort of grand and formidable breathing. There was a long and terrible silence; then, all at once, a long file of uplifted arms, brandishing sabres, appeared above the crest, and casques, trumpets, and standards, and three thousand heads with grey moustaches, shouting, "Vive l'Empereur!" All this cavalry debouched on the plateau, and it was like the beginning of an earthquake.

All at once, a tragic incident happened; on the English left, on our right, the head of the column of cuirassiers reared up with a frightful clamour. On arriving at the culminating point of the crest, ungovernable, utterly given over to fury and their course of extermination of the squares and cannon, the cuirassiers had just caught sight of a trench or grave,—a trench between them and the English. It was the sunken road of Ohain.

It was a frightful moment. The ravine was there, unexpected, yawning, directly under the horses' feet, two fathoms deep between its double slopes; the second file pushed the first into it, and the third pushed on the second; the horses reared and fell backward, landed on their haunches, slid down, all four feet in the air, crushing and overwhelming the riders; and there being no means of retreat,—the whole column being no longer anything more than a projectile,—the force which had been acquiring to crush the English crushed the French; the inexorable ravine could only yield when filled; horses and riders rolled there pell-mell, grinding each other, forming but one mass of flesh in this gulf: when this trench was full of living men, the rest marched over them and passed on. Nearly a third of Dubois's brigade fell into that abyss.

This began the loss of the battle.

A local tradition, which evidently exaggerates matters, says that two thousand horses and fifteen hundred men were buried in the sunken road of Ohain. This figure probably comprises all the other corpses which were flung into this ravine the day after the combat.

Let us note in passing that it was Dubois's sorely tried brigade which, an hour previously, making a charge to one side, had captured the flag of the Lunenburg battalion.

Napoleon, before giving the order for this charge of Milhaud's cuirassiers, had scrutinized the ground, but had not been able to see that hollow road, which did not even form a wrinkle on the crest of the plateau. Warned, nevertheless, and put on his guard by the little white chapel which marks its angle of juncture with the Nivelles highway, he had put a question as to the possibility of an obstacle, to the guide Lacoste. The guide had answered No. We might almost say that Napoleon's catastrophe originated in the shake of a peasant's head.

Other fatalities were yet to arise.

Was it possible for Napoleon to win that battle? We answer No. Why? Because of Wellington? Because of Blücher? No. Because of God.

Bonaparte victor at Waterloo does not harmonise with the law of the nineteenth century. Another series of facts was in preparation, in which there was no longer any room for Napoleon. The ill will of events had declared itself long before.

It was time that this vast man should fall.

The excessive weight of this man in human destiny disturbed the balance. This individual alone counted for more than the universal group. These plethoras of all human vitality concentrated in a single head; the world mounting to the brain of one man,—this would be mortal to civilization were it to last. The moment had arrived for the incorruptible and supreme equity to alter its plan. Probably the principles and the elements, on which the regular gravitations of the moral, as of the material, world depend, had complained. Smoking blood, overcrowded cemeteries, mothers in tears,—these are formidable pleaders. When the earth is suffering from too heavy a burden, there are mysterious groanings of the shades, to which the abyss lends an ear.

Napoleon had been denounced in the infinite, and his fall had been decided on. He embarrassed God.

Waterloo is not a battle; it is a transformation on the part of the Universe.

The battery was unmasked simultaneously with the ravine.

Sixty cannons and the thirteen squares darted lightning point-blank on the cuirassiers. The intrepid General Delort made the military salute to the English battery.

The whole of the flying artillery of the English had re-entered the squares at a gallop. The cuirassiers had not had even the time for reflection. The disaster of the hollow road had decimated, but not discouraged them. They belonged to that class of men who, when diminished in number, increase in courage.

Wathier's column alone had suffered in the disaster; Delort's column, which had been deflected to the left, as though he had a presentiment of an ambush, had arrived whole.

The cuirassiers hurled themselves on the English squares.

At full speed, with bridles loose, swords in their teeth, pistols in their hand,—such was the attack.

There are moments in battles in which the soul hardens the man until the soldier is changed into a statue, and when all flesh becomes granite. The English battalions, desperately assaulted, did not stir.

Then it was terrible.

All the faces of the English squares were attacked at once. A frenzied whirl enveloped them. That cold infantry remained impassive. The first rank knelt and received the cuirassiers on their bayonets, the second rank shot them down; behind the second rank the cannoneers charged their guns, the front of the square parted, permitted the passage of an eruption of grape-shot, and closed again. The cuirassiers replied by crushing them. Their great horses reared, stroke across the ranks, leaped over the bayonets and fell, gigantic, in the midst of these four living walls. The cannon-balls ploughed furrows in these cuirassiers; the cuirassiers made breaches in the squares. Files of men disappeared, ground to dust under the horses. The bayonets plunged into the bellies of these centaurs; hence a hideousness of wounds which has probably never been seen anywhere else. The squares, wasted by this mad cavalry, closed up their ranks without flinching. Inexhaustible in the matter of grape-shot, they created explosions in their assailants' midst. The form of this combat was monstrous. These squares were no longer battalions, they were craters; those cuirassiers were no longer cavalry, they were a tempest. Each square was a volcano attacked by a cloud; lava combated with lightning.

The extreme right square, the most exposed of all, being in the air, was almost annihilated at the very first attack. It was formed of the 75th regiment of Highlanders. The piper in the centre dropped his melancholy eyes, filled with the reflections of the forests and the lakes in profound inattention, while men were being exterminated around him, and seated on a drum, with his pibroch under his arm, played the Highland airs. These Scotchmen died thinking of Ben Lothian, as did the Greeks remembering Argos. The sword of a cuirassier, which hewed down the bagpipes and the arm which bore it, put an end to the song by killing the singer.

The cuirassiers, relatively few in number, and still further diminished by the catastrophe of the ravine, had almost the whole English army against them, but they multiplied themselves so that each man of them was equal to ten. Nevertheless, some Hanoverian battalions yielded. Wellington saw it, and thought of his cavalry. Had Napoleon at that same moment thought of his infantry, he would have won the battle. This forgetfulness was his great and fatal mistake.

All at once, the cuirassiers, who had been the assailants, found themselves assailed. The English cavalry was at their back. Before them two squares, behind them Somerset; Somerset meant fourteen hundred dragoons of the guard. On the right, Somerset had Dornberg with the German light-horse, and on his left, Trip with the Belgian carbineers; the cuirassiers attacked on the flank and in front, before and in the rear, by infantry and cavalry, had to face all sides. What did they care? They were a whirlwind. Their valour was indescribable.

In addition to this, they had behind them the battery, which was still thundering. It was necessary that it should be so, or they could never have been wounded in the back. One of their cuirasses, pierced on the shoulder by a ball, is in the Waterloo Museum.

For such Frenchmen nothing less than such Englishmen was needed. It was no longer a hand-to-hand *mêlée;* it was a shadow, a fury, a dizzy transport of souls and courage, a hurricane of lightning swords. In an instant the fourteen hundred dragoon guards numbered only eight hundred. Fuller, their lieutenant-colonel, fell dead. Ney rushed up with the lancers and Lefebvre-Desnouettes's light-horse. The plateau of Mont-Saint-Jean was captured, re-captured, captured again. The cuirassiers left the cavalry to return to the infantry; or, to put it more exactly, the whole of that formidable rout collared each other without releasing the other. The squares still held firm after a dozen assaults. Ney had four horses killed under him. Half the cuirassiers remained on the plateau. This struggle lasted two hours.

The English army was profoundly shaken. There is no doubt that, had they not been enfeebled in their first shock by the disaster of the hollow road, the cuirassiers would have overwhelmed the centre and decided the victory. This extraordinary cavalry petrified Clinton, who had seen Talavera and Bada-joz. Wellington, three-quarters vanquished, admired heroically. He said in an undertone, "Splendid!"

The cuirassiers annihilated seven squares out of thirteen, took or spiked sixty guns, and captured from the English regiments six flags, which three cuirassiers and three chasseurs of the Guard bore to the Emperor in front of the farm of La Belle-Alliance.

Wellington's situation had grown worse. This strange battle was like a duel between two savage, wounded men, each of whom, still fighting and still resisting, is expending all his blood.

Which will be the first to fall?

The conflict on the plateau continued.

What had become of the cuirassiers? No one could have told. One thing is certain, that on the day after the battle, a cuirassier and his horse were found dead among the woodwork of the scales for vehicles at Mont-Saint-Jean, at the very point where the four roads from Nivelles, Genappe, La Hulpe, and Brussels meet and intersect each other. This horseman had pierced the English lines. One of the men who picked up the body still lives at Mont-Saint-Jean. His name is Dehaye. He was eighteen years old at that time.

Wellington felt that he was yielding. The crisis was at hand.

The cuirassiers had not succeeded, since the centre was not broken through. As every one was in possession of the plateau, no one held it, and in fact it remained, to a great extent, in the hands of the English. Wellington held the village and the plain; Ney had only the crest and the slope. They seemed rooted in that fatal soil on both sides.

But the weakening of the English seemed irremediable. The haemor-rhage of that army was horrible. Kempt, on the left wing, demanded reinforcements. "There are none," replied Wellington. Almost at that same moment, a singular coincidence which depicts the exhaustion of the two armies, Ney demanded infantry from Napoleon, and Napoleon exclaimed, "Infantry! Where does he expect me to get it? Does he think I can make it?"

Nevertheless, the English army was in the worse plight of the two. The furious onsets of those great squadrons with cuirasses of iron and breasts of steel had crushed the infantry. A few men clustered round a flag marked the post of a regiment; some battalions were commanded only by a captain or a lieutenant; Alten's division, already so roughly handled at La Haie-Sainte, was almost destroyed; the intrepid Belgians of Van Kluze's brigade strewed the rye-fields all along the Nivelles road; hardly anything was left of those Dutch grenadiers, who, intermingled with Spaniards in our ranks in 1811, fought against Wellington; and who, in 1815, rallied to the English standard, fought against Napoleon. The loss in officers was considerable. Lord Uxbridge, who had his leg buried on the following day, had a fractured knee. If, on the French side, in that tussle of the cuirassiers, Delort, l'Héritier, Colbert, Dnop, Travers, and Blancard were disabled, on the side of the English there was Alten wounded, Barne wounded, Delancey killed, Van Meeren killed, Ompteda killed, the whole of Wellington's staff decimated, and England had the heaviest loss of it in that balance of blood. The second regiment of foot-guards had lost five lieutenant-colonels, four captains, and three ensigns; the first battalion of the 30th infantry had lost 24 officers and 1200 soldiers; the 79th Highlanders had lost 24 officers wounded, 18 officers killed, 450 soldiers killed. Cumberland's Hanoverian hussars, a whole regiment, with Colonel Hacke at its head, who was destined to be tried later on and cashiered, had turned bridle in the presence of the fray, and had fled to the forest of Soignes, spreading the rout as far as Brussels. The transports, ammunition-wagons, the baggage-wagons, the wagons filled with wounded, on seeing that the French were gaining ground and approaching the forest, rushed into it. The Dutch, mowed down by the French cavalry, cried, "Alarm!" From Vert-Coucou to Groentendael, a distance of nearly two leagues in the direction of Brussels, according to the testimony of eye-witnesses who are still alive, the roads were dense with fugitives. This panic was such that it attacked the Prince de Condé at Mechlin, and Louis XVIII at Ghent. With the exception of the feeble reserve echelonned behind the ambulance established at the farm of Mont-Saint-Jean, and of Vivian's and Vandeleur's brigades, which flanked the left wing, Wellington had no cavalry left. A number of batteries lay dismounted. These facts are attested by Siborne; and Pringle, exaggerating the disaster, goes so far as to say that the Anglo-Dutch army was reduced to thirty-four thousand men. The Iron Duke remained calm, but his lips blanched. Vincent, the Austrian commissioner, Alava, the Spanish commissioner, who were present at the battle in the English staff, thought the Duke lost. At five o'clock Wellington drew out his watch, and he was heard to murmur these sinister words, "Blücher, or night!"

It was about that moment that a distant line of bayonets gleamed on the heights in the direction of Frischemont.

This was the culminating point in this stupendous drama.

The awful mistake of Napoleon is well known. Groucy expected, Blücher arriving. Death instead of life.

Fate has these turns; the throne of the world was expected; it was Saint Helena that was seen.

If the little shepherd who served as guide to Bülow, Blücher's lieu-tenant, had advised him to debouch from the forest above Frischemont, instead of below Plancenoit, the form of the nineteenth century might, perhaps, have been different. Napoleon would have won the battle of Waterloo. By any other route than that below Plancenoit, the Prussian army would have come out upon a ravine impassable for artillery, and Bülow would not have arrived.

Now the Prussian general, Muttling, declares that one hour's delay, and Blücher would not have found Wellington on his feet. "The battle was lost."

It was time that Bülow should arrive, as we shall see. He had, more-over, been very much delayed. He had bivouacked at Dieu-le-Mont, and had set out at daybreak; but the roads were impassable, and his divisions stuck fast in the mud. The ruts were up to the axles of the cannons. Moreover, he had been obliged to pass the Dyle on the narrow bridge of Wavre; the street leading to the bridge had been fired by the French, so the caissons and ammunition-wag-ons could not pass between two rows of burning houses, and had been obliged to wait until the conflagration was extinguished. It was mid-day before Bülow's vanguard had been able to reach Chapelle-Saint-Lambert.

Had the action begun two hours earlier, it would have been over at four o'clock, and Blücher would have fallen on the battle won by Napoleon. Such are these immense risks proportioned to an infinite which we cannot comprehend.

The Emperor had been the first, as early as mid-day, to descry with his field-glass, on the extreme horizon, something which had attracted his atten-tion. He had said, "I see over there a cloud, which seems to me to be troops." Then he asked the Duc de Dalmatie, "Soult, what do you see in the direction of Chapelle-Saint-Lambert?" The marshal, looking through his glass, answered, "Four or five thousand men, Sire." It was evidently Grouchy. But it remained motionless in the mist. All the glasses of the staff had studied "the cloud" pointed out by the Emperor. Some said: "They are columns halting." The truth is, that the cloud did not move. The Emperor detached Domon's division of light cavalry to reconnoitre in that direction.

Bülow had not moved in fact. His vanguard was very feeble, and could accomplish nothing. He was obliged to wait for the main body of the army corps, and he had received orders to concentrate his forces, before entering into line; but at five o'clock, perceiving Wellington's peril, Blücher ordered Bülow to attack, and uttered these remarkable words: "We must let the English army breathe."

A little later, the divisions of Losthin, Hiller, Hacke, and Ryssel deployed before Lobau's corps, the cavalry of Prince William of Russia debouched from the Bois de Paris, Plancenoit was in flames, and the Prussian cannon-balls began to rain even upon the ranks of the guard in reserve behind Napoleon.

The rest is known,—the irruption of a third army; the battle broken to pieces; eighty-six cannon thundering simultaneously; Pirch the first coming up with Bülow; Zieten's cavalry led by Blücher in person, the French driven back; Marcognet swept from the plateau of Ohain; Durutte dislodged from Papelotte; Donzelot and Quiot retreating; Lobau attacked on the flank; a fresh battle precipitating itself on our dismantled regiments at nightfall; the whole English line resuming the offensive and thrust forward; the gigantic breach made in the French army; the English grape-shot and the Prussian grape-shot aiding each other; the extermination; disaster in front; disaster on the flank; the Guard entering the line in the midst of this terrible crumbling of all things.

Conscious that they were about to die, they shouted, "Long live the Emperor!" History records nothing more touching than that death rattle bursting forth in acclamations.

The sky had been overcast all day. All of a sudden, at that very moment,—it was eight o'clock in the evening,—the clouds on the horizon parted, and allowed the sinister red glow of the setting sun to pass through, athwart the elms on the Nivelles road. They had seen it rise at Austerlitz.

Each battalion of the Guard was commanded by a general for this final *dénouement*. Friant, Michel, Roguet, Harlet, Mallet, Poret de Morvan, were there. When the tall bearskins of the grenadiers of the Guard, with their large plaques bearing the eagle, appeared, symmetrical, in line, tranquil, in the midst of that combat, the enemy felt a respect for France; they thought they beheld twenty victories entering the field of battle, with wings outspread, and those who were the conquerors, believing themselves to be vanquished, retreated;

but Wellington shouted, "Up, Guards, and at them!" The red regiment of English Guards, lying flat behind the hedges, sprang up, a cloud of grape-shot riddled the tricoloured flag and whistled round our eagles; all hurled themselves forwards, and the supreme carnage began. In the darkness, the Imperial Guard felt the army losing ground around it, and in the vast shock of the rout it heard the desperate flight which had taken the place of the "Long live the Emperor!" and, with flight behind it, it continued to advance, more crushed, losing more men at every step it took. There were none who hesitated, no timid men in its ranks. The soldier in that troop was as much of a hero as the general. Not a man was missing in that heroic suicide.

Ney, bewildered, great with all the grandeur of accepted death, offered himself to all blows in that tempest. He had his fifth horse killed under him there. Perspiring, his eyes aflame, foam on his lips, with uniform unbuttoned, one of his epaulets half cut off by a sword-stroke from the horse-guard, his plaque with the great eagle dented by a bullet; bleeding, bemired, magnificent, a broken sword in his hand, he said, "Come and see how a Marshal of France dies on the field of battle!" But in vain; he did not die. He was haggard and angry. At Drouet d'Erlon he hurled this question, "Are you not going to get yourself killed?" In the midst of all that artillery engaged in crushing a handful of men, he shouted: "So there is nothing for me! Oh! I should like to have all these English bullets enter my chest!" Unhappy man, thou wert reserved for French bullets!

The rout in the rear of the Guard was melancholy.

The army yielded suddenly on all sides simultaneously.—Hougomont, La Haie-Sainte, Papelotte, Plancenoit. The cry, "Treachery!" was followed by a cry of "Save yourselves who can!" An army which is disbanding is like a thaw. All yields, splits, cracks, floats, rolls, falls, collides, is precipitated. The disintegration is unprecedented. Ney borrows a horse, leaps upon it, and without hat, cravat, or sword, dashes across the Brussels road, stopping both English and French. He strives to detain the army, he recalls it to its duty, he insults it, he clings to the route. He is overwhelmed. The soldiers fly from him, shouting, "Long live Marshal Ney!" Two of Durutte's regiments go and come in affright as though tossed back and forth between the swords of the Uhlans and the fusillade of the brigades of Kempt, Best, Pack, and Ryland; the worst of hand-to-hand conflicts is the defeat; friends kill each other in order to escape; squadrons and battalions break and disperse against each other, like the tremendous foam of battle. Lobau at one extremity, and Reille at the other, are drawn into the tide. In vain does Napoleon erect walls from what is left to him of his Guard; in vain does he expend in a last effort his last serviceable squadrons. Quiot retreats before Vivian, Kellermann before Vandeleur, Lobau before Bülow, Morand before Pirch, Domon and Subervic before Prince William of Prussia; Guyot, who led the Emperor's squadrons to the charge, falls beneath the feet of the English dragoons. Napoleon gallops past the line of fugitives, harangues, urges, threatens, entreats them. All the mouths which in the morning had shouted, "Long live the Emperor!" remain gaping; they hardly recognize him. The Prussian cavalry, newly arrived, dashes forwards, flies, hews, slashes, kills, exterminates. Horses lash out, the cannons flee; the soldiers of the artillery-train unharness the caissons and use the horses to make their escape; wagons overturned, with all four wheels in the air, block the road and occasion massacres. Men are crushed, trampled down, others walk over the dead and the living. Arms are lost. A dizzy multitude fills the roads, the paths, the bridges, the plains, the hills, the valleys, the woods, encumbered by this invasion of forty thousand men. Shouts, despair, knapsacks and guns flung among the wheat, passages forced at the point of the sword, no more comrades, no more officers, no more generals, an indescribable terror. Zeiten putting France to the sword at his leisure. Lions converted into goats. Such was the flight.

At Genappe, an effort was made to wheel about, to present a battle front, to draw up in line. Lobau rallied three hundred men. The entrance to the village was barricaded, but at the first volley of Prussian canister, all took to flight again, and Lobau was made prisoner. That volley of grape-shot can be seen to-day imprinted on the ancient gable of a brick building on the right of the road at a few minutes' distance before you reach Genappe. The Prussians threw themselves into Genappe, furious, no doubt, that they were not more entirely the conquerors. The pursuit was stupendous. Blücher ordered extermination. Roguet had set the lugubrious example of threatening with death any French grenadier who should bring him a Prussian prisoner. Blücher surpassed Roguet. Duchesme, the general of the Young Guard, hemmed in at the doorway of an inn at Genappe, surrendered his sword to a huzzar of death, who took the sword and slew the prisoner. The victory was completed by the assassination of the vanquished. Let us inflict punishment, since we are writing history; old Blücher disgraced himself. This ferocity put the finishing touch to the disaster. The desperate rout traversed Genappe, traversed Quatre-Bras, traversed Gosselies, traversed Frasnes, traversed Charleroi, traversed Thuin, and only halted at the frontier. Alas! and who, then, was fleeing in that manner? The Grand Army.

This vertigo, this terror, which downfall into ruin of the highest bravery which ever astounded history,—is that causeless? No. The shadow of an enormous right is projected across Waterloo. It is the day of destiny. The force which is mightier than man produced that day. Hence the terrified wrinkle of those brows; hence all those great souls surrendering their swords. Those who had conquered Europe have fallen prone on the earth, with nothing left to say nor to do, feeling the present shadow of a terrible presence. *Hoc erat in fatis.* That day the perspective of the human race was changed. Waterloo is the hinge of the nineteenth century. The disappearance of the great man was necessary for the advent of the great age, and he, who cannot be answered, took the responsibility on himself. The panic of heroes can be explained. In the battle of Waterloo there is something more than a cloud, there is something of the meteor.

At nightfall, in a meadow near Genappe, Bernard and Bertrand seized by the skirt of his coat and detained a man, haggard, pensive, sinister, gloomy, who, dragged to that point by the current of the rout, had just dismounted, had passed the bridle of his horse over his arm, and with wild eye was returning alone to Waterloo. It was Napoleon, the immense somnambulist of this dream which had crumbled, trying once more to advance.

Landing Zone X-Ray

From *Chickenhawk*

BY ROBERT MASON

FOR ALL WHO LIVED through the 1960s and early 1970s, the images of Huey choppers thudding into landing zones amid swirling dust, smoke, and exploding shell-fire are synonymous with the word Vietnam. Captured on TV news footage and in famous movies, the helicopters were leading players in the dramas that took place on the battlefields of the jungle.

This excerpt from chopper pilot Robert Mason's account of his Vietnam experiences will take you closer to the way it really was than any movie ever will. Mason was there—and he knows how to write. It doesn't get any more realistic than this!

★   ★   ★   ★   ★

"The longest week began on a sun-drenched Sunday morning in a small clearing, designated Landing Zone X-Ray, in the Chu Pong foothills. Intelligence had long suspected the Chu Pong massif of harboring a large Communist force fed from the Cambodian side of the border. X-Ray seemed like a likely spot to find the enemy, and so it was." I read this in *Time,* the week after the Tea Plantation incident.

The results of nearly two weeks of searching and probing by the Cav were hundreds of dead NVA soldiers and a very good idea of where to find the main force of three NVA regiments. On November 14 our battalion lifted the 1st Battalion, 7th Cavalry (Custer's old unit) into LZ X-Ray, where they were expected to make contact. Our sister company, the Snakes, made the first assault in the morning and received very little opposition. By early afternoon,

though, the two companies of the Seventh Cav they had lifted in had been surrounded, and suffered heavy casualties. Our company was assigned to support
the Snakes, to lift in reinforcements.

We picked up the troopers at the Tea Plantation, eight to each Huey. It
was easy to tell where we were going. Although we were still fifteen miles
away, the smoke was clearly visible from all the artillery, B-52 bombers, and
gunship support concentrated around the LZ to keep the grunts from being
overrun. As we cruised over the jungles and fields of elephant grass, I had the
feeling this was a movie scene: the gentle rise and fall of the Hueys as we
cruised, the perspective created by looking along the formation of ships to the
smoke on the horizon, the quiet. None of the crews talked on the radios. We
all listened to the urgent voices in the static as they called in air strikes and artillery on their own perimeters, then yelled that the rounds were hitting *in*
their positions.

LZ X-Ray could accommodate eight Hueys at once, so that was how
the ships were grouped in the air. Yellow and White in the first group; Orange
and Red in the second. Leese and I were Red Two. As we got closer to X-Ray,
the gap between us and the first group got bigger to allow time for them to
land, drop off troopers, and take off.

Five miles away, we dropped to low level. We were flying under the artillery fire going into the LZ.

A mile ahead of us, the first group was going over the approach end of
the LZ and disappearing into the smoke. Now the radios came alive with the
pilots' calling in where the fire was coming from. The gunners on all the ships
could hear this. Normally it was helpful, but this time, with the friendlies on
the ground, they could not fire back. Yellow and White were on the ground
too long. The artillery still pounded. The massif behind the LZ was completely
obscured by the pall of smoke. We continued our approach. Leese was on the
controls. I double- or triple-checked my sliding armor panel on my door side
and cursed the army once again for not giving us chest protectors. I put my
hands and feet near the controls and stared at the scene.

"Orange One, abort your landing. Fire in the LZ is too heavy," a
pathfinder called from X-Ray. Orange flight turned, and we followed. There
was a whole bunch of yelling on the radios. I heard two ships in the LZ call out
that they were hit badly. What a mess. Orange flight led us in a wide orbit two
miles away, still low level. Now A1-E's from the air force were laying heavy fire
at the front of the LZ along with the artillery and our own gunships. What
kept everybody from flying into each other I'll never know. Finally we heard
Yellow One call to take off, and we saw them emerge from the smoke on the

left side of the LZ, shy two ships. They had waited in the heavy fire while the crews of the two downed ships got on the other Hueys. One crew chief stayed, dead. One pilot was wounded.

We continued the orbit for fifteen minutes. I looked back at the grunts who were staring at the scene. They had no idea what was going on, because they had no headsets.

"Orange One, make your approach," the pathfinder called. Apparently a human-wave attack by the NVA on the LZ was stopped. "Orange One, all eight of the ships in your two flights are keyed to pick up wounded." "Keyed" meant that they had groups of wounded positioned to be loaded first.

"Roger. Red One copy?"

"Red One roger."

Orange One rolled out of the orbit and we followed. The A1-E's were gone, but our gunships came back to flank us on the approach. Even with the concentration of friendlies on the ground, the gunships could fire accurately enough with their flex guns and rockets, so the grunts allowed them to. Our own door gunners were not allowed to fire unless they saw an absolutely clear target.

We crossed the forward tree line into the smoke. The two slicks that had been shot down were sitting at the front of the LZ, rotors stopped. That made it a little tight for eight of us to get in, but it was okay. The grunts jumped off even before the skids hit the ground. Almost before our Hueys had settled into the grass, other grunts had dumped wounded men, some on stretchers, into our ships. No fire. At least nothing coming our way. Machine guns and hundreds of rifles crackled into a roar all around us as the grunts threw out withering cover fire. The pathfinder, hidden in the tree line somewhere, told us everybody was loaded and to take off to the left. Orange One rogered and led us out. Fifty yards past the perimeter, some of the ships took hits, and we cleared all our guns to fire. Our ship was untouched.

After we dropped off the wounded, Leese and I were delayed by taking some men to an artillery position, separating us from the rest of the company for a half hour.

We were on our way to rejoin them when we saw a fighter get hit near X-Ray. It was a prop-driven A1-E. This scene, too, was right out of the movies. Orange flames burst from the root of his right wing and billowed back toward the tail, turning into coal-black smoke. The flames flared thicker than the fuselage and in moments hid the multipaned canopy. The pilot was either dead or unconscious, for he did not eject. The plane screamed toward the ground from about 3000 feet, not more than half a mile from Leese and me.

Black smoke marked its path as it streaked into the jungle at a steep angle, exploding instantly, spreading wreckage, and bursting bombs, unspent ammo, and fire forward, knocking down trees.

I made the mistake of calling our headquarters to tell them of the crash.

"Roger, Red Two, wait one," was the answer in my phones.

"Ah, Red Two, Grunt Six has relayed instructions that you are to proceed to the site of the crash and inspect same."

I wanted to go flying around where an air-force plane just got shot down like I wanted to extend my tour. Leese advised flying by very fast and taking a quick look-see. I dumped the Huey from 3000 feet, using the speed of my dive to swoop over the burning swatch in the jungle.

I told headquarters to tell Grunt Six that nobody had jumped out before the plane had hit and that there now remained only some smoldering pieces of airplane and some exploding ammo in the middle of the burnt clearing.

"Ah, roger, Red Two, wait one."

Whenever they asked you to wait, you knew they were up to no good.

"Ah, Red Two, Grunt Six says roger. But the air force wants you to land and do an on-site inspection."

Leese shook his head. "Negative, HQ," I radioed, "this area is hot. We will return to do a slow fly-by and check it again, but we know there's nobody left." Leese nodded.

Now, you would think that that would be good enough. I had just volunteered the four of us in our lone Huey to fly back over a very hot area to double-check the obvious.

It was not good enough. The air-force commander, via a relay through our HQ radio, wanted more.

"Red Two, the air force wants you to land and inspect the crash site for survivors," announced the voice in my flight helmet.

I told them to wait one, that I was in the process of doing another fly-by to check it out.

While our guy at HQ got back to the air-force commander, Leese and I and Reacher and the nervous ex-grunt who was our gunner approached the crash site. I wanted to be sure this time. I slowed to about thirty miles an hour just above the trees surrounding the new clearing. I started to circle the smoke and flames below us when we heard explosions. Leese, who always stayed off the controls, said, "I got it." He took the controls and dumped the nose of the Huey to accelerate. "Probably just some leftover ammunition from the fighter exploding," he said, "but I want to come back around in a fast turn just in case." He glanced out his window. "Somebody shot down this guy, and they're still around here somewhere." Leese began a turn to the left to circle back to the smoke. He picked up speed fast, and when we got to the clearing again, he banked very hard to the left. We all sank into our seats feeling the pressure of at least two Gs as Leese put the Huey into an almost-90-degree bank. I looked across at him in the left seat, through his side window and directly down to the wreckage. I had never experienced such a maneuver in flight school. My first thought was that the Huey would disconnect from the rotors, that the Jesus nut would break.

The view was, however, unique and totally revealing. And we were moving so fast we would be harder to hit.

From this dizzy vantage point we could see a few metal parts that hadn't melted and the flashes of exploding ammo. We hoped that all his bombs had gone off in the crash. We radioed that the pilot was definitely dead.

"Ah, roger, Red Two, wait one." We circled at 2000 feet about a mile away.

"Red Two, this is Preacher Six." Major Williams was now on the horn. "I have just talked to the air force, and I agreed that you would land to do an on-site inspection."

Leese, in his capacity as aircraft commander, answered. "Preacher Six, Red Two. We have already confirmed that no one is at the crash site, alive or dead. We have already risked more than we should have to determine this."

Leese should have known better than to try to be logical.

"Whether you have risked enough is my decision, Red Two. You are ordered to proceed to the crash site and land. You will then have your crew get out and inspect the wreckage firsthand. Over and out."

There was silence. I'm sure Leese considered telling him to stuff it, but he had to play his role.

He played it correctly. "Affirmative."

We were now back at the wreckage, circling once again in a scrotum-stretching Leese special. The left side of the Huey was really straight down. After two of these furious turns, he pulled away to set up his approach. He had decided not to try to land in the wreckage-strewn clearing itself because we wouldn't be able to land far enough away from the fire and the exploding ammo. Just behind the point of impact, there was a natural thin spot in the jungle where a few bare, 75-foot trees stood. It certainly wasn't big enough to put a Huey there, but that's where he was headed. Leese was going to show me another trick.

He settled into a hundred-foot hover directly over the tall trees and moved around searching for the right spot to play lawnmower. He had Reacher and the gunner lean out to watch the very delicate tail rotor. He found what he liked and began to let the helicopter settle down into the trees.

He had picked the spot perfectly. The tail boom with the spinning rotor on the end had a clear slot to follow down to the ground. The main rotor only had to chop a few two-inch-thick branches off some trees, a maneuver not even hinted at in flight school. When they hit the first branches, it sounded like gunfire.

Splintered wood flew everywhere. Treetops towered above us as we chopped our way down. We settled to the ground amid swirling debris, ass end low on a gentle slope covered with dense undergrowth. There was a moment of silence as the twigs and leaves settled around us. Nothing had been broken.

Reacher and the gunner grabbed their rifles and leapt into the thick tangle of weeks, galloping toward the still-exploding wreckage. The cords from their flight helmets trailed behind them.

Leese and I sat at the bottom of the vertical tunnel he had cut, our heads swiveling on nervous lookout. So far, only the sound of exploding ammo occasionally popped over the sound of the Huey. Reacher and the gunner disappeared through the thicket of trees between us and the wreckage.

We waited.

Whump! Whump, whump! Mortars! From wherever they were hiding, the NVA launched their worst.

We were alone. HQ had not sent a gunship for escort or even another slick to watch over us. Leese and I looked at each other as the mortars got closer. His mouth was thin and his jaw was tight. I wondered if this was as bad as landing gliders. In the dense foliage around us I heard the mortars crashing heavily, shaking the air, searching for us. They sounded like the footfalls of a drunken giant. A big crunch nearby, then one to the side, then another behind us as the invisible giant staggered around trying to stomp us. The NVA were very good with their mortars, but it took time to zero in on a new target like us. Since they couldn't see us from where they were, they had to walk the rounds back and forth until they got us.

Just when my fear was at an all-time high, Reacher and the gunner finally broke through the thicket to release us from the trap. They were both pale with fear as they dove on board. Leese had never let the Huey relax, so to speak. He had been ready to go at any second. As the two men hit the deck, Leese went.

He climbed back up through his tunnel in the trees like an express elevator and nosed the Huey over hard just as the rotor cleared the treetops. A mortar went off below just as our tail cleared the last tree.

Reacher told us that there was not even a little piece of the pilot left, and the air-force commander was finally satisfied. "Not only that," I fantasized he would write to the widow, "but I sent four suckers from the army right back in there to make sure your husband was dead."

Leese and I joined our company for the next lift after a trip to the Turkey Farm for refueling.

X-Ray was quiet this time. We dropped off the troopers and picked up wounded. At the hospital tent next to the runway at Holloway, I couldn't believe how many bodies were piling up outside the tent. Williams radioed that Leese and I and another ship could fly over to our camp and shut down because he wouldn't need us for the last lift in. I looked at the pile of dead, and shivered.

Back at our camp, Sergeant Bailey leaned out of the operations tent and yelled that the company was on its way back to Holloway. Two pilots had been hit.

Leese and I had been laying back for ten minutes at the Big Top, drinking coffee and enjoying every minute away from the gaggle. As Bailey yelled, I noticed the whole battalion on the horizon coming up from the south. Getting closer, the swarm was so noisy it sounded like a war all by itself. It wasn't too hard to imagine how the VC kept track of where we were.

The battalion broke into trail formation a few miles south, and the string of Hueys looped around, landing from the west. Leese and I were downwind from the flight line, and a warm, sweet breeze of burning kerosene from the turbines drifted by us.

The Hueys lined up side by side. Engines were shut down, and the pilots jumped out, carrying their gear. The crew chiefs waited patiently to tie the blades down and postflight their machines. As the pilots got closer, we could hear some whooping and yelling in their midst. It wasn't what we expected to hear after the news of the wounded.

At the Big Top, it was obvious why they were happy. The two wounded pilots, both from the other platoon, were walking with them, grinning and laughing with the rest. The blood from their wounds had dried in their hair and on their faces.

Both men had been hit in the head on the last lift. One had been shot from the front and the other from the side. Both were clutching their helmets, pointing at the holes. One guy had had a bullet hit the visor knob on the forehead portion of his flight helmet. The bullet had crushed his helmet and glanced off. His scalp was bleeding.

The other lucky soul walked around holding his helmet with a finger stuck into the holes on each side of it. Dried blood matted his hair on each side of his head. It was a magician's illusion. The bullet had to have gone through his head, from what he could see. We wanted to know the trick.

"I figured it out on the way back," he said. "I mean, after I stopped feeling for the holes on each side of my head and asking Ernie if I was still alive!" He was still pale, but he laughed. "The bullet hit while we were on short final to X-Ray. Luckily, Ernie was flying. It felt like somebody had hit me on the head with a bat. It blurred my vision. First I thought that a bullet had hit me on the helmet and somehow bounced off. Ernie first noticed the blood. He'd turned to tell me about a round going through the canopy in front of him when he saw it." I could imagine the guy seeing the jagged hole in the side of his friend's flying helmet, blood dripping down his neck. "I reached up to feel my helmet and felt the hole on the right side, but Ernie said the blood was coming from the other side. I put my left hand up and felt *that* hole! I pulled both hands down quickly, and they were both bloody! I felt the helmet again. Two holes all right. Two wounds all right. One on each side of my head. I couldn't believe I was still alive!" He passed the helmet around while he continued his story. "See, it hit here." He pointed in front of his right ear. "The bullet hit this ridge of bone and deflected up between my scalp and the inside of my helmet. Then"—he shook his head in disbelief—"then it circled around inside the top of the helmet and hit this ridge of bone on my left side." He pointed. "It was deflected out here, through the helmet and on through the canopy in front of Ernie!" He beamed. I saw the path the bullet made as it tore its way around through the padding on the inside of the helmet and the two wounds on each side of his head. I shook my head. God again?

As soon as he finished his story, a Jeep drove him and the other pilot across the airstrip to the hospital tent. As I watched them go, I saw the eastern sky fill with a huge formation of helicopters coming from the direction of An Khe. The Cav was sending the 227th to join us. That's about as near to full strength as the Cav got.

I joined Resler and the rest of the pilots going over to the compound for chow. About a hundred of us walked across the runway, spread out, talking to our buddies under the twilight sky. We passed the hospital tent, where the smell of blood was strong and body bags concealing grotesquely contorted corpses waited in the shadows.

The next morning, Leese and I stayed behind when the company left. We left a half hour later, to go on a single-ship mission before joining them later.

We had an easy mission to an artillery unit. We were supposed to drop off some radios, the mail, and the unit's commander, who was dropping by to talk shop with his boys. When he was finished, we were to take him back to Pleiku and then join our company.

The grunts were in the middle of a fire mission. Twenty steel barrels grouped on the north side of the clearing pointed eagerly toward the sky in the south. Concussion rings sprang away from the muzzles in the high humidity. The guns rocked back. They were shooting at targets five miles away.

They cleared us to come in, but kept on firing. The landing spot was in front of the guns.

Landing at artillery positions was a thrill. They were always in the middle of a fire mission, and they would keep firing until the ship was just about in front of the first tube. Naturally the final decision about what was too close for comfort was entirely up to the man pulling the lanyard on the cannon. The timing varied a lot. It depended on the mood of the gunner, which in turn depended on whether or not a helicopter had ever blown his tent away.

This was only my second landing into an artillery position. I set up my approach to the clearing in front of the guns and cautiously crept in, constantly reminding them on the radio that I was coming. As I crossed the trees, they were still firing. I glanced at the blasting muzzles on my left and realized that we were beginning to line up on the barrels. They stopped firing. I looked into the black muzzles and watched smoke drift lazily out as I flew through the still-turbulent air in front of them.

Someone decided to resume firing.

I was so close to the guns, looking right down their barrels when they went off, that I thought they had made a mistake and blown us apart. The sound went through me. My chest vibrated. The shock of the explosion rocked the helicopter. I landed and checked the seat. Clean.

The artillery commander told us he'd be about an hour, so I got out and walked around the place.

Twenty 105mm howitzers were grouped together on one side of the circular clearing. They took up about one fourth of the available space, the rest being kept clear for helicopters.

Spent brass casings glittered in the grass. They took these, eventually, to a large cargo net laid out near the middle of the clearing to be carried away by a Chinook when it was full.

I walked around behind the guns to watch the crews work. They were in the middle of a big salvo, going toward X-Ray, and the pace was hectic. The explosions were more than loud; they shook my body and my brains. I stuffed toilet paper in my ears and kept my mouth open. This was supposed to keep your eardrums from bursting.

One man near each gun took a chain of four or five powder bags out of the shell casings and tore off one of them. He threw it into a nearby fire, where it flashed brilliantly. The strength of the charge was controlled by discarding packets not needed for the distance they were shooting. After adjusting the charge, the man put the round—the business end of the package containing high explosives or white phosphorus—onto the open end of the brass casing. Ready to fire, the shell was stacked on a pile near the gun crew.

A hundred shirtless men worked, sweating, in practiced synchronization in the hot, stagnant air of the clearing. I watched them fire round after round in a fifteen-minute barrage that finally ended when the command "Cease fire" was shouted down the line.

When the thunder stopped, the quiet was startling. The men in the crews began clearing away spent casings and rearranging some of the litter around them, but they were clearly interested in the outcome of their efforts. I heard calls of "How'd we do?"

The aerial observer several miles away, at their target, radioed the news. "A hit. Body count over 150." A few isolated cheers sprang from among the twenty crews. Their sweat-covered backs glistened in the sun as they sat down for a smoke break.

Theirs was an odd war. Working feverishly in tree-walled clearings dotted here and there, away from everyone else, their enemy remained unseen, and the measure of their success or failure was a radio call from an aerial observer counting bodies. The work was hard and the noise was oppressive. During the month-long battle of Ia Drang valley, it went on twenty-four hours a day. Could a man ever really sleep in such cacophony? I tried it once and couldn't.

I talked to some guys in the crews, and they liked their job, especially as an alternative to being a trooper or a door gunner on a Huey. Their only real danger, aside from their guns blowing up, was being overrun. So far this hadn't happened in the Cav.

They asked me a lot of questions about what was happening. They could see the big flights of choppers heading south. They were having more fire missions with big body counts. The pace was quickening. They were excited about the idea of trapping the NVA. Maybe, just maybe, the enemy could be surrounded and killed. Maybe after suffering such a defeat, they would give up. We could all go home. It seemed possible. We were winning, weren't we?

The number of wounded we were carrying was growing fast. That week Leese and I flew more than a hundred wounded to the hospital tent. Other slicks carried a similar number.

When there was room and time, we carried the dead. They had low priority because they were no longer in a hurry. Sometimes they were thrown on board in body bags, but usually not. Without the bags, blood drained on the deck and filled the Huey with a sweet smell, a horribly recognizable smell. It was nothing compared to the smell of men not found for several days. We had never carried so many dead before. We were supposed to be winning now. The NVA were trapped and being pulverized, but the pile of dead beside the hospital tent was growing. Fresh recruits for graves registration arrived faster than they could be processed.

Back at our camp, I was feeling jittery after seeing too much death. I heard that two pilots had got caught on the ground.

Nate and Kaiser had gone to rescue them. Nate was almost in tears as he talked to us in the Big Top. "The stupid assholes. They had been relieved to return for fuel. But you know Paster and Richards: typical gunship pilots. Somehow they think their flex guns make them invulnerable. Anyway, on the flight back they were alone and spotted some VC or NVA or somebody on the ground and decided to attack. Nobody knows how long they were flying around there, because they called after they got hit. When Kaiser and I got there about ten minutes later, the Huey was just sitting there in a clearing looking fine. There were two gunships with us, and they circled around first and took no fire. Kaiser and I went behind the grounded ship. When we landed, I saw a red mass of meat hanging off a tree branch. It turned out to be Paster, hanging by his feet with his skin ripped off. There was nobody else around. The guns kept circling around and a Dust Off landed behind us. I got out, Kaiser stayed with the ship. The medic jumped out and ran with me." Nate kept patting his breast pockets, looking for his pipe. He never found it. "Paster's skin hung down in sheets and covered his head. The bastards had even cut off his cock. They must have just started on Richards, because we found him lying half naked about a hundred feet away in the elephant grass. His head was almost off." Nate stopped for a second, looking pale. "I almost threw up. Richards and I went to flight school together. The medics cut Paster down and stuffed him into a body bag." He shook his head, holding back tears. "Remember how Richards always bragged about how he knew he'd survive in the jungle if he got shot down? Shit, he even went to jungle school in Panama. If anybody'd be able to get away, it'd be Richards."

Nate's story hit hard. I remembered Richards and his jungle-school patch. Big deal, jungle expert. You got a hundred feet on your one big chance to evade the enemy. All that training down the drain. The thought of his wasting all that training brought tears to my eyes.

The pace remained hectic. The next day several assaults were made to smaller LZs near X-Ray to broaden our front against the NVA. Farris was assigned the command ship in a company-size flight, a mix of ships from the Snakes and the Preachers. We were going to a small, three-ship LZ. He picked me to be his pilot.

Everyone was tense. Radio conversations were terse. The grunts in the back looked grim. Even Farris looked worried. The NVA were being surrounded, and we knew they had to fight.

Farris and I would be in the first group of three to land. The company, each ship carrying eight grunts, trailed out behind us.

As the flight leader, Farris had the option to fly from any position in his flight. He chose the second ship. A theory from the developmental days of the air-assault concept said that the flight commander supposedly got a better idea about what was happening from the middle or even the end of the formation. Really big commanders flew high above us, for the best view of all.

I think this was my first time as a command-ship pilot, and I was all for survival. I would've been very happy flying the brigade commander up there at 5000 feet, or Westmoreland to his apartment in Saigon. It's amazing how many places I considered being besides there.

In assaults, we usually started drawing fire at 1000 feet, sometimes at 500. This time we didn't.

At 500 feet, on a glide path to the clearing, smoke from the just completed prestrike by our artillery and gunships drifted straight up in the still air. There had to be one time when the prep actually worked and everybody was killed in the LZ. I hoped this might be it.

Fighting my feeling of dread, I went through the automatic routine of checking the smoke drift for wind direction. None. We approached from the east, three ships lined up in a trail, to land in the skinny LZ. But it was too quiet!

At 100 feet above the trees, closing on the near end of the LZ, the door gunners in Yellow One started firing. They shot into the trees at the edge of the clearing, into bushes, anywhere they suspected the enemy was hiding. There was no return fire. The two gunships on each side of our flight opened up with their flex guns. Smoke poured out of them as they crackled. My ears rang with the loud but muffled popping as my door gunners joined in with the rest. I ached to have my own trigger. With so many bullets tearing into the LZ, it was hard to believe anyone on the ground could survive.

The gunships had to stop firing as we flared close to the ground because we could be hit by ricocheting bullets. Still no return fire. Maybe they *were* all dead! Could this be the wrong spot?

My adrenaline was high, and I was keenly aware of every movement of the ship. I waited for the lurch of dismounting troopers as the skids neared the ground. They were growling and yelling behind me, psyched for battle. I could hear them yelling above all the noise. I still can.

My landing was synchronized with the lead ship, and as our skids hit the ground, so did the boots of the growling troops.

At the same instant, the uniformed regulars from the North decided to spring their trap. From at least three different directions, they opened up on our three ships and the off-loading grunts with machine-gun crossfire. The LZ was suddenly alive with their screaming bullets. I tensed on the controls, involuntarily leaning forward, ready to take off. I had to fight the logical reaction to leave immediately. I was light on the skids, the troops were out. Let's go! Farris yelled on the radio for Yellow One to go. They didn't move.

The grunts weren't even making it to the trees. They had leapt out, screaming murderously, but now they dropped all around us, dying and dead. The lead ship's rotors still turned, but the men inside did not answer. I saw the sand spurt up in front of me as bullets tore into the ground. My stomach tightened to stop them. Our door gunners were firing over the prone grunts at phantoms in the trees.

A strange quietness happened in my head. The scene around me seemed far away. With the noise of the guns, the cries of the gunners about everybody being dead, and Farris calling for Yellow One to go, I thought about bullets coming through the Plexiglas, through my bones and guts and through the ship and never stopping. A voice echoed in the silence. It was Farris yelling "Go! Go! Go!"

I reacted so fast that our Huey snapped off the ground. My adrenaline seemed to power the ship as I nosed over hard to get moving fast. I veered to the right of the deadly quiet lead ship, still sitting there. The door gunners fired continuously out both sides. The tracers coming at me now seemed as thick as raindrops. How could they miss? As a boy I made a game of dodging raindrops in the summer showers. I always got hit eventually. But not this time. I slipped over the treetops and stayed low for cover, accelerating. I veered left and right fast, dodging, confounding, like Leese had taught me, and when I was far enough away, I swooped up and away from the nightmare. My mind came back, and so did the sound.

"What happened to Yellow Three?" a voice said. It was still on the ground.

The radios had gone wild. I finally noticed Farris's voice saying, "Negative, White One. Veer left. Circle back." Farris had White One lead the rest of the company into an orbit a couple of miles away. Yellow One and Yellow Three were still in the LZ.

I looked down at the two ships sitting quietly on the ground. Their rotors were turning lazily as their turbines idled. The machines didn't care, only the delicate protoplasm inside them cared. Bodies littered the clearing, but some of the thirty grunts we had brought in were still alive. They had made it to cover at the edge of the clearing.

Farris had his hands full. He had twelve more ships to get in and unloaded. Then the pilot of Yellow Three called. He was still alive, but he thought his partner was dead. His crew chief and gunner looked dead, too. He could still fly.

Two gunships immediately dove down to escort him out, machine guns blazing. It was a wonderful sight to see from a distance.

Only Yellow One remained on the ground. She sat, radios quiet, still running. There was room behind her to bring in the rest of the assault.

A grunt who found himself still alive got to a radio. He said that he and a few others could keep some cover fire going for the second wave.

Minutes later, the second group of three ships was on its way in, and Farris told me to return to the staging area. I flew back a couple of miles to a big field, where I landed and picked up another load of wildeyed boys.

They also growled and yelled. This was more than just the result of training. They were motivated. We all thought that this was the big push that might end it all. By the time I made a second landing to the LZ, the enemy machine guns were silent. This load would at least live past the landing.

Somebody finally shut down Yellow One's turbine when we left. Nobody in the crew could. They were all patiently waiting to be put into body bags for the trip home.

Why I didn't get hit I'll never know. I must have read the signs right. Right? They started calling me "Lucky" after that mission.

Custer and the Little Bighorn

From *Son of the Morning Star*

BY EVAN S. CONNELL

THIS IS THE STORY of how Gen. George Armstrong Custer and about 250 troopers of the U.S. Seventh Cavalry rode into legend and history on Sunday, June 25, 1876, in the valley of the Little Bighorn in Montana Territory.

Arguably, Evan Connell's book *Son of the Morning Star,* from which this excerpt is taken, is the best written and best researched work ever done on Custer and the Little Bighorn. To me the book is an engaging pleasure to read, even though you know what the outcome will be, with much the same type of storytelling skill that has made Sebastian Junger's *The Perfect Storm* a permanent fixture on nonfiction bestseller lists in recent years.

Custer and his men rode out of Fort Lincoln on June 22, forked stars-and-stripes guidons flying, a band playing the jaunty Irish tune "Garry Owen" Custer adored. They were bound for the vicinity of the Rosebud on an Indian-killing sweep involving three separate forces—Generals Crook, Terry and Custer, and Gibbon. This was the same vicinity where, on June 17, Sioux forces under Crazy Horse, accompanied by Cheyennes, had beaten off General Crook's ("Three-Stars Crook," the Indians called him) bluecoats. Crook had retired to his base camp on Goose Creek to await reinforcements from Custer, Terry, or Gibbon.

As Custer and his troopers rode into the Rosebud area, they did not know that the Sioux and Cheyennes had moved to the Little Bighorn because of herds of antelope and good grass reported to be there. Nor did he know the vast size of the Indian encampment, which included far more warriors, and different warriors, than had been involved in the fight with Crook on the 17th. Custer thought that somewhere in the vicinity of the Rosebud he would encounter a Sioux force of perhaps 1,500 braves. According to the noted histo-

140

rian Dee Brown, in *Bury My Heart at Wounded Knee,* the encampment on the Little Bighorn probably included 10,000 Sioux and Cheyenne with 3,000 or 4,000 warriors. Even if the Crook, Gibbon, and Terry-Custer columns had been together, they would have faced a formidable task in attacking the massed Indians. Instead, the Cavalry forces were scattered, with Gibbon on the Yellowstone, Crook at Goose Creek, and the Terry-Custer columns approaching from Fort Lincoln, near Bismarck in the Dakota Territory.

When Custer and his scouts crossed the obvious tracks of a large Indian force moving toward the Little Bighorn late on June twenty-fourth, he immediately discussed plans to follow the clearly defined trail over the divide into the valley of the Little Bighorn the following day, hide there, and attack on the twenty-sixth. That plan was never carried out. When he struck the outskirts of the Indian encampment on the twenty-fifth, Custer could not contain himself. He ordered Maj. Marcus Reno to launch an immediate attack, which he planned to follow with his own troops. Once the fight began, Reno and his men were routed, and Custer, not knowing his flank forces had crumbled, rode to his doom. (Reno would later be courtmartialed in a controversial trial.) Obviously, the Indians' scouts had been aware of Custer's approach long before the first shots were fired.

George Armstrong Custer and the troops of the 7th Cav. had ridden into the valley of the Little Bighorn to kill as many Indians as they could. This time, the Indians were in a position to defend themselves. And they did—with a vengeance!

★   ★   ★   ★   ★

These days the slope is quiet. Not many tourists congregate on Custer's ridge. They clog Yosemite and swarm at the lip of the Grand Canyon like colonies of iridescent beetles, but the Little Bighorn is a formidable drive from anywhere. Excepting Crow Agency, the nearest town is Hardin—fifteen miles northwest at the junction of the Little Bighorn and the Bighorn. Fifty miles beyond Hardin is Billings. From Billings to Great Falls or Butte is more than two hundred miles.

Strangely wrinkled umber hills half-enclose the site. If one overlooks highway I-90 and a spatter of rural buildings it might as well be Mongolia, there is such vast indifference beneath this bone-yellow sky. North of the battleground are a motel, coffee shop, gas pumps, and the Crow Agency rodeo stadium. To the east above a succession of waterless ravines the blunt brown Wolf Mountains slant toward nothing. Sixty or eighty miles south the snowy

Bighorns hang like a motionless cloud. And to the west—beyond Bozeman, very far west—one can make out the long rugged spine of the Rockies.

Imported evergreens and the deep luxuriant grass of Custer National Cemetery seem incongruous on this terra cotta hillside. Years ago there was thick vegetation, but sheepherders used the slope and sheep do not leave much, so any kind of moisture runs off quickly. Without irrigation this rectangular oasis would wither, the trees would shrivel. Every day the militant shadows of these spruce trees darken the graves of Major Reno, of the scout Curly, of Captain Fetterman who chased a band of Sioux away from Fort Kearny, and of many other soldiers.

The place where Custer died is surrounded by a black iron fence—an inclined plot whose midsummer custodians are grasshoppers, crickets, flies, and a few undistinguished little birds. Insects flicker across the weeds, except during hail-swept interludes, while a honey-warm sun pours down.

Pvt. Coleman wrote: "25th the sun rose this Morning with every appearance of it being verry hot . . ."

A month later Lt. Bradley wrote for the Helena *Herald:*

Probably never did hero who had fallen upon the field of battle appear so much to have died a natural death. His expression was rather that of a man who had fallen asleep and enjoyed peaceful dreams, than of one who had met his death amid such fearful scenes as that field had witnessed, the features being wholly without ghastliness or any impress of fear, horror or dispair. . . .

Although Bradley was the first to look down upon the general he was soon followed by many others, and because their descriptions are so much alike it is possible to recreate the scene very much as it must have been. Gerard, for example, preceded the troops. "He found the naked bodies of two soldiers, one across the other, and Custer's naked body in a sitting posture between and leaning against them, his upper right arm along and on the topmost body, his right forearm and hand supporting his head in an inclining posture like one resting or asleep. . . ." Other reports indicate that Custer was seen with his right leg flung across a dead soldier, the heel resting on a horse carcass, the fingers of his right hand extended as though he had been holding a pistol—which suggests that someone lowered him from the upright posture noted by Gerard. But these discrepancies are slight.

He lay just south or southwest of the monument. He had been shot twice: in the left side beneath the heart and in the left temple. Either would have been fatal, but he probably was killed by the shot in the side because this wound was bloody. The hole in his temple was clean, a shot meant to guarantee that he was not feigning death. There was also a wound in his right forearm, but this might have been caused by the bullet emerging from his body. Benteen, who took a close look, did not think the wounds were caused by .45 caliber bullets, so it seems likely that he was hit the first time from some distance by a Henry rifle or a Winchester.

Sgt. Knipe said he lay across two or three dead soldiers with only a portion of his back touching the ground. Except for socks he had been undressed, as were the men around him. The bottom of one of his boots lay nearby, but the upper part was missing—which certainly means that a squaw sliced off the tops to make purses or moccasins. Knipe said he lay at the peak of the ridge, somewhat higher than the enclosed cluster of tablets. No matter. From within the black iron fence or from the peak of the ridge it is easy to imagine what he saw: an enormous village beside the Little Bighorn stretched out as though in subjugation at his feet.

With the possible exception of one fingertip, he had not been mutilated. So the public was told. But there are said to be unpublished letters detailing various disfigurements: thighs slashed to the bone, ears slit, arrows driven in the groin. Supposedly this information was withheld out of regard for Elizabeth, and even now may be too disagreeable for publication.

Why he escaped scalping has never been determined. For a long time many Americans thought he had earned this respect by his courage. Terry's men allegedly saw a mark on his cheeks, put there by an unidentified chief as a warning to the squaws that he should be left alone, but this appears to be no more than a white man's tale. Many Indians were consulted and their answers noted. From a warrior's point of view the Son of the Morning Star had an unattractive head. The hair was sparse because he was growing prematurely bald and what remained had been cut short. A number of braves might have inspected him and decided the hair was not worth keeping.

By one account he walked along the ridge carrying his white hat, leading his horse by the bridle, after everybody else was dead. Several Indians rose up and killed him but did not take the scalp, nor even touch the body, because they thought he was insane.

A Canadian identified as "Mr. Macdonald" said he had been told by Indians that Custer was not mutilated because of his buckskin suit; they mistook him for a hunter who was visiting the troops and was therefore innocent.

Lt. Col. William Bowen was told by Benteen that when Rain in the Face saw Custer's body he shook the right hand of the corpse and exclaimed,

"My poor friend!" It was Rain, according to Col. Bowen, who saved Custer from further humiliation.

He is said to have shot himself, the ultimate proof of cowardice, and today many people believe it. That he did so can be verified by numerous testimonials. For instance, an army officer in Wyoming was told by an old Indian that he—the old Indian—was hiding in a buffalo wallow near the battlefield and saw Custer commit suicide. Buffalo seldom wallow on hillsides, but never mind. No powder burn was observed on his temple, but never mind. A righthanded man is not apt to shoot himself in the left temple, but never mind. These days it is stylish to denigrate the general, whose stock sells for nothing. Nineteenth-century Americans thought differently. At that time he was a cavalier without fear and beyond reproach.

Several facts can be sifted from the myth. There is no doubt that G. A. C. and his brother Tom were buried by Sgt. John Ryan of M Company, assisted by Corporals Harrison Davis and Frank Neeley and Private James H. Seaver. They dug a wide, shallow grave about eighteen inches deep at the foot of the knoll where the earth was soft and arranged the brothers side by side, covering their bodies with blankets and canvas tent sections. Dirt was shoveled over them and a travois found in the village was turned upside down on top, loaded with rocks and pegged to the ground. A large basket found with the travois may have been left on the grave to serve as a marker. Ryan is ambiguous about this, but states categorically that nobody else received such a fine burial. He states also that both bullets struck General Custer on the right side; however, testimony from men who examined the body more closely seems to indicate that on this point Ryan was mistaken.

Another point of dispute among scholars concerns the horse Vic, whether it was a stallion or a mare. Elizabeth, who saw the animal many times and should be considered an authority, alludes to it as a horse; yet old John Burkman years afterward persisted in calling Vic a mare: "Hadn't I orter know, Bud, seein' 's how I've curried her and trimmed her fetlocks and polished her hoofs time and time agin?"

Elizabeth said Vic was a Kentucky thoroughbred "found dead beside his devoted master." Well, just possibly Victor/Victoria emerged from the fight between the knees of a Santee Sioux named Walks Under the Ground—one of several Indians who claimed to have killed the soldier chief. Walks Under did come out with a blaze-faced sorrel, which properly describes the horse. By another account some unidentified Unkpapa recognized Vic among the captured animals and appropriated it. Still, the old Miniconjou known as Dewey Beard or Iron Hail, who lived almost forever—until 1955—Dewer Beard claimed to have seen a blaze-faced sorrel with white stockings tied by the reins to Custer's wrist, so maybe Elizabeth was right.

Col. Homer Wheeler and Capt. John Bourke visited the battlefield in 1877. Wheeler said they located the graves of General Custer and Tom, of Autie Reed, adjutant W. W. Cooke, and correspondent Mark Kellogg. Wheeler believed the remains of their horses lay nearby. He and Bourke cut off all four hooves of the animal supposedly ridden by Custer. Bourke had his pair turned into inkstands, one of which he donated to a museum in Philadelphia. Wheeler put his pair into a grain sack which was either lost or stolen while he was campaigning against the Nez Perces.

Lt. Edward McClernand, who arrived with Terry and Gibbon, was shown a dead horse lying about fifty yards from the last stand. Somebody told him this was Vic. From the position of the legs McClernand surmised that Vic must have been galloping, and because the head lay in the direction of the last stand it seemed to him that Custer would have been thrown to the ground, but got up and sprinted those last fifty yards in his boots: "I do not say that such was the case. . . ."

To these enigmas, and perhaps a grain sack stuffed with others, the general alone might provide answers.

Pvt. Coleman contemplated the horror on the ridge, and as usual he describes a scene more forcibly than his literate superiors. Now, he begins:

Comes the most heartrendering tale of all. As I have said before General Custer with five Companies went below the Village to Cut them off as he Supposed but instead he was Surrounded and all of them Killed to a Man 14 officers and 250 Men Their the Bravest General of Modder times met his death with his two Brothers Brotherinlaw and Nephew not 5 yards apart Surrounded by 42 Men of E Company. Oh what a slaughter how Manny homes are Made desolate by the Sad disaster eavery one of them were Scalped and otherwise Mutilated but the General he lay with a smile on his face. . . .

All three bluecoat armies—Crook, Terry, Gibbon—were under surveillance by Sioux and Cheyennes. The Terry-Custer column might have been watched from the day it left Fort Lincoln, and there is no doubt that hostile scouts observed the *Far West* at the mouth of Rosebud Creek several days before the battle. They also reported soldiers traveling up the Rosebud; and on the morning of June 25, two or three hours before Custer crossed the fatal divide, it is almost certain they knew exactly where he was and the size of his regiment. The only thing that surprised them was the speed of his advance.

Not many Indians were alarmed. Just a few days earlier they had fought Three Stars Crook, and although they had defeated him there was a chance he might return. Yet they could not imagine that Crook, or any white general, would attack such a large camp. It is said that about noon of the twenty-fourth a Sans Arc herald went around crying: "Soldiers will be here tomorrow!" Nobody paid much attention.

A Cheyenne prophet named Box Elder saw the advancing regiment in a dream and when he awoke he tried to warn everybody, but other Cheyennes mocked him by howling—implying that he had gone mad and should be fed to the wolves.

A Miniconjou named Standing Bear went for a swim on the morning of the fight. When he got back to his lodge one of his uncles advised him to collect the horses right away because something might happen.

An Oglala named Joseph White Cow Bull slept late. When he got up he asked an old woman for breakfast and while he was eating she told him there would be a battle. "How do you know, grandmother?" he asked. She refused to talk about it. Not long after this he was visiting friends at the Cheyenne camp when they heard shots and saw dust in the air and an Oglala rode by calling out that soldiers had attacked the Unkpapa circle. Joseph and three Cheyenne friends were getting ready to join the Unkpapas when they saw Custer's battalion on the ridge, so instead of riding south they went east toward the river. An old warrior named Mad Wolf tried to stop them, saying there were too many bluecoats, but a Cheyenne—Bobtail Horse—replied: "Uncle, only the earth and the heavens last long." Joseph and his friends then continued east, all four singing their death songs.

Soldiers—pink and hairy—came riding down a coulee. Joseph noticed one in a big hat and a buckskin jacket who rode a blaze-faced sorrel with white stockings. Beside him rode a soldier with a flag. This man in buckskin looked across the river and shouted, which caused the bluecoats to charge. Joseph and the Cheyennes slid off their ponies and began to shoot. Bobtail Horse hit a soldier who fell out of the saddle into the water. Joseph hit the one in buckskin. He, too, fell out of the saddle and when this happened many soldiers reined up, gathering around him. After that it was difficult to see anything because other Indians were arriving and the air filled with smoke.

This story of four braves challenging Custer's battalion has been told various ways. They might have been searching the valley for injured warriors when Custer appeared on the ridge, so they splashed across a ford and rode some distance up Medicine Tail coulee before starting to fight.

Just what occurred is now forgotten, but almost certainly three or four young Indians did confront five picked companies of the elite Seventh—an act of suicidal defiance which may have affected Custer's battle plan. Not that they could intimidate him, but he had no way of knowing how many other hostiles lay in wait. Those four might have looked like decoys, so he withdrew.

How surprised the Indians were by almost simultaneous assaults on opposite ends of the village is impossible to say. Ten or fifteen thousand people had camped beside the river and there is no reason to suppose they would all agree. Most of them were startled and disconcerted. Others probably had been wondering if Crook would try again. Some must have realized it was not Crook's army. Some had heard about Custer and might have guessed this was his regiment.

Tribal leaders had talked about what to do if the camp was threatened. Their decision seems to have been that they would wait to see how the soldiers behaved.

Scouts watched the regiment cross the divide and later observed it separate into battalions. Gall himself watched Custer's five companies ride along the bluffs east of the river. He said they kicked up a lot of dust. They rode out of sight but soon reappeared. He said they were mounted on white horses, which must be an incorrect translation of his words, or else he was referring to Lt. Smith's gray horse company, or to the fact that among the grays and browns were a few white horses belonging to musicians who dismounted at the Powder River depot. Gall thought these soldiers looked nice, riding as if they were on parade. He and his Unkpapas continued to watch them, meanwhile rounding up the pony herd in case the bluecoats meant to cause trouble. He had no idea who was leading these men, or if they intended to start a fight.

In 1919 a Miniconjou, Feather Earring, said to General H. L. Scott: "If Custer had come up and talked with us, we had all agreed we would have surrendered and gone in with him." During subsequent conversations Feather Earring emphasized that if Custer had approached diplomatically the Indians would have gone back to the reservation. This was confirmed years later by other Indians. General Scott observed that such a method of dealing with the hostiles had not occurred to anybody.

The entire expedition might have been unnecessary. A Sioux chief whose name has been awkwardly translated as Pretty Voice Eagle spoke with Custer just before the army left Fort Lincoln. Whether this chief also spoke with General Terry is not clear, but he was very clear about the fact that he led a delegation of his people to Custer in an attempt to avoid a battle. He asked Custer to promise that he would not fight the Sioux. Custer promised.

. . . and we asked him to raise his hand to God that he would not fight the Sioux, and he raised his hand. After he raised his hand to God that he would not fight the Sioux he asked me to go west with my delegation to see these roaming Sioux, and tell them to come back to the reservation, that he would give them food, horses, and clothing. After we got through talking, he soon left the agency, and we soon heard that he was fighting the Indians and that he and all his men were killed. If Custer had given us time we would have gone out ahead of him, but he did not give us time. If we had gone out ahead of Custer he would not have lost himself nor would his men have been killed. I did all I could to persuade the Ree scouts not to go. . . .

Capt. Bourke once remarked that some people learn quickly, others learn slowly, "preachers, school-teachers, and military people most slowly of all."

Many Indians at the Little Bighorn were so convinced of trouble that tribal leaders posted guards east of the river to prevent ambitious young men from riding out to locate the troops and drench themselves in glory by being the first to count coup. About sundown on the evening before the fight these guards made themselves visible on the ridge. Despite this warning, several braves sneaked across the river and got up into the hills. The next day they were riding around looking for soldiers when they heard the shots fired by Reno's troops in the valley.

Crazy Horse did not behave as usual. Ordinarily he was composed, even when battle was imminent, but it is said that this morning he rode back and forth, hurried into his lodge, and quickly reappeared with his medicine bag. After moistening one hand he dipped it in maroon pigment and printed a hand on each side of his pony's hips. On both sides of the neck he drew an arrow and a bloody scalp. All of which suggests intuitive knowledge of things to come, or else he had been talking with Oglala scouts who told him what to expect. Most Indians, however, seem to have felt secure in the belief that only a great fool would attack.

Low Dog thought it must be a false alarm when he heard about soldiers charging the Unkpapa circle.

Iron Thunder could not believe the truth until a few bullets whizzed by.

Chief Red Horse and several women felt so unconcerned that they were away from the village digging tipsina—wild turnip—a knobby root filled with starch, when they noticed a dust cloud and saw Reno's troops.

A female cousin of Sitting Bull, Pte-San-Waste-Win, usually translated as Mrs. Spotted Horn Bull, said that by the time the turnip diggers got back to the village everybody could see the flash of sabers, which is a puzzling remark. Not one cavalryman, with the possible exception of DeRudio, carried a saber. What she saw might have been sunlight glinting on gun barrels.

Rain in the Face had been invited to a feast. The guests were eating when they heard bluecoat guns, which did not sound like their own. Rain habitually carried a stone-headed war club, even to parties, but he rushed back to his lodge for a gun, his bow, and a quiver of arrows. Then he hopped on his pony and was about to ride south when he and his friends saw troops on the eastern ridge. While riding against these troops they discovered a young woman—Tashenamini, Moving Robe—riding with them. Her brother had been killed during the fight with Crook and now she was holding her brother's war staff above her head. Rain declared that she looked as pretty as a bird. "Behold, there is among us a young woman!" he called out, because this would make everybody brave. "Let no young man hide behind her garment!"

Custer's soldiers were almost surrounded by the time Rain got there. They had dismounted, he said, but climbed back on their horses, dismounted again, and split into several companies. They were shooting very fast. After a while some of them began riding toward Reno's troops, but Indians followed them like blackbirds following a hawk.

The Cheyenne chief Two Moon told Hamlin Garland in 1898 that he was trying to reassure a bunch of frightened women when Custer's men arrived, cloaked with dust: "While I was sitting on my horse I saw flags coming up over the hill to the east. . . ."

When it was all over Two Moon and four Sioux chiefs rode through the valley and across the hillside counting dead bluecoats. He explained through an interpreter, Wolf Voice, that one Indian carried a little bundle of sticks: "When we came to dead men, we took a little stick and gave it to another man, so we counted the dead. There were three hundred and eighty-eight." However, Two Moon told a different story sixteen years later. This time he said they went to the river to cut willow sticks. An Indian was assigned to throw down a stick beside each dead soldier, then the sticks were picked up and counted: "It was about six times we had to cut willow sticks, because we kept finding men all along the ridge. We counted four hundred and eighty-eight. . . ."

Either way the number has been inflated, but how to explain this seems impossible. As Robert Utley points out, meanings are difficult to convey from one language to another. "Testimony delivered from an aboriginal frame of reference risked serious distortion in the process."

Three hundred and eighty-eight. Four hundred and eighty-eight. What did Two Moon actually say? What did he mean?

In a communiqué from the north bank of the Yellowstone, dated July 9, 1876, General Terry wrote that two hundred sixty-eight officers, men, and civilians were killed, fifty-two wounded—which may or may not be accurate. Company rosters were kept by first sergeants and five of these sergeants—Edwin Bobo, James Butler, Frederick Hohmeyer, Michael Kenney, Frank Varden—died with Custer. When the bodies of these men were stripped the company rosters disappeared.

In 1927 a Northern Cheyenne woman, Kate Bighead, told Dr. Thomas Marquis about the battle. She spoke in sign language, which Marquis had learned while working as a government doctor on the Cheyenne reservation. He transcribed the story she delivered with her hands.

When she was young, she related, she lived with the southern branch of the tribe in Oklahoma. Early one morning during the winter of 1868, after a big storm, soldiers led by General Custer attacked Black Kettle's village on the Washita. She ran barefoot across the snow to escape being killed. Next spring, while the Cheyennes were camped on a branch of the Red River, General Custer returned. He smoked a peace pipe and said he would not fight anymore. The chiefs told him that if he broke this promise he surely would be killed, and they gave him the name Hi-es-tzie, which means Long Hair.

She saw him often, she told Dr. Marquis. One time the general came very close while she was mounting her pony and she looked at him. He had deep eyes and wavy red hair. He wore a buckskin suit with a big white hat. She was then twenty-two years old and she thought he was handsome. She admired him. All the Cheyenne women thought he was handsome.

She had a cousin, Me-o-tzi, who sometimes went riding with General Custer. The Cheyennes were pleased that Me-o-tzi was important to him. Later, after he went away, quite a few young Cheyennes wanted to marry her but Me-o-tzi said General Custer was her husband. She told them he had promised to come back for her. She waited seven years. During those years Kate Bighead joined the northern branch of the tribe so she did not know what happened when Me-o-tzi learned of Custer's death, but she was told that the girl gashed her legs and chopped off her hair.

Joseph White Cow Bull also gave an account of Me-o-tzi, which differed from the story told by Kate Bighead. According to Joseph, Me-o-tzi was at the Little Bighorn with her seven-year-old son—called Yellow Hair or Yellow Bird because of light streaks in his hair. Joseph said he knew her. In fact, he said, he was courting her.

This legend of Custer's child by a Cheyenne woman turns up again and again, like a will-o'-the-wisp at dusk, as though the Indians did not want their enemy absolutely eliminated, and it cannot be proved or disproved. Nor is it possible after such a long time to establish the presence or absence of Me-o-tzi at the Little Bighorn. This comely girl whose silken tresses, the general said, rivaled in color the blackness of a raven—was she in Oklahoma or with northern relatives in Montana? Kate Bighead told Dr. Marquis that about a year after the battle Me-o-tzi married a white man named Isaac. They had several children and Me-o-tzi died in Oklahoma in January of 1921, but among the Cheyennes her name lived on. One of Kate's granddaughters was called Me-o-tzi, and friends liked to tease this girl by saying she was Custer's Indian wife.

On the day of the battle Kate had gone to visit Miniconjou friends at the upper end of the camp. She found them bathing in the river. All at once two boys ran by shouting that soldiers were coming. Kate did not identify these boys, except as Sioux. They may have been grandsons of the Santee chief Inkpaduta—Scarlet Point—who was in his sixties or seventies and blind. An early history of Minnesota states that he was seventy-five at the time of the Little Bighorn, although Gall and Mazamane both said he was sixty-one. Whatever his age, he and two of his grandsons were fishing from the riverbank when Reno's battalion trotted down the valley. The boys might have rushed around trying to warn people before leading their grandfather back to the village. If so, these could have been the boys Kate mentioned.

Old Inkpaduta never did have good eyesight. In 1862 after the Minnesota massacre he pointed out and ordered the murder of a man in a blue coat whom he took to be a ranking officer with General Sibley. The marked man was in fact a regimental surgeon. Anyway, despite age and blindness, Inkpaduta was a chief with authority. His Santees were among the first to challenge Reno; and this venomous old figurehead, exuding hatred for every white-skinned human on earth, may have been the dominant chief until Gall arrived.

As for Kate, terribly frightened, at first she tried to hide; but then she ran toward the Cheyenne circle more than a mile downstream. She ran by young men painting themselves for war, women hurriedly pulling down teepees and loading pack horses. She saw a woman screaming and jumping up and down because she could not find her child.

Later, when Custer's troops appeared, Kate asked her brother for a pony so she could cross the river to watch the fight and encourage their nephew, Noisy Walking. She wanted to sing strongheart songs for him. He had tied a red scarf around his neck to identify himself because he knew she would want to see how well he fought.

At the place where there is now a monument with an iron fence the soldiers got off their horses. This place had no trees, she told Dr. Marquis, and the smoke from the soldiers' guns showed exactly where they were. But they had trouble seeing the Indians because arrows do not make smoke and because arrows were shot high in the air instead of straight at the enemy. Thousands of arrows dropped from the sky, sticking in horses and in the backs of soldiers, and while the Indians shot arrows they crawled up gullies—getting closer and closer—because each one wanted to count coup on a living enemy.

After a while no more bullets came from that place. The Indians thought all of the soldiers were dead and began running toward them, but seven soldiers jumped up and ran downhill toward the river with Sioux and Cheyenne warriors chasing them. Kate did not know what happened to these soldiers. She heard afterward that they shot themselves, as did many who stayed on the ridge hiding behind dead horses. She watched one shoot himself by holding a revolver against his head. Then another did the same, and another. She watched several pairs of them shoot each other in the breast. She said that for a little while the Indians stayed where they were and just looked at these white men shooting each other. She thought the soldiers had gone crazy. She thought it was their punishment for attacking a peaceful village. One soldier sat on the ground and rubbed his head as if he could not understand what was happening. Three Sioux ran up to him. They stretched him out on his back. They did this slowly and she wondered what they would do next. Two of them held his arms while the third one cut off his head with a sheath knife.

When the battle ended she rode around looking for her nephew. Many soldiers were alive. Indians were cutting off their arms and legs.

She found her nephew in a gulch halfway to the river. He had been shot and stabbed. That night he died.

During the battle most of the women and children and old men watched from the benchlands to the west, ready to run away if the soldiers won, or come back to the village if the Indians won. It was hard to tell who was winning. They saw a band of riders cross the river and come toward them. These riders were dressed in blue and they were on American horses. The people watching from the benchlands thought these were soldiers. Women began screaming. Some fainted. Others started to run. One woman seized her two little boys and ran into a gully, but she was so excited that she picked them up by the feet and slung them across her shoulders upside down. After a while, though, everybody could see that the horsemen were their own warriors bringing the weapons and horses and clothing of dead soldiers.

Six Cheyennes were killed in this battle, Kate said, and twenty-four Sioux. More would have been killed if the soldiers had not gone crazy.

According to the Bismarck *Tribune* extra of July 6: "The Indian dead were great in number. . . . The Indians were severely punished." Reno opened the battle "most gallantly, driving back repeatedly the Indians who charged in their front. . . ." And from the bluff to which he had retreated, the hostile assaults "were each time repulsed with heavy slaughter." Lonesome Charley by himself wiped out a platoon: ". . . emptying several chambers of his revolver, each time bringing a red-skin before he was brought down—shot through the heart." None of this happened to be true, but the *Trib* was providing nourishment for the folks at home, which is necessary if citizens are to remain enthusiastic about a distant campaign.

Just how many Indians were killed at the Little Bighorn could no more be determined than the United States government could determine a century later how many Asiatics gave up the ghost in a remote jungle. Col. W. S. Nye noticed while interviewing old Indians how seldom they mentioned battle deaths. He thought this was not an attempt to deceive or to minimize losses, just that Indians had a tendency to report only what they themselves had seen or what they had been told by a relative. Then, too, they were reluctant to pronounce the names of dead men, a superstition which made Anglo score-keeping difficult. Whatever the exact body count, it must have been shockingly low by wasichu standards.

David Humphreys Miller, who consulted dozens of old warriors, produced a list of thirty-two dead. Now that they are long gone, their exploits and even their personalities forgotten by all except a few descendants, their names would be meaningless if not for the images they evoke.

These were Cheyennes killed at the Little Bighorn: Black Cloud, Whirlwind, Left Hand, Owns-Red-Horse, Flying By, Mustache, Noisy Walking, Limber Bones, Hump Nose, Black Bear, Swift Cloud, Lame White Man.

Unkpapa Sioux: White Buffalo, Rectum, Hawk Man, Swift Bear, Red Face, Long Road.

Oglalas: White Eagle, Many Lice, Bad-Light-Hair, Young Skunk, Black White Man.

Sans Arcs: Two Bears, Standing Elk, Long Robe, Cloud Man, Elk Bear, Long Dog.

Miniconjoux: High Horse, Long Elk.

Two Kettle: Chased-by-Owls.

The most important Indian to be killed—a Southern Cheyenne chief, Lame White Man—was shot and scalped by a Sioux who mistook him for a Ree or a Crow. He may have been wearing a captured blue coat, a whim that cost his life, although his grandson John Stands in Timber said he was mistaken for a Custer scout because he rushed into battle without braiding his hair. He had been taking a sweat bath when Reno attacked and instead of dressing properly he wrapped a blanket around his waist, grabbed his moccasins, a belt, and a gun.

Wooden Leg, that peripatetic fighter and reconteur, came across Lame White Man's half-hidden body and thought at first it must be a scalped Crow or Shoshone. But then he thought he recognized the form. "I backed away and went to find my brother. . . ." The two of them returned, got off their ponies, rolled the body on its back, and looked closely. They agreed it was Lame White Man—shot through the breast, stabbed many times. Other Cheyennes rode up. All agreed it was the chief. He had been killed and scalped by a Sioux. Because the Cheyennes did not know what to say about this accident they kept quiet.

So much gunsmoke and dust obscured the field it would have been hard to recognize one's best friend. An Arapaho named Left Hand came upon a wounded Indian—perhaps a Ree—whom he attacked with a lance as sharp as an arrow. The lance went clear through this enemy, who fell across a pile of dead soldiers: "Afterward I found out he was a Sioux, and the Sioux were going to kill me. . . ."

Hideous things appeared. Through the dust came a bloody Sioux, leaving the fight. Wooden Leg saw him walk toward a ravine. "He wabbled dizzily as he moved along. He fell down, got up, fell down again, got up again. As he passed near to where I was I saw that his whole lower jaw was shot away. The sight of him made me sick. I had to vomit. . . ."

On the second day, when the chiefs learned of more soldiers approaching, they decided to leave.

Late that afternoon the tribes began moving south. They traveled most of the night before stopping to rest. They went up the Little Bighorn, down the Rosebud, eastward to the Tongue, then farther east to the Powder.

Where the Sioux and Cheyennes separated is not known, probably somewhere along the Powder. Before going their own ways they held a parade. They had a bugle, maybe more than one, and several warriors rode big gray horses which they had captured. They rode in a line, pretending to be American cavalrymen. They wore Seventh Cavalry uniforms, except for boots and pants which they did not like. One warrior carried a guidon.

After this parade the Cheyennes continued north to the Yellowstone, which they called the Elk. Here they discovered the bodies of two Indians—an old Sioux and his squaw—huddled in some bushes as though they had been trying to hide. Around them were the tracks of metal-shod horses. The old man and the old woman had been shot in the back. The old man was scalped. Here, too, the Cheyennes discovered a cache of food: bacon, rice, beans, coffee, sugar, crackers, dried apples, and corn. A steamboat came up the river while they were helping themselves to food and several warriors shot at the boat just for fun. Kate Bighead told Dr. Marquis that months afterward, when they learned they had fought Custer, they joked about him, saying, "It is too bad we killed him, for it must have been him, our friend, who left all of the good food. . . ."

She might have seen Custer during the battle. She was not certain. She said two Southern Cheyenne women were at the Little Bighorn and when the fighting ended they went to the battlefield. They saw Custer. They knew him well. They had known him in Oklahoma. They recognized him even though his hair was short and his face was dirty. While they stood looking down at him a bunch of Sioux warriors came by and wanted to cut up his body, but these women made signs telling the warriors he was a relative. They did this because of Me-o-tzi. The Sioux then cut off one of his fingertips.

Kate said these two women punctured Custer's eardrums with a sewing awl. They did this to improve his hearing because he had not been able to hear what he was told in Oklahoma seven years before. When he smoked a pipe with Medicine Arrow and Little Robe they told him that if he broke his promise and again made war on the Cheyennes he would be killed. "Through almost sixty years," Kate signaled with her hands, "many a time I have thought of Hi-es-tzie as the handsome man I saw in the South. And I have often wondered if, when I was riding among the dead where he was lying, my pony may have kicked dirt upon his body."

Omaha Beach

From *D-Day, The Climactic Battle of World War II*

BY STEPHEN E. AMBROSE

At the core, the American citizen soldiers knew the difference between right and wrong, and they didn't want to live in a world in which wrong prevailed. So they fought, and won, and we all of us, living and yet to be born, must be forever profoundly grateful.

—Stephen E. Ambrose, *Citizen Soldiers*

P ROSE LIKE THIS quote from Stephen Ambrose has deservedly made his books and name frequent listings on best-seller lists during the 1990s. With *D-Day,* from which this chapter has been excerpted, and others like *Citizen Soldiers,* Ambrose has earned a spectacular reputation as one of the finest military historians ever. In addition, his book on the Lewis and Clark Expedition—*Undaunted Courage*—is regarded as a classic work on the opening of the American west.

Of all the enemy fire on D-Day, Tuesday, June 6, 1944, the deadliest came from German guns on Omaha Beach sectors dubbed in Army parlance Charlie, Dog Green, Dog White, Dog Red, Easy Green, Easy Red, Fox Green, and Fox Red. Here, on shoals of stones leading up to cliffs, infantrymen fought their way through murderous artillery, machine gun, mortar and small-arms fire poured down on them from the high ground above. They were victorious—at a horrific cost. This is their story.

★　　★　　★　　★　　★

If the Germans were going to stop the invasion anywhere, it would be at Omaha Beach. It was an obvious landing site, the only sand beach between the mouth of the Douve to the west and Arromanches to the east, a distance of almost forty kilometers. On both ends of Omaha the cliffs were more or less perpendicular.

The sand at Omaha Beach is golden in color, firm and fine, perfect for sunbathing and picnicking and digging, but in extent the beach is constricted. It is slightly crescent-shaped, about ten kilometers long overall. At low tide, there is a stretch of firm sand of 300 to 400 meters in distance. At high tide, the distance from the waterline to the one- to three-meter bank of shingle (small round stones) is but a few meters.

In 1944 the shingle, now mostly gone, was impassable to vehicles. On the western third of the beach, beyond the shingle, there was a part-wood, part-masonry seawall from one to four meters in height (now gone). Inland of the seawall there was a paved, promenade beach road, then a V-shaped antitank ditch as much as two meters deep, then a flat swampy area, then a steep bluff that ascended thirty meters or more. A man could climb the bluff, but a vehicle could not. The grass-covered slopes appeared to be featureless when viewed from any distance, but in fact they contained many small folds or irregularities that proved to be a critical physical feature of the battlefield.

There were five small "draws" or ravines that sloped gently up to the tableland above the beach. A paved road led off the beach at exit D-1 to Vierville; at Les Moulins (exit D-3) a dirt road led up to St.-Laurent; the third draw, exit E-1, had only a path leading up to the tableland; the fourth draw, E-3, had a dirt road leading to Colleville; the last draw had a dirt path at exit F-1.

No tactician could have devised a better defensive situation. A narrow, enclosed battlefield, with no possibility of outflanking it; many natural obstacles for the attacker to overcome; an ideal place to build fixed fortifications and a trench system on the slope of the bluff and on the high ground looking down on a wide, open killing field for any infantry trying to cross no-man's-land.

The Allied planners hated the idea of assaulting Omaha Beach, but it had to be done. This was as obvious to Rommel as to Eisenhower. Both commanders recognized that if the Allies invaded in Normandy, they would have to include Omaha Beach in the landing sites; otherwise the gap between Utah and the British beaches would be too great.

The waters offshore were heavily mined, so too the beaches, the promenade (which also had concertina wire along its length), and the bluff. Rommel had placed more beach obstacles here than at Utah. He had twelve strong points holding 88s, 75s, and mortars. He had dozens of Tobruks and machine-gun pillboxes, supported by an extensive trench system.

Everything the Germans had learned in World War I about how to stop a frontal assault by infantry Rommel put to work at Omaha. He laid out the firing positions at angles to the beach to cover the tidal flat and beach shelf with crossing fire, plunging fire, and grazing fire, from all types of weapons. He prepared artillery positions along the cliffs at either end of the beach, capable of delivering enfilade fire from 88s all across Omaha. The trench system included underground quarters and magazines connected by tunnels. The strong points were concentrated near the entrances to the draws, which were further protected by large cement roadblcoks. The larger artillery pieces were protected to the seaward by concrete wing walls. There was not one inch of the beach that had not been presighted for both grazing and plunging fire.

Watching the American landing craft approach, the German defenders could hardly believe their eyes. "Holy smoke—here they are!" Lieutenant Frerking declared. "But that's not possible, that's not possible." He put down his binoculars and rushed to his command post in a bunker near Vierville.

"Landing craft on our left, off Vierville, making for the beach," Cpl. Hein Severloh in *Widerstandsnesten* 62 called out. "They must be crazy," Sergeant Krone declared. "Are they going to swim ashore? Right under our muzzles?

The colonel of the artillery regiment passed down a strict order: "Hold your fire until the enemy is coming up to the waterline."

All along the bluff, German soldiers watched the landing craft approach, their fingers on the triggers of machine guns, rifles, artillery fuses, or holding mortar rounds. In bunker 62, Frerking was at the telephone, giving the range to gunners a couple of kilometers inland: "Target Dora, all guns, range four-eight-five-zero, basic direction 20 plus, impact fuse."

Capt. Robert Walker of HQ Company, 116th Regiment, 29th Division, later described the defenses in front of Vierville: "The cliff-like ridge was covered with well-concealed foxholes and many semipermanent bunkers. The bunkers were practically unnoticeable from the front. Their firing openings were toward the flank so that they could bring flanking crossfire to the beach as well as all the way up the slope of the bluff. The bunkers had diagrams of fields of fire, and these were framed under glass and mounted on the walls beside the firing platforms."

A. J. Liebling, who covered the invasion for the *New Yorker,* climbed the bluff a few days after D-Day. "The trenches were deep, narrow, and so convoluted that an attacking force at any point could be fired on from several directions," he wrote. "Important knots in the system, like the command post and mortar emplacements, were of concrete. The command post was sunk at least twenty-five feet into the ground and was faced with brick on the inside. The garrison had slept in underground bombproofs, with timbered ceilings and wooden floors." To Liebling, it looked like "a regular Maginot Line."

Four things gave the Allies the notion that they could successfully assault this all-but-impregnable position. First, Allied intelligence said that the fortifications and trenches were manned by the 716th Infantry Division, a low-quality unit made up of Poles and Russians with poor morale. At Omaha, intelligence reckoned that there was only one battalion of about 800 troops to man the defenses.

Second, the B-17s assigned to the air bombardment would hit the beach with everything they had, destroying or at least neutralizing the bunkers and creating craters on the beach and bluff that would be usable as foxholes for the infantry. Third, the naval bombardment, culminating with the LCT(R)s' rockets, would finish off anything left alive and moving after the B-17s finished. The infantry from the 29th and 1st divisions going into Omaha were told that their problems would begin when they got to the top of the bluff and started to move inland twoard their D-Day objectives.

The fourth cause for confidence that the job would be done was that 40,000 men with 3,500 motorized vehicles were scheduled to land at Omaha on D-Day.

In the event, none of the above worked. The intelligence was wrong; instead of the contemptible 716th Division, the quite-capable 352nd Division was in place. Instead of one German battalion to cover the beach, there were three. The cloud cover and late arrival caused the B-17s to delay their release until they were as much as five kilometers inland; not a single bomb fell on the beach or bluff. The naval bombardment was too brief and generally inaccurate, and in any case it concentrated on the big foritications above the bluff. Finally, most of the rockets fell short, most of them landing in the surf, killing thousands of fish but no Germans.

Captain Walker, on an LCI, recalled that just before H-Hour, "I took a look toward the shore and my heart took a dive. I couldn't believe how peaceful, how untouched, and how tranquil the scene was. The terrain was green. All buildings and houses were intact. The church steeples were proudly and defiantly standing in place.★ 'Where,' I yelled to no one in particular, 'is the damned Air Corps?' "

★At the pre-assault briefing, Walker had been told, "The mock-up shows the land behind the beach as green, but it won't look that way on D-Day. The pulverizing from the bombing, naval shells, and rockets will turn it brown. And don't depend on those village curch steeples as landmarks, because all buildings will be flattened.

The Overlord plan for Omaha was elaborate and precise. It had the 116th Regiment of the 29th Division (attached to the 1st Division for this day only) going in on the right (west), supported by C Company of the 2nd Ranger Battalion. The 16th Regiment of the 1st Division would go in on the left. It would be a linear attack, with the two regiments going in by companies abreast. There were eight sectors, from right to left named Charlie, Dog Green, Dog White, Dog Red, Easy Green, Easy Red, Fox Green, and Fox Red. The 116th's sectors ran from Charlie to Easy Green.

The first waves would consist of two battalions from each of the regiments, landing in a column of companies, with the third battalion coming in behind. Assault teams would cover every inch of beach, firing M-1s, .30-caliber machine guns, BARs, bazookas, 60mm mortars, and flamethrowers. Ahead of the assault teams would be DD tanks, Navy underwater demolition teams, and Army engineers. Each assault team and the supporting units had specific tasks to perform, all geared to opening the exits. As the infantry suppressed whatever fire the Germans could bring to bear, the demolition teams would blow the obstacles and mark the paths through them with flags, so that as the tide came in the coxswains would know where it was safe to go.

Next would come the following waves of landing craft, bringing in reinforcements on a tight, strict schedule designed to put firepower ranging from M-1s to 105 mm howitzers into the battle exactly when needed, plus more tanks, trucks, jeeps, medical units, traffic-control people, headquarters, communication units—all the physical support and administrative control required by two overstrength divisions of infantry conducting an all-out offensive.

By H plus 120 minutes the vehicles would be driving up the opened draws to the top of the bluff and starting to move inland twoard their D-Day objectives, first of all the villages of Vierville, St.-Laurent, and Colleville, then heading west toward Pointe-du-Hoc or south to take Trevières, eight kilometers from Omaha.

Eisenhower's little aphorism that plans are everything before the battle, useless once it is joined, was certainly the case at Omaha. Nothing worked according to the plan, which was indeed useless the moment the Germans opened fire on the assault forces, and even before.

With the exception of Company A, 116th, no unit landed where it was supposed to. Half of E Company was more than a kilometer off target, the other half more than two kilometers to the east of its assigned sector. This was a consequence of winds and tide. A northwest wind of ten to eighteen knots created waves of three to four feet, sometimes as much as six feet, which pushed the landing craft from right to left. So did the tidal current, which with the rising tide (dead low tide at Omaha was 0525) ran at a velocity of 2.7 knots.

By H-Hour, not only were the boats out of position, but the men in them were cramped, seasick, miserable. Most had climbed down their rope nets into the craft four hours or more earlier. The waves came crashing over the gunwales. Every LCVP and LCA (landing craft assault, the British version of the Higgins boat) shipped water. In most of them, the pumps could not carry the load, so the troops had to bail with their helmets.

At least ten of the 200 boats in the first wave swamped; most of the troops were picked up later by Coast Guard rescue craft, often after hours in the water; many drowned. Another disheartening sight to the men in the surviving boats was the glimpse of GIs struggling in life preservers and on rafts, personnel from the foundered DD tanks.

In general, the men of the first wave were exhausted and confused even before the battle was joined. Still, the misery caused by the spray hitting them in the face with each wave and by their seasickness was such that they were eager to hit the beach, feeling that nothing could be worse than riding on those damned Higgins boats. The only comforting thing was those tremendous naval shells zooming over their heads—but even they were hitting the top of the bluff or further inland, not the beach or the slope. At H minus five minutes the fire lifted.

Chief Electrician's Mate Alfred Sears was in the last LCVP of sixteen in the first wave. Going in, the ensign had told him "all the German strong points will be knocked out by the time we hit the beach." Sears went on, "We were so confident of this, that on the way in most of my men and I were sitting on top of the engine room decking of the landing craft, enjoying the show, fascinated by the barrage from the rocket ships. About one thousand rockets shattered the beach directly where we were to land. It looked pretty good."

Lt. Joe Smith was a Navy beachmaster. His job was to put up flags to guide the landing craft from A Company, 116th Regiment. His Higgins boat may have been the first to hit the beach. "The Germans let us alone on the beach. We didn't know why, we could see the Germans up there looking down on us; it was a weird feeling. We were right in front of a German 88 gun emplacement, but fortuantely for us they were set to cover down the beach and not toward the sea, so they could not see us."

A Higgins boat carrying an assault team from A Company came in behind Smith. The men in it figured that what they had been told to expect had come true: the air and naval bombardments had wiped out the opposition. The ramp went down.

"Target Dora—fire!" Lieutenant Frerking shouted into the telephone. When the battery opened fire, eager German gunners throughout the area pulled their triggers. To Frerking's left there were three MG-42 positions; to his front a fortified mortar position; on the forward slopes of the bluff infantrymen in trenches. They exploded into action.

"We hit the sandbar," Electrician's Mate Sears recalled, "dropped the ramp, and then all hell poured loose on us. The soldiers in the boat received a hail of machine-gun bullets. The Army lieutenant was immediately killed, shot through the head."

In the lead Company A boat, LCA 1015, Capt. Taylor Fellers and every one of his men were killed before the ramp went down. It just vaporized. No one ever learned whether it was the result of hitting a mine or getting hit by an 88.

"They put their ramp down," Navy beachmaster Lt. Joe Smith said of what he saw, "and a German machine gun or two opened up and you could see the sand kick up right in front of the boat. No one moved. The coxswain stood up and yelled and for some reason everything was quiet for an instant and you could hear him as clear as a bell, he said, 'For Christ's sake, fellas, get out! I've got to go get another load.' "

All across the beach, the German machine guns were hurling fire of monstrous proportions on the hapless Americans. (One gunner with Lieutenant Frerking at strong point 62 fired 12,000 rounds that morning.) Because of the misplaced landings, the GIs were bunched together, with large gaps between groups, up to a kilometer in length, which allowed the Germans to concentrate their fire. As the Higgins boats and larger LCIs approached the beach, the German artillery fired at will, from the Tobruks and fortifications up the draws and on top of the bluff and from the emplacements on the beach.

Motor Machinst Charles Jarreau, Coast Guard, was on LCI 94. His skipper was an "old man" of thirty-two years, a merchant mariner who did things his own way. His nickname was "Popeye." He had stashed a supply of J&B scotch aboard and told the cook that his duty that day was to go around to the crew "and keep giving them a drink until they didn't want anymore or until we ran out; essentially we drank most of the day. Didn't have any food, but I drank all day and didn't get the least bit intoxicated. It had absolutely no effect."

LCI 94 was in the first wave, right behind the Navy demolition teams and the beach-marking crew. "By this time, it was getting pretty hot. Popeye looked at our sign and said, 'Hell, I'm not going in there, we'll never get off that beach.' So he aborted the run. The rest of the LCIs in our flotilla went in where they were supposed to go and none of them got off the beach. They were all shot up. Which made our skipper go up in our esteem by one hell of a lot."

Popeye cruised down the beach about 100 meters, turned toward shore, dropped his stern anchor, and went in at one-third speed until he ran aground twenty meters or so offshore. The ramps went down and the men from the 116yh moved down them. As they disembarked, the ship lightened. Popeye had his engines put into reverse, used the small Briggs & Stratton motor to pull on the anchor chain, and backed off. Five men from his twenty-six-man crew were dead, killed by machine-gun fire. Twenty of the 200 infantrymen were killed before they reached the beach.

Pvt. John Barnes, Company A, 116th, was in an LCA. As it approached the shore, line abreast with eleven other craft, someone shouted, "Take a look! This is something that you will tell your grandchildren!"

If we live, Barnes thought.

Ahead, he could see the single spire of the church at Vierville. A Company was right on target. The LCA roared ahead, breasting the waves. "Suddenly, a swirl of water wrapped around my ankles, and the front of the craft dipped down. The water quickly reached our waist and we shouted to the other boats on each side. The waved in return. Our boat just fell away below me. I squeezed the CO2 tube in my life belt. The buckle broke and it popped away. I turned to grab the back of the man behind me. I was going down under. I climbed on his back and pulled myself up in a panic. Heads bobbed up above the water. We could see the other boats moving off toward shore."

Some men had wrapped Mae Wests around their weapons and inflated them. Barnes saw a rifle floating by, then a flamethrower with two Mae Wests around it. "I hugged it tight but still seemed to be going down. I couldn't keep my head above the surface. I tried to pull the release straps on my jacket but I couldn't move. Lieutenant Gearing grabbed my jacket and used his bayonet to cut the straps and release me from the weight. I was all right now. I could swim."

The assault team was about a kilometer offshore. Sergeant Laird wanted to swim in, but Lieutenant Gearing said, "No, we'll wait and get picked up by some passing boat." But none would stop; the coxswains' orders were to go on in and leave the rescue work to others.

After a bit, "we heard a friendly shout of some Limey voice in one of the LCAs. He stopped, his boat was empty. He helped us to climb on board. We recognized the coxswain. He was from the *Empire Javelin*. He wouldn't return to the beach. We asked how the others made out. He said he had dropped them off OK. We went back to the *Empire Javelin,* which we had left at 0400 that morning. How long had it been? It seemed like just minutes. When I thought to ask, it was 1300."

Barnes and his assault team were extraordinarily lucky. About 60 percent of the men of Company A came from one town, Bedford, Virginia; for Bedford, the first fifteen minutes at Omaha was an unmitigated disaster. Companies G and F were supposed to come in to the immediate left of Company A, but they drifted a kilometer further east before landing, so all the Germans around the heavily defended Vierville draw concentrated their fire on Company A. When the ramps on the Higgins boats dropped, the Germans just poured the machine-gun, artillery, and mortar fire on them. It was a slaughter. Of the 200-plus men of the company, only a couple of dozen survived, and virtually all of them were wounded.

Sgt. Thomas Valance survived, barely. "As we came down the ramp, we were in water about knee-high and started to do what we were trained to do, that is, move forward and then crouch and fire. One problem was we didn't quite know what to fire at. I saw some tracers coming from a concrete emplacement which, to me, looked mammoth. I never anticipated any gun emplacements being that big. I shot at it but there was no way I was going to knock out a German concrete emplacement with a .30-caliber rifle."

The tide was coming in, rapidly, and the men around Valance were getting hit. He found it difficult to stay on his feet—like most infantrymen, he was badly overloaded, soaking wet, exhausted, trying to struggle though wet sand and avoid the obstacles with mines attached to them. "I abandoned my equipment, which was dragging me down into the water.

"It became evident rather quickly that we weren't going to accomplish very much. I remeber floundering in the water with my hand up in the air, trying to get my balance, when I was first shot through the palm of my hand, then through the knuckle.

"Pvt. Henry Witt was rolling over toward me. I remember him saying, 'Sergeant, they're leaving us here to die like rats. Just to die like rats.'"

Valance was hit again, in the left thigh by a bullet that broke his hip bone. He took two additional flesh wounds. His pack was hit twice, and the chin strap on his helmet was severed by a bullet. He crawled up the beach "and staggered up against the seawall and sort of collapsed there and, as a matter of fact, spent the whole day in that same position. Essentially my part in the invasion was ended by having been wiped out as most of my company was. The bodies of my buddies were washing ashore and I was the one live body in amongst so many of my friends, all of whom were dead, in many cases very severely blown to pieces."

On his boat, Lt. Edward Tidrick was first off. As he jumped from the ramp into the water he took a bullet through his throat. He staggered to the sand, flopped down near Pvt. Leo Nash, and raised himself up to gasp, "Advance with the wire cutters!" At that instant, machine-gun bullets ripped Tidrick from crown to pelvis.

By 0640 only one officer from A Company was alive, Lt. E. Ray Nance, and he had been hit in the heel and the belly. Every sergeant was either dead or wounded. On one boat, when the ramp was dropped every man in the thirty-man assault team was killed before any of them could get out.

Pvt. George Roach was an assistant flamethrower. He weighed 125 pounds. He carried over 100 pounds of gear ashore, including his M-1 rifle, ammunition, hand grenades, a five-gallon drum of flamethrower fluid, and assorted wrenches and a cylinder of nitrogen.

"We went down the ramp and the casualty rate was very bad. We couldn't determine where the fire was coming from, whether from the top of the bluff or from the summer beach-type homes on the shore. I just dropped myself into the sand and took my rifle and fired it at this house and Sergeant Wilkes asked, 'What are you firing at?' and I said, 'I don't know.' "

The only other live member of his assault team Roach could see was Pvt. Gil Murdoch. The two men were lying together behind an obstacle. Murdoch had lost his glasses and could not see. "Can you swim?" Roach asked.

"No."

"Well, look, we can't stay here, there's nobody around here that seems to have any idea of what to do. Let's go back in the water and come in with the tide." They fell back and got behind a knocked-out tank. Both men were slightly wounded. The tide covered them and they hung onto the tank. Roach started to swim to shore; a coxswain from a Higgins boat picked him up about halfway in. "He pulled me on board, it was around 1030. And I promptly fell asleep."

Roach eventually got up to the seawall, where he helped the medics. The following day, he caught up with what remained of his company. "I met General Cota and I had a brief conversation with him. He asked me what company I was with and I told him and he just shook his head. Company A was just out of action. When we got together, there were eight of us left from Company A ready for duty."

(Cota asked Roach what he was going to do when the war was over. "Someday I'd like to go to college and graduate," Roach replied. "I'd like to go to Fordham." Five years to the day later, Roach did graduate from Fordham. "Over the years," he said in 1990, "I don't think there has been a day that has gone by that I haven't thought of those men who didn't make it.")

Sgt. Lee Polek's landing craft was about to swamp as it approached the shore. Everyone was bailing with helmets. "We yelled to the crew to take us in, we would rather fight than drown. As the ramp dropped we were hit by machine-gun and rifle fire. I yelled to get ready to swim and fight. We were getting direct fire right into our craft. My three squad leaders in front and others were hit. Some men climbed over the side. Two sailors got hit. I got off in water only ankle deep, tried to run but the water was suddenly up to my hips. I crawled to hide behind a steel beach obstacle. Bullets hit off it, others hit more of my men. Got up to the beach to crawl behind the shingle and a few of my men joined me. I took a head count and there was only eleven of us left, from the thirty on the craft. As the tide came in we took turns running out to the water's edge to drag wounded men to cover. Some of the wounded were hit again while on the beach. More men crowding up and crowding up. More people being hit by shellfire. People trying to help each other.

"While we were huddled there, I told Jim Hickey that I would like to live to be forty years old and work forty hours a week and make a dollar an hour (when I joined up I was making thrity-seven-and-a-half cents an hour). I felt, boy, I would really have it made at $40 a week.

"Jim Hickey still calls me from New York on June 6 to ask, 'Hey, Sarge, are you making forty bucks per yet?'"

Company A had hardly fired a weapon. Almost certainly it had not killed any Germans. It had expected to move up the Vierville draw and be on top of the bluff by 0730, but at 0730 its handful fo survivors were huddled up against the seawall, virtually without weapons. It had lost 96 percent of its effective strength.

But its sacrifice was not in vain. The men had brought in rifles, BARs, grenades, TNT charges, machine guns, mortars and mortar rounds, flamethrowers, rations, and other equipment. Ths was now strewn across the sand at Dog Green. The weapons and equipment would make a life-or-death difference to the following waves of infantry, coming in at higher tide and having to abandon everything to make their way to shore.

F Company, 116th, supposed to come in at Dog Red, landed near its target, astride the boundary between Dog Red and Easy Green. But G Company, supposed to be to the right of F at Dog White, drifted far left, so the two companies came in together, directly opposite the heavy fortifications at Les Moulins. There was a kilometer or so gap to each side of the inter-mixed companies, which allowed the German defenders to concentrate their fire.

For the men of F and G companies, the 200 meters or more journey from the Higgins boats to the shingle was the longest and most hazardous trip they had ever experienced, or ever would. The lieutenant commanding the assault team on Sgt. Harry Bare's boat was killed and the ramp went down. "As ranking noncom," Bare related, "I tried to get my men off the boat and make it somehow to get under the seawall. We waded to the sand and threw ourselves down and the men were frozen, unable to move. My radioman had his head blown off three yards from me. The beach was covered with bodies, men with no legs, no arms—God it was awful."

When Bare finally made it to the seawall, dodging and ducking behind beach obstacles to get there, "I tried to get the men organized. There were only six out of my boat alive. I was soaking wet, shivering, but trying like hell to keep control. I could feel the cold fingers of fear grip me."

On the boat coming in, Pvt John Robertson of F Company was throwing up over the side. His sergeant yelled at him to get his head down. Robertson replied, "I'm dying of seasickness, it won't make much difference."

The coxswain hit a sandbar and shouted that he was unloading and getting the hell out of there. The ramp went down and "our guys started jumping out in water up to their necks." Robertson was toward the rear of the boat. He saw his leader, Lieutenant Hilscher, get killed by an exploding shell. Then the flamethrower got blown up. Robertson jumped out. Despite his sixty pounds of ammunition and other equipment, he managed to struggle his way inland, to where the water was about a foot deep. "I just lay there wondering what I was going to do."

"It wasn't long when I made a quick decision. Behind me, coming at me, was a Sherman tank with pontoons wrapped around it. I had two chices; get run over by the tank or run through the machine-gun fire and the shelling. How I made it, I'll never know. But I got to the shingle and tried to survive."

When Sgt. Warner Hamlett of F Company made it to the shore, he found that the weight of wet clothes, sand, and equipment made it difficult to run. He could hear men shouting, "Get off the beach!" and realized "our only chance was to get off as quick as possible, because there we were sitting ducks."

He stumbled forward and saw a hole and jumped in. He landed on top of Pvt. O.T. Grimes.★

A shell exploded within ten meters of Hamlett and blew his rifle from his hands while sending his helmet flying off his head. Crawling on his elbows and knees, he retrieved his rifle and helmet, then waited to regain his strength "and to see if my legs would support my weight." They did. By short leaps and advances, using obstacles for protection, he worked his way toward the shingle. While he was resting behind an obstacle, "Private Gillingham, a young soldier, fell beside me, white with fear. He seemed to be begging for help with his eyes.

"I said, 'Gillingham, let's stay separated, 'cause the Germans will fire at two quicker than they will at one.' He remained silent as I jumped and ran forward again."

A shell burst between them. "It took Gillingham's chin off, including the bone, except for a small piece of flesh. He tried to hold his chin in place as he ran toward the shingle. He made it and Bill Hawkes and I gave him his morphine shot. We stayed with him for approximately thrity minutes until he died. The entire time he remained conscious and aware that he was dying."

From the beach, to the GIs, that shingle looked like the most desirable place in the world to be at that moment. But when they reached it, they found concertina wire covering it, no way to get across without blowing the wire, nothing on the other side but more death and misery. And although they were now protected from machine-gun and rifle fire coming down from the German trenches on the bluff, they were exposed to mortar fire. The few who made it had no organization, little or no leadership (Lieutenant Wise of F Company, one of the few officers to make it to the wall, was trying to force a gap in the concertina when he was hit by a bullet in the forehead and killed), only a handful of weapons. They could but huddle and hope for follow-up waves to bring in bangalore torpedoes to blow the wire.

E Company, 116th, landed farthest from its target. Scheduled to come in at Easy Green, it actually landed on the boundary between Easy Red and Fox Green, a kilometer off and intermixed with men from the 16th Regiment, 1st Division. Pvt. Harry Parley was a flamethrower, so far as he is aware "the

---

★"On our recent 1987 annual reunion," Hamlett said, "O.T. told me his back still hurt because of my heavy boot."

only flamethrower to come off the beach unscathed."* He landed with a pistol, a holster, a shovel, a Mae West, a raincoat, a canteen, a block of dynamite, and his eighty-pound flamethrower.

"As our boat touched sand and the ramp went down," Parley recalled, "I became a visitor to hell." Boats on either side were getting hit by artillery. Some were burning, others sinking. "I shut everything out and concentrated on following the men in front of me down the ramp and into the water."

He immediately sank. "I was unable to come up. I knew I was drowning and made a futile attempt to unbuckle the flamethrower harness." A buddy grabbed his flamethrower and pulled Parley forward, to where he could stand. "Then slowly, half-drowned, coughing water, and dragging my feet, I began walking toward the chaos ahead."

He had 200 meters to go to the beach. He made it, exhausted. Machine-gun fire was hitting the beach. As it hit the sand "it made a 'sip sip' sound like someone sucking on their teeth. To this day I don't know why I didn't dump the flamethrower and run like hell for shelter. But I didn't." He was behind the other members of the team. "Months later, trying to analyze why I was able to safely walk across the beach while others running ahead were hit, I found a simple answer. The Germans were directing their fire down onto the beach so that the line of advancing attackers would run into it and, since I was behind, I was ignored. In short, the burden on my back may well have saved my life."

When Parley reached the shingle, he found chaos. "Men were trying to dig or scrape trenches or foxholes for protection from the mortars. Others were carrying or helping the wounded to shelter. We had to crouch or crawl on all fours when moving about. To communicate, we had to shout above the din of the shelling from both sides as well as the explosions on the beach. Most of us were in no condition to carry on. We were just trying to stay alive.

"The enormity of our situation came as I realized that we had landed in the wrong sector and that many of the people around me were from other units and stangers to me. What's more, the terrain before us was not what I had been trained to encounter. I remember removing my flamethrower and trying to dig a trench while lying on my stomach. Failing that, I searched and found a discarded BAR. But we could see nothing above us to return the fire. We were the targets."

Parley lay behind the shingle, "scared, worried, and often praying. Once or twice I was able to control my fear enough to race across the sand to

---

*Pvt. Charles Neighbor, of E Company, was an assistant flamethrower who made it ashore and took over when his No. 1 became a casualty.

drag a helpless GI from drowning in the incoming tide. That was the extent of my bravery that morning." Not true, as will be seen.

Capt. Lawrence Madill of E Company was urging his men forward. "One of the episodes I remember the most was debarking from the landing craft and trying to take shelter from the enemy fire behind one of their obstacles," recalled Walter A. Smith. "Captain Madill came up behind me and others, ordering all that could move to get off the beach. I looked up at him and his left arm appeared to be almost blown off."

Madill made it to the seawall, where he discovered that one of his company mortars had also made it but had no ammunition. He ran back to the beach to pick up some rounds. As he was returning, he was hit by machine-gun fire. Before he died, Madill gasped, "Senior noncom, take the men off the beach."

As what was left of A, F, G, and E companies of the 116th huddled behind obstacles or the shingle, the following waves began to come in: B and H companies at 0700, D at 0710, C, K, I, and M at 0720. No one came in on target. The coxswains were trying to dodge obstacles and incoming shells, while the smoke drifted in and out and obscured the landmarks and what few marker flags there were on the beach.

On the command boat for B Company, the CO, Capt. Ettore Zappacosta, heard the British coxswain cry out, "We can't go in there. We can't see the landmarks. We must pull off."

Zappacosta pulled his Colt .45 and ordered, "By God, you'll take this boat straight in."

The coxswain did. When the ramp dropped, Zappacosta was first off. He was immediately hit. Medic Thomas Kenser saw him bleeding from hip and shoulder. Kenser, still on the ramp, shouted, "Try to make it in! I'm coming." But the captain was already dead. Before Kenser could jump off the ramp he was shot dead. Every man in the boat save one (Pvt. Robert Sales) was either killed or wounded before reaching the beach.

Nineteen-year-old Pvt. Harold Baumgarten of B Company got a bullet through the top of his helmet while jumping from the ramp, then another hit the receiver of his M–1 as he carried it at port arms. He waded through the waist-deep water as his buddies fell alongside him.

"I saw Pvt. Robert Ditmar of Fairfield, Connecticut, hold his chest and heard him yell, 'I'm hit, I'm hit!' I hit the ground and watched him as he continued to go forward about ten more yards. He tripped over an obstacle and, as he fell, his body made a complete turn and he lay sprawled on the damp sand with his head facing the Germans, his face looking skyward. He was yelling, 'Mother, Mom.'

"Sgt. Clarence 'Pilgrim' Robertson had a gaping wound in the upper right corner of his forehead. He was walking crazily in the water. Then I saw him get down on his knees and start praying with his rosary beads. At this moment, the Germans cut him in half with their deadly crossfire."

Baumgarten had drawn a Star of David on the back of his field jacket, with "The Bronx, New York" written on it—that would let Hitler know who he was. He was behind an obstacle. He saw the reflection from the helmet of one of the German riflemen on the bluff "and took aim and later on I found out I got a bull's eye on him." That was the only shot he fired because his damaged rifle broke in two when he pulled the trigger.

Shells were bursting about him. "I raised my head to curse the Germans when an 88 shell exploded about twenty yards in front of me, hitting me in my left cheek. It felt like being hit with a baseball bat only the results were much worse. My upper jaw was shattered, the left cheek blown open. My upper lip was cut in half. The roof of my mouth was cut up and teeth and gums were laying all over my mouth. Blood poured freely from the gaping wound."

The tide was coming in. Baumgarten washed his face with the cold, dirty Channel water and managed not to pass out. The water was rising about an inch a minute (between 0630 and 0800 the tide rose eight feet) so he had to get moving or drown. He took another hit, from a bullet, in the leg. He moved forward in a dead man's float with each wave of the incoming tide. He finally reached the seawall where a medic dressed his wounds. Mortars were coming in, "and I grabbed the medic by the shirt to pull him down. He hit my hand away and said, 'You're injured now. When I get hurt you can take care of me.' "*

Sgt. Benjamin McKinney was a combat engineer attached to C Company. When his ramp dropped, "I was so seasick I didn't care if a bullet hit me between the eyes and got me out of my misery." As he jumped off the ramp, "rifle and machine-gun fire hit it like rain falling." Ahead, "it looked as if all the first wave were dead on the beach." He got to the shingle. He and Sergeant Storms saw a pillbox holding a machine gun and a rifleman about thirty meters to the right, spraying the beach with their weapons. Storms and McKinney crawled toward the position. McKinney threw hand grenades as Storms put

---

*Baumgarten was wounded five times that day, the last time by a bullet in his right knee as he was being carried on a stretcher to the beach for evacuation. He went on to medical school and became a practicing physician. He concluded his oral history, "Happily, in recent years when I've been back to Normandy, especially on Sept. 17, 1988, when we dedicated a monument to the 29th Division in Vierville, I noted that the French people really appreciated us freeing them from the Germans, so it made it all worthwhile."

rifle fire into it. Two Germans jumped out; Storms killed them. The 116th was starting to fight back.

At 0730 the main command group of the 116th began to come in, including the regimental commander, Col. Charles Canham, and the assistant commander of the 29th Division, Brig. Gen. Norman Cota. They were in an LCVP with an assault team from Company K. The boat got hung up on a beach obstacle to which a Teller mine was attached. Although the boat rose and fell in the swells, by some miracle the mine did not go off, but the LCVP was under heavy machine-gun, mortar, and light-cannon fire. Three men, including Maj. John Sours, the regimental S-4, were instantly killed as the ramp went down.

Pvt. Felix Branham was in that boat. "Colonel Canham had a BAR and a .45 and he was leading us in," Branham said. "There he was firing and he got his BAR shot out of his hand and he reached and he used his .45. He was the bravest guy."

The scene the commanders saw as they struggled their way to the beach was described by Cota's aide-de-camp, Lt. J. T. Shea, in a letter he wrote ten days later: "Although the leading elements of the assault had been on the beach for approximately an hour, none had progressed farther than the seawall at the inland border of the beach. [They] were clustered under the wall, pinned down by machine-gun fire, and the enemy was beginning to bring effective mortar fire to bear on those hidden behind the wall." The beach was jammed with the dead, the dying, the wounded, and the disorganized.

When Cota got to the wall, he made an immediate and critical command decision. He saw at once that the plan to go up the draws was obsolete. It simply could not be done. Nor could the men stay where they were. They had to get over the shingle, get through the heavily mined swamp, and climb the bluff to drive the Germans from their trenches and take the draws from the inland side.

Lieutenant Shea described Cota's actions: "Exposing himself to enemy fire, General Cota went over the seawall giving encouragement, directions, and orders to those about him, personally supervised the placing of a BAR, and brought fire to bear on some of the enemy positions of the bluff that faced them. Finding a belt of barbed wire inside the seawall, General Cota personally supervised placing a bangalore torpedo for blowing the wire and was one of the first three men to go through the wire."

Six mortar shells fell into the immediate area. They killed three men and wounded two others, but Cota was unharmed. "At the head of a mixed column of troops he threaded his way to the foot of the high ground beyond the beach and started the troops up the high ground where they could bring effective fire to bear on the enemy positions." Behind him, engineers with mine detectors began marking a path through the minefield, using white tape.

Some of the boats in the follow-up waves got in relatively unscathed. It was a question of luck and numbers. The luck was avoiding mined obstacles, now well underwater. The numbers of boats coming in meant that the Germans could no longer concentrate their fire; they had too many targets. By 0730 what was supposed to have happened with the first wave was beginning to take place—the assault teams were coming forward on every sector of the beach (not always or even usually the right one).

Others had bad luck. LCI 92, approaching Dog White about 0740, was hit in the stern by an 88 as it made its first attempt to get through the obstacles. Sgt. Debs Peters of the 121st ECB was on the craft. He recalled, "We lost headway and turned sideways in the waves and were parallel to the beach for a few seconds. We were hit directly midship and blew up. Those of us on deck were caught on fire with flaming fuel oil and we just rolled overboard. I fell into the water and went down like a rock." He inflated his Mae West and popped to the surface.

"The Germans were raking the whole area with machine-gun fire. I held onto one of those poles until I could get my breath, then moved to another one. I finally got within about fifty yards of the shore. Now the tide was in full, it almost reached the road."

When Peters reached the beach "I was loaded so heavy with water and sand that I could just stagger about." He got behind a tank; it got hit by an 88. Shrapnel wounded the man beside him and hit Peters in the cheek. He was lucky; he was one of the few survivors from LCI 92.

Capt. Robert Walker of HQ Company was on LCI 91, just behind LCI 92. (LCI 94, the one "Popeye" the skipper decided not to take in on that sector, was just to the left of LCIs 91 and 92.) As it approached the beach, LCI 91 began taking rifle and machine-gun fire. Maneuvering through the obstacles, the LCI got caught on one of the pilings and set off the Teller mine. The explosion tore off the starboard landing ramp.

The skipper tried to back off. Walker moved to the port-side ramp, only to find it engulfed in flames. A man carrying a flamethrower had been hit by a bullet; another bullet had set the jellied contents of his fuel tank on fire. Screaming in agony, he dove into the sea. "I could see that even the soles of his boots were on fire." Men around him also burned; Walker saw a couple of riflemen "with horrendous drooping face blisters."

The skipper came running to the front deck, waving his arms and yelling "Everybody over the side." Walker jumped into water about eight feet deep. He was carrying so much equipment that despite two Mae Wests he could not stay afloat. He dropped his rifle, then his helmet, then his musette bag, which enabled him to swim to where he could touch bottom.

"Here I was on Omaha Beach. Instead of being a fierce, well-trained, fighting infantry warrior, I was an exhausted, almost helpless, unarmed survivor of a shipwreck." When he got to waist-deep water he got on his knees and crawled the rest of the way. Working his way forward to the seawall, he saw the body of Captain Zappacosta. At the seawall, "I saw dozens of soldiers, mostly wounded. The wounds were ghastly to see."

(Forty-nine years later, Walker recorded that the scene brought to his mind Tennyson's lines in "The Charge of the Light Brigade," especially "Cannon to right of them/Cannon to left of them/Cannon in front of them/Volley'd and thunder'd." He added that so far as he could tell every GI knew the lines, "Theirs not to reason why/Theirs but to do and die," even if the soldiers did not know the source. Those on Omaha Beach who had committed the poem to memory surely muttered to themselves, "Some one had blunder'd.")

Walker came to Cota's conclusion. Any place was better than this; the plan was *kaput;* he couldn't go back; he set out on his own to climb the bluff. He picked up an M-1 and a helmet from a dead soldier and moved out. "I was alone and completely on my own."

Maj. Sidney Bingham (USMA 1940) was CO 2nd Battalion, 116th. When he reached the shingle he was without radio, aide, or runner. His S-3 was dead, his HQ Company commander wounded, his E Company commander dead, his F Company commander wounded, his H Company commander killed, "and in E Company there were some fifty-five killed out of a total of something just over 200 who landed."

Bingham was overwhelmed by a feeling of "complete futility. Here I was, the battalion commander, unable for the most part to influence action or do what I knew had to be done." He set out to organize a leaderless group from F Company and get it moving up the bluff.

By this time, around 0745, unknown others were doing the same, whether NCOs or junior officers or, in some cases, privates. Staying on the beach meant certain death; retreat was not possible; someone had to lead; men took the burden on themselves and did. Bingham put it this way: "The individual and small-unit initiative carried the day. Very little, if any, credit can be accorded company, battalion, or regimental commanders for their tactical prowess and/or their coordination of the action."

Bingham did an analysis of what went wrong for the first and second waves. Among other factors, he said, the men were in the Higgins boats far too long. "Seasickness occasioned by the three or four hours in LCVPs played havoc with any idealism that may have been present. It markedly decreased the combat effectiveness of the command."

In addition, "The individual loads carried were in my view greatly excessive, hindered mobility, and in some cases caused death by drowning." In his view, "If the enemy had shown any sort of enthusiasm and moved toward us, they could have run us right back into the Channel without any trouble."

From June 6, 1944, on to 1990, Bingham carried with him an unustified self-criticism: "I've often felt very ashamed of the fact that I was so completely inadequate as a leader on the beach on that frightful day." That is the way a good battalion commander feels when he is leading not much more than a squad—but Bingham got that squad over the shingle and into an attack against the enemy, which was exactly the right thing to do, and the only thing he could do under the circumstances.

The Germans did not counterattack for a number of reasons, some of them good ones. First, they were not present in sufficient strength. General Kraiss had but two of his infantry battalions and one artillery battalion on the scene, about 2,000 men, or less than 250 per kilometer. Second, he was slow to react. Not until 0735 did he call up his division reserve, *Kampfgruppe Meyer* (named for the CO of the 915th Regiment of Kraiss's 352nd Division), and then he decided to commit only a single battalion, which did not arrive until midday. He was acting on a false assumption: that his men had stopped the invasion at Omaha. Third, the German infantrymen were not trained for assaults, only to hold their positions and keep firing.

One German private who was manning an MG 42 on top of the bluff put it this way, in a 1964 radio interview: "It was the first time I shoot at living men. I don't remember exactly how it was: the only thing I know is that I went to my machine gun and I shoot, I shoot, I shoot."

The sacrifice of good men that morning was just appalling. Capt. Walter Schilling of D Company, who had given a magnificent briefing to his magnificently trained men, was in the lead boat in the third wave. He was as good a company CO as there was in the U.S. Army. The company was coming into a section of the beach that had no one on it; there was no fire; Schilling remarked to Pvt. George Kobe, "See, I told you it was going to be easy." Moments later, before the ramp went down, Schilling was killed by a shell.

Lt. William Gardner was the company executive officer, a West Point graduate described by Sgt. John Robert Slaughter as "young, articulate, handsome, tough, and aggressive. He possessed all the qualities to become a high-ranking officer in the Army." The ramp went down on his boat some 150 meters from shore. The men got off without loss. Gardner ordered them to spread out and keep low. He was killed by machine-gun fire before he made the shore.

Sgt. Slaughter's boat was bracketed by German artillery fire. At 100 meters from shore, the British coxswain said he had to lower the ramp and everyone should get out quickly. Sgt. Willard Norfleet told him to keep going: "These men have heavy equipment and you *will* take them all the way in."

The coxswain begged, "But we'll *all* be killed!"

Norfleet unholstered his .45 Colt pistol, put it to the sailor's head and ordered, "All the way in!" The coxswain proceeded.

Sergeant Slaughter, up at the front of the boat, was thinking, If this boat don't hurry up and get us in, I'm going to die from seasickness. The boat hit a sandbar and stopped.

"I watched the movie *The Longest Day,*" Slaughter recalled, "and they came charging off those boats and across the beach like banshees but that isn't the way it happened. You came off the craft, you hit the water, and if you didn't get down in it you were going to get shot."

The incoming fire was horrendous. "This turned the boys into men," Slaughter commented. "Some would be very brave men, others would soon be dead men, but all of those who survived would be frightened men. Some wet their britches, others cried unashamedly, and many just had to find it within theselves to get the job done." In a fine tribute to Captain Shilling, Slaughter concluded, "This is where the discipline and training took over."

Slaughter made his way toward shore. "There were dead men floating in the water and there were live men acting dead, letting the tide take them in." Most of Company D was in the water a full hour, working forward. Once he reached shore, for Slaughter "getting across the beach to the shingle became an obsession." He made it. "The first thing I did was to take off my assault jacket and spread my raincoat so I could clean my rifle. It was then I saw bullet holes in my raincoat. I lit my first cigarette [they were wrapped in plastic]. I had to rest and compose myself becaue I became weak in my knees.

"Colonel Canham came by with his right arm in a sling and a .45 Colt in his left hand. He was yelling and screaming for the officers to get the men off the beach. 'Get the hell off this damn beach and go kill some Germans.' There was an officer taking refuge from an enemy mortar barrage in a pillbox. Right in front of me Colonel Canham screamed, 'Get your ass out of there and show some leadership.' "To another lieutenant he roared, "Get these men off their dead asses and over that wall."

This was the critical moment in the battle. It was an ultimate test: could a democracy produce young men tough enough to take charge, to lead? As Pvt. Carl Weast put it, "It was simple fear that stopped us at that shingle and we lay there and we got butchered by rocket fire and by mortars for no damn reason other than the fact that there was nobody there to lead us off that god-damn beach. Like I say, hey man, I did my job, but somebody had to lead me."

Sgt. William Lewis remembered cowering behind the shingle. Pvt. Larry Rote piled in on top of Lewis. He asked, "Is that you shaking, Sarge?"

"Yeah, damn right!"

"My God," Rote said. "I thought it was me!" Lewis commented, "Rote was shaking all right."

They huddled together with some other men, "just trying to stay alive. There was nothing we could do except keep our butts down. Others took cover behind the wall."

All across Omaha, the men who had made it to the shingle hid behind it. Then Cota, or Canham, or a captain here, a lieutenant there, a sergeant someplace else, began to lead. They would cry out, "Follow me!" and start moving up the bluff.

In Sergeant Lewis's case, "Lt. Leo Van de Voort said, 'Let's go, goddamn, there ain't no use staying here, we're all going to get killed!' The first thing he did was to run up to a gun emplacement and throw a grenade in the embra-sure. He returned with five or six prisoners. So then we thought, hell, if he can do that, why can't we. That's how we got off the beach."

That was how most men got off the beach. Pvt. Raymond Howell, an engineer attached to D Company, described his thought process. He took some shrapnel in helmet and hand. "That's when I said, bullshit, if I'm going to die, to hell with it I'm not going to die here. The next bunch of guys that go over the goddamn wall, I'm going with them. If I'm gonna be infantry, I'm gonna be infantry. So I don't know who else, I guess all of us decided well, it is time to start."

The Drums of the Fore and Aft

BY RUDYARD KIPLING

ARGUABLY, HE WAS the most prolific and popular writer on the subject of war in the English-speaking world during his lifetime (1865–1936). He observed military life on the farthermost outposts of the British Empire and filled page after page with prose and verse that captured with empathy and wit the indomitable spirit and exploits of the English and Gurkha soldiers he knew so well. From his beloved England to the shoulders of the Himalayas, the jungles of Burma, the scorched reaches of the Sudan, the veldt of South Africa, Kipling wrote tirelessly about what he saw and felt. Novels, short stories, verse, fables, even children's stories—his talented pen poured the images onto the pages in gushes of great literature, praised to the heavens in literary and academic circles and enjoyed by satisfied and grateful readers.

Kipling anticipated and dreaded the coming of World War I, and saw his worst nightmare become a reality. His son was killed at age eighteen, serving in France in 1915 as a commissioned officer with the Irish Guards. His body was never found. Like many others, he was presumably blown to bits or buried by shell-fire. Afterwards, Kipling went on writing about the war, including melancholy verses in which he tried to put his anguish into words in a way that would be universally felt and not remembered as autobiographical personal tragedy. Perhaps his most famous verse in remembering the fallen is the ever-poignant "Recessional," which appears on this book's dedication page, though ironically it was written prior to his son's untimely death.

"Guns of the Fore and Aft" was published in *Wee Willie Winkie and Other Stories.* There is neither a specific regiment of that name nor are specific battles depicted. Instead, Kipling uses his powers of invention to draw from several engagements that really happened in the second Afghan War of 1878–80, including heroic stands against overwhelming odds and disastrous and panic-stricken collapses. The story is one of my personal favorites and has not appeared in many anthologies.

$$\star \quad \star \quad \star \quad \star \quad \star$$

In the Army List they still stand as 'The Fore and Fit Princess Hohenzollern-Sigmaringen-Anspach's Merthyr-Tydfilshire Own Royal Loyal Light Infantry, Regimental District 329A', but the Army through all its barracks and canteens knows them now as the 'Fore and Aft'. They may in time do something that shall make their new title honourable, but at present they are bitterly ashamed, and the man who calls them 'Fore and Aft' does so at the risk of the head which is on his shoulders.

Two words breathed into the stables of a certain Cavalry Regiment will bring the men out into the streets with belts and mops and bad language; but a whisper of 'Fore and Aft' will bring out this regiment with rifles.

Their one excuse is that they came again and did their best to finish the job in style. But for a time all their world knows that they were openly beaten, whipped, dumb-cowed, shaking, and afraid. The men know it; their officers know it; the Horse Guards know it, and when the next war comes the enemy will know it also. There are two or three regiments of the Line that have a black mark against their names which they will then wipe out; and it will be excessively inconvenient for the troops upon whom they do their wiping.

The courage of the British soldier is officially supposed to be above proof, and, as a general rule, it is so. The exceptions are decently shovelled out of sight, only to be referred to in the freshet of unguarded talk that occasionally swamps a Mess-table at midnight. Then one hears strange and horrible stories of men not following their officers, of orders being given by those who had no right to give them, and of disgrace that, but for the standing luck of the British Army, might have ended in brilliant disaster. These are unpleasant stories to listen to, and the Messes tell them under their breath, sitting by the big wood fires, and the young officer bows his head and thinks to himself, please God, his men shall never behave unhandily.

The British soldier is not altogether to be blamed for occasional lapses; but this verdict he should not know. A moderately intelligent General will waste six months of mastering the craft of the particular war that he may be waging; a Colonel may utterly misunderstand the capacity of his regiment for three months after it has taken the field; and even a Company Commander may err and be deceived as to the temper and temperament of his own handful: wherefore the soldier, and the soldier of to-day more particularly, should not be blamed for falling back. He should be shot or hanged afterwards—to encourage the others; but he should not be vilified in newspapers, for that is want of tact and waste of space.

He has, let us say, been in the service of the Empress for, perhaps, four years. He will leave in another two years. He has no inherited morals, and four years are not sufficient to drive toughness into his fibre, or to teach him how holy a thing is his Regiment. He wants to drink, he wants to enjoy himself—in India he wants to save money—and he does not in the least like getting hurt. He has received just sufficient education to make him understand half the purport of the orders he receives, and to speculate on the nature of clean, incised, and shattering wounds. Thus, if he is told to deploy under fire preparatory to an attack, he knows that he runs a very great risk of being killed while he is deploying, and suspects that he is being thrown away to gain ten minutes' time. He may either deploy with desperate swiftness, or he may shuffle, or bunch, or break, according to the discipline under which he has lain for four years.

Armed with imperfect knowledge, cursed with the rudiments of an imagination, hampered by the intense selfishness of the lower classes, and unsupported by any regimental associations, this young man is suddenly introduced to an enemy who in Eastern lands is always ugly, generally tall and hairy, and frequently noisy. If he looks to the right and the left and sees old soldiers—men of twelve years' service, who, he knows, know what they are about—taking a charge, rush, or demonstration without embarrassment, he is consoled and applies his shoulder to the butt of his rifle with a stout heart. His peace is the greater if he hears a senior, who has taught him his soldiering and broken his head on occasion, whispering: 'They'll shout and carry on like this for five minutes. Then they'll rush in, and then we've got 'em by the short hairs!'

But, on the other hand, if he sees only men of his own term of service turning white and playing with their triggers, and saying: 'What the Hell's up now?' while the Company Commanders are sweating into their sword-hilts and shouting: 'Front-rank, fix bayonets! Steady there—steady! Sight for three hundred—no, for five! Lie down, all! Steady! Front-rank kneel!' and so forth, he becomes unhappy; and grows acutely miserable when he hears a comrade turn over with the rattle of fire-irons falling into the fender, and the grunt of a pole-axed ox. If he can be moved about a little and allowed to watch the effect of his own fire on the enemy he feels merrier, and may be then worked up to the blind passion of fighting, which is, contrary to general belief, controlled by a chilly Devil and shakes men like ague. If he is not moved about, and begins to feel cold at the pit of the stomach, and in that crisis is badly mauled, and hears orders that were never given, he will break, and he will break badly; and of all things under the light of the sun there is nothing more terrible than a broken British regiment. When the worst comes to the worst and the panic is really epidemic, the men must be e'en let go, and the Company Commanders had better escape to the enemy and stay there for safety's sake. If they can be made to come again they are not pleasant men to meet; because they will not break twice.

About thirty years from this date, when we have succeeded in half-educating everything that wears trousers, our Army will be a beautifully unreliable machine. It will know too much and it will do too little. Later still, when all men are at the mental level of the officer of to-day, it will sweep the earth. Speaking roughly, you must employ either blackguards or gentlemen, or, best of all, blackguards commanded by gentlemen, to do butcher's work with efficiency and despatch. The ideal soldier should, of course, think for himself—the *Pocket-book* says so. Unfortunately, to attain this virtue he has to pass through the phase of thinking *of* himself, and that is misdirected genius. A blackguard may be slow to think for himself, but he is genuinely anxious to kill, and a little punishment teaches him how to guard his own skin and perforate another's. A powerfully prayerful Highland Regiment, officered by rank Presbyterians, is, perhaps, one degree more terrible in action than a hard bitten thousand of irresponsible Irish ruffians led by most improper young unbelievers. But these things prove the role—which is that the midway men are not to be trusted alone. They have ideas about the value of life and an upbringing that has not taught them to go on and take the chances. They are carefully unprovided with a backing of comrades who have been shot over, and until that backing is reintroduced, as a great many Regimental Commanders intend it shall be, they are more liable to disgrace themselves than the size of the Empire or the dignity of the Army allows. Their officers are as good as good can be, because their training begins early, and God has arranged that a clean-run youth of the British middle classes shall, in the matter of backbone, brains, and bowels, surpass all other youths. For this reason a child of eighteen will stand up, doing nothing, with a tin sword in his hand and joy in his heart until he is dropped. If he dies, he dies like a gentleman. If he lives, he writes Home that he has been 'potted', 'sniped', 'chipped', or 'cut over', and sits down to besiege Government for a wound-gratuity until the next little war breaks out, when he perjures himself before a Medical Board, blarneys his Colonel, burns incense round his Adjutant, and is allowed to go to the Front once more.

Which homily brings me directly to a brace of the most finished little fiends that ever banged drum or tootled fife in the Band of a British regiment. They ended their sinful career by open and flagrant mutiny and were shot for it. Their names were Jakin and Lew—Piggy Lew—and they were bold, bad drummer-boys, both of them frequently birched by the Drum-Major of the Fore and Fit.

Jakin was a stunted child of fourteen, and Lew was about the same age. When not looked after, they smoked and drank. They swore habitually after the manner of the Barrack-room, which is cold swearing and comes from between clinched teeth; and they fought religiously once a week. Jakin had sprung from some London gutter and may or may not have passed through Dr. Barnardo's hands ere he arrived at the dignity of drummer-boy. Lew could remember nothing except the regiment and the delight of listening to the Band from his earliest years. He hid somewhere in his grimy little soul a genuine love for music, and was most mistakenly furnished with the head of a cherub: insomuch that beautiful ladies who watched the Regiment in church were wont to speak of him as a 'darling'. They never heard his vitriolic comments on their manners and morals, as he walked back to barracks with the Band and matured fresh causes of offence against Jakin.

The other drummer-boys hated both lads on account of their illogical conduct. Jakin might be pounding Lew, or Lew might be rubbing Jakin's head in the dirt, but any attempt at aggression on the part of an outsider was met by the combined forces of Lew and Jakin; and the consequences were painful. The boys were the Ishmaels of the corps, but wealthy Ishmaels, for they sold battles in alternate weeks for the sport of the barracks when they were not pitted against other boys; and thus they amassed money.

On this particular day there was dissension in the camp. They had just been convicted afresh of smoking, which is bad for little boys who use plug tobacco, and Lew's contention was that Jakin had 'stunk so 'orrid bad from keepin' the pipe in 'is pocket,' that he and he alone was responsible for the birching they were both tingling under.

'I tell you I 'id the pipe back o' barracks,' said Jakin pacifically.

'You're a bloomin' liar,' said Lew without heat.

'You're a bloomin' little barstard,' said Jakin, strong in the knowledge that his own ancestry was unknown.

Now there is one word in the extended vocabulary of barrack-room abuse that cannot pass without comment. You may call a man a thief and risk nothing. You may even call him a coward without finding more than a boot whiz past your ear, but you must not call a man a bastard unless you are prepared to prove it on his front teeth.

'You might ha' kep' that till I wasn't so sore,' said Lew sorrowfully, dodging round Jakin's guard.

'I'll make you sorer,' said Jakin genially, and got home on Lew's alabaster forehead. All would have gone well and this story, as the books say, would never have been written, had not his evil fate prompted the Bazar-Sergeant's son, a long, employless man of five-and-twenty, to put in an appearance after the first round. He was eternally in need of money, and knew that the boys had silver.

'Fighting again,' said he. 'I'll report you to my father, and he'll report you to the Colour-Sergeant.'

'What's that to you?' said Jakin with an unpleasant dilation of the nostrils.

'Oh! nothing to *me*. You'll get into trouble, and you've been up too often to afford that.'

'What the Hell do you know about what we've done?' asked Lew the Seraph. '*You* aren't in the Army, you lousy, cadging civilian.'

He closed in on the man's left flank.

'Jes' 'cause you find two gentlemen settlin' their diff'rences with their fists you stick in your ugly nose where you aren't wanted. Run 'ome to your 'arf-caste slut of a Ma—or we'll give you what-for,' said Jakin.

The man attempted reprisals by knocking the boys' heads together. The scheme would have succeeded had not Jakin punched him vehemently in the stomach, or had Lew refrained from kicking his shins. They fought together, bleeding and breathless, for half an hour, and, after heavy punishment, triumphantly pulled down their opponent as terriers pull down a jackal.

'Now,' gasped Jakin, 'I'll give you what-for.' He proceeded to pound the man's features while Lew stamped on the outlying portions of his anatomy. Chivalry is not a strong point in the composition of the average drummer-boy. He fights, as do his betters, to make his mark.

Ghastly was the ruin that escaped, and awful was the wrath of the Bazar-Sergeant. Awful, too, was the scene in Orderly-Room when the two reprobates appeared to answer the charge of half-murdering a 'civilian'. The Bazar-Sergeant thirsted for a criminal action, and his son lied. The boys stood to attention while the black clouds of evidence accumulated.

'You little devils are more trouble than the rest of the Regiment put together,' said the Colonel angrily. 'One might as well admonish thistledown, and I can't well put you in cells or under stoppages. You must be birched again.'

'Beg y' pardon, Sir. Can't we say nothin' in our own defence, Sir?' shrilled Jakin.

'Hey! What? Are you going to argue with *me?*' said the Colonel.

'No, Sir,' said Lew. 'But if a man come to you, Sir, and said he was going to report you, Sir, for 'aving a bit of a turn-up with a friend, Sir, an' wanted to get money out o' *you,* Sir—'

The Orderly-Room exploded in a roar of laughter. 'Well?' said the Colonel.

'That was what that measly *jarnwar* there did, Sir, and 'e'd 'a' *done* it, Sir, if we 'adn't prevented 'im. We didn't 'it 'im much, Sir. 'E 'adn't no manner o' right to interfere with us, Sir. I don't mind bein' birched by the Drum-Major, Sir, nor yet reported by *any* Corp'ral, but I'm—but I don't think it's fair, Sir, for a civilian to come an' talk over a man in the Army.'

A second shout of laughter shook the Orderly-Room, but the Colonel was grave.

'What sort of characters have these boys?' he asked of the Regimental Sergeant-Major.

'Accordin' to the Bandmaster, Sir,' returned that revered official—the only soul in the Regiment whom the boys feared—'they do everything *but* lie, Sir.'

'Is it like we'd go for that man for fun, Sir?' said Lew, pointing to the plaintiff.

'Oh, admonished—admonished!' said the Colonel testily, and when the boys had gone he read the Bazar-Sergeant's son a lecture on the sin of unprofitable meddling, and gave orders that the Bandmaster should keep the Drums in better discipline.

'If either of you comes to practice again with so much as a scratch on your two ugly little faces,' thundered the Bandmaster, 'I'll tell the Drum-Major to take the skin off your backs. Understand that, you young devils.'

Then he repented of his speech for just the length of time that Lew, looking like a seraph in red worsted embellishments, took the place of one of the trumpets—in hospital—and rendered the echo of a battle-piece. Lew certainly was a musician, and had often in his more exalted moments expressed a yearning to master every instrument of the Band.

'There's nothing to prevent your becoming a Bandmaster, Lew,' said the Bandmaster, who had composed waltzes of his own, and worked day and night in the interests of the Band.

'What did he say?' demanded Jakin after practice.

'Said I might be a bloomin' Bandmaster, an' be asked in to 'ave a glass o' sherry-wine on Mess-nights.'

'Ho! Said you might be a bloomin' non-combatant, did 'e! That's just about wot 'e would say. When I've put in my boy's service—it's a bloomin' shame that doesn't count for pension—I'll take on as a privit. Then I'll be a Lance in a year—knowin' what I know about the ins an' outs o' things. In three years I'll be a bloomin' Sergeant. I won't marry then, not me! I'll 'old on and learn the orf'cers' ways an' apply for exchange into a reg'ment that doesn't know all about me. Then I'll be a bloomin' orf'cer. Then I'll ask you to 'ave a glass o' sherry-wine, *Mister* Lew, an' you'll bloomin' well 'ave to stay in the hanty-room while the Mess-Sergeant brings it to your dirty 'ands.'

''S'pose I'm going to be a Bandmaster? Not I, quite. I'll be a orf'cer too. There's nothin' like taking to a thing an' stickin' to it, the Schoolmaster says. The Reg'ment don't go 'ome for another seven years. I'll be a Lance then or near to.'

Thus the boys discussed their futures, and conducted themselves piously for a week. That is to say, Lew started a flirtation with the Colour-Sergeant's daughter, aged thirteen—'not,' as he explained to Jakin, 'with any intention o' matrimony, but by way o' keepin' my 'and in.' And the black-haired Cris Delighan enjoyed that flirtation more than previous ones, and the other drummer-boys raged furiously together, and Jakin preached sermons on the dangers of 'bein' tangled along o' petticoats'.

But neither love nor virtue would have held Lew long in the paths of propriety had not the rumour gone abroad that the Regiment was to be sent on active service, to take part in a war which, for the sake of brevity, we will call 'The War of the Lost Tribes'.

The barracks had the rumour almost before the Mess-room, and of all the nine hundred men in barracks not ten had seen a shot fired in anger. The Colonel had, twenty years ago, assisted at a Frontier expedition; one of the Majors had seen service at the Cape; a confirmed deserter in E Company had helped to clear streets in Ireland; but that was all. The Regiment had been put by for many years. The overwhelming mass of its rank and file had from three to four years' service; the non-commissioned officers were under thirty years old; and men and sergeants alike had forgotten to speak of the stories written in brief upon the Colours—the New Colours that had been formally blessed by an Archbishop in England ere the Regiment came away.

They wanted to go to the Front—they were enthusiastically anxious to go—but they had no knowledge of what war meant, and there was none to tell them. They were an educated regiment, the percentage of school-certifi-cates in their ranks was high, and most of the men could do more than read and write. They had been recruited in loyal observance of the territorial idea; but they themselves had no notion of that idea. They were made up of drafts from an over-populated manufacturing district. The system had put flesh and muscle upon their small bones, but it could not put heart into the sons of those who for generations had done over-much work for over-scanty pay, had sweated in drying-rooms, stooped over looms, coughed among white-lead, and shivered on lime-barges. The men had found food and rest in the Army, and now they were going to fight 'niggers'—people who ran away if you shook a stick at them. Wherefore they cheered lustily when the rumour ran, and the shrewd, clerkly non-commissioned officers speculated on the chances of batta and of saving their pay. At Headquarters men said: 'The Fore and Fit have never been under fire within the last generation. Let us, therefore, break them in eas-ily by setting them to guard lines of communication.' And this would have been done but for the fact that British Regiments were wanted—badly wanted—at the Front, and there were doubtful Native Regiments that could fill the minor duties. 'Brigade 'em with two strong Regiments,' said Headquar-ters. 'They may be knocked about a bit, but they'll learn their business before they come through. Nothing like a night-alarm and a little cutting-up of strag-glers to make a Regiment smart in the field. Wait till they've had half-a-dozen sentries' throats cut.'

The Colonel wrote with delight that the temper of his men was ex-cellent, that the Regiment was all that could be wished, and as sound as a bell. The Majors smiled with a sober joy, and the subalterns waltzed in pairs down the Mess-room after dinner, and nearly shot themselves at revolver-practice. But there was consternation in the hearts of Jakin and Lew. What was to be done with the Drums? Would the Band go to the Front? How many of the Drums would accompany the Regiment?

They took counsel together, sitting in a tree and smoking.

'It's more than a bloomin' toss-up they'll leave us be'ind at the Depôt with the women. You'll like that,' said Jakin sarcastically.

''Cause o' Cris, y' mean? Wot's a woman, or a 'ole bloomin' depôt o' women, 'longside o' the chanst of field-service? You know I'm as keen on goin' as you,' said Lew.

'Wish I was a bloomin' bugler,' said Jakin sadly. 'They'll take Tom Kidd along, that I can plaster a wall with, an' like as not they won't take us.'

'Then let's go an' make Tom Kidd so bloomin' sick 'e can't bugle no more. You 'old 'is 'ands an' I'll kick him,' said Lew, wriggling on the branch.

'That ain't no good neither. We ain't the sort o' characters to pre-soom on our rep'tations—they're bad. If they leave the Band at the Depôt we don't go, and no error *there*. If they take the Band we may get cast for med-ical unfitness. Are you medical fit, Piggy?' said Jakin, digging Lew in the ribs with force.

'Yus,' said Lew with an oath. 'The Doctor says you 'eart's weak through smokin' on an empty stummick. Throw a chest an' I'll try yer.'

Jakin threw out his chest, which Lew smote with all his might. Jakin turned very pale, gasped, crowed, screwed up his eyes, and said—'That's all right.'

'You'll do,' said Lew. 'I've 'eard o' men dyin' when you 'it 'em fair on the breastbone.'

'Don't bring us no nearer goin', though,' said Jakin. 'Do you know where we're ordered?'

'Gawd knows, an' 'E won't split on a pal. Somewhere up to the Front to kill Paythans—hairy big beggars that turn you inside out if they get 'old o' you. They say their women are good-lookin', too.'

'Any loot?' asked the abandoned Jakin.

'Not a bloomin' anna, they say, unless you dig up the ground an' see what the niggers 'ave 'id. They're a poor lot.' Jakin stood upright on the branch and gazed across the plain.

'Lew,' said he, 'there's the Colonel coming. 'Colonel's a good old beg-gar. Let's go an' talk to 'im.'

Lew nearly fell out of the tree at the audacity of the suggestion. Like Jakin he feared not God, neither regarded he Man, but there are limits even to the audacity of drummer-boy, and to speak to a Colonel was—

But Jakin had slid down the trunk and doubled in the direction of the Colonel. That officer was walking wrapped in thought and visions of a C.B.—yes, even a K.C.B., for had he not at command one of the best Regiments of the Line—the Fore and Fit? And he was aware of two small boys charging down upon him. Once before it had been solemnly reported to him that 'the Drums were in a state of mutiny', Jakin and Lew being the ringleaders. This looked like an organized conspiracy.

The boys halted at twenty yards, walked to the regulation four paces, and saluted together, each as well-set-up as a ramrod and little taller.

The Colonel was in a genial mood; the boys appeared very forlorn and unprotected on the desolate plain, and one of them was handsome.

'Well?' said the Colonel, recognizing them. 'Are you going to pull me down in the open? I'm sure I never interfere with you, even though'—he sniffed suspiciously—'you have been smoking.'

It was time to strike while the iron was hot. Their hearts beat tumultuously.

'Beg y' pardon, Sir,' began Jakin. 'The Reg'ment's ordered on active service, Sir?'

'So I believe,' said the Colonel courteously.

'Is the Band goin', Sir?' said both together. Then, without pause, 'We're goin', Sir, ain't we?'

'You!' said the Colonel, stepping back the more fully to take in the two small figures. 'You! You'd die in the first march.'

'No, we wouldn't, Sir. We can march with the Reg'ment anywheres—p'rade an' anywhere else,' said Jakin.

'If Tom Kidd goes 'e'll shut up like a clasp-knife,' said Lew. 'Tom 'as very-close veins in both 'is legs, Sir.'

'Very how much?'

'Very-close veins, Sir. That's why they swells after long p'rade, Sir. If 'e can go, we can go, Sir.'

Again the Colonel looked at them long and intently.

'Yes, the Band is going,' he said as gravely as though he had been addressing a brother officer. 'Have you any parents, either of you two?'

'No, Sir,' rejoicingly from Lew and Jakin. 'We're both orphans, Sir. There's no one to be considered of on our account, Sir.'

'You poor little sprats, and you want to go up to the Front with the Regiment, do you? Why?'

'I've wore the Queen's Uniform for two years,' said Jakin. 'It's very 'ard, Sir, that a man don't get no recompense for doin' of 'is dooty, Sir.'

'An'—an' if I don't go, Sir,' interrupted Lew, 'the Bandmaster 'e says 'e'll catch an' make a bloo— a blessed musician o' me, Sir. Before I've seen any service, Sir.'

The Colonel made no answer for a long time. Then he said quietly: 'If you're passed by the Doctor I daresay you can go. I shouldn't smoke if I were you.'

The boys saluted and disappeared. The Colonel walked home and told the story to his wife, who nearly cried over it. The Colonel was well pleased. If that was the temper of the children, what would not the men do?

Jakin and Lew entered the boys' barrack-room with great stateliness, and refused to hold any conversation with their comrades for at least ten minutes. Then, bursting with pride, Jakin drawled: 'I've bin intervooin' the Colonel. Good old beggar is the Colonel. Says I to 'im, "Colonel," says I, "let me go to the Front, along o' the Reg'ment."—"To the Front you shall go," says 'e, "an' I only wish there was more like you among the dirty little devils that bang the bloomin' drums." Kidd, if you throw your 'courtrements at me for tellin' you the truth to your own advantage, your legs'll swell.'

None the less there was a battle-royal in the barrack-room, for the boys were consumed with envy and hate, and neither Jakin nor Lew behaved in conciliatory wise.

'I'm goin' out to say adoo to my girl,' said Lew, to cap the climax. 'Don't none o' you touch my kit because it's wanted for active service; me bein' specially invited to go by the Colonel.'

He strolled forth and whistled in the clump of trees at the back of the Married Quarters till Cris came to him, and, the preliminary kisses being given and taken, Lew began to explain the situation.

'I'm goin' to the Front with the Reg'ment,' he said valiantly.

'Piggy, you're a little liar,' said Cris, but her heart misgave her, for Lew was not in the habit of lying.

'Liar yourself, Cris,' said Lew, slipping an arm round her. 'I'm goin'. When the Reg'ment marches out you'll see me with 'em, all galliant and gay. Give us another kiss, Cris, on the strength of it.'

'If you'd on'y 'a' stayed at the Depôt—where you *ought* to ha' bin— you could get as many of 'em as—as you dam please,' whimpered Cris, putting up her mouth.

'It's 'ard, Cris. I grant you it's 'ard. But what's a man to do? If I'd 'a' stayed at the Depôt, you wouldn't think anything of me.'

'Like as not, but I'd 'ave you with me, Piggy. An' all the thinkin' in the world isn't like kissin'.'

'An' all the kissin' in the world isn't like 'avin' a medal to wear on the front o' your coat.'

'*You* won't get no medal.'

'Oh yus, I shall though. Me an' Jakin are the only actin—drummers that'll be took along. All the rest is full men, an' we'll get our medals with them.'

'They might ha' taken anybody but you, Piggy. You'll get killed— you're so venturesome. Stay with me, Piggy darlin', down at the Depôt, an' I'll love you true, for ever.'

'Ain't you goin' to do that *now*, Cris? You said you was.'

'O' course I am, but t' other's more comfortable. Wait till you've growed a bit, Piggy. You aren't no taller than me now.'

'I've bin in the Army for two years an' I'm not goin' to get out of a chanst o' seein' service, an' don't you try to make me do so. I'll come back,

Cris, an' when I take on as a man I'll marry you—marry you when I'm a Lance.'

'Promise, Piggy?'

Lew reflected on the future as arranged by Jakin a short time previously, but Cris's mouth was very near to his own.

'I promise, s'elp me Gawd!' said he.

Cris slid an arm round his neck.

'I won't 'old you back no more, Piggy. Go away an' get your medal, an' I'll make you a new button-bag as nice as I know how,' she whispered.

'Put some o' your 'air into it, Cris, an' I'll keep it in my pocket so long's I'm alive.'

Then Cris wept anew, and the interview ended. Public feeling among the drummer-boys rose to fever pitch and the lives of Jakin and Lew became unenviable. Not only had they been permitted to enlist two years before the regulation boy's age—fourteen—but, by virtue, it seemed, of their extreme youth, they were now allowed to go to the Front—which thing had not happened to acting-drummers within the knowledge of boy. The Band which was to accompany the Regiment had been cut down to the regulation twenty men, the surplus returning to the ranks. Jakin and Lew were attached to the Band as supernumeraries, though they would much have preferred being Company buglers.

'Don't matter much,' said Jakin, after the medical inspection. 'Be thankful that we're 'lowed to go at all. The Doctor 'e said that if we could stand what we took from the Bazar-Sergeant's son we'd stand pretty nigh anything.'

'Which we will,' said Lew, looking tenderly at the ragged and ill-made housewife that Cris had given him, with a lock of her hair worked into a sprawling 'L' upon the cover.

'It was the best I could,' she sobbed. 'I wouldn't let mother nor the Sergeants' tailor 'elp me. Keep it always, Piggy, an' remember I love you true.'

They marched to the railway station, nine hundred and sixty strong, and every soul in cantonments turned out to see them go. The drummers gnashed their teeth at Jakin and Lew marching with the Band, the married women wept upon the platform, and the Regiment cheered its noble self black in the face.

'A nice level lot,' said the Colonel to the Second-in-Command as they watched the first four companies entraining.

'Fit to do anything,' said the Second-in-Command enthusiastically. 'But it seems to me they're a thought too young and tender for the work in hand. It's bitter cold up at the Front now.'

'They're sound enough,' said the Colonel. 'We must take our chance of sick casualties.'

So they went northward, ever northward, past droves and droves of camels, armies of camp followers, and legions of laden mules, the throng thickening day by day, till with a shriek the train pulled up at a hopelessly congested junction where six lines of temporary track accommodated six forty-waggon trains; where whistles blew, Babus sweated, and Commissariat officers swore from dawn till far into the night amid the wind-driven chaff of the fodder-bales and the lowing of a thousand steers.

'Hurry up—you're badly wanted at the Front,' was the message that greeted the Fore and Fit, and the occupants of the Red Cross carriages told the same tale.

''Tisn't so much the bloomin' fightin',' gasped a headbound trooper of Hussars to a knot of admiring Fore and Fits. ''Tisn't so much the bloomin' fightin', though there's enough o' that. It's the bloomin' food an' the bloomin' climate. Frost all night 'cept when it hails, an' biling sun all day, an' the water stinks fit to knock you down. I got my 'ead chipped like a egg; I've got pneumonia too, an' my guts is all out o' order. 'Tain't no bloomin' picnic in those parts, I can tell you.'

'Wot are the niggers like?' demanded a private.

'There's some prisoners in that train yonder. Go an' look at 'em. They're the aristocracy o' the country. The common folk are a dashed sight uglier. If you want to know what they fight with, reach under my seat an' pull out the long knife that's there.'

They dragged out and beheld for the first time the grim, bone-handled, triangular Afghan knife. It was almost as long as Lew.

'That's the thing to jint ye,' said the trooper feebly. 'It can take off a man's arm at the shoulder as easy as slicin' butter. I halved the beggar that used that 'un, but there's more of his likes up above. They don't understand thrustin', but they're devils to slice.'

The men strolled across the tracks to inspect the Afghan prisoners. They were unlike any 'niggers' that the Fore and Fit had ever met—these huge, black-haired, scowling sons of the Beni-Israel. As the men stared the Afghans spat freely and muttered one to another with lowered eyes.

'My eyes! Wot awful swine!' said Jakin, who was in the rear of the procession. 'Say, old man, how you got *puckrowed,* eh? *Kiswasti* you wasn't hanged for your ugly face, hey?'

The tallest of the company turned, his leg-irons clanking at the movement, and stared at the boy. 'See!' he cried to his fellows in Pushtu. 'They send children against us. What a people, and what fools!'

'*Hya!*' said Jakin, nodding his head cheerily. 'You go down-country. *Khana* get, *peenikapanee* get—live like a bloomin' Rajah *ke marfik*. That's a better *bundobust* than baynit get it in your innards. Good-bye, ole man. Take care o' your beautiful figure-'ed, an' try to look *kushy*.'

The men laughed and fell in for their first march, when they began to realize that a soldier's life was not all beer and skittles. They were much impressed with the size and bestial ferocity of the niggers whom they had now learned to call 'Paythans', and more with the exceeding discomfort of their own surroundings. Twenty old soldiers in the corps would have taught them how to make themselves moderately snug at night, but they had no old soldiers, and, as the troops on the line of march said, 'they lived like pigs'. They learned the heart-breaking cussedness of camp-kitchens and camels and the depravity of an E. P. tent and a wither-wrung mule. They studied animalculae in water, and developed a few cases of dysentery in that study.

At the end of their third march they were disagreeably surprised by the arrival in their camp of a hammered iron slug which, fired from a steady rest at seven hundred yards, flicked out the brains of a private seated by the fire. This robbed them of their peace for a night, and was the beginning of a long-range fire carefully calculated to that end. In the daytime they saw nothing except an unpleasant puff of smoke from a crag above the line of march. At night there were distant spurts of flame and occasional casualties, which set the whole camp blazing into the gloom and, occasionally, into opposite tents. Then they swore vehemently, and vowed that this was magnificent but not war.

Indeed it was not. The Regiment could not halt for reprisals against the sharpshooters of the countryside. Its duty was to go forward and make connection with the Scotch and Gurkha troops with which it was brigaded. The Afghans knew this, and knew too, after their first tentative shots, that they were dealing with a raw regiment. Thereafter they devoted themselves to the task of keeping the Fore and Fit on the strain. Not for anything would they have taken equal liberties with a seasoned corps—with the wicked little Gurkhas, whose delight it was to lie out in the open on a dark night and stalk their stalkers—with the terrible, big men dressed in women's clothes, who could be heard praying to their God in the nightwatches, and whose peace of mind no amount of sniping could shake—or with those vile Sikhs, who marched so ostentatiously unprepared, and who dealt out such grim reward to those who tried to profit by that unpreparedness. This white regiment was different—quite different. It slept like a hog, and, like a hog, charged in every direction when it was roused. Its sentries walked with a footfall that could be heard for a quarter of a mile; would fire at anything that moved—even a driven donkey—and when they had once fired, could be scientifically 'rushed' and laid out a horror and an offence against the morning sun. Then there were camp-followers who straggled and could be cut up without fear. Their shrieks would disturb the white boys, and the loss of their services would inconvenience them sorely.

Thus, at every march, the hidden enemy became bolder and the regiment writhed and twisted under attacks it could not avenge. The crowning triumph was a sudden night-rush ending in the cutting of many tent-ropes, the collapse of the sodden canvas, and a glorious knifing of the men who struggled and kicked below. It was a great deed, neatly carried out, and it shook the already shaken nerves of the Fore and Fit. All the courage that they had been required to exercise up to this point was the 'two o'clock in the morning courage'; and, so far, they had only succeeded in shooting their own comrades and losing their sleep.

Sullen, discontented, cold, savage, sick, with their uniforms dulled and unclean, the Fore and Fit joined their Brigade.

'I hear you had a tough time of it coming up,' said the Brigadier. But when he saw the hospital-sheets his face fell.

'This is bad,' said he to himself. 'They're as rotten as sheep.' And aloud to the Colonel—'I'm afraid we can't spare you just yet. We want all we have, else I should have given you ten days to recover in.'

The Colonel winced. 'On my honour, Sir,' he returned, 'there is not the least necessity to think of sparing us. My men have been rather mauled and upset without a fair return. They only want to go in somewhere where they can see what's before them.'

'Can't say I think much of the Fore and Fit,' said the Brigadier in confidence to his Brigade-Major. 'They've lost all their soldiering, and, by the trim of them, might have marched through the country from the other side. A more fagged-out set of men I never put eyes on.'

'Oh, they'll improve as the work goes on. The parade gloss has been rubbed off a little, but they'll put on field polish before long,' said the Brigade-Major. 'They've been mauled, and they don't quite understand it.'

They did not. All the hitting was on one side, and it was cruelly hard hitting with accessories that made them sick. There was also the real sickness that laid hold of a strong man and dragged him howling to the grave. Worst of all, their officers knew just as little of the country as the men themselves, and looked as if they did. The Fore and Fit were in a thoroughly unsatisfactory condition, but they believed that all would be well if they could once get a fair go-in at the enemy. Pot-shots up and down the valleys were unsatisfactory, and the bayonet never seemed to get a chance. Perhaps it was as well, for a long-limbed Afghan with a knife had a reach of eight feet, and could carry away lead that would disable three Englishmen.

The Fore and Fit would like some rifle-practice at the enemy—all seven hundred rifles blazing together. That wish showed the mood of the men.

The Gurkhas walked into their camp, and in broken, barrack-room English strove to fraternise with them; offered them pipes of tobacco and stood them treat at the canteen. But the Fore and Fit, not knowing much of the nature of the Gurkhas, treated them as they would treat any other 'niggers', and the little men in green trotted back to their firm friends the Highlanders, and with many grins confided to them: 'That dam white regiment no dam use. Sulky—ugh! Dirty—ugh! *Hya,* any tot for Johnny?' Whereat the Highlanders smote the Gurkhas as to the head, and told them not to vilify a British Regiment, and the Gurkhas grinned cavernously, for the Highlanders were their elder brothers and entitled to the privileges of kinship. The common soldier who touches a Gurkha is more likely to have his head sliced open.

Three days later the Brigadier arranged a battle according to the rules of war and the peculiarity of the Afghan temperament. The enemy were massing in inconvenient strength among the hills, and the moving of many green standards warned him that the tribes were 'up' in aid of the Afghan regular troops. A squadron and a half of Bengal Lancers represented the available Cavalry, and two screw-guns borrowed from a column thirty miles away, the Artillery at the General's disposal.

'If they stand, as I've a very strong notion they will, I fancy we shall see an infantry fight that will be worth watching,' said the Brigadier. 'We'll do it in style. Each regiment shall be played into action by its Band, and we'll hold the Cavalry in reserve.'

'For *all* the reserve?' somebody asked.

'For all the reserve; because we're going to crumple them up,' said the Brigadier, who was an extraordinary Brigadier, and did not believe in the value of a reserve when dealing with Asiatics. Indeed, when you come to think of it, had the British Army consistently waited for reserves in all its little affairs, the boundaries of Our Empire would have stopped at Brighton beach.

That battle was to be a glorious battle.

The three regiments debouching from three separate gorges, after duly crowning the heights above, were to converge from the centre, left, and right upon what we will call the Afghan army, then stationed towards the lower extremity of a flat-bottomed valley. Thus it will be seen that three sides of the valley practically belonged to the English, while the fourth was strictly Afghan property. In the event of defeat the Afghans had the rocky hills to fly to, where the fire from the guerrilla tribes in aid would cover their retreat. In the event of victory these same tribes would rush down and lend their weight to the rout of the British.

The screw-guns were to shell the head of each Afghan rush that was made in close formation, and the Cavalry, held in reserve in the right valley, were to gently stimulate the breakup which would follow on the combined attack. The Brigadier, sitting upon a rock overlooking the valley, would watch the battle unrolled at his feet. The Fore and Fit would debouch from the central gorge, the Gurkhas from the left, and the Highlanders from the right, for the reason that the left flank of the enemy seemed as though it required the most hammering. It was not every day that an Afghan force would take ground in the open, and the Brigadier was resolved to make the most of it.

'If we only had a few more men,' he said plaintively, 'we could surround the creatures and crumple 'em up thoroughly. As it is, I'm afraid we can only cut them up as they run. It's a great pity.'

The Fore and Fit had enjoyed unbroken peace for five days, and were beginning, in spite of dysentery, to recover their nerve. But they were not happy, for they did not know the work in hand, and had they known, would not have known how to do it. Throughout those five days in which old soldiers might have taught them the craft of the game, they discussed together their misadventures in the past—how such an one was alive at dawn and dead ere the dusk, and with what shrieks and struggles such another had given up his soul under the Afghan knife. Death was a new and horrible thing to the sons of mechanics who were used to die decently of zymotic disease; and their careful conservation in barracks had done nothing to make them look upon it with less dread.

Very early in the dawn the bugles began to blow, and the Fore and Fit, filled with a misguided enthusiasm, turned out without waiting for a cup of coffee and a biscuit; and were rewarded by being kept under arms in the cold while the other regiments leisurely prepared for the fray. All the world knows that it is ill taking the breeks off a Highlander. It is much iller to try to make him stir unless he is convinced of the necessity for haste.

The Fore and Fit waited, leaning upon their rifles and listening to the protests of their empty stomachs. The Colonel did his best to remedy the default of lining as soon as it was borne in upon him that the affair would not begin at once, and so well did he succeed that the coffee was just ready when—the men moved off, their Band leading. Even then there had been a mistake in time, and the Fore and Fit came out into the valley ten minutes before the proper hour. Their Band wheeled to the right after reaching the open, and retired behind a little rocky knoll still playing while the regiment went past.

196 . The Greatest War Stories Ever Told

It was not a pleasant sight that opened on the uninstructed view, for the lower end of the valley appeared to be filled by an army in position—real and actual regiments attired in red coats, and—of this there was no doubt—firing Martini-Henry bullets which cut up the ground a hundred yards in front of the leading company. Over that pock-marked ground the regiment had to pass, and it opened the ball with a general and profound courtesy to the piping pickets; ducking in perfect time, as though it had been brazed on a rod. Being half capable of thinking for itself, it fired a volley by the simple process of pitching its rifle into its shoulder and pulling the trigger. The bullets may have accounted for some of the watchers on the hillside, but they certainly did not affect the mass of enemy in front, while the noise of the rifles drowned any orders that might have been given.

'Good God!' said the Brigadier, sitting on the rock high above all. 'That battalion has spoilt the whole show. Hurry up the others, and let the screw-guns get off.'

But the screw-guns, in working round the heights, had stumbled upon a wasps' nest of a small mud fort which they incontinently shelled at eight hundred yards, to the huge discomfort of the occupants, who were unaccustomed to weapons of such devilish precision.

The Fore and Fit continued to go forward, but with shortened stride. Where were the other regiments, and why did these niggers use Martinis? They took open order instinctively, lying down and firing at random, rushing a few paces forward and lying down again, according to the regulations. Once in this formation, each man felt himself desperately alone, and edged in towards his fellow for comfort's sake.

Then the crack of his neighbour's rifle at his ear led him to fire as rapidly as he could—again for the sake of the comfort of the noise. The reward was not long delayed. Five volleys plunged the files in banked smoke impenetrable to the eye, and the bullets began to take ground twenty or thirty yards in front of the firers, as the weight of the bayonet dragged down and to the right arms wearied with holding the kick of the jolting Martini. The Company Commanders peered helplessly through the smoke, the more nervous mechanically trying to fan it away with their helmets.

'High and to the left!' bawled a Captain till he was hoarse. 'No good! Cease firing, and let it drift away a bit.'

Three and four times the bugles shrieked the order, and when it was obeyed the Fore and Fit looked that their foe should be lying before them in mown swaths of men. A light wind drove the smoke to leeward, and showed the enemy still in position and apparently unaffected. A quarter of a ton of lead had been buried a furlong in front of them, as the ragged earth attested.

That was not demoralizing to the Afghans, who have not European nerves. They were waiting for the mad riot to die down, and were firing quietly into the heart of the smoke. A private of the Fore and Fit spun up his company shrieking with agony, another was kicking the earth and gasping, and a third, ripped through the lower intestines by a jagged bullet, was calling aloud on his comrades to put him out of his pain. These were the casualties, and they were not soothing to hear or see. The smoke cleared to a dull haze.

Then the foe began to shout with a great shouting, and a mass—a black mass—detached itself from the main body, and rolled over the ground at horrid speed. It was composed of, perhaps, three hundred men, who would shout and fire and slash if the rush of their fifty comrades who were determined to die carried home. The fifty were Ghazis, half maddened with drugs and wholly mad with religious fanaticism. When they rushed the British fire ceased, and in the lull the order was given to close ranks and meet them with the bayonet.

Any one who knew the business could have told the Fore and Fit that the only way of dealing with a Ghazi rush is by volleys at long ranges; because a man who means to die, who desires to die, who will gain heaven by dying, must, in nine cases out of ten, kill a man who has a lingering prejudice in favour of life. Where they should have closed and gone forward, the Fore and Fit opened out and skirmished, and where they should have opened out and fired, they closed and waited.

A man dragged from his blankets half awake and unfed is never in a pleasant frame of mind. Nor does his happiness increase when he watches the whites of the eyes of three hundred six-foot fiends upon whose beards the foam is lying, upon whose tongues is a roar of wrath, and in whose hands are yard-long knives.

The Fore and Fit heard the Gurkha bugles bringing that regiment forward at the double, while the neighing of the Highland pipes came from the right. They strove to stay where they were, though the bayonets wavered down the line like the oars of a ragged boat. Then they felt body to body the amazing physical strength of their foes; a shriek of pain ended the rush, and the knives fell amid scenes not to be told. The men clubbed together and smote blindly—as often as not at their own fellows. Their front crumpled like paper, and the fifty Ghazis passed on; their backers, now drunk with success, fighting as madly as they.

Then the rear ranks were bidden to close up, and the subalterns dashed into the stew—alone. For the rear ranks had heard the clamour in front, the yells and the howls of pain, and had seen the dark stale blood that makes afraid. They were not going to stay. It was the rushing of the camps over again. Let their officers go to Hell, if they chose; they would get away from the knives.

'Come on!' shrieked the subalterns, and their men, cursing them, drew back, each closing into his neighbour and wheeling round.

Charteris and Devlin, subalterns of the last company, faced their death alone in the belief that their men would follow.

'You've killed me, you cowards,' sobbed Devlin and dropped, cut from the shoulder-strap to the centre of the chest, and a fresh detachment of his men retreating, always retreating, trampled him under foot as they made for the pass whence they had emerged . . .

'I kissed her in the kitchen and I kissed her in the hall.
Child'un, child'un, follow me!
"Oh Golly", said the cook, "is he gwine to kiss us all?"
Halla—Halla—Halla—Hallelujah!'

The Gurkhas were pouring through the left gorge and over the heights at the double to the invitation of their Regimental Quick-step. The black rocks were crowned with dark green spiders as the bugles gave tongue jubilantly:—

'In the morning! In the morning *by* the bright light!
When Gabriel blows his trumpet in the morning!'

The Gurkha rear companies tripped and blundered over loose stones. The front-files halted for a moment to take stock of the valley and to settle stray boot-laces. Then a happy little sigh of contentment soughed down the ranks, and it was as though the land smiled, for behold there below were the enemy, and it was to meet them that the Gurkhas had doubled so hastily. There was much enemy. There would be amusement. The little men hitched their *kukris* well to hand, and gaped expectantly at their officers as terriers grin ere the stone is cast for them to fetch. The Gurkhas' ground sloped downward to the valley, and they enjoyed a fair view of the proceedings. They sat upon the boulders to watch, for their officers were not going to waste their wind in as-sisting to repulse a Ghazi rush more than half a mile away. Let the white men look to their own front.

'Hi yi!' said the Subadar-Major, who was sweating profusely. 'Dam fools yonder, stand close-order! This is no time for close order, it is the time for volleys. Ugh!'

Horrified, amused, and indignant, the Gurkhas beheld the retirement of the Fore and Fit with a running chorus of oaths and commentaries.

'They run! The white men run! Colonel Sahib, may *we* also do a little running?' murmured Runbir Thappa, the Senior Jemadar.

But the Colonel would have none of it. 'Let the beggars cut up a little,' said he wrathfully. 'Serves 'em right. They'll be prodded into facing round in a minute.' He looked through his field-glasses, and caught the glint of an officer's sword.

'Beating 'em with the flat—damned conscripts! How the Ghazis are walking into them!' said he.

The Fore and Fit, heading back, bore with them their officers. The narrowness of the pass forced the mob into solid formation, and the rear-rank delivered some sort of a wavering volley. The Ghazis drew off, for they did not know what reserves the gorge might hide. Moreover, it was never wise to chase white men too far. They returned as wolves return to cover, satisfied with the slaughter that they had done, and only stopping to slash at the wounded on the ground. A quarter of a mile had the Fore and Fit retreated, and now, jammed in the pass, were quivering with pain, shaken and demoralized with fear, while the officers, maddened beyond control, smote the men with the hilts and the flats of their swords.

'Get back! Get back, you cowards—you women! Right about face—column of companies, form—you hounds!' shouted the Colonel, and the subalterns swore aloud. But the Regiment wanted to go—to get anywhere out of the range of those merciless knives. It swayed to and fro irresolutely with shouts and outcries, while from the right the Gurkhas dropped volley after volley of cripple-stopper Sniper bullets at long range into the mob of the Ghazis returning to their own troops.

The Fore and Fit Band, though protected from direct fire by the rocky knoll under which it had sat down, fled at the first rush. Jakin and Lew would have fled also, but their short legs left them fifty yards in the rear, and by the time the Band had mixed with the regiment, they were painfully aware that they would have to close in alone and unsupported.

'Get back to that rock,' gasped Jakin. 'They won't see us there.'

And they returned to the scattered instruments of the Band, their hearts nearly bursting their ribs.

'Here's a nice show for *us*,' said Jakin, throwing himself full length on the ground. 'A bloomin' fine show for British Infantry! Oh, the devils! They've gone an' left us alone here! Wot'll we do?'

Lew took possession of a cast-off water bottle, which naturally was full of canteen rum, and drank till he coughed again.

'Drink,' said he shortly. 'They'll come back in a minute or two—you see.'

Jakin drank, but there was no sign of the regiment's return. They could hear a dull clamour from the head of the valley of retreat, and saw the Ghazis slink back, quickening their pace as the Gurkhas fired at them.

'We're all that's left of the Band, an' we'll be cut up as sure as death,' said Jakin.

'I'll die game, then,' said Lew thickly, fumbling with his tiny drummer's sword. The drink was working on his brain as it was on Jakin's.

''Old on! I know somethin' better than fightin',' said Jakin, 'stung by the splendour of a sudden thought' due chiefly to rum. 'Tip our bloomin' cowards yonder the word to come back. The Paythan beggars are well away. Come on, Lew! We won't get 'urt. Take the fife an' give me the drum. The Old Step for all your bloomin' guts are worth! There's a few of our men comin' back now. Stand up, ye drunken little defaulter. By your right—quick march!'

He slipped the drum-sling over his shoulder, thrust the fife into Lew's hand, and the two boys marched out of the cover of the rock into the open, making a hideous hash of the first bars of the 'British Grenadiers'.

As Lew had said, a few of the Fore and Fit were coming back sullenly and shamefacedly under the stimulus of blows and abuse. Their red coats shone at the head of the valley, and behind them were wavering bayonets. But between this shattered line and the enemy, who with Afghan suspicion feared that the hasty retreat meant an ambush, and had not moved therefore, lay half a mile of level ground dotted only with the wounded.

The tune settled into full swing and the boys kept shoulder to shoulder, Jakin banging the drum as one possessed. The one fife made a thin and pitiful squeaking, but the tune carried far, even to the Gurkhas.

'Come on, you dogs!' muttered Jakin to himself. 'Are we to play forhever?' Lew was staring straight in front of him and marching more stiffly than ever he had done on parade.

And in bitter mockery of the distant mob, the old tune of the Old Line shrilled and rattled:—

'Some talk of Alexander,

And some of Hercules;
Of Hector and Lysander,
And such great names as these!'

There was a far-off clapping of hands from the Gurkhas, and a roar from the Highlanders in the distance, but never a shot was fired by British or Afghan. The two little red dots moved forward in the open parallel to the enemy's front.

'But of all the world's great heroes
There's none that can compare,
With a tow-row-row-row-row-row,
To the British Grenadier!'

The men of the Fore and Fit were gathering thick at the entrance to the plain. The Brigadier on the heights far above was speechless with rage. Still no movement from the enemy. The day stayed to watch the children.

Jakin halted and beat the long roll of the Assembly, while the fife squealed despairingly.

'Right about face! Hold up, Lew, you're drunk,' said Jakin. They wheeled and marched back:——

'Those heroes of antiquity
Ne'er saw a cannon-ball,
Nor knew the force o' powder'

'Here they come!' said Jakin. 'Go on, Lew':——

'To scare their foes withal!'

The Fore and Fit were pouring out of the valley. What officers had said to men in that time of shame and humiliation will never be known; for neither officers nor men speak of it now.

'They are coming anew!' shouted a priest among the Afghans. 'Do not kill the boys! Take them alive, and they shall be of our faith.'

But the first volley had been fired, and Lew dropped on his face. Jakin stood for a minute, spun round and collapsed, as the Fore and Fit came forward, the curses of their officers in their ears, and in their hearts the shame of open shame.

Half the men had seen the drummers die, and they made no sign. They did not even shout. They doubled out straight across the plain in open order, and they did not fire.

'This,' said the Colonel of Gurkhas softly, 'is the real attack, as it should have been delivered. Come on, my children.'

'Ulu-lu-lu-lu!' squealed the Gurkhas, and came down with a joyful clicking of *kukris*—those vicious Gurkha knives.

On the right there was no rush. The Highlanders, cannily commending their souls to God (for it matters as much to a dead man whether he has been shot in a Border scuffle or at Waterloo), opened out and fired according to their custom, that is to say, without heat and without intervals, while the screw-guns, having disposed of the impertinent mud fort aforementioned, dropped shell after shell into the clusters round the flickering green standards on the heights.

'Charrging is an unfortunate necessity,' murmured the Colour-Sergeant of the right company of the Highlanders. 'It makes the men sweer so—but I am thinkin' that it will come to a charrge if these black devils stand much longer. Stewarrt, man, you're firing into the eye of the sun, and he'll not take any harm for Government ammuneetion. A foot lower and a great deal slower! What are the English doing? They're very quiet there in the centre. Running again?'

The English were not running. They were hacking and hewing and stabbing, for though one white man is seldom physically a match for an Afghan in a sheepskin or wadded coat, yet, through the pressure of many white men behind, and a certain thirst for revenge in his heart, he becomes capable of doing much with both ends of his rifle. The Fore and Fit held their fire till one bullet could drive through five or six men, and the front of the Afghan force gave on the volley. They then selected their men, and slew them with deep gasps and short hacking coughs, and groanings of leather belts against strained bodies, and realized for the first time that an Afghan attacked is far less formidable than an Afghan attacking: which fact old soldiers might have told them.

But they had no old soldiers in their ranks.

The Gurkhas' stall at the bazar was the noisiest, for the men were engaged—to a nasty noise as of beef being cut on the block—with the *kukri,* which they preferred to the bayonet; well knowing how the Afghan hates the half-moon blade.

As the Afghans wavered, the green standards on the mountain moved down to assist them in a last rally. This was unwise. The Lancers chafing in the right gorge had thrice despatched their only subaltern as galloper to report on the progress of affairs. On the third occasion he returned, with a bullet-graze on his knee, swearing strange oaths in Hindustani, and saying that all things were ready. So that squadron swung round the right of the Highlanders with a wicked whistling of wind in the pennons of its lances, and fell upon the remnant just when, according to all the rules of war, it should have waited for the foe to show more signs of wavering.

But it was a dainty charge, deftly delivered, and it ended by the Cavalry finding itself at the head of the pass by which the Afghans intended to retreat; and down the track that the lances had made streamed two companies of the Highlanders, which was never intended by the Brigadier. The new development was successful. It detached the enemy from his base as a sponge is torn from a rock, and left him ringed about with fire in that pitiless plain. And as a sponge is chased round the bath-tub by the hand of the bather, so were the Afghans chased till they broke into little detachments much more difficult to dispose of than large masses.

'See!' quoth the Brigadier. 'Everything has come as I arranged. We've cut their base, and now we'll bucket 'em to pieces.'

A direct hammering was all that the Brigadier had dared to hope for, considering the size of the force at his disposal; but men who stand or fall by the errors of their opponents may be forgiven for turning Chance into Design. The bucketing went forward merrily. The Afghan forces were upon the run—the run of wearied wolves who snarl and bite over their shoulders. The red lances dipped by twos and threes, and, with a shriek, up rose the lance-butt, like a spar on a stormy sea, as the trooper cantering forward cleared his point. The Lancers kept between their prey and the steep hills, for all who could were trying to escape from the valley of death. The Highlanders gave the fugitives two hundred yards' law, and then brought them down, gasping and choking, ere they could reach the protection of the boulders above. The Gurkhas followed suit; but the Fore and Fit were killing on their own account, for they had penned a mass of men between their bayonets and a wall of rock, and the flash of the rifles was lighting the wadded coats.

'We cannot hold them, Captain Sahib!' panted a Rissaldar of Lancers. 'Let us try the carbine. The lance is good, but it wastes time.'

They tried the carbine, and still the enemy melted away—fled up the hills by hundreds when there were only twenty bullets to stop them. On the heights the screw-guns ceased firing—they had run out of ammunition—and the Brigadier groaned, for the musketry fire could not sufficiently smash the retreat. Long before the last volleys were fired the doolies were out in force looking for the wounded. The battle was over, and, but for want of fresh troops, the Afghans would have been wiped off the earth. As it was they counted their dead by hundreds, and nowhere were the dead thicker than in the track of the Fore and Fit.

But the Regiment did not cheer with the Highlanders, nor did they dance uncouth dances with the Gurkhas among the dead. They looked under their brows at the Colonel as they leaned upon their rifles and panted.

'Get back to camp, you. Haven't you disgraced yourselves enough for one day? Go and look to the wounded. It's all you're fit for,' said the Colonel. Yet for the past hour the Fore and Fit had been doing all that mortal commander could expect. They had lost heavily because they did not know how to set about their business with proper skill, but they had borne themselves gallantly, and this was their reward.

A young and sprightly Colour-Sergeant, who had begun to imagine himself a hero, offered his water-bottle to a Highlander, whose tongue was black with thirst. 'I drink with no cowards,' answered the youngster huskily, and, turning to a Gurkha, said, '*Hya,* Johnny! Drink water got it?' The Gurkha grinned and passed his bottle. The Fore and Fit said no word.

They went back to camp when the field of strife had been a little mopped up and made presentable, and the Brigadier, who saw himself a Knight in three months, was the only soul who was complimentary to them. The Colonel was heart-broken, and the officers were savage and sullen.

'Well,' said the Brigadier, 'they are young troops of course, and it was not unnatural that they should retire in disorder for a bit.'

'Oh, my only Aunt Maria!' murmured a junior Staff Officer. 'Retire in disorder! It was a bally run!'

'But they came again, as we all know,' cooed the Brigadier, the Colonel's ashy-white face before him, 'and they behaved as well as could possibly be expected. Behaved beautifully, indeed. I was watching them. It isn't a matter to take to heart, Colonel. As some German General said of his men, they wanted to be shooted over a little, that was all.' To himself he said—'Now they're blooded I can give 'em responsible work. It's as well that they got what they did. Teach 'em more than any amount of rifle flirtations, that will—later—run alone and bite. Poor old Colonel, though!'

All that afternoon the heliograph winked and flickered on the hills, striving to tell the good news to a mountain forty miles away. And in the evening there arrived, dusty, sweating, and sore, a misguided Correspondent who had gone out to assist at a trumpery village-burning, and who had read off the message from afar, cursing his luck the while.

'Let's have the details somehow—as full as ever you can, please. It's the first time I've ever been left this campaign,' said the Correspondent to the Brigadier, and the Brigadier, nothing loth, told him how an Army of Communication had been crumpled up, destroyed, and all but annihilated by the craft, strategy, wisdom, and foresight of the Brigadier.

But some say, and among these be the Gurkhas who watched on the hillside, that that battle was won by Jakin and Lew, whose little bodies were borne up just in time to fit two gaps at the head of the big ditch-grave for the dead under the heights of Jagai.

Sink the Bismarck!

BY C. S. FORESTER

T HIS IS A STORY of the most desperate chances, of the loftiest patriotism and of the highest professional skills, of a gamble for the domination of the world in which human lives were the stakes on the green gaming table of the ocean. There was a pursuit without precedent in the history of navies; there were battles fought in which the defeated gained as much glory as the victors, and in which the most unpredictable bad luck was counterbalanced by miraculous good fortune. For six days that pursuit lasted, days of unrelenting storm, of tossing gray seas and lowering clouds, without a single gleam of sunshine to lighten the setting of the background of tragedy. Those actors in the tragedy who played their parts at sea did so to the unceasing accompaniment of shrieking wind, leaping waves, flying spray, and bitter cold."

In that introduction to *Sink the Bismarck!*, the distinguished English writer C. S. Forester has set the stage for one of the greatest naval dramas of all time. The stakes could not be higher. The time is May 1941. Britain is hanging on against Germany by sheer guts. The great German battleship *Bismarck* breaks into the North Atlantic from Gdynia in the Baltic Sea, makes its way past Norway to the Denmark Straits and promptly takes on Britain's HMS *Hood*. The *Hood* is blown to pieces with a single shot, a devastating loss of life for the English and a strategic disaster. Now it appears that the *Bismarck* will be on the loose on the high seas, sinking English shipping at will.

But other British fighting ships are in pursuit, and eventually a torpedo plane from one of them is in position to at least damage the mighty *Bismarck*. Minor though the damage is, it is the beginning of the end.

We pick up the chase as German Admiral Lutjens, in overall command, and Captain Lindemann, in command of the *Bismarck,* watch for attacking British forces. It will be dark soon, and their escape to the high seas will probably be successful after that.

C. S. Forester (1899–1966) has written so many great novels about action on the high seas—the Hornblower series, *The Good Shepherd*—that his nonfiction is often overshadowed. As you will see, however, his storytelling talents were very much in evidence in getting real history onto the printed page.

★　★　★　★　★

In the *Bismarck,* Lutjens and Lindemann were looking at the gray sky.

"They should have attacked two hours ago," said Lindemann.

"One of the unpredictable accidents of war, I expect," said Lutjens. "One more hour of daylight . . . That's all."

At this moment came the yell of "Plane on the starboard bow!" followed by the roar of the alarm. The AA guns turned and began to fire, but the deafening racket was pierced by further cries: "Plane on the port beam. Plane on the starboard quarter."

Lindemann was giving rapid helm orders, which, transmitted down the voice-pipe, were translated into violent action by the helmsman at the wheel. The ship turned and twisted, to leave behind her a boiling, curved wake. There was a crash and a great jet of water at the bow as one torpedo exploded there; but the ship fought on without apparent damage. Then came a Swordfish, swooping at the stern as she swung; the wake of her dropped torpedo was clearly visible. On the wing of the bridge, Lutjens was shaking his fists at the plane.

"Hard a-port. Hard a-port!" shouted Lindemann, but there was not time to check the turn. The torpedo hit on her swinging stern, bursting close by the rudder in a shower of spray. A frightful vibration made itself felt throughout the ship, as if the whole vast structure would shake itself to pieces, and she heeled over madly as she continued in a tight turn.

"Starboard! Starboard!" shouted Lindemann.

Down below, the helmsman was struggling with the wheel while the compass before him still went swinging round over the card.

"I can't move the wheel, sir!" he said. "Rudder's jammed!"

On the bridge the vibration still continued and the ship still circled. A telephone squawked and the officer of the watch answered it.

"Engine room, sir," he said to the captain.

"Captain," said Lindemann calmly into the telephone. "Yes. . . . Yes. . . . Very well."

The shattering vibration ceased as he hung up, and some of the speed of the ship fell away.

"Portside engines stopped, sir," he said to the admiral. "Portside propellers were thrashing against some obstruction."

"Yes," said Lutjens.

Another telephone was squawking.

"Damage Control, sir," said the officer of the watch.

"Captain," said Lindemann into the telephone. "Yes. . . . Yes. . . . Very well, get going on that."

Then he turned to Lutjens.

"Steering flat is flooded, sir. Steering engine out of action."

"What about the hand steering?"

"They've just been trying it, sir, but the rudder's jammed right over. They're trying to clear it now."

"The fate of the Reich depends on getting that rudder clear," said Lutjens.

In the War Room in London the senior officers were gathered round a chart of a different sort. This was on a scale so large that it showed mostly blank ocean, with only a hint of the coast of France and Spain on the right-hand side. But pinned upon the blank area were several tabs, marked, conspicuously, *Bismarck, King George V, Rodney,* FORCE H, VIAN'S DESTROYERS; and leading up to each tab were the black lines of the tracks of those ships during the last several hours. The only other feature of the map was a wide arc of a circle marking the limit of air cover from France.

A junior officer came over with a message in his hand.

"*Sheffield* has *Bismarck* in sight now, sir," he said, making an adjustment to *Bismarck*'s position. "She's reporting position, course and speed."

"How long before she's under air cover now?" demanded the admiral.

Someone swept with his dividers from *Bismarck*'s position to the arc. "A hundred and seventy-two miles, sir."

"Less than seven hours before she's safe!" said the rear admiral.

"And only an hour of daylight. What the devil's *Ark Royal* up to?"

"Here's a most immediate signal coming through now, sir," said an officer, "from *Sheffield:* HAVE SIGHTED SWORDFISH ATTACKING. *Bismarck* FIRING."

"That's *Ark Royal*'s planes," said the admiral.

"Come on, men! Come on!" said the air vice marshal.

"Most immediate from *Sheffield* again: *Bismarck* CIRCLING."

"That's something gained, anyway," said the rear admiral.

"Not enough to matter," said the admiral.

"Most immediate from *Sheffield:* ATTACK APPARENTLY COMPLETED. SWORDFISH RETURNING."

The rear admiral began to speak, but the admiral checked him, as the officer was still speaking.

"*Bismarck* STILL CIRCLING."

"Then the attack's not over," said the rear admiral.

"There's something odd," said the admiral.

The signals were clattering down the tubes to be opened hastily, but they were all, clearly, merely confirmations of what the young officer was announcing from his telephone.

"*Bismarck* HEADING NORTH."

"Heading north? Heading *north?* That's straight for *Rodney,*" said the admiral.

"Perhaps she's still avoiding a plane *Sheffield* can't see," said the rear admiral.

"I wonder . . ." said the admiral.

"ESTIMATE *Bismarck's* SPEED AT 10 KNOTS."

"That hardly sounds likely," said the admiral.

"It must be pretty well dark there now."

Another young officer at the telephones spoke:

"Most immediate signal coming through from *Ark Royal,* sir."

"It's time we heard from her."

"FIRST FIVE AIRCRAFT RETURNING REPORT NO HITS."

The air vice marshal struck his fist into his hand, but the message went on.

"SHADOWING AIRCRAFT REPORTS *Bismarck* COURSE NORTH, SPEED 9 KNOTS."

"Something's happened to her, for sure," said the admiral.

"AIRCRAFT REPORTS HIT ON *Bismarck's* STARBOARD BOW."

"Good! Good!" said the air vice marshal.

"But that wouldn't account for it," said the rear admiral.

"*Sheffield* reporting, sir," said the first young officer: "*Bismarck* COURSE NORTH, SPEED 9 KNOTS."

"There's no doubt about it, then," said the rear admiral.

"*Ark Royal* reporting, sir," said the second officer; "AIRCRAFT REPORTS HIT ON *Bismarck* RIGHT AFT."

"That's it, then!" said the rear admiral.

"Yes, that's it. Propellers or rudder, or both," said the admiral.

"*Bismarck* COURSE NORTH, SPEED 10 KNOTS."

"There's a heavy sea running and she can't turn her stern to it," said the admiral.

"Vian'll be up to her in an hour," said the rear admiral. "He'll keep her busy during the night."

"And *King George V* and *Rodney* will be up to her by daylight," said the admiral. "I think we've got her. I think we have."

"Hooray!" said the air vice marshal again.

"*Sheffield* reporting, sir: HAVE SIGHTED VIAN'S DESTROYERS PREPARING TO ATTACK."

"Hooray!" said the air vice marshal again.

"Many men are going to die very soon," said the admiral.

"Any orders for Captain Vian, sir?"

There was only a moment's pause before that question was answered.

"No," said the admiral. "We all know Vian, and he knows his business. He won't lose touch with her. If she stays crippled he won't have to force the pace too much—he can bring in the battleships to get her at dawn. If she manages to repair herself he'll have to attack all-out."

"Not so easy with that sea running," said the rear admiral. "And *Bismarck*'s got a good radar, apparently. The darkness will hamper him and won't hamper her."

"That won't stop Vian from attacking," said the rear admiral. "*Bismarck* is certainly going to have a lively night."

"All the better for our battleships tomorrow, then. Her crew must be worn out already, and another sleepless night . . . But I'm not going to count our chickens before they're hatched. We don't know *all* that's going on."

Deep down in the stern of the *Bismarck* all was dark except for the beams of electric hand-lamps. There was the sound of water washing back and forth, and the gleam of it, reflected from the lamps, came and went. The working party there was faintly visible. For a few seconds could be seen a man in emergency diving kit disappearing into the surging water. A little farther forward a seaman was stringing an emergency wire which brought light to the dark spaces, so that now the dark water was illuminated as the sea surged backward and forward, roaring through the incredible confusion of twisted steel. There were pumps at work as the diver emerged, blood streaming from his lacerated shoulders. He made his report to the officer there, who went back to use the telephone against a dark bulkhead; to reach these a watertight door was opened for him and shut behind him, although, before it closed, the water came pouring in over the coaming with the movement of the ship. A working party was laboring to shore up the bulkhead, and he had to sign to the men to cease their deafening labor before he could make himself understood at the telephone switchboard.

In the chartroom of the *Bismarck* the captain was receiving the message.

"Yes," he said. "Yes. Very well."

Then when he replaced the telephone he addressed Lutjens and the staff officers gathered there.

"They don't think any repair can be effected," he went on. "Furthermore, unless we keep our bows to sea they think the bulkhead will give way, and flood the next series of compartments. So we must hold this course as best we can."

"That means we go forward to meet our fate instead of trying to run away from it," said Lutjens. "That is what our Führer would like."

The chief of staff came forward with a bunch of signal forms in his hand.

"Berlin has just sent in a long message, a résumé of all the intelligence they can gather," he said. "The *King George V* is some fifty miles from us now, bearing northwesterly."

The assitant chief of staff opened the reference book to display a series of pictures.

"Fourteen-inch guns, speed 28 knots, 35,000 tons. Completed last year. Admiral Tovey's flagship; Captain Patterson."

"*Renown* and *Ark Royal*—"

"That's Force H," said Lutjens. "We know about them."

"And there's a force of destroyers, probably under Captain Vian—the man who captured the *Altmark*—close to us to the northward. From the position Berlin gives, they ought to be in sight now."

"No doubt they soon will be," said Lutjens. "I was hoping we might have a quiet night before our battle tomorrow."

"The men are falling asleep at their posts, as you know, sir," said Lindemann.

"Yes," said Lutjens.

"And there's the *Rodney*," went on the chief of staff. "She's in touch with the *King George V,* and may even have joined her by now."

The assistant chief of staff opened the reference book at another page. "Sixteen-inch guns, speed 24 knots, 35,000 tons, completed soon after the last war. Captain Dalrymple Hamilton."

"Twenty years old," and Lutjens. "And I know her well. I lunched on board her in '24 at Malta when I was a young lieutenant."

It called for no effort on the part of Lutjens to conjure up the memory before his mind's eye. The heat and the dazzling sunshine and the smooth water of the harbor—all so different from this bitter cold and tossing sea and gray sky—and the spotless battleship, glittering with fresh paint and polished brasswork; the white handropes, the white uniforms, the dazzling gold lace; the bosun's mates lined up with their calls to their lips; the welcoming group of officers on the quarterdeck as Lutjens followed his captain on board; the salutes and the handshakes, the introductions and the formalities, before the English captain led the way below to a wide airy cabin, the armchairs gay with chintz, the table covered with white lines, the glassware sparkling.

"That was the peacetime Navy" said Lutjens.

If Lutjens could have seen the *Rodney* now, as she plowed over the sea towards him, he would hardly have recognized her. A British lieutenant and an American naval lieutenant were at that moment on the boat deck of the *Rodney* looking around them at the ship.

"A battle's the last thing we expected," said the Englishman.

"That's what it looks like," said the American.

His eyes traveled over the boat deck and the upper deck. They were piled with wooden cases secured in every available space.

"This Lend-Lease of yours," said the Englishman. "Very kind of you to refit us, I know. We couldn't do without it. But we have to bring half our refitting stores with us, the things you can't supply because of our different standards."

"I know about that," said the American.

"Those are pom-pom mountings," said the Englishman.

"They look more like the Pyramids," said the American. They were eying at the moment two enormous wooden cases that towered up beside them on the boat deck.

"We've five hundred invalids on board for Canada," went on the Englishman. "They'll see another battle before they see Canada, anyway, and their wishes haven't been consulted about it."

"Me too," replied the American mildly. "I'm only supposed to be quietly showing you the way to Boston."

"That's the old *Rodney* for you," said the Englishman. "She can't even start off on a quiet trip to America without crossing the bows of a German battleship. We always try to do our guests well—entertainment regardless of expense. You'll see fireworks tomorrow."

"Very kind of you," said the American.

"Mind you," went on the Englishman, "it may not be quite as lavish as we'd like. We haven't had time for a refit for two years. We're old and we're dingy. But we'll show you something good tomorrow, all the same. When those fellows talk—"

He pointed down to the turrets where the main armament crews were exercising. It was a moment of indescribable menace, as the sixteen-inch guns trained and elevated.

That was the same moment that Admiral Lutjens looked round at the rather depressed faces all round him, and went on: "Now, gentlemen, there's no need to despair. Three days ago we fought two battleships and won a tremendous victory. Now we face two battleships again. Our fighting capacity is unimpaired. We can sink this *King George V* and this Admiral Tovey. We can make this *Rodney* run away like the *Prince of Wales*. By noon tomorrow there'll be such an assembly of U-boats around us that no one will dare to attack us. We aren't fighting a battle of despair. We're fighting for victory. And for the German Navy, the Reich, and the Führer!"

It appeared as if his fighting words had some effect. Heads were raised higher again, and there was animation in the faces of those he addressed. Lindemann looked at the clock.

"Another half-hour of daylight," he said. "I'll have food issued to the men while there's time, before we darken ship."

"Always the thoughtful officer, Lindemann," said Lutjens.

And so the last meal was served out and carried round to the men at their posts during the last minutes of daylight. There were men who went on sleeping—men of that half of the crew who were allowed to sleep after the alarm of the attack by the Swordfish had ended, who flung themselves down on the steel decks in their aching longing for sleep. There were men who took a few mouthfuls of food. There were men who ate eagerly, with appetite. And there were the men struggling with damage repair below, who had no chance either to eat or sleep.

But darkness closed down from the gray sky so abruptly that even the half-hour of which Lutjens had spoken was cut short. The alarm roared through the ship. The sleepers whom even the alarm could not now rouse were shaken or kicked awake.

The voice-pipe spoke abruptly to the group in the chartroom: *"Destroyer on the starboard bow"*— and directly afterwards: *"Destroyer on the port bow."*

Outside, the darkened ship was suddenly illuminated by the flash of the secondary armament. The guns bellowed. That was the beginning of a dreadful night. As the hands of the clock crept slowly round, alarm followed alarm. *"Destroyer to port!"* *"Destroyer to starboard!"*

In the outer blackness, Vian's five destroyers—four British and one Polish—had made their way to shadowing positions encircling the *Bismarck*. It was not so easy to do in that howling wind and over that rough sea. The destroyers that made their way to *Bismarck*'s port side had to head directly into the waves.

The captain and navigating officer on the bridge of the leading destroyer felt the frightful impact as the successive seas crashed upon the forecastle, and the spray that flew aft was so solid that it was impossible to see anything as they looked forward.

"We can't keep it up," said the captain. "Slow to 18 knots."

At that speed the destroyer could just withstand the battering of the seas—although the plight of the men in exposed situations was horrible—and she could go heaving and plunging forward. The lookouts straining their eyes through the darkness could see nothing, could not pick out the smallest hint of the vast bulk of the *Bismarck* battling the waves. The lookout peering over the starboard bow was conscious of nothing—strive as he would—except roaring darkness and hurtling spray. Yet as he watched, the darkness was suddenly rent by the long vivid flashes of gunfire—pointed, as it seemed to him, directly into his eyes. Four second later—no more—the howl of the wind was augmented by the scream of shells overhead; the sea all about the destroyer was torn into wilder confusion still by a hail of splashes, and plainly through the lurching and staggering of the ship could be felt the sharper impact of shell fragments against the frail hull.

"Port fifteen," said the captain, and the destroyer swung away abruptly. Before her turn was completed the long flashes of the *Bismarck*'s guns appeared again in the darkness, and close under the destroyer's stern the salvo plunged into the sea to raise splashes brief-lived in the brisk wind.

"Good shooting in the dark," said the captain.

"That's their radar."

The destroyer's turn had taken her into the trough of the sea, and now she was rolling fantastically, far over, first on one side and then on the other, as the steep waves heaved her over.

"We'll try again," said the captain. "Starboard fifteen."

Another series of long flames, but longer and brighter than the preceding ones, stabbed into the darkness over there, yet no salvo splashed about them.

"One of the others is getting it," remarked the navigator.

"That's their fifteen-inch," said the captain. "They're using their secondary armament for us and the main battery on the other side."

The destroyer put her nose into a sea and something much solider than spray came hurtling aft to cascade against the bridge.

"We can't take that," said the captain. "Turn two points to port and slow to 15 knots."

A few seconds after the order had been given the gun flashes lit the sky to starboard again, and close beside the starboard bow the salvo hit the water.

"Just as well we made that turn," said the captain. "That's good shooting."

"And we haven't even seen her yet!" marveled the navigator.

"They haven't seen us either," said the captain. "This is modern warfare."

It was modern warfare. Far down below decks in the *Bismarck*, walled in by armor plate, a group of officers and men sat at tables and switchboards. Despite the vile weather outside, despite the wind and the waves, it was almost silent in here; in addition to the quiet orders and announcements of the radar fire-control team there could only be heard the low purring of the costly instruments they handled. Centered in the room was the yellow-green eye of the radar, echoing the impressions received by the aerial at the masthead a hundred feet above; the room was half dark to enable the screen to be seen clearly. And in accordance with what that screen showed, dials were turned and pointers were set and reports were spoken into telephones; save for the uniforms, it might have been a gathering of medieval wizards performing some secret rite—but it was not the feeble magic of trying to cause an enemy to waste away by sticking pins into his waxen image or of attempting to summon up fiends from the underworld. These incantations let loose a thousand foot tons of energy from the *Bismarck*'s guns and hurled instant death across ten miles of raging sea. It was as a result of what that eye saw that the exhausted men of the *Bismarck* forced themselves into renewed activity to serve the guns, although there were actually men who fell asleep with the guns bellowing in their very ears. Now and then, a dazzling flash, star shells soared up from the destroyers and hung over the doomed battleship, lighting her up as if it were day. Sometimes there would be a shadowy glimpse of the destroyers racing to get into position, their bow-waves gleaming except when the heavy seas burst over their bows. Even Lutjens himself was overtaken by sleep as he sat in the control room, nodding off in his chair while the guns fired, and pulling himself up with a jerk. Once when he roused himself he called a staff officer to his side.

"Send this to Berlin at once. We SHALL FIGHT TO THE LAST. LONG LIVE THE FÜHRER."

In the War Room in London the rear admiral entered after an absence.

"Vian's still engaging her," explained one of the officers.

"*Bismarck*'s still transmitting," said another.

"What's the weather report?"

"No change, sir. Wind force 8, westerly. High sea running, low cloud, visibility poor."

"*King George V* will sight her soon enough."

Back in the control room of the *Bismarck,* Lutjens was nodding off again in his chair. His head sank lower and lower, and after a while he gave up the struggle and settled back into a sound sleep. It lasted very little time, however, because the chief of staff came to him and laid a hand on his shoulder.

"Sunrise in half an hour, sir."

"I shall go on the bridge," said Lutjens. "I think a breath of fresh air will do me good."

"Your overcoat, sir," said his flag lieutenant as he went out.

"Do you think I shall need it?" asked Lutjens, but he put it on nevertheless.

Outside, the faint light was increasing. As ever, the wind was shrieking round them; the ship was rolling heavily in the waves, with the spray flying in sheets.

"Good morning, Admiral," said Lindemann.

"Good morning, Captain," said Lutjens.

"Destroyers out of range on the starboard bow, sir," said Lindemann. "And there's a cruiser somewhere to the northward of us. I'm sure she's the *Norfolk.*"

"That was the ship that sighted us in Denmark Strait," said Lutjens. "Still with us, is she?"

One of the lookouts blinked himself awake and stared forward through his binoculars. "Ship right ahead! Two ships right ahead!"

Lutjens and Lindemann trained their glasses forward.

"Battleships?" asked Lutjens.

"I think so, sir. Battleships."

The lookout in *King George V* was staring through his glasses.

"Ship right ahead!"

The lookout in *Rodney* reported.

"Ship bearing green 5!"

"That's *Bismarck!*" said an officer on the bridge of *Rodney.*

Down the voice-pipe, over the head of the quartermaster at the wheel of the *Rodney,* came a quiet order.

"Port ten."

"Port ten, sir," repeated the quartermaster, turning his wheel.

Up in the gunnery control tower the captain's voice made itself heard in the gunnery officer's earphones.

"We are turning to port. Open fire when your guns bear."

The gunnery officer looked down at the gun ready lights. He looked through his glasses with the pointer fixed upon the silhouette of the *Bismarck.*

"Fire!" he said.

Out on the wing of the bridge stood the American officer and the British lieutenant, glasses to their eyes. Below them, just as on the evening before, the sixteen-inch guns were training round and reaching upwards towards extreme elevation. Then came the incredible roar and concussion of the salvo. The brown cordite smoke spurted out from the muzzles, to be borne rapidly away by the wind as the shells took their unseen way on their mission of death.

"Short but close. Damned close," said the Englishman; the last words were drowned by the din of the second salvo, and he did not speak again during the brief time of flight. But when he spoke it was in a voice high-pitched with excitement. "A hit! A hit! At the second salvo! I told you the old *Rodney*—"

Again his words were drowned by the roar of the guns, and he forced himself to keep his glasses steady on the target. Next it was the American who spoke.

"Another hit," he said. "She doesn't stand a chance now."

Down in the radar room of the *Bismarck* the same disciplined team was still at work.

"Range seventeen thousand meters," said the rating at the screen.

There was a roar like thunder then, all about them, as the first salvo hit the *Bismarck*. The lights went out and came on, went out and came on, and the yellow-green eye of the radar screen abruptly went lifeless. The rating there reached for other switches, clicked them on and off; he tried another combination.

"Radar not functioning, sir," he announced.

"You've tried the after aerial?" asked the officer.

"Yes, sir. No result."

"No connection with gunnery control, sir," announced another rating.

"No connection with—" began another rating, but another rolling peal of thunder cut off his words, and again the lights flickered. "No connection with the bridge, sir."

"Very well."

"No connection with the charthouse, sir."

"Very well."

The first wisps of smoke had begun to enter the radar room through the ventilating system. Wisp after wisp it came, seeping in thicker and thicker, swirling in, while the lights burned duller and duller. And peal after peal of thunder shook the whole structure, the shock waves causing the wreaths of smoke to eddy abruptly with each impact, and a section of paneling fell from the bulkhead with a sudden clatter. It was as if the witches' Sabbath in which they had been engaged had now roused the infernal forces for their own destruction. Throughout the doomed ship the lights were burning low and smoke was creeping in thicker and thicker.

In the War Room the young officer was repeating the messages heard on the telephone.

"Most immediate from *Norfolk*. *Rodney* HAS OPENED FIRE. . . . *King George V* HAS OPENED FIRE. . . . *Bismarck* IS RETURNING THE FIRE. . . . *Bismarck* HIT. . . . *Bismarck* HIT AGAIN."

It was almost possible for the men listening in the War Room to visualize what was actually going on. As the *Bismarck* trained her guns round, she was surrounded by a forest of splashes from *Rodney's* salvo, and before she could fire, the splashes from *King George V's* salvo surrounded her. Hardly had her guns spoken before a shell hit the second turret from forward and burst with a roar and a billow of smoke. The blast and the fragments swept everywhere about the bridge. The fabric was left a twisted litter of stanchions, and lying huddled and contorted in it were a number of corpses, among them those of Lindemann—conspicious by its Knight's Cross—and of Lutjens.

The voice of the officer at the telephone went on describing what was going on. "*Bismarck* ON FIRE AFT. . . . *Bismarck* HIT. . . . *Bismarck* HIT. . . . *Bismarck's* FORE TURRET OUT OF ACTION." Another officer broke in.

"*Ark Royal* signaling, sir: ALL PLANES AWAY."

"*Ark Royal?* I can't believe her planes will find anything to do. But quite right to send them in."

On the flight deck of the *Ark Royal* the sound of the gunfire was plainly to be heard, loudly, in the intervals of the Swordfish revving up their engines and taking off. Conditions were as bad as ever as the ship heaved and plunged in the rough sea under a lowering gray sky, yet somehow the lumbering aircraft managed to get away, and circle, and get into formation, and head northwards, low over the heaving sea and close under the dripping clouds. It was only a few seconds before the leader saw what he was looking for. There was a long bank of black smoke lying on the surface of the water, spreading and expanding from the denser and narrower nucleus to the northward, and it was towards that nucleus that he headed his plane.

"My God!" said the leader.

The smoke was pouring from the battered, almost shapeless hull of the *Bismarck,* stripped of her upper works, mast, funnels, bridge and all. Yet under the smoke, plainly in the dull gray light, he could see a forest—a small grove, rather—of tall red flames roaring upward from within the hull. But it was not the smoke nor the flames that held the eye, strangely enough, but the ceaseless dance of tall jets of water all about her. Two battleships were flinging shells at her both from their main and from their secondary armaments; and from the cruisers twenty eight-inch guns were joining in. There was never a moment when she was not ringed in by the splashes of the near-misses, but when the leader forced his eye to ignore the distraction of this wild water dance he saw something else: from bow to stern along the tortured hull he could see a continual coming and going of shellbursts, volcanoes of flame and smoke. From that low height, as the Swordfish closed in, he could see everything. He could see the two fore-turrets useless, one of them with the roof blown clean off and the guns pointing over side at extreme elevation, the other with the guns fore and aft drooping at extreme depression. Yet the aftermost turret was still in action; even as he watched, he saw one of the guns in it fling out a jet of smoke towards the shadowy form of the *King George V;* down there in the steel turret, nestling among the flames, some heroes were still contriving to load and train and fire. And he saw something else at the last moment of his approach. There were a few tiny, foreshortened figures visible here and there, scrambling over the wreckage, incredibly alive amid the flames and the explosions, leaping down from the fiery hull into the boiling sea.

He swung the Swordfish away from the horrible sight, to lead the way back to the *Ark Royal.* While that bombardment was going on there was no chance of a frail plane delivering a successful torpedo attack. He had seen the climax of the manifestation of sea power, the lone challenger overwhelmed by a colossal concentration of force. He was not aware of the narrowness of the margin of time and space, of how in the British battleships the last few tons of oil fuel were being pumped towards the furnaces, of German U-boats hastening, just too late, from all points in the North Atlantic to try to intervene in the struggle, of German air power chafing at the bit unable to take part in a battle only a few miles beyond their maximum range.

While the squadron was being led back to the Ark Royal, the officer at the telephone in the War Room was continuing to announce the signals coming through.

"*Bismarck* HIT AGAIN. . . . SHE IS ONLY A WRECK NOW. . . . *King George V* AND *Rodney* TURNING AWAY."

In the War Room people looked sharply at each other at that piece of news. The admiral looked at the clock.

"That's the last minute they could stay. They'll only have just enough oil fuel to get them home. Not five minutes to spare."

"Here's a signal from the flag, sir," interposed another young officer. "Ships with torpedoes go in and sink her."

"And here's *Norfolk* again," said the first young officer. "*Dorsetshire* GOING IN."

Bismarck lay, a shattered, burning, sinking hulk, as *Dorsetshire* approached. At two miles she fired two torpedoes which burst on *Bismarck's* starboard side. At a mile and a half she fired another which burst on the port side of the wreck. *Bismarck* rolled over and sank, leaving the surface covered with debris and struggling men.

"*Bismarck* SUNK," said the young officer in the War Room. "*Bismarck* SUNK."

Those words of the young officer were spoken in a hushed voice, and yet their echoes were heard all over the world. In a hundred countries radio announcers hastened to repeat those words to their audiences. In a hundred languages, newspaper headlines proclaimed, *Bismarck* SUNK to a thousand million readers. Frivolous women heard those words unhearing; unlettered peasants heard them uncomprehending, even though the destinies of all of them were changed in that moment. Stock exchange speculators revised their plans. Prime ministers and chiefs of state took grim note of those words. The admirals of a score of navies prepared to compose memoranda advising their governments regarding the political and technical conclusions to be drawn from them. And there were wives and mothers and children who heard those words as well, just as Nobby's mother had heard about the loss of the *Hood*.

The Battle at Borodino

From *War and Peace*

BY LEO TOLSTOY

T HIS EXCERPT FROM Tolstoy's masterpiece focuses on the 1812 battle that gave Napoleon's invading French army a "technical" victory, with the final roads to Moscow clear. But, as Tolstoy describes the campaign, Napoleon's forces at Borodino suffered mortal wounds that reduced its cohesive effectiveness to a condition Tolstoy likes to a mortally wounded animal, enraged but crippled.

Napoleon did enter Moscow and burned as much of it as he could. He did not, however, destroy the Russian army, his larger objective. When he began his retreat from Moscow after a few weeks, his stricken army began to bleed to death under attacks along the old Smolensk road, leading to the eventual downfall of Napoleonic France.

Much of this part of the story is told from the viewpoint of Prince Andrew Bolkonski, one of the leading fictional characters in *War and Peace*. Prince Andrew will later succumb to the wounds he sustains in the action at Borodino.

★　★　★　★　★

Prince Andrew's regiment was among the reserves which till after one o'clock were stationed inactive behind Semënovsk, under heavy artillery fire. Toward two o'clock the regiment, having already lost more than two hundred men, was moved forward into a trampled oatfield in the gap between Semënovsk and the Knoll Battery, where thousands of men perished that day and on which an intense, concentrated fire from several hundred enemy guns was directed between one and two o'clock.

Without moving from that spot or firing a single shot the regiment here lost another third of its men. From in front and especially from the right, in the unlifting smoke the guns boomed, and out of the mysterious domain of smoke that overlay the whole space in front, quick hissing cannon balls and slow whistling shells flew unceasingly. At times, as if to allow them a respite, a quarter of an hour passed during which the cannon balls and shells all flew overhead, but sometimes several men were torn from the regiment in a minute and the slain were continually being dragged away and the wounded carried off.

With each fresh blow less and less chance of life remained for those not yet killed. The regiment stood in columns of battalion, three hundred paces apart, but nevertheless the men were always in one and the same mood. All alike were taciturn and morose. Talk was rarely heard in the ranks, and it ceased altogether every time the thud of a successful shot and the cry of "stretchers!" was heard. Most of the time, by their officers' order, the men sat on the ground. One, having taken off his shako, carefully loosened the gathers of its lining and drew them tight again; another, rubbing some dry clay between his palms, polished his bayonet; another fingered the strap and pulled the buckle of his bandolier, while another smoothed and refolded his leg bands and put his boots on again. Some built little houses of the tufts in the plowed ground, or plaited baskets from the straw in the cornfield. All seemed fully absorbed in these pursuits. When men were killed or wounded, when rows of stretchers went past, when some troops retreated, and when great masses of the enemy came into view through the smoke, no one paid any attention to these things. But when our artillery or cavalry advanced or some of our infantry were seen to move forward, words of approval were heard on all sides. But the liveliest attention was attracted by occurrences quite apart from, and unconnected with, the battle. It was as if the minds of these morally exhausted men found relief in everyday, commonplace occurrences. A battery of artillery was passing in front of the regiment. The horse of an ammunition cart put its leg over a trace. "Hey, look at the trace horse! . . . Get her leg out! She'll fall. . . . Ah, they don't see it!" came identical shouts from the ranks all along the regiment. Another time, general attention was attracted by a small brown dog, coming heaven knows whence, which trotted in a preoccupied manner in front of the ranks with tail stiffly erect till suddenly a shell fell close by, when it yelped, tucked its tail between its legs, and darted aside. Yells and shrieks of laughter rose from the whole regiment. But such distractions lasted only a moment, and for eight hours the men had been inactive, without food, in constant fear of death, and their pale and gloomy faces grew ever paler and gloomier.

Prince Andrew, pale and gloomy like everyone in the regiment, paced up and down from the border of one patch to another, at the edge of the meadow beside an oatfield, with head bowed and arms behind his back. There was nothing for him to do and no orders to be given. Everything went on of itself. The killed were dragged from the front, the wounded carried away, and the ranks closed up. If any soldiers ran to the rear they returned immediately and hastily. At first Prince Andrew, considering it his duty to rouse the courage of the men and to set them an example, walked about among the ranks, but he soon became convinced that this was unnecessary and that there was nothing he could teach them. All the powers of his soul, as of every soldier there, were unconsciously bent on avoiding the contemplation of the horrors of their situation. He walked along the meadow, dragging his feet, rustling the grass, and gazing at the dust that covered his boots; now he took big strides trying to keep to the footprints left on the meadow by the mowers, then he counted his steps, calculating how often he must walk from one strip to another to walk a mile, then he stripped the flowers from the wormwood that grew along a boundary rut, rubbed them in his palms, and smelled their pungent, sweetly bitter scent. Nothing remained of the previous day's thoughts. He thought of nothing. He listened with weary ears to the ever-recurring sounds, distinguishing the whistle of flying projectiles from the booming of the reports, glanced at the tiresomely familiar faces of the men of the first battalion, and waited. "Here it comes . . . this one is coming our way again!" he thought, listening to an approaching whistle in the hidden region of smoke. "One, another! Again! It has hit. . . ." He stopped and looked at the ranks. "No, it has gone over. But this one has hit!" And again he started trying to reach the boundary strip in sixteen paces. A whizz and a thud! Five paces from him, a cannon ball tore up the dry earth and disappeared. A chill ran down his back. Again he glanced at the ranks. Probably many had been hit—a large crowd had gathered near the second battalion.

"Adjutant!" he shouted. "Order them not to crowd together."

The adjutant, having obeyed this instruction, approached Prince Andrew. From the other side a battalion commander rode up.

"Look out!" came a frightened cry from a soldier and, like a bird whirring in rapid flight and alighting on the ground, a shell dropped with little noise within two steps of Prince Andrew and close to the battalion commander's horse. The horse first, regardless of whether it was right or wrong to show fear, snorted, reared almost throwing the major, and galloped aside. The horse's terror infected the men.

"Lie down!" cried the adjutant, throwing himself flat on the ground.

Prince Andrew hesitated. The smoking shell spun like a top between him and the prostrate adjutant, near a wormwood plant between the field and the meadow.

"Can this be death?" thought Prince Andrew, looking with a quite new, envious glance at the grass, the wormwood, and the streamlet of smoke that curled up from the rotating black ball. "I cannot, I do not wish to die. I love life—I love this grass, this earth, this air. . . ." He thought this, and at the same time remembered that people were looking at him.

"It's shameful, sir!" he said to the adjutant. "What . . ."

He did not finish speaking. At one and the same moment came the sound of an explosion, a whistle of splinters as from a breaking window frame, a suffocating smell of powder, and Prince Andrew started to one side, raising his arm, and fell on his chest. Several officers ran up to him. From the right side of his abdomen, blood was welling out making a large stain on the grass.

The militiamen with stretchers who were called up stood behind the officers. Prince Andrew lay on his chest with his face in the grass, breathing heavily and noisily.

"What are you waiting for? Come along!"

The peasants went up and took him by his shoulders and legs, but he moaned piteously and, exchanging looks, they set him down again.

"Pick him up, lift him, it's all the same!" cried someone.

They again took him by the shoulders and laid him on the stretcher.

"Ah, God! My God! What is it? The stomach? That means death! My God!"—voices among the officers were heard saying.

"It flew a hair's breadth past my ear," said the adjutant.

The peasants, adjusting the stretcher to their shoulders, started hurriedly along the path they had trodden down, to the dressing station.

"Keep in step! Ah . . . those peasants!" shouted an officer, seizing by their shoulders and checking the peasants, who were walking unevenly and jolting the stretcher.

"Get into step, Fëdor . . . I say, Fëdor!" said the foremost peasant.

"Now that's right!" said the one behind joyfully, when he had got into step.

"Your excellency! Eh, Prince!" said the trembling voice of Timòkhin, who had run up and was looking down on the stretcher.

Prince Andrew opened his eyes and looked up at the speaker from the stretcher into which his head had sunk deep and again his eyelids drooped.

The militiamen carried Prince Andrew to the dressing station by the wood, where wagons were stationed. The dressing station consisted of three tents with flaps turned back, pitched at the edge of a birch wood. In the wood, wagons and horses were standing. The horses were eating oats from their movable troughs and sparrows flew down and pecked the grains that fell. Some crows, scenting blood, flew among the birch trees cawing impatiently. Around the tents, over more than five acres, bloodstained men in various garbs stood, sat, or lay. Around the wounded stood crowds of soldier stretcher-bearers with dismal and attentive faces, whom the officers keeping order tried in vain to drive from the spot. Disregarding the officers' orders, the soldiers stood leaning against their stretchers and gazing intently, as if trying to comprehend the difficult problem of what was taking place before them. From the tents came now loud angry cries and now plaintive groans. Occasionally dressers ran out to fetch water, or to point out those who were to be brought in next. The wounded men awaiting their turn outside the tents groaned, sighed, wept, screamed, swore, or asked for vodka. Some were delirious. Prince Andrew's bearers, stepping over the wounded who had not yet been bandaged, took him, as a regimental commander, close up to one of the tents and there stopped, awaiting instructions. Prince Andrew opened his eyes and for a long time could not make out what was going on around him. He remembered the meadow, the wormwood, the field, the whirling black ball, and his sudden rush of passionate love of life. Two steps from him, leaning against a branch and talking loudly and attracting general attention, stood a tall, handsome, black-haired noncommissioned officer with a bandaged head. He had been wounded in the head and leg by bullets. Around him, eagerly listening to his talk, a crowd of wounded and stretcher-bearers was gathered.

"We kicked *him* out from there so that he chucked everything, we grabbed the King himself!" cried he, looking around him with eyes that glittered with fever. "If only reserves had come up just then, lads, there wouldn't have been nothing left of him! I tell you surely. . . ."

Like all the others near the speaker, Prince Andrew looked at him with shining eyes and experienced a sense of comfort. "But isn't it all the same now?" thought he. "And what will be there, and what has there been here? Why was I so reluctant to part with life? There was something in this life I did not and do not understand."

One of the doctors came out of the tent in a bloodstained apron, holding a cigar between the thumb and little finger of one of his small bloodstained hands, so as not to smear it. He raised his head and looked about him, but above the level of the wounded men. He evidently wanted a little respite. After turning his head from right to left for some time, he sighed and looked down.

"All right, immediately," he replied to a dresser who pointed Prince Andrew out to him, and he told them to carry him into the tent.

Murmurs arose among the wounded who were waiting.

"It seems that even in the next world only the gentry are to have a chance!" remarked one.

Prince Andrew was carried in and laid on a table that had only just been cleared and which a dresser was washing down. Prince Andrew could not make out distinctly what was in that tent. The pitiful groans from all sides and the torturing pain in his thigh, stomach, and back distracted him. All he saw about him merged into a general impression of naked, bleeding human bodies that seemed to fill the whole of the low tent, as a few weeks previously, on that hot August day, such bodies had filled the dirty pond beside the Smolénsk road. Yes, it was the same flesh, the same *chair à canon,* the sight of which had even then filled him with horror, as by a presentiment.

There were three operating tables in the tent. Two were occupied, and on the third they placed Prince Andrew. For a little while he was left alone and involuntarily witnessed what was taking place on the other two tables. On the nearest one sat a Tartar, probably a Cossack, judging by the uniform thrown down beside him. Four soldiers were holding him, and a spectacled doctor was cutting into his muscular brown back.

"Ooh, ooh, ooh!" grunted the Tartar, and suddenly lifting up his swarthy snub-nosed face with its high cheekbones, and baring his white teeth, he began to wriggle and twitch his body and utter piercing, ringing, and prolonged yells. On the other table, round which many people were crowding, a tall well-fed man lay on his back with his head thrown back. His curly hair, its color, and the shape of his head seemed strangely familiar to Prince Andrew. Several dressers were pressing on his chest to hold him down. One large, white, plump leg twitched rapidly all the time with a feverish tremor. The man was sobbing and choking convulsively. Two doctors—one of whom was pale and trembling—were silently doing something to this man's other, gory leg. When he had finished with the Tartar, whom they covered with an overcoat, the spectacled doctor came up to Prince Andrew, wiping his hands.

He glanced at Prince Andrew's face and quickly turned away.

"Undress him! What are you waiting for?" he cried angrily to the dressers.

His very first, remotest recollections of childhood came back to Prince Andrew's mind when the dresser with sleeves rolled up began hastily to undo the buttons of his clothes and undressed him. The doctor bent down over the wound, felt it, and sighed deeply. Then he made a sign to someone, and the torturing pain in his abdomen caused Prince Andrew to lose consciousness. When he came to himself the splintered portions of his thighbone had been extracted, the torn flesh cut away, and the wound bandaged. Water was being sprinkled on his face. As soon as Prince Andrew opened his eyes, the doctor bent over, kissed him silently on the lips, and hurried away.

After the sufferings he had been enduring, Prince Andrew enjoyed a blissful feeling such as he had not experienced for a long time. All the best and happiest moments of his life—especially his earliest childhood, when he used to be undressed and put to bed, and when leaning over him his nurse sang him to sleep and he, burying his head in the pillow, felt happy in the mere consciousness of life—returned to his memory, not merely as something past but as something present.

The doctors were busily engaged with the wounded man the shape of whose head seemed familiar to Prince Andrew: they were lifting him up and trying to quiet him.

"Show it to me. . . . Oh, ooh . . . Oh! Oh, ooh!" his frightened moans could be heard, subdued by suffering and broken by sobs.

Hearing those moans Prince Andrew wanted to weep. Whether because he was dying without glory, or because he was sorry to part with life, or because of those memories of a childhood that could not return, or because he was suffering and others were suffering and that man near him was groaning so piteously—he felt like weeping childlike, kindly, and almost happy tears.

The wounded man was shown his amputated leg stained with clotted blood and with the boot still on.

"Oh! Oh, ooh!" he sobbed, like a woman.

The doctor who had been standing beside him, preventing Prince Andrew from seeing his face, moved away.

"My God! What is this? Why is he here?" said Prince Andrew to himself.

In the miserable, sobbing, enfeebled man whose leg had just been amputated, he recognized Anatole Kurágin. Men were supporting him in their arms and offering him a glass of water, but his trembling, swollen lips could not grasp its rim. Anatole was sobbing painfully. "Yes, it is he! Yes, that man is somehow closely and painfully connected with me," thought Prince Andrew, not yet clearly grasping what he saw before him. "What is the connection of that man with my childhood and my life?" he asked himself without finding an answer. And suddenly a new unexpected memory from that realm of pure and loving childhood presented itself to him. He remembered Natásha as he had seen her for the first time at the ball in 1810, with her slender neck and arms and with a frightened happy face ready for rapture, and love and tenderness for her, stronger and more vivid than ever, awoke in his soul. He now remembered the connection that existed between himself and this man who was dimly gazing at him through tears that filled his swollen eyes. He remembered everything, and ecstatic pity and love for that man overflowed his happy heart.

Prince Andrew could no longer restrain himself and wept tender loving tears for his fellow men, for himself, and for his own and their errors.

"Compassion, love of our brothers, for those who love us and for those who hate us, love of our enemies; yes, that love which God preached on earth and which Princess Mary taught me and I did not understand—that is what made me sorry to part with life, that is what remained for me had I lived. But now it is too late. I know it!"

The terrible spectacle of the battlefield covered with dead and wounded, together with the heaviness of his head and the news that some twenty generals he knew personally had been killed or wounded, and the consciousness of the impotence of his once mighty arm, produced an unexpected impression on Napoleon who usually liked to look at the killed and wounded, thereby, he considered, testing his strength of mind. This day the horrible appearance of the battlefield overcame that strength of mind which he thought constituted his merit and his greatness. He rode hurriedly from the battlefield and returned to the Shevárdino knoll, where he sat on his campstool, his sallow face swollen and heavy, his eyes dim, his nose red, and his voice hoarse, involuntarily listening, with downcast eyes, to the sounds of firing. With painful dejection he awaited the end of this action, in which he regarded himself as a participant and which he was unable to arrest. A personal, human feeling for a brief moment got the better of the artificial phantasm of life he had served so long. He felt in his own person the sufferings and death he had witnessed on the battlefield. The heaviness of his head and chest reminded him of the possibility of suffering and death for himself. At that moment he did not desire Moscow, or victory, or glory (what need had he for any more glory?). The one thing he wished for was rest, tranquillity, and freedom. But when he had been on the Semënovsk heights the artillery commander had proposed to him to bring several batteries of artillery up to those heights to strengthen the fire on the Russian troops crowded in front of Knyazkóvo. Napoleon had assented and had given orders that news should be brought him of the effect those batteries produced.

An adjutant came now to inform him that the fire of two hundred guns had been concentrated on the Russians, as he had ordered, but that they still held their ground.

"Our fire is mowing them down by rows, but still they hold on," said the adjutant.

"They want more! . . ." said Napoleon in a hoarse voice.

"Sire?" asked the adjutant who had not heard the remark.

"They want more!" croaked Napoleon frowning. "Let them have it!"

Even before he gave that order the thing he did not desire, and for which he gave the order only because he thought it was expected of him, was being done. And he fell back into that artificial realm of imaginary greatness, and again—as a horse walking a treadmill thinks it is doing something for itself—he submissively fulfilled the cruel, sad, gloomy, and inhuman role predestined for him.

And not for that day and hour alone were the mind and conscience darkened of this man on whom the responsibility for what was happening lay more than on all the others who took part in it. Never to the end of his life could he understand goodness, beauty, or truth, or the significance of his actions which were too contrary to goodness and truth, too remote from everything human, for him ever to be able to grasp their meaning. He could not disavow his actions, belauded as they were by half the world, and so he had to repudiate truth, goodness, and all humanity.

Not only on that day, as he rode over the battlefield strewn with men killed and maimed (by his will as he believed), did he reckon as he looked at them how many Russians there were for each Frenchman and, deceiving himself, find reason for rejoicing in the calculation that there were five Russians for every Frenchman. Not on that day alone did he write in a letter to Paris that "the battlefield was superb," because fifty thousand corpses lay there, but even on the island of St. Helena in the peaceful solitude where he said he intended to devote his leisure to an account of the great deeds he had done, he wrote:

"The Russian war should have been the most popular war of modern times: it was a war of good sense, for real interests, for the tranquillity and security of all; it was purely pacific and conservative.

"It was a war for a great cause, the end of uncertainties and the beginning of security. A new horizon and new labors were opening out, full of well-being and prosperity for all. The European system was already founded; all that remained was to organize it.

"Satisfied on these great points and with tranquillity everywhere, I too should have had my *Congress* and my *Holy Alliance.* Those ideas were stolen from me. In that reunion of great sovereigns we should have discussed our interests like one family, and have rendered account to the peoples as clerk to master.

"Europe would in this way soon have been, in fact, but one people, and anyone who traveled anywhere would have found himself always in the common fatherland. I should have demanded the freedom of all navigable rivers for everybody, that the seas should be common to all, and that the great standing armies should be reduced henceforth to mere guards for the sovereigns.

"On returning to France, to the bosom of the great, strong, magnificent, peaceful, and glorious fatherland, I should have proclaimed her frontiers immutable; all future wars purely *defensive,* all aggrandizement *antinational.* I should have associated my son in the Empire; my *dictatorship* would have been finished, and his constitutional reign would have begun.

"Paris would have been the capital of the world, and the French the envy of the nations!

"My leisure then, and my old age, would have been devoted, in company with the Empress and during the royal apprenticeship of my son, to leisurely visiting, with our own horses and like a true country couple, every corner of the Empire, receiving complaints, redressing wrongs, and scattering public buildings and benefactions on all sides and everywhere."

Napoleon, predestined by Providence for the gloomy role of executioner of the peoples, assured himself that the aim of his actions had been the peoples' welfare and that he could control the fate of millions and by the employment of power confer benefactions.

"Of four hundred thousand men who crossed the Vistula," he wrote further of the Russian war, "half were Austrians, Prussians, Saxons, Poles, Bavarians, Württembergers, Mecklenburgers, Spaniards, Italians, and Neapolitans. The Imperial army, strictly speaking, was one third composed of Dutch, Belgians, men from the borders of the Rhine, Piedmontese, Swiss, Genevese, Tuscans, Romans, inhabitants of the Thirty-second Military Division, of Bremen, of Hamburg, and so on: it included scarcely a hundred and forty thousand who spoke French. The Russian expedition actually cost France less than fifty thousand men; the Russian army in its retreat from Vilna to Moscow lost in the various battles four times more men than the French army; the burning of Moscow cost the lives of a hundred thousand Russians who died of cold and want in the woods; finally, in its march from Moscow to the Oder the

Russian army also suffered from the severity of the season; so that by the time it reached Vilna it numbered only fifty thousand, and at Kálisch less than eighteen thousand."

He imagined that the war with Russia came about by his will, and the horrors that occurred did not stagger his soul. He boldly took the whole responsibility for what happened, and his darkened mind found justification in the belief that among the hundreds of thousands who perished there were fewer Frenchmen than Hessians and Bàvarians.

Several tens of thousands of the slain lay in diverse postures and various uniforms on the fields and meadows belonging to the Davydov family and to the crown serfs—those fields and meadows where for hundreds of years the peasants of Borodinó, Górki, Shevárdino, and Semënovsk had reaped their harvests and pastured their cattle. At the dressing stations the grass and earth were soaked with blood for a space of some three acres around. Crowds of men of various arms, wounded and unwounded, with frightened faces, dragged themselves back to Mozháysk from the one army and back to Valúevo from the other. Other crowds, exhausted and hungry, went forward led by their officers. Others held their ground and continued to fire.

Over the whole field, previously so gaily beautiful with the glitter of bayonets and cloudlets of smoke in the morning sun, there now spread a mist of damp and smoke and a strange acid smell of saltpeter and blood. Clouds gathered and drops of rain began to fall on the dead and wounded, on the frightened, exhausted, and hesitating men, as if to say: "Enough, men! Enough! Cease . . . bethink yourselves! What are you doing?"

To the men of both sides alike, worn out by want of food and rest, it began equally to appear doubtful whether they should continue to slaughter one another; all the faces expressed hesitation, and the question arose in every soul: "For what, for whom, must I kill and be killed? . . . You may go and kill whom you please, but I don't want to do so any more!" By evening this thought had ripened in every soul. At any moment these men might have been seized with horror at what they were doing and might have thrown up everything and run away anywhere.

But though toward the end of the battle the men felt all the horror of what they were doing, though they would have been glad to leave off, some incomprehensible, mysterious power continued to control them, and they still brought up the charges, loaded, aimed, and applied the match, though only one artilleryman survived out of every three, and though they stumbled and panted with fatigue, perspiring and stained with blood and powder. The cannon balls flew just as swiftly and cruelly from both sides, crushing human bodies, and that terrible work which was not done by the will of a man but at the will of Him who governs men and worlds continued.

Anyone looking at the disorganized rear of the Russian army would have said that, if only the French made one more slight effort, it would disappear; and anyone looking at the rear of the French army would have said that the Russians need only make one more slight effort and the French would be destroyed. But neither the French nor the Russians made that effort, and the flame of battle burned slowly out.

The Russians did not make that effort because they were not attacking the French. At the beginning of the battle they stood blocking the way to Moscow and they still did so at the end of the battle as at the beginning. But even had the aim of the Russians been to drive the French from their positions, they could not have made this last effort, for all the Russian troops had been broken up, there was no part of the Russian army that had not suffered in the battle, and though still holding their positions they had lost *one half* of their army.

The French, with the memory of all their former victories during fifteen years, with the assurance of Napoleon's invincibility, with the consciousness that they had captured part of the battlefield and had lost only a quarter of their men and still had their Guards intact, twenty thousand strong, might easily have made that effort. The French who had attacked the Russian army in order to drive it from its position ought to have made that effort, for as long as the Russians continued to block the road to Moscow as before, the aim of the French had not been attained and all their efforts and losses were in vain. But the French did not make that effort. Some historians say that Napoleon need only have used his Old Guards, who were intact, and the battle would have been won. To speak of what would have happened had Napoleon sent his Guards is like talking of what would happen if autumn became spring. It could not be. Napoleon did not give his Guards, not because he did not want to, but because it could not be done. All the generals, officers, and soldiers of the French army knew it could not be done, because the flagging spirit of the troops would not permit it.

It was not Napoleon alone who had experienced that nightmare feeling of the mighty arm being stricken powerless, but all the generals and soldiers of his army whether they had taken part in the battle or not, after all their experience of previous battles—when after one tenth of such efforts the enemy had fled—experienced a similar feeling of terror before an enemy who, after losing HALF his men, stood as threateningly at the end as at the beginning of the battle. The moral force of the attacking French army was exhausted. Not that sort of victory which is defined by the capture of pieces of material fastened to sticks, called standards, and of the ground on which the troops had stood and were standing, but a moral victory that convinces the enemy of the moral superiority of his opponent and of his own impotence was gained by the Russians at Borodinó. The French invaders, like an infuriated animal that has in its onslaught received a mortal wound, felt that they were perishing, but could not stop, any more than the Russian army, weaker by one half, could help swerving. By the impetus gained, the French army was still able to roll forward to Moscow, but there, without further effort on the part of the Russians, it had to perish, bleeding from the mortal wound it had received at Borodinó. The direct consequence of the battle of Borodinó was Napoleon's senseless flight from Moscow, his retreat along the old Smolénsk road, the destruction of the invading army of five hundred thousand men, and the downfall of Napoleonic France, on which at Borodinó for the first time the hand of an opponent of stronger spirit had been laid.

Les Braves Gens (The Brave Men)

From *Goodbye, Darkness*

BY WILLIAM MANCHESTER

EFORE THE SANDS of Iwo Jima, there was Tarawa. In 1943, already
fully bloodied in places like Guadalcanal, long before they would ultimately plant the flag on the summit of Mt. Suribachi in Iwo in
February 1945, the U.S. Marines floundered through tidal flats into
hell on Tarawa.

This account of one of the most devastating battles ever fought is from
William Manchester's brilliant and gripping book on his service as a Marine in
World War II, *Goodbye, Darkness.* The book is a mixture of memories of actual
fighting in which Manchester was involved, histories of other battles, and impressions of battlefields as he visits them long after the war. The title is an expression of Manchester's ultimate relief from the frequent nightmares of the
war he endured for many years.

William Manchester's many outstanding works include, *Death of a
President,* on the assassination of President Kennedy; *American Caesar,* on General Douglas MacArthur; and *The Last Lion,* a biography of Winston Churchill.

★   ★   ★   ★   ★

Americans at home thought all the island battlefields in the Pacific were pretty
much alike: jungly, rainy, with deep white beaches ringed by awnings of palm
trees. That was true of New Guinea and the Solomons, but most of Admiral
Nimitz's central Pacific offensive, which opened in the autumn of 1943, was
fought over very different ground. Only the palms and the pandanus there
evoke memories of the South Pacific, and the pandanus do not flourish because rain seldom falls. A typical central Pacific island, straddling the equator, is
a small platform of coral, sparsely covered with sand and scrub bush, whose
highest point rises no more than a few feet above the surf line. Tarawa (pro-

nounced *TAR-uh-wuh*), like most of the land formations in this part of the world, is actually an atoll, a triangular group of thirty-eight islands circled by a forbidding coral reef and sheltering, within the triangle, a dreamy lagoon. The fighting was on one of Tarawa's isles, Betio (*BAY-she-oh*), because that was where the priceless Japanese airstrip was. Betio is less than half the size of Manhattan's Central Park. No part of it is more than three hundred yards from the water. A good golfer can drive a ball across it at almost any point.

Tarawa is in the Gilbert Islands. Nimitz's real objective was Kwajalein, in the Marshall Islands, over five hundred miles to the northwest. The largest atoll in the world, sixty-five miles long, Kwajalein would provide the Americans with an immense anchorage and a superb airdrome. But Tarawa and its sister atoll Makin (pronounced *MUG-rin*) had to fall first. Unlike the Marshalls, which had been mandated to Japan in the Treaty of Versailles, and which Hirohito's troops had spent twenty years arming to the teeth, the Gilberts, where Tarawa was, had been a British crown colony. The Nips had arrived there two days after Pearl Harbor. Colonel Vivien Fox-Strangeways, the resident British administrator, had fled Tarawa in a small launch, dashing from island to island by day and holing up in coves by night until a British ship picked him up in the Ellice Islands, to the south. Since then the only Allied contact with the Gilberts had been the ineffectual foray by Carlson's Raiders on Makin. Carlson reported that he hadn't encountered much resistance. By the autumn of 1943 that was no longer true. Carlson, ironically, had been the agent of change. Warned by his strike, the enemy had strengthened the defenses of the Gilberts, particularly those on Tarawa's Betio. The Japanese needed that airstrip there. It is a sign of their determination that they had chosen Betio's beach to site the British coastal defense guns they had captured at Singapore.

Everyone knew that Tarawa—which is to say Betio—would be tough. The reef was formidable. The enemy had mined it. The beach bristled with huge guns, concrete obstacles, and barbed-wire concertinas designed to force invaders into the fire zone of cannon and machine guns. That was only part of the problem, but it was the part known to Spruance and his staff before the first wave of Marines went in. The greater problem was the reef. The only craft which could cross a jutting reef, even after the mines had been defused, were what we called "amphtracs"—amphibious tractors. Driven by propellers, they could move through water at four knots; their caterpillar tracks would carry them over land, including the reef ledge, at twenty miles per hour. Twenty Marines could ride in each amphtrac. The landing force needed all it could get. But there were few available, and Spruance's staff, notably Rear Admiral Turner, took a sanguine view of the tidal problem anyway.

Using 1841 charters, they assured the Marines that at H-hour the reef would be covered by five feet of water, which meant that a loaded Higgins boat, drawing between three and four feet, could cross it. Therefore there would be enough amphtracs for the first wave, though, they conceded, there would be none for those following.

This defies understanding. A landing in spring would have been another matter, but Fox-Strangeways had described Betio's low, dodging autumn tides to the Americans. Major F. L. G. Holland, a New Zealander who had lived on Tarawa for fifteen years, said the tide might be as little as three feet. And the night before the Betio attack Rota Onorio, now Speaker of the Gilberts' House of Assembly and then a fourteen-year-old boy, paddled his dugout out to the Allied fleet and told naval officers that tomorrow the reef would be impassable, even at high tide. He, Fox-Strangeways, and Holland were ignored. Then, in the morning, the situation worsened when the fleet's timetable began to come apart. The transports carrying the Marines were trapped between Spruance's battleship bombardment and the replying fire from the enemy's shore guns. They moved, delaying the landing and missing the tide. Next it was discovered that the battleship captains and the carrier commanders had failed to consult one another; the ships' thirty-five-minute salvos ended to permit the carrier planes to come in, but the planes, whose pilots had been given another schedule, were a half hour late. That permitted the Jap batteries to open up on the transports, further delaying the landing waves. The air strike was supposed to last thirty minutes. It lasted seven. Finally, everyone awaited what was supposed to be the last touch in softening up the beach defenses, a massive B-24 raid from a base in the Ellice Islands. They waited. And waited. The B-24s never arrived. H-hour was delayed by forty-three more precious minutes.

Both the American *and* the Japanese troops were commanded by admirals—the defenders of the atoll were members of the Japanese Special Landing Forces: Japanese Marines, wearing the distinctive crysanthemum-and-anchor emblem on their helmets—and confidence was high, both on the flagship offshore and in the beach's headquarters bunker. The admiral commanding the American bombardment told Marine officers: "Gentlemen, we will not neutralize Betio. We will not destroy it. We will obliterate it!" A Marine general, Julian C. Smith, replied: "Even though you navy officers do come in to about a thousand yards, I remind you that you have a little armor. I want you to know that Marines are crossing that beach with bayonets, and the only armor they will have is a khaki shirt." But despite scheduling blunders the warships and warplanes seemed to be doing their best to prepare the way for the landing force. Three U.S. battleships, five cruisers, and nine destroyers had plastered the shore with three thousand tons of high explosives—roughly ten tons per acre. Yet the Japanese admiral remained confident. He had said that "a million men cannot take Tarawa in a hundred years." Each of his underground pillboxes was built with steel and reinforced concrete, covered with coconut logs and coral, invisible to the American bombers and warships. Underground tunnels, invulnerable even to direct hits, connected the pillboxes and blockhouses. Fourteen huge coastal guns, including the eight-inchers from Singapore, led an orchestra of fifty fieldpieces. Over a hundred machine-gun nests were zeroed in on the lip of a four-foot coconut-log and coral-block seawall. The Japs doubted that any of the U.S. assault troops would ever reach the beach, however. The reef standing between them and the Allied fleet was wider than Betio itself. And the Japanese, unlike the Americans, possessed accurate tide tables.

The struggle for the island began in the early hours of Saturday, November 20, 1943. By 4:30 a.m. the Marines assigned to the first wave had descended their cargo nets, jumped into Higgins boats, and transferred to amphtracs, which began forming for the assault. Japanese ashore were aware of dark hulks in the night but were waiting until the Americans committed themselves to the isle's sea beach or its lagoon side. At 4:41 a.m. a Nip coastal defense gun fired a red-star cluster over the six U.S. transports. Now they knew: it was to be the lagoon side. Our naval gunfire had been stunning—one Marine said, "It's a wonder the whole goddam island doesn't fall apart and sink"—but it had ended an hour earlier. Two U.S. destroyers laying down a smoke screen for the Marines were shelling the beach, but against such defenses tin-can fire was ineffectual. Japs who had been braced for an approach from the sea leapt into prepared positions facing the lagoon. Now the American Marines would confront 4,836 Japanese, most of them Jap Marines.

Amphtrac coxswains found the seventeen-mile-long, nine-mile-wide lagoon choppy, its current strong, and their screws baffled by a riptide, a tug created by large volumes of water being sucked through underwater gaps in the reef. Instants later, they discovered that the Japs had somehow survived the bombardment. At three thousand yards from shore enemy artillery opened up on them; at two thousand yards they came under fire from long-range machine guns, and at eight hundred yards, as their awkward vehicles, half tanks, half boats, waddled over the reef, they were greeted by everything the enemy had, including sniper fire and heavy mortars. The amphtracs, performing as expected, came on. The Higgins boats behind them were stranded on the reef. They lowered their ramps, and the Marines stepped into chest-deep water. Robert Sherrod, then a *Time* war correspondent, has recalled: "It was painfully slow, wading in such deep water. And we had seven hundred yards to walk slowly into this machine-gun fire, looming into larger targets as we rose onto high ground." Aboard one of the American warships a naval officer wrote in his log: "The water seemed never clear of tiny men . . . slowly wading beachward. . . . They kept falling, falling, falling . . . singly, in groups, and in rows." Yet they trudged on, keeping their formations, "calm," in Sherrod's words, "even disdainful of death . . . black dots of men, holding their weapons high above their heads, moving at a snail's pace, never faltering." At Balaklava Pierre Bosquet had said of the Light Brigade: *"C'est magnifique, mais ce n'est pas la guerre."* And at Sedan in the Franco-Prussian War, where the French cavalry charged the Krupp guns again and again, until the last of them lay writhing in their own blood beside the carcasses of their slaughtered mounts, the King of Prussia had lowered his spyglass and murmured: *"Ah, les braves gens!"* Tarawa was more ghastly than magnificent, and it was certainly war, yet after all these years the bravery of its men is still wondrous.

There was a ramshackle, cribwork pier, long and narrow, jutting out from the beach. As shelters the pier's coconut stanchions were pitifully inadequate, but they were better than nothing, and those who reached them unwounded thought themselves lucky. There they crouched, with shellfire pealing in their ears, amid geysers of water from new shells and the smaller splashes from machine guns in the bunkers and Jap snipers tied in the trees overhead, while the precise American invasion plan fell apart. The troops in the amphtracs were luckier than those jumping from the Higgins boats stranded on the coral-reef apron, but in this fire storm danger was merely relative; there was no real safety for anyone. Unprotected by counterbattery fire from the U.S. fleet, which could not risk hitting Americans, five out of every six amphtracs were destroyed or disabled. Some reached the wrong beaches. Some, their coxswains dead, ran amok, spinning crazily and hurling seasick men into the surf. Some toppled into shell holes. And some blew up when enemy bullets pierced their fuel tanks. A survivor of the first wave remembers: "Amphtracs were hit, stopped, and burst into flames, with men jumping out like torches." Craft which survived were shuttling back and forth from the reef, carrying the wounded out and reinforcements in. The commander of the assault, Colonel David M. Shoup, a bullnecked, red-faced fighter who was also a scholar and poet, was wading toward shore when he hailed an amphtrac, ordered its crew to help him toss the Marine corpses in it overboard, rode in, and then set his command post in the shadow of the pier pilings, issuing orders while standing waist-deep in water with two other officers and a sergeant. Shrapnel riddled Shoup's legs; he winced and then braced himself, waving away a corpsman. Other drenched Marines who had made it ashore huddled, terrified, beneath the four-foot seawall. Two brave amphtrac coxswains punched a gap in the long wall. Marines following them actually established a precarious toehold at the edge of the airstrip, about fifty yards inland, but their waterlogged radios didn't work and so Shoup was unaware of their position. Closer to him, another coxswain trying to climb the wall succeeded only in jamming his amphtrac treads against it. The men who had reached the beach alive seemed doomed. One later said that it felt "like being in the middle of a pool table without any pockets."

It was now noon. Because the tide had been misjudged, the Higgins boats couldn't even mount the reef now. Most of the amphtracs had been destroyed. One of them completely disappeared in a shell burst. "It had been there," recalls a Marine who was nearby, "and then suddenly it was not. In its place, for a split second, there was a blur in the air, and then there was nothing." One horrified coxswain lost his mind. On his way in, with bullets rattling on his hull, he screamed, "This is as far as I go!" He dropped his ramp and twenty Marines bowed by weapons and ammunition drowned in fifteen feet of water. A battalion commander elsewhere raised his pistol as he waded in and cried to the men behind him: "Come on, these bastards can't stop us!" A Nambu ripped open his rib cage, killing him instantly. Another battalion commander, gravely wounded in shallow water, crawled on top of a pile of dead Americans to avoid drowning in the incoming tide. He was found there the following afternoon, still alive but raving.

Enemy fire, writes Morison, "was horribly accurate; several times it dropped a shell right on a landing craft just as the ramp came down, spreading a pool of blood around the boat." The Marine dead became part of the terrain; they altered tactics; they provided defilade, and when they had died on barbed-wire obstacles, live men could avoid the wire by crawling over them. Even so, the living were always in some Jap's sights. There were many agents of death on Tarawa: snipers, machine gunners, artillery shells, mortar bursts, the wire, or drowning as a result of stepping into holes in the coral. As the day wore on, the water offshore was a grotesque mass of severed heads, limbs, and torsos. If a body was intact, you could tell which wave it had been in; the freshly killed were limp, with only their scalps and arms visible in the swells, but those who had died in the first hour floated stiffly, like kayaks, showing faces, or pieces of faces. If they had lost all their blood they were marble white, and the stench of their putrefaction soon hung over them. Most of those still alive cowered where they were. One who didn't, a corporal and a professional baseball pitcher in civilian life, crouched beside an amphtrac that Japs were trying to stop with hand grenades. As the grenades sailed in, he fielded them and flung them back as fastballs. Then one took a home-team bounce. Before he could grab it, it exploded. Later his hand was amputated. His example awed his men but did not inspire them. Real leadership was impossible. In a typical company, five of six officers were dead and all the sergeants dead or wounded. The survivors were bunched in little groups of three or four, trembling, sweating, and staring the thousand-yard stare of combat.

By early afternoon, with the tide falling, virtually all in the fourth wave, including 37-millimeter guns and their crews, were blocked by the reef. Some coxswains found holes in the coral; the others would be unable to move until night fell and the tide rose. The fifth wave landed its Sherman tanks on the reef; they plunged into four feet of water on the lee side and churned gamely on. Ashore, the survivors of four assault battalions held a lumpy arc about 300 yards wide which at places, owing to individual acts of heroism, reached a maximum depth of about 150 yards. Shoup had moved his command post fifteen yards in from the surf. His legs streaked with blood, he was standing exactly three feet from a Japanese blockhouse, but owing to the angle of its gunports, he couldn't reach the enemy and they couldn't reach him. Here and there officers and NCOs were shoving and kicking—literally kicking—dazed Marines inland. All the news was bad. The most dismaying reports came from the west, or right, of the island. The seawall was useless in the cove there; a sweeping cross fire enfiladed our riflemen. The battalion commander in the cove, seeing that his men ashore were being scythed by machine gunners, held the rest of them on the reef. He radioed Shoup: "Unable to land. Issue in doubt." After a silence he radioed: "Boats held up on reef of right flank Red One. Troops receiving heavy fire in water." Shoup replied: "Land Red Beach Two"—to the left—"and work west." Another silence from the battalion commander, then: "We have nothing left to land." The officers around Shoup stared at one another. There had been seven hundred men in that battalion. How could there be *nothing* left?

In fact about a hundred of the men were still alive, but in the chaos on the beach, with most radios still sodden or jammed, no one, including Shoup, knew of local successes. There was that tenuous hold on the end of the runway. It lay on the left flank of the assault, east of the pier. There was also the battalion of Major Henry P. "Jim" Crowe, a redheaded mustang, and it had landed intact, thanks to the covering fire of two destroyers. Except for the force on the runway tip, Crowe's men were pinned down on the beach by fire from Jap pillboxes, but he could have silenced them with flamethrowers and TNT satchel charges if he had had enough of them. Chagrin yielded to alarm when an enemy tank appeared, clanking toward the battalion. Two U.S. 37-millimeter antitank guns were offshore in a sunken landing craft. The men hauled them through the languid surf and then, with all hands lifting, the two nine-hundred-pound guns were thrown over the seawall just in time to drive the tank back. On the other end of the Marine position, Major Michael P. Ryan, leading a ragtag force of men who had made it ashore and supported by the 75-millimeter guns of two tanks, overran several enemy positions. But Ryan, too, lacked flamethrowers and TNT. Finding that he couldn't reach Shoup to call for reinforcements, he pulled back to a defense perimeter about five hundred yards deep. On Tarawa that was a victory.

Messages between the troops ashore and the hovering fleet also went astray. In desperation, Shoup sent out an officer (Evans Carlson) in an undamaged amphtrac to beg for men, water, and ammunition. Carlson didn't reach the battleship *Maryland* until late in the evening. By then, however, the plight of the force ashore had become obvious to General Smith, who had been anxiously following the sketchy reports from his CP on the battleship. Smith radioed his senior, Marine General Holland M. Smith, who, aboard the *Pennsylvania,* was commanding both the Makin and Tarawa assaults. His message to Holland Smith was: "Issue in doubt." He wanted the Sixth Marines, which were being held in reserve. Meanwhile he was organizing cooks, field musics, typists, motor transport men, specialists, and staff officers into an improvised battalion which he intended to lead ashore if reinforcements were denied him. But he got the Sixth Marines. At the time it was thought they might just swing the balance, but Shoup's position was at best precarious, and the Japanese were by now notorious for their night counterattacks.

As darkness fell, five thousand Marines on the beach awaited death or terror. Ryan's and Crowe's men were wired in and Shoup held a shallow, boxlike perimeter at the base of the pier. Everything, including ammunition, was in short supply. The beach was covered with shattered vehicles, the dead, the dying, and the wounded awaiting evacuation. Five 75-millimeter pack howitzers were ashore and a few medium tanks; that and the 37-millimeter guns was about it. The tropical moon was only a quarter full, but fuel dumps burning all over Betio provided a lurid, flickering light. Corpsmen worked through the night, ferrying casualties to the reef in large rubber rafts; other rafts brought water, blood plasma, ammunition, and reinforcements to the pier. The men on the perimeter, who thought they were ready for anything, were shocked to find their foxholes raked by machine-gun fire from the sea. Japs had swum out to disabled amphtracs abandoned there and were firing at the Marines' backs. To the Americans that seemed the ultimate blow. Demoralized, they expected a banzai charge at any moment. To their astonishment it didn't come. The night passed quietly. The Japanese had problems, too. Naval gunfire hadn't obliterated the island, but it had inflicted heavy casualties on Nips outside their bunkers. And it had destroyed their communications. Great as Shoup's radio problems were, the Japanese commander's were worse. He couldn't get *any* messages through.

Seawalls are to beachheads what sunken roads—as at Waterloo and Antietam—are to great land battles. They provide inexpressible relief to assault troops who can crouch in their shadows, shielded for the moment from flat-trajectory fire, and they are exasperating to the troops' commanders because they bring the momentum of an attack to a shattering halt. On Tarawa the survival of the American force depended upon individual decisions to risk death. Wellington said, "The whole art of war consists of getting at what is on the other side of the hill." If no one vaulted over the wall, no Marine would leave Betio alive. Naturally everyone wanted others to take the chance. In the end, some did—not many, but a few—and they were responsible for the breakthrough. In defense of those who chose to remain until the odds were shorter it should be said that Tarawa was exceptional. In most instances frontal attacks are unnecessary. Cunning is more effective than daring. Even on Betio, even after the reef blunder and the failure to bombard the enemy until the last possible moment, permitting the shift of defenders to prepared positions on the lagoon side, there was a way out. Ryan provided it. He had turned the Jap flank. If Shoup's radio had worked he would have known that and could have strengthened Ryan, rolling up the Nip defenses from the rear. So the instincts of the rifleman who hides behind the wall are usually sound. At least that is what I tell myself whenever I think of Tubby Morris.

My seawall was on Oroku. There was no reef to speak of, and though enemy fire was heavy as the Higgins boats brought us in—we were soaked with splashes from near misses, and we could hear the small-arms lead pinging on our hulls—we lost very few men in the landing. Then we saw the seawall and thanked God for it. It was built of sturdy logs and stood over five feet high. Incongruously, an enormous scarlet vine rioted over the lower half of it. Between there and the surf line the beach was about ten feet deep. It looked wonderful. I was prepared to spend the rest of my life on those ten feet. A braver man, I knew, would try to skirt the wall and find Jap targets. But enemy machine gunners knew where we were. Nambus were chipping at the top of the wall; you could see the splinters. Even if I hadn't been determined to save my own skin, which I certainly was, there were other reasons for staying put. I was surrounded by the Raggedy Ass Marines, the least subordinate of fighters.

I knew that if I went up I would be alone. Furthermore, it seemed possible, even probable, that the Firt Battalion, on our extreme right, could envelop the Nips. The seawall tapered off in that direction, and the map showed an inlet where our men had room to move around. Anyhow, I was going to give them their chance and all the time they wanted.

That was when Tubby arrived in the third wave. He had been in my officer candidate class at Quantico, and unlike me he had been commissioned. Now he was a second lieutenant, a replacement officer making his debut as a leader, or presumed leader, of seasoned troops. If there is a more pitiful role in war, I don't know it. Troops are wary of untested officers, and the Raggedy Ass Marines were contemptuous of them. Some of them, like me, remembered him from Quantico. He hadn't changed since we had last seen him; he was a stubby, brisk youth, in his early twenties but already running to fat around the jowls and belly. He had the sleek peach complexion of a baby and a perpetual frown, not of petulance but of concentration. I hadn't known him well. He had the megalomania of undersized men. He was like one of those boys who always do their homework at school and never let you copy. He had been an overachiever, determined to please his superiors, but there had been many like him at Quantico. Here, however, he was unique. Among men who prided themselves on the saltiness—shabbiness—of their uniforms, his was right off the quartermaster's shelf. I wondered whether he had been disappointed when they told him not to wear his bars in combat, for whatever his other failings he was, and was soon to prove, courageous.

He caught his breath, looked around, and said, "I'm your new officer." I grinned, held out my hand, and said, "Hi, Tubby." That was stupid of me. He glared and kept his own hand on his trouser seam. Standing cockily like a bantam rooster—the wall was just high enough to let him stand—he crisply asked, "Sergeant, are these your men?" The Raggedy Asses grinned at one another. The very thought of belonging to *anyone* amused them. I felt cold. This wasn't the good-natured Tubby I had known. This was trouble. I said, "Tubby—" and he cut me off: "Slim, I am an officer and I expect to be treated with proper military courtesy." That broke the men up. He heard their stifled chuckles and looked around furiously. It was an insane situation. Here we were, in the middle of a battle, and Tubby seemed to expect a salute, if not homage, from me. There wasn't much room, but I said in a low voice, "Let's talk this over," moved away a few feet, and knelt. He bridled, but came over and squatted beside me. I told him that I didn't want to undermine him, that I hadn't meant to sound familiar, and that I was sorry. His jaw muscles were working. He said, "You should be." Anger stirred in me. Looking back, I see that my motives were less selfless than I thought then. My sympathy for his position, though genuine, was tained by resentment at taking orders from this little man whose background was no different from mine, by irrational scorn of junior officers who hadn't yet proved themselves, and by the arrogance which combat veterans feel toward all green replacements, especially platoon leaders. At that moment, however, all I saw was that there was bound to be a certain stiffness between us which we would probably work around in time. Then I learned that for Tubby there wasn't much time. He said, "Don't tell me. Show me. I'm going to lead these people over the top, and I want you with me."

He actually said "over the top." We didn't talk like that. He must have heard it from his father. World War I soldiers left their trenches to go over the top, over the parapet, into no-man's-land. Then the implication of what he had said hit me. I whispered, "You mean over this wall?" He nodded once, a quick little jerk of his head. He said, "That's where the Japs are. You can't kill them if you can't see them." I felt numb. I said, "Look, Tubby—Lieutenant—I think—" He snapped, "You're not paid to think. You're paid to take orders." I considered saying the hell with it. But this was literally a matter of life or imminent death. I tried again, earnestly: "Going up there would be suicide. The First Bat's down there," I said, pointing. "Give them a chance to turn the Nips' flank and roll up those machine-gun nests." He growled, "What's the matter with *this* battalion?" I said, "We're pinned down, so the action is on the flanks." I could see I wasn't convincing him, and I said hoarsely, "Tubby, I know they didn't teach you that at Quantico, but that's how we do it here. You're not on some fucking parade ground. You can't just pump your fist up and down and expect the men to spring up. They won't do it. *They won't do it.* I've been out here a long time, Tubby. I *know.*"

He stared at me for a long time, as though waiting for me to blink first. I blinked and blinked again. Letting his voice rise, he said, "You're scared shitless, aren't you?" I nodded emphatically. His voice rose higher. All the guys could hear him now. He said, "That's why I put up bars and you're just an NCO. They could tell the difference between us in O.C. I've got balls and you haven't." There was just a tremor in his voice, and it dawned on me that he himself was petrified—he was masking his fear with his rudeness to me. But what he said next smothered my compassion. He sneered, and keeping his voice in the same register, he said: "I know your kind, Bub. You think we couldn't hear you back there in the squad bay, masturbating every night? Did you think they'd give a Marine Corps commission to a masturbator? Only thing I couldn't make out was how you dried the come. I figured you had a handkerchief." I heard a titter from Bubba. I'm sure Bubba had never masturbated. His father, the Alabama preacher in whose steps he hoped to follow, had shown him the way to what he called "Nigra poontang" when he reached adolescence. But I wasn't interested in Bubba's good opinion. What Tubby had done, and it was unforgivable, was make me look ridiculous in the eyes of all my men. He knew that was wrong. They *had* taught *that* at Quantico. By mocking me he had contaminated both of us. I thought: *Since I am a dog, beware my fangs.* He and I were through. He was past saving now. His longevity would be less than a Jap's. No one could lengthen it for him. I've kept telling myself that all these years, but there will always be a tug of guilt.

Rising in one swift motion, he wiped his hands on his sturdy thighs, stood with arms akimbo, and barked: "Men, I know you'd like to stay here. I would myself. But those yellow bastards down the beach are killing your buddies." He didn't even realize that a combat man's loyalty is confined to those around him, that as far as the Raggedy Ass Marines were concerned the First Battalion might as well have belonged to a separate race. He said, "Our duty lies up there." He pointed. He went on: "That's what we call a target of opportunity, lads." He paused, and his pouter-pigeon breast swelled. I wondered if he was trying to imitate Chesty Puller, that legendary Marine hero who is said to have boasted that he would win a Medal of Honor if he had to bring home a seabag full of dog tags. Tubby said, "I'm not going to ask any of you people to do what I don't do. I'm going up first. Your sergeant will—" He checked himself. "It's your sergeant's job to see that every man follows me." I was still down on one knee, eyes averted, running sand through my fingers. I wanted no part of this. He asked, "Any questions?"

They looked up at him glassily. He hesitated, probably wondering whether he should threaten them with courts-martial. Then he turned and sprang at the seawall. He was too short. He couldn't get a footing. He tried to stick one boondocker in a vine crotch, but the V was too tight. He could only wedge his toe in sideways, and that didn't give him the right leverage. Panting, he tried again and again. He turned to me, his face flushed. He said, "Help me." He must have hated to ask. I certainly hated his asking. I felt an insane urge to laugh, which I knew would turn into weeping. I looked into his wide eyes and said, "My legs are too shaky." It was true. He said between his teeth, "I'll take care of you later." He turned, pointed to Bubba, and said, "You, over here." Bubba came over and linked his hands. Tubby put in a foot, as if into a stirrup, swung up, rolled atop the wall, and rose till he stood sideways. Both his hands were pointing. His left forefinger was pointed down at us, his right forefinger at the Japs. It was a Frederic Remington painting. He breathed deeply and yelled, *"Follow me!"*

The men's faces still were turned up, expressionless. Nobody moved. I stood beneath the wall, my arms outstretched, waiting to catch what would be left. At that moment the slugs hit him. It was a Nambu; it stitched him vertically, from forehead to crotch. One moment he was looming above us in that heroic pose; in the next moment red pits blossomed down him, four on his face alone, and a dozen others down his uniform. One was off center; it slammed in the Marine Corps emblem over his heart; the gunner knew his job. Blood had just begun to stream from there, from his face, from his belly, and from his groin, when he collapsed, tottering on the edge and falling and whumping in my arms face up. His features were disappearing beneath a spreading stain, and he was trying to blink the blood out of his eyes. But he could see. He saw me. He choked faintly: "You . . . you . . . you . . ." Then he gagged and he was gone.

I looked away, feeling queasy. My blouse was wet with gore. Mo Crocker and Dusty Rhodes took Tubby from me and gently laid him out. There was no malice in the section. They mourned him as they would have mourned any casualty. They—and I above all—had merely been unwilling to share his folly. It was followed by savage irony. We had scarcely finished trussing him up in a poncho when we heard the sound of cheering to our right. The First Bat had turned the Jap flank. You could just see the bobbing of the camouflaged helmet covers and the moving line of smoke, and you could hear the snuffling of the tanks as their drivers shifted gears. I raged as I had raged over the death of Zepp. It was the sheer futility of it which was unbearable. Then I was diverted, as death in its grisly mercy diverts you, by the necessity of disposing of the corpse. I said to Knocko, "Pass the word to Buck Rogers—" Suddenly I realized that Buck might not still be alive, and that because Tubby had arrived so recently, his name might be unknown at the CP anyhow. Instead, I said, "The new lieutenant is dead. Pass the word to the nearest officer."

One of the problems at Tarawa was the uniforms. When General Smith said the Marines' armor would be limited to khaki, he was speaking figuratively. The men actually wore new jungle suits, camouflaged green on one side and brown on the other, presumably for use if the Marine Corps found itself fighting in the Sahara Desert. But the designers of the suits had neglected to make them porous. Wearing them was like being wrapped in plastic. The men would have sweated that first night on Betio whatever they wore—they were just ninety miles from the equator—but in those suits they lost pounds, and greeted the dawn gaunt and shrunken. In the early light, they saw that their lines were intact. That heartened them, and led many to conclude that the crisis was past. They were wrong. As the struggle resumed its ferocity, Sherrod heard on all sides the *pi-ing* of enemy rifles rippling the air and the *ratatatata* and the *brrrp* of their machine guns. In five minutes he saw six Marines die. He wrote: "This is worse, far worse than it was yesterday." The battleship *Maryland,* with communications restored, radioed Shoup, asking him if he had enough men. He said he didn't and added: "Imperative you land ammunition, water, rations and medical supplies. . . . Imperative you get all types of ammunition to all landing parties immediately." The corpsmen ran out of bandages. Shoup ordered them to wade out to the reef and strip dead Marines of first-aid kits that all men carried on their belts. At midmorning he told Sherrod: "We're in a mighty tough spot." At 11:00 a.m. he radioed General Julian Smith: "Situation doesn't look good ashore."

The immediate problem was bringing in reinforcements from the Sixth Marines. They had been waiting in Higgins boats for nearly twenty hours, trying to find a way past or over the reef. The Japs on the stranded amphtracs were still in position, firing seaward now, their .303-caliber copper bullets hitting with remarkable accuracy whenever men on the landing craft peered over their bulkheads. Nambus seemed to be firing on all sides. One was set up on a Jap privy built over the water. The greatest danger, however, came from the hulk of an old freighter to the right of the pier, about seven hundred yards out. From here the enemy could smash the fuel tanks of landing craft, exploding them, and zero in on the Sixth Marines as they jumped out into the water and started trudging in. There were 800 Marines when they started; 450 made it to the beach.

Marines already ashore rocked the freighter with 75-millimeter pack howitzers and 81-millimeter mortars, and dive-bombers from U.S. carriers tried to take it out, but it seemed indestructible. A naval officer on one Higgins boat suggested to debarking men that they keep the boat between them and the hulk, as a shield, but, as the officer recalls, "They told us to follow the plan and retire so other waves could get to help them." It was at this point that the erratic Betio tide began to rise, threatening the wounded men lying on the reef with drowning. A salvage crew from the transport *Sheridan,* rescuing them, encountered about thirty-five Marines, unharmed but lacking weapons. The skipper offered to evacuate them. They shook their heads, asking only that the crew "bring back something to fight with." During the five hours needed to land the First Battalion of the Eighth Marines—the last of the reinforcements—its casualties were greater than those of any battalion reaching shore the day before.

The survivors strengthened Ryan's end of the beachhead. At daybreak, his communication with the fleet reestablished, he had called in a barrage of five-inch shells from a destroyer offshore. With those salvos and fire from two tanks, he recovered the ground that he had yielded the previous afternoon; pushing on, he crossed the airfield and established an anchor on Betio's south shore. This time Shoup learned of Ryan's progress and altered his tactics to exploit it. As Tarawa's tide turned, the tide of the battle was at last turning with it. The freighter hulk was annihilated by concentrated fire. Jim Crowe's mortars and a seemingly invincible tank christened "Colorado" were cracking pillboxes open. Flamethrowers, suddenly plentiful, licked at spider holes and bunkers. One two-story concrete blockhouse, intact despite point-blank fire from a destroyer, was knocked out when a Marine tank crawled up to the entrance and blasted away. Over three hundred charred corpses were later found inside. The western half of Betio was now in American hands. Shoup radioed the fleet: "Casualties many; percentage dead not known: we are winning."

The Japanese didn't think so. They laid down such heavy howitzer fire on Shoup's left flank, resting on a Burns-Philip Company wharf, that any U.S. advance there was out of the question. The enemy didn't know about the cargoes of equipment, supplies, and plasma coming in over the now-submerged reef, or that another battalion had reached Ryan—the first to stream ashore with few casualties and dry weapons. The Nips' will to resist was as inflexible as ever. As American firepower drove them back and back on the eastern half of the island, their snipers scampered up palm trees or lay among their dead comrades, feigning death until they could leap up and attack Marines whose backs were to them. Monday night they launched three vicious counterattacks against the Marine line, which now lay athwart the entire island. Despite naval gunfire and Marine artillery, some Japs penetrated the American perimeter. Hand-to-hand fighting followed, with Kabars and bayonets. A Marine lieutenant sent back word: "We're killing them as fast as they come at us, but we can't hold much longer. We need reinforcements." He was told: "We haven't got them to send you. You've got to hold."

They did; Tuesday morning they counted 325 Jap bodies around their foxholes. At the time it was impolitic to pay the slightest tribute to the enemy, and Nip determination, their refusal to say die, was commonly attributed to "fanaticism." In retrospect it is indistinguishable from heroism. To call it anything less cheapens the victory, for American valor was necessary to defeat it. There were brave Marines, too, men who didn't commit suicide, as Tubby did, but who knew the risk, decided an objective was worth it, and never looked back. There was Jim Crowe, charging and shouting over his shoulder, "You'll never get the Purple Heart a-laying in those foxholes, men!" There was Lieutenant William "Hawk" Hawkins, who knocked out machine guns by standing in full view of the gunners and firing into pillbox slits, then tossing in grenades to finish off the Nips inside. He was wounded by a mortar burst and told a corpsman: "I came here to kill Japs, not to be evacuated." Still erect in the terrible heat, Hawk blew up three more pillboxes before a shell killed him. And there was Lieutenant Alexander Bonnyman, an officer of engineers who could have left the fighting to the infantry but who chose to attack the enemy's huge headquarters fortress bunker with five of his men. They climbed up the tough, stringy weeds of the slope outside to reach the roof, the highest point on the island. A door opened and a horde of Japanese poured out to drive him off. Bonnyman remained standing for thirty seconds, firing a carbine and then a flamethrower before he fell, mortally wounded. He had held the erupting Nips off just long enough for his men to drop grenades into the strongpoint's ventilation system. When the grenades exploded, more Nips swarmed up. Shells and small-arms fire drove them back. A bulldozer sealed the entry. Gasoline was poured in vents still open and ignited by TNT. The Marines heard the blasts, then screams, then nothing. Inside were nearly two hundred Japanese corpses.

One of them was that of the Jap admiral commanding Betio's defenses. His faith in Tarawa's impregnability had been based on the assumption that if he were attacked, Tokyo would send him warships, warplanes, and more troops. His superior had assured him that Tarawa would be "a hornet's nest for the Yankees." He couldn't imagine what had gone wrong. We know now. Because of America's twin-pronged drive, the men and equipment which had been earmarked for him had gone to Bougainville, under assault by the Third Marine Division, and to MacArthur's objectives in New Guinea. Shortly before Bonnyman's feat, the doomed admiral had radioed Tokyo: "Our weapons have been destroyed, and from now on everyone is attempting a final charge. . . . May Japan exist for ten thousand years!" Leaderless now, the remaining Nips formed for the first of those suicidal banzai charges or took their lives in a sick ritual which would soon be familiar to American assault troops all over the Pacific: lying down, jamming the muzzle of an Arisaka rifle in the mouth, and squeezing the trigger with the big toe. By Tuesday Japanese resistance had collapsed. Except for seventeen Nips who surrendered, all were dead or fugitives, running across the reef to other islands in Tarawa's atoll, where they were soon pursued and shot. Tokyo's commentators eulogized them as "flowers of the Pacific" and quickly turned to other news, as well they might. Tarawa had been a Nipponese disaster. Already Hellcats were landing on Betio's airstrip, named Hawkins Field for Hawk. At 1:10 P.M. Tuesday the battle was officially ended. It had lasted seventy-six hours, and the only dispute about it now was whether the island's bird-shaped fragment of coral was worth the price the Americans had paid.

All Quiet on the Western Front

BY ERICH MARIA REMARQUE

ERNEST HEMINGWAY ONCE called World War I "the most colossal, murderous, mismanaged butchery that has ever taken place on earth."

"Papa" Hemingway isn't likely to draw any return fire over that one. The literature that lines shelf after shelf describes suicidal attacks by waves and waves of men walking into machine gun and artillery fire across open ground on "no man's land"—and being cut down like rows of wheat—without a prayer of a chance of achieving their objectives. Endless mud, disease, hunger, and pain made the trenches hell on earth. In many cases, the orders of bombastic, self-aggrandizing, insensitive fools in command sent the finest young men of England, France, and Germany to their dooms.

One of the famous accounts of life in the trenches as seen through the eyes of a common soldier was written about a German soldier by Erich Maria Remarque. *All Quiet on the Western Front* is an enduring classic. This excerpt is from the final pages of the book.

★　★　★　★　★

We count the weeks no more. It was winter when I came up, and when the shells exploded the frozen clods of earth were just as dangerous as the fragments. Now the trees are green again. Our life alternates between billets and the front. We have almost grown accustomed to it; war is a cause of death like cancer and tuberculosis, like influenza and dysentery. The deaths are merely more frequent, more varied and terrible.

Our thoughts are clay, they are moulded with the changes of the days;—when we are resting they are good; under fire, they are dead. Fields of craters within and without.

Everyone is so, not only ourselves here—the things that existed before are no longer valid, and one practically knows them no more. Distinctions, breeding, education are changed, are almost blotted out and hardly recognizable any longer. Sometimes they give an advantage for profiting by a situation;—but they also bring consequences along with them, in that they arouse prejudices which have to be overcome. It is as though formerly we were coins of different provinces; and now we are melted down, and all bear the same stamp. To re-discover the old distinctions, the metal itself must be tested. First we are soldiers and afterwards, in a strange and shamefaced fashion, individual men as well.

It is a great brotherhood, which to a condition of life arising out of the midst of danger, out of the tension and forlornness of death, adds something of the good-fellowship of the folk-song, of the feeling of solidarity of convicts, and of the desperate loyalty to one another of men condemned to death—seeking in a wholly unpathetic way a fleeting enjoyment of the hours as they come. If one wants to appraise it, it is at once heroic and banal—but who wants to do that?

It is this, for example, that makes Tjaden spoon down his ham-and-pea soup in such tearing haste when an enemy attack is reported, simply because he cannot be sure that in an hour's time he will still be alive. We have discussed at length, whether it is right or not to do so. Kat condemns it, because, he says, a man has to reckon with the possibility of an abdominal wound, and that is more dangerous on a full stomach than on an empty one.

Such things are real problems, they are serious matters to us, they cannot be otherwise. Here, on the borders of death, life follows an amazingly simple course, it is limited to what is most necessary, all else lies buried in gloomy sleep;—in that lies our primitiveness and our survival. Were we more subtly differentiated we must long since have gone mad, have deserted, or have fallen. As in a polar expedition, every expression of life must serve only the preservation of existence, and is absolutely focussed on that. All else is banished because it would consume energies unnecessarily. That is the only way to save ourselves. In the quiet hours when the puzzling reflection of former days, like a blurred mirror, projects beyond me the figure of my present existence, I often sit over against myself, as before a stranger, and wonder how the unnameable active principle that calls itself Lie has adapted itself even to this form. All other expressions lie in a winter sleep, life is simply one continual watch against the menace of death;—it has transformed us into unthinking animals in order to give us the weapon of instinct—it has reinforced us with dullness, so that we do not go to pieces before the horror, which would overwhelm us if we had clear, conscious thought—it has awakened in us the sense of comradeship, so that we escape the abyss of solitude—it has lent us the indifference of wild creatures, so that in spite of all we perceive the positive in every moment, and store it up as a reserve against the onslaught of nothingness. Thus we live a closed, hard existence of the utmost superficiality, and rarely does an incident strike out a spark. But then unexpectedly a flame of grievous and terrible yearning flares up.

Those are the dangerous moments. They show us that the adjustment is only artificial, that it is not simple rest, but sharpest struggle for rest. In the outward form of our life we are hardly distinguishable from Bushmen; but whereas the latter can be so always, because they are so truly, and at best may develop further by exertion of their spiritual forces, with us it is the reverse;— our inner forces are not exerted toward regeneration, but toward degeneration. The Bushmen are primitive and naturally so, but we are primitive in an artificial sense, and by the virtue of the utmost effort.

And at night, waking out of a dream, overwhelmed and bewitched by the crowding faces, a man perceives with alarm how slight is the support, how thin the boundary that divides him from the darkness. We are little flames poorly sheltered by frail walls against the storm of dissolution and madness, in which we flicker and sometimes almost go out. Then the muffled roar of the battle becomes a ring that encircles us, we creep in upon ourselves, and with big eyes stare into the night. Our only comfort is the steady breathing of our comrades asleep, and thus we wait for the morning.

Every day and every hour, every shell and every death cuts into this thin support, and the years waste it rapidly. I see how it is already gradually breaking down around me.

There is the mad story of Detering.

He was one of those who kept himself to himself. His misfortune was that he saw a cherry tree in a garden. We were just coming back from the front-line, and at a turning of the road near our new billets, marvellous in the morning twilight, stood this cherry tree before us. It had no leaves, but was one white mass of blossom.

In the evening Detering was not to be seen. Then at last he came back and had a couple of branches of cherry blossom in his hand. We made fun of him, and asked whether he was going to a wedding. He made no answer, but laid them on his bed. During the night I heard him making a noise, he seemed to be packing. I sensed something amiss and went over to him. He made out it was nothing, and I said to him: "Don't do anything silly, Detering."

"Ach, why—it's merely that I can't sleep—"

"What did you pick the cherry branches for?"

"I might have been going to get some more cherry branches," he replied, evasively—and after a while: "I have a big orchard with cherry trees at home. When they are in blossom, from the hay loft they look like one single sheet, so white. It is just the time."

"Perhaps you will get leave soon. You may even be sent back as a farmer."

He nodded, but he was far away. When these peasants are excited they have a curious expression, a mixture of cow and yearning god, half stupid and half rapt. In order to turn him away from his thoughts I asked him for a piece of bread. He gave it to me without a murmur. That was suspicious, for he is usually tight-fisted. So I stayed awake. Nothing happened; in the morning he was as usual.

Apparently he had noticed that I had been watching him;—but the second morning after he was gone. I noticed it but said nothing, in order to give him time; he might perhaps get through. Various fellows have already got into Holland.

But at roll call he was missed. A week after we heard that he had been caught by the field gendarmes, those despicable military police. He had headed toward Germany, that was hopeless, of course—and, of course, he did everything else just as idiotically. Anyone might have known that his flight was only home-sickness and a momentary aberration. But what does a court-martial hundreds of miles behind the front-line know about it? We have heard nothing more of Detering.

But sometimes it broke out in other ways, this danger, these pent-up things, as from an overheated boiler. It will be enough to tell how Berger met his end.

Our trenches have now for some time been shot to pieces, and we have an elastic line, so that there is practically no longer any proper trench warfare. When attack and counter-attack have waged backwards and forwards there remains a broken line and a bitter struggle from crater to crater. The front-line has been penetrated, and everywhere small groups have established themselves, the fight is being carried on from small clusters of shell-holes.

We are in a crater, the English are coming down obliquely, they are turning our flank and working in behind us. We are surrounded. It is not easy to surrender, fog and smoke hang over us, no one would recognize that we wanted to give ourselves up, and perhaps we don't want to, a man doesn't even know himself at such moments. We hear the explosions of the hand-grenades coming toward us. Our machine-gun sweeps over the semicircle in front of us. The cooling-water evaporates, we hastily pass round the case, every man urinates in it, and thus we again have water, and are able to continue firing. But behind us the attack crashes ever nearer.

A few minutes and we are lost.

Then, at closest range, a second machine-gun bursts out. It is set up in a crater alongside us; Berger has fetched it, and now the counter-attack comes over from behind; we are set free and make contact with the rear.

Afterwards, as we lie in comparatively good cover, one of the food-carriers reports that a couple of hundred yards distant there lies a wounded messenger-dog.

"Where?" asks Berger.

The other describes the place to him. Berger goes off either to fetch the beast in or to shoot it. Six months ago he would not have cared, he would have been reasonable. We try to prevent him. Then, as he goes off grimly, all we can say is: "You're mad," and let him go. For these cases of front-line madness become dangerous if one is not able to fling the man to the ground and hold him fast. And Berger is six feet and the most powerful man in the company.

He is absolutely mad for he has to pass through the barrage; but this lightning that lowers somewhere above us all has struck him and made him demented. It affects others so that they begin to rave, to run away—there was one man who even tried to dig himself into the ground with hands, feet, and teeth.

It is true, such things are often simulated, but the pretence itself is a symptom. Berger, who means to finish off the dog, is carried off with a wound in the pelvis, and one of the fellows who carry him gets a bullet in the cheek while doing it.

Müller is dead. Someone shot him point blank with a Verey light in the stomach. He lived for half an hour, quite conscious, and in terrible pain.

Before he died he handed over his pocketbook to me, and bequeathed me his boots—the same that he once inherited from Kemmerich. I wear them, for they fit me quite well. After me Tjaden will get them, I have promised them to him.

We have been able to bury Müller, but he is not likely to remain long undisturbed. Our lines are falling back. There are too many fresh English and American regiments over there. There's too much corned beef and white wheaten bread. Too many new guns. Too many aeroplanes.

But we are emaciated and starved. Our food is so bad and mixed up with so much substitute stuff that it makes us ill. The factory owners in Germany have grown wealthy;—dysentery dissolves our bowels. The latrine poles are always densely crowded; the people at home ought to be shown these grey, yellow, miserable, wasted faces here, these bent figures from whose bodies the colic wrings out the blood, and who with lips trembling and distorted with pain, grin at one another and say: "It is not much sense pulling up one's trousers again—"

Our artillery is fired out, it has too few shells and the barrels are so worn that they shoot uncertainly, and scatter so widely as even to fall on ourselves. We have too few horses. Our fresh troops are anaemic boys in need of rest, who cannot carry a pack, but merely know how to die. By thousands. They understand nothing about warfare, they simply go on and let themselves be shot down. A single flyer routed two companies of them for a joke, just as they came fresh from the train—before they had ever heard of such a thing as cover.

"Germany ought to be empty soon," says Kat.

We have given up hope that some day an end may come. We never think so far. A man can stop a bullet and be killed; he can get wounded, and then the hospital is his next stop. There, if they do not amputate him, he sooner or later falls into the hands of one of those staff surgeons who, with the War Service Cross in his buttonhole, says to him: "What, one leg a bit short? If you have any pluck you don't need to run at the front. The man is A1. Dismiss!"

Kat tells a story that has travelled the whole length of the front from the Vosges to Flanders;—of the staff surgeon who reads the names on the list, and when a man comes before him, without looking up says: "A1. We need soldiers up there." A fellow with a wooden leg comes up before him, the staff surgeon again says A1—"And then," Kat raises his voice, "the fellow says to him: 'I already have a wooden leg, but when I go back again and they shoot off my head, then I will get a wooden head made and become a staff surgeon.'" This answer tickles us all immensely.

There may be good doctors, and there are, lots of them; all the same, every soldier some time during his hundreds of inspections falls into the clutches of one of these countless hero-grabbers who pride themselves on changing as many C3's and B3's as possible into A1's.

There are many such stories, they are mostly far more bitter. All the same, they have nothing to do with mutiny or lead-swinging. They are merely honest and call a thing by its name; for there is a very great deal of fraud, injustice, and baseness in the army.—Is it nothing that regiment after regiment returns again and again to the ever more hopeless struggle, that attack follows attack along the weakening, retreating, crumbling line?

From a mockery the tanks have become a terrible weapon. Armoured they come rolling on in long lines, and more than anything else embody for us war's horror.

We do not see the guns that bombard us; the attacking lines of the enemy infantry are men like ourselves; but these tanks are machines, their caterpillars run on as endless as the war, they are annihilation, they roll without feeling into the craters, and climb up again without stopping, a fleet of roaring, smoke-belching armour-clads, invulnerable steel beasts squashing the dead and the wounded—we shrivel up in our thin skin before them, against their colossal weight our arms are sticks of straw, and our hand-grenades matches.

Shells, gas clouds, and flotillas of tanks—shattering, starvation, death.

Dysentery, influenza, typhus—murder, burning, death.

Trenches, hospitals, the common grave—there are no other possibilities.

In one attack our company commander, Bertinck, falls. He was one of those superb front-line officers who are foremost in every hot place. He was with us for two years without being wounded, so that something had to happen in the end.

We occupy a crater and get surrounded. The stink of petroleum or oil blows across with the fumes of powder. Two fellows with a flame-thrower are seen, one carries the tin on his back, the other has the hose in his hands from which the fire spouts. If they get so near that they can reach us we are done for, we cannot retreat at the moment.

We open fire on them. But they work nearer and things begin to look bad. Bertinck is lying in the hole with us. When he sees that we cannot escape because under the sharp fire we must make the most of this cover, he takes a rifle, crawls out of the hole, and lying down propped on his elbows, he takes aim. He fires—the same moment a bullet smacks into him, they have got him. Still he lies and aims again;—once he shifts and again takes his aim; at last the rifle cracks. Bertinck lets the gun drop and says: "Good," and slips back into the hole. The hindermost of the two flame-throwers is hit, he falls, the hose slips away from the other fellow, the fire squirts about on all sides and the man burns.

Bertinck has a chest wound. After a while a fragment smashes away his chin, and the same fragment has sufficient force to tear open Leer's hip. Leer groans as he supports himself on his arm, he bleeds quickly, no one can help him. Like an emptying tube, after a couple of minutes he collapses.

What use is it to him now that he was such a good mathematician at school?

The months pass by. The summer of 1918 is the most bloody and the most terrible. The days stand like angels in gold and blue, incomprehensible, above the ring of annihilation. Every man here knows that we are losing the war. Not much is said about it, we are falling back, we will not be able to attack again after this big offensive, we have no more men and no more ammunition.

Still the campaign goes on—the dying goes on—

Summer of 1918—Never has life in its niggardliness seemed to us so desirable as now;—the red poppies in the meadows round our billets, the smooth beetles on the blades of grass, the warm evenings in the cool, dim rooms, the black, mysterious trees of the twilight, the stars and the flowing waters, dreams and long sleep—O Life, life, life!

Summer of 1918—Never was so much silently suffered as in the moment when we depart once again for the front-line. Wild, tormenting rumours of an armistice and peace are in the air, they lay hold on our hearts and make the return to the front harder than ever.

Summer of 1918—Never was life in the line more bitter and more full of horror than in the hours of the bombardment, when the blanched faces lie in the dirt, and the hands clutch at the one thought: No! No! Not now! Not now at the last moment!

Summer of 1918—Breath of hope that sweeps over the scorched fields, raging fever of impatience, of disappointment, of the most agonizing terror of death, insensate question: Why? Why do they not make an end? And why do these rumours of an end continue to fly about?

There are so many airmen here, and they are so sure of themselves that they give chase to single individuals, just as though they were hares. For every one German plane there come at least five English and American. For one hungry, wretched German soldier come five of the enemy, fresh and fit. For one Germany army loaf there are fifty tins of canned beef over there. We are not beaten, for as soldiers we are better and more experienced; we are simply crushed and driven back by overwhelmingly superior forces.

Behind us lie rainy weeks—grey sky, grey fluid earth, grey dying. If we go out, the rain at once soaks through our overcoat and clothing;—and we remain wet all the time we are in the line. We never get dry. Those who still wear high boots tie sand bags round the top so that the mud does not pour in so fast. The rifles are caked, the uniforms caked, everything is fluid and dissolved, the earth one dripping, soaked, oily mass in which lie the yellow pools with red spiral streams of blood and into which the dead, wounded, and survivors slowly sink down.

The storm lashes us, out of the confusion of grey and yellow the hail of splinters whips forth the childlike cries of the wounded, and in the night shattered life groans wearily to the silence.

Our hands are earth, our bodies clay and our eyes pools of rain. We do not know whether we still live.

Then the heat sinks heavily into our shell-holes like a jelly-fish, moist and oppressive, and on one of these late summer days, while bringing food, Kat falls. We two are alone. I bind up his wound; his shin seems to be smashed. It has got the bone, and Kat groans desperately: "At last—just at the last—"

I comfort him. "Who knows how long the mess will go on yet! Now you are saved—"

The wound begins to bleed fast. Kat cannot be left by himself while I try to find a stretcher. Anyway, I don't know of a stretcher-bearer's post in the neighbourhood.

Kat is not very heavy; so I take him up on my back and start off to the dressing-station with him.

Twice we rest. He suffers acutely on the way. We do not speak much. I have opened the collar of my tunic and breathe heavily, I sweat and my face is swollen with the strain of carrying. All the same I urge him to let us go on, for the place is dangerous.

"Shall we go on again, Kat?"

"Must, Paul."

"Then come."

I raise him up, he stands on the uninjured leg and supports himself against a tree. I take up the wounded leg carefully, then he gives a jump and I take the knee of the sound leg also under my arm.

The going is more difficult. Often a shell whistles across. I go as quickly as I can, for the blood from Kat's wound drips to the ground. We cannot shelter ourselves properly from the explosions; before we can take cover the danger is all over.

We lie down in a small shell-hole to rest. I give Kat some tea from my water bottle. We smoke a cigarette. "Well, Kat," I say gloomily, "we are going to be separated."

He is silent and looks at me.

"Do you remember, Kat, how we commandeered the goose? And how you brought me out of the barrage when I was still a young recruit and was wounded for the first time? I cried then. Kat, that is almost three years ago."

He nods.

The anguish of solitude rises up in me. When Kat is taken away I will not have one friend left.

"Kat, in any case we must see one another again, if it is peace time before you come back."

"Do you think that I will be marked A1 again with this leg?" he asks bitterly.

"With rest it will get better. The joint is all right. It may limp a bit."

"Give me another cigarette," he says.

"Perhaps we could do something together later on, Kat." I am very miserable, it is impossible that Kat—Kat my friend, Kat with the drooping shoulders and the poor, thin moustache, Kat, whom I know as I know no other man, Kat with whom I have shared these years—it is impossible that perhaps I shall not see Kat again.

"In any case give me your address at home, Kat. And here is mine, I will write it down for you."

I write his address in my pocketbook. How forlorn I am already, though he still sits here beside me. Couldn't I shoot myself quickly in the foot so as to be able to go?

Suddenly Kat gurgles and turns green and yellow. "Let us go on," he stammers.

I jump up, eager to help him, I take him up and start off at a run, a slow steady pace, so as not to jolt his leg too much.

My throat is parched; everything dances red and black before my eyes, I stagger on doggedly and pitilessly and at last reach the dressing-station.

There I drop down on my knees, but have still enough strength to fall on to the side where Kat's sound leg is. After a few minutes I straighten myself up again. My legs and my hands tremble. I have trouble in finding my water bottle, to take a pull. My lips tremble as I try to drink. But I smile—Kat is saved.

After a while I begin to sort out the confusion of voices that falls on my ears.

"You might have spared yourself that," says an orderly.

I look at him without comprehending.

He points to Kat. "He is stone dead."

I do not understand him. "He has been hit in the shin," I say.

The orderly stands still. "That as well."

I turn round. My eyes are still dulled, the sweat breaks out on me again, it runs over my eyelids. I wipe it away and peer at Kat. He lies still. "Fainted," I say quickly.

The orderly whistles softly. "I know better than that. He is dead. I'll lay any money on that."

I shake my head: "Not possible. Only ten minutes ago I was talking to him. He has fainted."

Kat's hands are warm, I pass my arm under his shoulders in order to rub his temples with some tea. I feel my fingers become moist. As I draw them away from behind his head, they are bloody. "You see—" The orderly whistles once more through his teeth.

On the way without my having noticed it, Kat has caught a splinter in the head. There is just one little hole, it must have been a very tiny, stray splinter. But it has sufficed. Kat is dead.

Slowly I get up.

"Would you like to take his pay-book and his things?" the lance-corporal asks me.

I nod, and he gives them to me.

The orderly is mystified. "You are not related, are you?"

No, we are not related. No, we are not related.

Do I walk? Have I feet still? I raise my eyes, I let them move round, and turn myself with them, one circle, one circle, and I stand in the midst. All is as usual. Only the Militiaman Stanislaus Katczinsky has died.

Then I know nothing more.

It is autumn. There are not many of the old hands left. I am the last of the seven fellows from our class.

Everyone talks of peace and armistice. All wait. If it again proves an illusion, then they will break up; hope is high, it cannot be taken away again without an upheaval. If there is not peace, then there will be revolution.

I have fourteen days' rest, because I have swallowed a bit of gas; in a little garden I sit the whole day long in the sun. The armistice is coming soon, I believe it now too. Then we will go home.

Here my thoughts stop and will not go any farther. All that meets me, all that floods over me are but feelings—greed of life, love of home, yearning of the blood, intoxication of deliverance. But no aims.

Had we returned home in 1916, out of the suffering and the strength of our experiences we might have unleashed a storm. Now if we go back we will be weary, broken, burnt out, rootless, and without hope. We will not be able to find our way any more.

And men will not understand us—for the generation that grew up before us, though it has passed these years with us here, already had a home and a calling; now it will return to its old occupations, and the war will be forgotten—and the generation that has grown up after us will be strange to us and push us aside. We will be superfluous even to ourselves, we will grow older, a few will adapt themselves, some others will merely submit, and most will be bewildered;—the years will pass by and in the end we shall fall into ruin.

But perhaps all this that I think is mere melancholy and dismay, which will fly away as the dust, when I stand once again beneath the poplars and listen to the rustling of their leaves. It cannot be that it has gone, the yearning that made our blood unquiet, the unknown, the perplexing, the oncoming things, the thousand faces of the future, the melodies from dreams and from books, the whispers and divinations of women, it cannot be that this has vanished in bombardment, in despair, in brothels.

Here the trees show gay and golden, the berries of the rowan stand red among the leaves, country roads run white out to the sky-line, and the canteens hum like beehives with rumours of peace.

I stand up.

I am very quiet. Let the months and years come, they bring me nothing more, they can bring me nothing more. I am so alone, and so without hope that I can confront them without fear. The life that has borne me through these years is still in my hands and my eyes. Whether I have subdued it, I know not. But so long as it is there it will seek its own way out, heedless of the will that is within me.

He fell in October, 1918, on a day that was so quiet and still on the whole front, that the army report confined itself to the single sentence: All quiet on the Western Front.

He had fallen forward and lay on the earth as though sleeping. Turning him over one saw that he could not have suffered long; his face had an expression of calm, as though almost glad the end had come.

Pickett's Charge

From *The Killer Angels*

BY MICHAEL SHAARA

I
F EVER A BOOK deserved the avalanches of praise heaped upon it over the years, the late Michael Shaara's *The Killer Angels* more than qualifies for the distinction. Shaara's life was cut short by illness in 1988 (he was born in 1929), but he lived to see his work receive public and critical acclaim. His book was published in 1974 and earned the Pulitzer Prize in 1975. Today, Shaara's son Jeff carries on his father's work, with new excellent novels of the Civil War in the same style pioneered by his dad.

The Killer Angels is a re-creation of the Battle of Gettysburg that resonates with drama and authenticity. It absolutely ranks among the greatest war stories ever written, and if you said you felt it was the best of them all, not many folks would feel like arguing with you.

This excerpt contains the climatic events of the battle—the action known forever as Pickett's Charge that took place on the third afternoon of the battle, Friday, July 3, 1863. Since the battle began on Wednesday, with Lee's forces ironically approaching Gettysburg from the North and West and the Union forces from the South, General Robert E. Lee and his second in command, Lt. Gen. James Longstreet, have been in serious disagreement over the question of strategy. Since the Union Army occupies the high ground on a ridge—Cemetery Ridge—running South from the town of Gettysburg to the prominent Little and Big Round Top hills, Longstreet favors a swing to the right. Get between the Union Army and Washington, he urges Lee, then chop them to pieces when they are forced to assault the Army of Northern Virginia's defensive positions. Longstreet has never forgotten the writhing fire with which Rebel sharpshooters slaughtered Union troops making bold assaults against their lines at the Battle of Fredericksburg.

Lee will not be dissuaded. On at least three occasions, he repeats to Longstreet, in effect, that with the enemy right in front of him he is going to attack. As the noted historian Shelby Foote relates, "Lee's blood was up. And when his blood was up, there was no stopping him."

On the first day, the helter-skelter fighting saw the Confederates almost break through the town and take the ridge. But by the time the battle commenced on the second day, General George G. Meade's reinforcements had strengthened the Union line and once again it held, this time against ferocious attacks at the Round Tops, the peach orchard, and wheat field areas on the Confederate right.

Now, on the third day, Lee still will not resort to feints and trickery. He expects one more major push—this time straight up the middle, straight up Cemetery Ridge—will break the back of Meade's forces. Longstreet, visualizing murderous fire pouring down on the men from the Union lines and the hills as they cross the open terrain, feels in his heart the attack is doomed.

As this excerpt begins, Longstreet's worst fears have become reality. The Confederate forces have been mauled by withering fire as they try to advance up Cemetery Ridge. Now Longstreet can only watch in pain as the survivors retreat.

★ ★ ★ ★ ★

Longstreet sat on a rail fence, hugging his chest with both arms. He suspended thinking; his mind was a bloody vacancy, like a room in which there has been a butchering. He tried once formally to pray, but there was no one there and no words came, and over and over he said to himself, Heavenly Father, Heavenly Father. He watched the battle dissolve to nightmare: the neat military lines beginning to come apart as they crossed the road and no order beyond that but black struggling clots and a few flags in the smoke, tilting like sails above a white sea, going down one by one. A shell burst near Longstreet and he felt the hot brutal breath, and then the sounds of battle were softer, the smoke began to blanket the field. But there was still a few flags moving toward the top of the hill. Longstreet put glasses to his eyes, saw ghost figures stumbling in white smoke, yellow blaze of cannon, black flakes of men spattering upward into a white sky, and then the smoke was too thick and he could not see anything and it was like going blind. A paralysis came over him. He sat staring off into the white sea where the guns still flashed and boomed softly, at a great distance, until he saw the first men beginning to come back out of the smoke. They came slowly up the long green slope, a ragged crowd of men. No one was running. They were moving with slow set stubborn unstoppable looks on their faces, eyes down, guns dragging the ground, and they were moving slowly but steadily, even though the Union guns had elevated and shells were still falling on them as they came back up the field. The smoke parted for a vision: the green field dirtied a vast mile with lumped bodies, white and red, and far across the field the whole army falling back in a speckled flood across the road to the safety of the woods, and there at the top of the hill one flag erect near the center of the Union line. Then that flag was down in the smoke, and Longstreet could no longer see, and the retreat began to flood by him.

The men parted as they passed him, not looking at him. He sat on an island in the stream of retreating men. He made no attempt to stop them. A man rode up on a black horse, a frantic man with blood on his face: Harry Bright, Pickett's staff. He was screaming. Longstreet stared at him. The man went on screaming. Longstreet made out: Pickett was asking for support. Longstreet shook his head, wordlessly, pointed down at the field. Bright did not yet understand. Longstreet said patiently, "Nine brigades went in. That's all we have." There was nothing to send now, no further help to give, and even if Lee on the other side would send support now it would be too late. Longstreet hugged his chest. He got down off the fence. A black horse rode up out of the smoke: familiar spot on a smoky forehead, blood bubbling from a foaming chest: Garnett's mount. Longstreet nodded. He told Bright to instruct Pickett to fall back. He sent word for a battery to move down the slope in front of him, to fire uphill and protect Pickett as he retreated.

The wind had changed. The smoke was blowing back across the field against his face. The guns were easing off. The men streamed by: nightmare army, faces gray and cold, sick. Longstreet felt a cold wind blowing in his brain. He stood up. He had sat long enough. He looked up to see Fremantle. A moment ago the man had been cheering wildly, not understanding what was happening. How he was holding out a silver flask. Longstreet shook his head. It was all done. Along with all the horror of loss, and the weariness, and all the sick helpless rage, there was coming now a monstrous disgust. He was through. They had all died for nothing and he had sent them. He thought: a man is asked to bear too much. And he refused. He began slowly to walk forward. He was all done. He would find a gun somewhere and take a walk forward. He walked down the long slope in front of him toward that one battery that was still firing toward the blue line. He saw a rifle by a dead man, the man missing a leg and the leg nearby, bent and chewed at the knee, and the rifle clean and new and cold. He bent down to pick it up, and when he looked up he saw Lee.

The old man was riding the gray horse across the open ground in front of the trees. He had taken his hat off and the white hair and the unmistakable white head were visible from a long way off. He was walking the horse slowly along the ground among the first rows of dead where the cannon had begun to take them as they stepped out of the trees, and the retreating men were slowed at the sight of him. Longstreet stopped. The old man reined up and stood for a moment immobile, head turned eastward toward the enemy, the gray hat on the horn of the saddle. He sat there motionless as a statue and the men coming back began to turn toward him. He sat looking down, talking to them. Longstreet stood watching him. He knew that he would never forgive the old man, never. He stood paralyzed holding the rifle and tears were running down his cheeks. The old man saw him and began riding toward him. Longstreet could hear him: "It is all my fault, it is all my fault," and men were already arguing with him and shaking their heads in rage and shame, but Lee said, "We shall rest and try it again another day. Now you must show good order. Never let them see you run."

There were men all around him, some of them crying. A tall man in a gray beard was pleading with Lee to let them attack again. A bony boy in a ripped and bloody shirt had hold of the halter of his horse and was insisting that the General move to the rear. Lee said again, "It is all my fault," but they were shaking their heads. Lee saw Longstreet.

Longstreet waited, the rifle in his hand. Lee rode slowly forward. A crowd of men was gathering now, a hundred or more. The stream to the rear had slowed. Now it was quieter and the nearby cannon were no longer firing and Lee came forward out of the smoke and the nightmare. His face was hard and red, his eyes bright and hot; he had a stiff, set look to him and both hands held hard to the saddle horn and when he looked at Longstreet his eyes had nothing in them. The old man stopped the horse and pointed east. He said in a soft, feathery voice, "I think they are forming over there, General. I think they may attack."

Longstreet nodded. The old man's voice was very soft; Longstreet could hardly hear. Lee looked down on him from a long way away. Longstreet nodded again. There was motion in front of him and suddenly he saw George Pickett, bloodstained. His hat was gone; his hair streamed like a blasted flower. His face was pale; he moved his head like a man who has heard too loud a sound. He rode slowly forward. Lee turned to meet him. Longstreet was vaguely amazed that Pickett was still alive. He heard Pickett say something to Lee. George turned and pointed back down the hill. His face was oddly wrinkled.

Lee raised a hand. "General Pickett, I want you to reform your Division in the rear of this hill."

Pickett's eyes lighted as if a sudden pain had shot through him. He started to cry. Lee said again with absolute calm, "General, you must look to your Division."

Pickett said tearfully, voice of a bewildered angry boy, "General Lee, I have no Division." He pointed back down the hill, jabbing at the blowing smoke, the valley of wrecked men, turned and shuddered, waving, then saying, "Sir? What about my men?" as if even now there was still something Lee could do to fix it. "What about my men? Armistead is gone. Garnett is gone. Kemper is gone. All my colonels are gone. General, *every one.* Most of my men are gone. Good God, sir, what about my men?"

Longstreet turned away. Enough of this. He looked for his horse, beckoned. The groom came up. Longstreet could look down across the way and see blue skirmishers forming across his front. The land sloped to where the one battery was still firing uphill into the smoke. Longstreet nodded. I'm coming. He felt a tug at his leg, looked down: Sorrel. Let me go, Major. The staff was around him, someone had the reins of the horse. Longstreet felt the gathering of the last great rage. He looked down slowly and pulled at the reins slowly and said carefully, "Major, you better let this damned horse go."

And then he pointed.

"They're coming, do you see? I'm going to meet them. I want you to put fire down on them and form to hold right here. I'm going down to meet them."

He rode off down the hill. He moved very quickly and the horse spurred and it was magnificent to feel the clean air blow across your face, and he was aware suddenly of the cold tears blurring his eyes and tried to wipe them away, Old Hero shying among all the dead bodies. He leaped a fence and became aware of a horse following and swung and saw the face of Goree, the frail Texan trailing him like the wind. Ahead of him the guns were firing into a line of blue soldiers and Longstreet spurred that way and Goree pulled alongside, screaming, "What are your orders, General? Where you want me to go?"

A shell blew up in front of him. He swerved to the right. Goree was down and Longstreet reined up. The bony man was scrambling, trying to get to his feet. Rifle fire was beginning to pluck at the air around them. Longstreet saw some of the staff riding toward him, trying to catch up. He rode to Goree and looked down but he couldn't say anything more, no words would come, and he couldn't even stop the damn tears, and Goree's eyes looking up, filled with pain and sorrow and pity, was another thing he would remember as long as he lived, and he closed his eyes.

The staff was around him, looking at him with wild eyes. Someone again had the bridle of his horse. Bullets still plucked the air: song of the dark guitar. He wanted to sleep. Someone was yelling, "Got to pull back," and he shook his head violently, clearing it, and turned back to the guns, letting the mind begin to function. "Place the guns," he bawled, "bring down some guns." He began directing fire. He took another shell burst close by and again the great drone filled his ears and after that came a cottony murmury rush, like a waterfall, and he moved in a black dream, directing the fire, waiting for them to come, trying to see through the smoke where the shells were falling. But the firing began to stop. The storm was ending. He looked out through the smoke and saw no more blue troops; they had pulled back. He thought, to God: if there is any mercy in you at all you will finish it now.

But the blue troops pulled back, and there was no attack.

After a while Longstreet sat on a fence. He noticed the rifle still in his hand. He had never used it. Carefully, he placed it on the ground. He stared at it for a while. Then he began to feel nothing at all. He saw the dirt-streaked face of T. J. Goree, watching him.

"How are you?" Longstreet said.

"Tolerable."

Longstreet pointed uphill. "They aren't coming."

Goree shook his head.

"Too bad," Longstreet said.

"Yes, sir."

"Too bad," Longstreet said again.

"Yes, sir. We got plenty canister left. If they hit us now we could sure make it hot for them."

Longstreet nodded. After a moment Goree said, "General, I tell you plain. There are times when you worry me."

"Well," Longstreet said.

"It's no good trying to get yourself killed, General. The Lord will come for you in His own time."

Longstreet leaned back against a fencepost and stared up into the sky. For a moment he saw nothing but the clean and wondrous sky. He sat for a moment, coming back to himself. He thought of Lee as he had looked riding that hill, his hat off so that the retreating men could see him and recognize him. When they saw him they actually stopped running. From Death itself.

It was darker now. Late afternoon. If Meade was coming he would have to come soon. But there was no sign of it. A few guns were still firing a long way off; heartbroken men would not let it end. But the fire was dying; the guns ended like sparks. Suddenly it was still, enormously still, a long pause in the air, a waiting, a fall. And then there was a different silence. Men began to turn to look out across the smoldering field. The wind had died; there was no motion anywhere but the slow smoke drifting and far off one tiny flame of a burning tree. The men stood immobile across the field. The knowledge began to pass among them, passing without words, that it was over. The sun was already beginning to set beyond new black clouds which were rising in the west, and men came out into the open to watch the last sunlight flame across the fields. The sun died gold and red, and the final light across the smoke was red, and then the slow darkness came out of the trees and flowed up the field to the stone wall, moving along above the dead and the dying like ths shadowing wing of an enormous bird, but still far off beyond the cemetery there was golden light in the trees on the hill, a golden blow over the rocks and the men in the last high places, and then it was done, and the field was gray.

Longstreet sat looking out across the ground to the green rise of the Union line and he saw a blue officer come riding along the crest surrounded by flags and a cloud of men, and he saw troops rising to greet him.

"They're cheering," Goree said bitterly, but Longstreet could not hear. He saw a man raise a captured battle flag, blue flag of Virginia, and he turned from the sight. He was done. Sorrel was by his side, asking for orders. Longstreet shook his head. He would go somewhere now and sleep. He thought: couldn't even quit. Even that is not to be allowed. He mounted the black horse and rode back toward the camp and the evening.

With the evening came a new stillness. There were no guns, no music. Men sat alone under ripped branchless trees. A great black wall of cloud was gathering in the west, and as the evening advanced and the sky grew darker they could begin to see the lightning although they could not yet hear the thunder. Longstreet functioned mechanically, placing his troops in a defensive line. Then he sat alone by the fire drinking coffee. Sorrel brought the first figures from Pickett's command.

Armistead and Garnett were dead; Kemper was dying. Of the thirteen colonels in Pickett's Division seven were dead and six were wounded. Longstreet did not look at the rest. He held up a hand and Sorrel went away.

But the facts stayed with him. The facts rose up like shattered fenceposts in the mist. The army would not recover from this day. He was a professional and he knew that as a good doctor knows it, bending down for perhaps the last time over a doomed beloved patient. Longstreet did not know what he would do now. He looked out at the burial parties and the lights beginning to come on across the field like clusters of carrion fireflies. All that was left now was more dying. It was final defeat. They had all died and it had accomplished nothing, the wall was unbroken, the blue line was sound. He shook his head suddenly, violently, and remembered the old man again, coming bareheaded along the hill, stemming the retreat.

After a while Lee came. Longstreet did not want to see him. But the old man came in a cluster of men, outlined under that dark and ominous sky, the lightning blazing beyond his head. Men were again holding the bridle of the horse, talking to him, pleading; there was something oddly biblical about it, and yet even here in the dusk of defeat there was something else in the air around him; the man brought strength with his presence: doomed and defeated, he brought nonetheless a certain majesty. And Longstreet, knowing that he would never quite forgive him, stood to meet him.

Lee dismounted. Longstreet looked once into his face and then dropped his eyes. The face was set and cold, stonelike. Men were speaking. Lee said, "I would like a few moments alone with General Longstreet." The men withdrew. Lee sat in a camp chair near the fire and Longstreet sat and they were alone together. Lee did not speak. Longstreet sat staring at the ground, into the firelight. Lightning flared; a cool wind was blowing. After a while Lee said, "We will withdraw tonight."

His voice was husky and raw, as if he had been shouting. Longstreet did not answer. Lee said, "We can withdraw under cover of the weather. If we can reach the river, there will be no more danger."

Longstreet sat waiting, his mind vacant and cold. Gradually he realized that the old man was expecting advice, an opinion. But he said nothing. Then he looked up. The old man had his hand over his eyes. He looked vaguely different. Longstreet felt a chill. The old man said slowly, "Peter, I'm going to need your help."

He kept his hand over his eyes, shading himself as if from bright sunlight. Longstreet saw his take a deep breath and let it go. Then he realized that Lee had called him by his nickname. Lee said, "I'm really very tired."

Longstreet said quickly, "What can I do?"

Lee shook his head. Longstreet had never seen the old man lose control. He had not lost it now, but he sat there with his hand over his eyes and Longstreet felt shut away from his mind and in that same moment felt a shudder of enormous pity. He said, "General?"

Lee nodded. He dropped the hand and glanced up once quickly at Longstreet, eyes bright and black and burning. He shook his head again. He raised both palms, a gesture almost of surrender, palms facing Longstreet, tried to say something, shook his head for the last time. Longstreet said, "I will take care of it, General We'll pull out tonight."

"I thought . . ." Lee said huskily.

Longstreet said, "Never mind."

"Well," Lee said. He took a long deep breath, faced the firelight. "Well, now we must withdraw."

"Yes."

They sat for a while in silence. Lee recovered. He crossed his legs and sat looking into the fire and the strength came back, the face smoothed calm again and grave, the eyes silent and dark. He said, "We must look to our own deportment. The spirit of the Army is still very good."

Longstreet nodded.

"We will do better another time."

Longstreet shook his head instinctively. He said, "I don't think so."

Lee looked up. The eyes were clearer now. The moment of weakness had come and passed. What was left was a permanent weariness. A voice in Longstreet said: let the old man alone. But there had been too much death; it was time for reality. He said slowly, "I don't think we can win it now."

After a moment Lee nodded, as if it were not really important. He said, "Perhaps."

"I don't think—" Longstreet raised his hands—"I don't know if I can go on leading them. To die. For nothing."

Lee nodded. He sat for a long while with his hands folded in his lap, staring at the fire, and the firelight on his face was soft and warm. Then he said slowly, "They do not die for us. Not for us. That at least is a blessing." He spoke staring at the fire. "Each man has his own reason to die. But if they go on, I will go on." He paused. "It is only another defeat." He looked up at Longstreet, lifted his hands, palms out, folded them softly, slowly. "If the war goes on—and it will, it will—what else can we do but go on? It is the same question forever, what else can we do? If they fight, we will fight with them. And does it matter after all who wins? Was that ever really the question? Will God ask that question, in the end?" He put his hands on his thighs, started painfully to rise.

He got to his feet, laboring. Longstreet reached forward instinctively to help him. Lee said, embarrassed, "Thank you," and then where Longstreet held his arm he reached up and covered Longstreet's hand. He looked into Longstreet's eyes. Then he said, "You were right. And I was wrong. And now you must help me see what must be done. Help us to *see*. I become . . . very tired."

"Yes," Longstreet said.

They stood a moment longer in the growing dark. The first wind of the coming storm had begun to break over the hills and the trees, cold and heavy and smelling of rain. Lee said, "I lectured you yesterday, on war."

Longstreet nodded. His mind was too full to think.

"I was trying to warn you. But . . . you have no Cause. You and I, we have no Cause. We have only the army. But if a soldier fights only for soldiers, he cannot ever win. It is only the soldiers who die."

Lee mounted the gray horse. Longstreet watched the old man clear his face and stiffen his back and place the hat carefully, formally on his head. Then he rode off into the dark. Longstreet stood watching him out of sight. Then he turned and went out into the field to say goodbye, and when that was done he gave the order to retreat.

★ ★ ★ ★ ★

Editor's Postscript: On the evening of July 3 and the following day, when Lee's retreat began, Union General George G. Meade did not mount a serious attack to cut Lee off and destroy the Confederate Army. Abraham Lincoln later said in dismay, "I was deeply mortified by the escape of Lee across the Potomac . . . because I believe General Meade and his nobel army had expended all the skill, toil, and blood, up to the ripe harvest, and then let the crop go to waste."

Faith at Sea

BY IRWIN SHAW

LTHOUGH IRWIN SHAW's World War II novel *The Young Lions* will probably always be his most-remembered work of that period, his mastery of the short-story form was very much in evidence in recalling the war.

Mainly in *The New Yorker,* Shaw (1913–1984) published such memorable war stories as "Act of Faith," "Retreat" and my personal favorite, "Faith at Sea."

Shaw wrote many successful novels, including the popular *Rich Man, Poor Man.* He also created an outstanding original screen story, "Fire Down Below," starring Rita Hayworth, Jack Lemmon, and Robert Mitchum.

★　★　★　★　★

LIEUTENANT PETER GIFFORD LAWRENCE stood on the foredeck of the *SS Rascoe,* holding on lightly to the canvas-sheathed three-inch gun as the bow dipped and trembled in the harsh chop of the North Atlantic. Twelve men of the gun crew stood at ease before him, shifting easily with the soaring lift and fall of the *SS Rascoe* as she chewed busily into the slate waves that had been hacking at her for six days, getting stronger and stronger as the 6,000-ton tramp steamer ploughed at nine knots toward England.

"The duties of the gun captain," Constantini was chanting, like a child in school. "A, on manning gun, reports through sight-setter to group control officer when gun is ready. B, operates plug as necessary. C, calls 'Ready,' to pointer when breech is closed . . ."

Lawrence only half listened as Constantini's voice droned on, in the regular Thursday afternoon gunnery class that Lawrence conducted to keep the Navy gun crew alert and interested on the long, monotonous trips. He looked at the twelve men outlined in mufflers and coats, against the low-hanging cold sun. These, plus the four men on duty now at the rear gun, had been given him by the Navy to guard the gray and shabby and valuable life of the SS *Rascoe,* and as always, when he saw them assembled he felt with a mixture of amusement and pity how old he was.

He was only thirty-five, but except for Farrell, the Chief Petty Officer, who was older than he, and Benson, the gunner's mate, who was twenty-five, all the men were twenty-one or under, their faces bronzed and unlined and boyish, always solemn and youthfully important when they were assembled like this for any official function, and especially solemn today because they had lost the convoy the night before in a storm and were now plodding over the gray wastes toward port, vulnerable and alone.

"He is responsible for the conduct, efficiency and spirit of the crew," Constantini was saying, "and must be made to realize that he is the representative of his battery officer."

"Very good," Lawrence said. "Harris."

"Yes, sir." Harris stood stiffly at attention.

"The duties of the sight setter."

"To set the sights," Harris rattled off glibly, "and to transmit all communications between gun and group control officer."

Lawrence looked up over Harris's head to the bridge. Captain Linsey, his beard patchy and crooked in the wind, was peering angrily down at what he called the Navy kindergarten.

"To call 'Set,' " Harris was saying, "to pointer when sights have been set . . ."

Suddenly Harris stopped. Lawrence turned from looking at Linsey on the bridge. The man next to Harris, William Doneger, was on his knees by Harris's side, gripping Harris's arm with a tortured, clutching hand. Harris stood there stupidly, frightened, looking blankly at the sweating tense face.

"Doneger . . ." Lawrence started toward him. Doneger let loose his grip and dropped, bent over and rocking, to the deck.

Constantini sank swiftly to his knees and took Doneger's head in his hands, tenderly.

"What is it?" Lawrence kneeled beside the two of them, with the other men crowded silent and helpless around them.

Doneger looked up at him wildly, the sweat breaking from his forehead, even in this bitter winter evening.

"He's been sick all day, sir," Constantini said, his hands almost unconsciously going slowly and soothingly over his friend's forehead. "Terrible bellyache, sir."

Lawrence looked down at the suffering boy. His lips were bleeding from biting them and his face had grown terribly, greenly pale, morbid and alarming in the cold Atlantic dusk. His legs pulled spasmodically and unreasonably as he lay on the wet deck.

"Let's get him below," Lawrence said. "To my quarters." There was no doctor on board and Lawrence's quarters had the medical chest and served as clinic for the Navy men.

Constantini got Doneger under the armpits and one of the other men got him around the knees and they started down with him. Constantini was a broad, powerful boy and held his friend firmly and lightly and maneuvered him delicately up the steps, his face tense and wary as he attempted to beat the cruel roll of the ship which at any moment threatened to smash the sick boy against a bulkhead.

Lawrence looked out across the ocean for a last survey. The water hissed by the *SS Rascoe* and the gray waves piled endlessly and monotonously on top of each other and the clouds came down, and that was all. He swallowed a little drily, thinking of Doneger lying racked and contorted in his room, then braced his shoulders consciously and walked slowly toward his quarters.

When he opened the door, Doneger was lying on the extra berth and Constantini was whispering to him, a steady, soft stream of comforting words. Constantini had a deep melodious voice, like a singer, and it sounded like a lullaby as he whispered to his friend.

"Nothing at all, William, nothing at all." He was the only one on the ship who called Doneger William. All the other men called him Bill and Billy, but Constantini gave him his full and proper name, like a doting mother, at all times. "Something you ate. I've had bellyaches in my time. . . ." Constantini was seventeen years old. "I thought I was going to split down the middle and two hours later I'd be out eating two plates of spaghetti and a quart of dago red. . . ."

When he saw Lawrence come into the room, he stopped his whispering and stood up at attention, trying to make his face impassive and military. But he had a child's face with deep soft-brown Italian eyes, with heavy curled black eyelashes, and a full, almost girlish mouth, and the military mask at the moment was not deceptive.

Lawrence looked down at the suffering boy. Doneger looked up at him wanly. "Sorry, sir," he whispered.

"Sssh," Lawrence said.

"He's been puking, sir," Constantini said. "All day, sir . . ."

Lawrence sighed and sat down on the berth next to Doneger. That's what it's going to turn out to be, he thought, as he put his hand on the boy's side. The worst possible thing . . .

The right side was swollen and tight and Doneger jumped even with the slightest pressure.

"He has a very sensitive belly, sir," Constantini was speaking quickly and anxiously, as though somehow his words and explanations could make the disease less. "I took him to my cousin's wedding and he got drunk faster than anyone else, even faster than the sixteen-year-old girls . . . We had a stew yesterday that was a little greasy and maybe . . ."

"He has appendicitis, Salvatore," Lawrence said slowly.

Constantini looked at his friend's face in silence. Doneger closed his eyes. Lying down here, in the warm stateroom, on a dry bed, he seemed more comfortable, better able to meet the pain.

"Everything will be all right, William," Constantini murmured to Doneger. "The Lieutenant has already diagnosed the disease."

The door opened and Captain Linsey came in. He stood above Doneger, staring down at him, without a word, his mouth curled, as always when he had anything to do with the Navy men on board his ship, into a sour and ancient snarl.

"Sick," Linsey said. "This son-of-a-bitch is very sick."

"Yes," Lawrence said. Captain Linsey would make amusing conversation after the war at dinner parties in Boston. Crusty old merchant seadog. Ignored the Navy. Ignored the war, even in the middle of a pack of submarines.

"This son-of-a-bitch'll die." Captain Linsey leaned over and peered harshly into the pale suffering face.

Very amusing after the war at dinner parties, Lawrence thought. Right now I'd like to kill him.

"We'll take care of him," Lawrence said.

Suddenly Captain Linsey poked Doneger in the side with a huge, wrinkled finger. Doneger cried and jumped. "Sorry, Sonny," Captain Linsey said. He turned to Lawrence. "Ready to bust. Boy out with me on the way to Wilhelmshaven in 1931 died in three days. Same thing."

Out of the corner of his eye, Lawrence saw Constantini look quickly down at Doneger, then look up and take a long, deep breath.

"Please," Lawrence said. "I'll come up to the bridge later and you can tell me whatever you . . ."

"This son-of-a-bitch needs an operation."

"There's no doctor on board."

Captain Linsey sucked at the wet ends of his mustache, looked with crazy slyness at Lawrence. "We won't make port for seven days. At least. He ain't going to last no week."

I'd like to kill him, Lawrence thought, looking up at Captain Linsey's old, harsh seaman's face. I'd like to kill him, but he's right, he's right.

"I thought we could freeze it," Lawrence said. "After all, we have ice. Maybe it'll subside . . ."

"Too late." Captain Linsey wagged his head finally. "Surgery. Surgery or nothing."

"There're no surgeons here," Lawrence said loudly. "If you insist on arguing, let's get out of this room."

"You ever see an operation?" Captain Linsey asked.

"Yes." Lawrence's brother-in-law was a fashionable surgeon and over a period of ten years Lawrence had seen seven or eight operations. "That isn't the same thing."

"There was a Dutchman we took to Capetown in 1927," Captain Linsey said. "A doctor. Studied in America. He left a book on board. All kinds of operations. Every once in a while I read in it Very interesting reading. I bet it's got appendicitis in it."

"That's ridiculous," Lawrence stood up and went over to the door. "Thank you for your interest, Captain . . ."

Captain Linsey touched Doneger's head. "Fever. I bet it's over 104. An operation really isn't so much. A little common sense and a little nerve. What the hell, what has this boy got to lose?" He leaned close to Doneger and spoke with surprising softness. "Sonny, you got any objections to being operated on?"

Doneger stared at Constantini. Constantini turned away, giving no answer one way or another with his eyes.

"I have no objections," Doneger said faintly.

Captain Linsey strode briskly toward the door. "I'll send the book down," he said cheerfully. "We'll save the son-of-a-bitch yet." He clapped Lawrence on the back. "I'd do it myself only I'm old and jumpy and I've drunk too much whisky in my day. I'll be on the bridge. I'll keep this tub as steady as possible."

He went out quickly.

Lawrence closed his eyes so that he wouldn't have to look at Doneger or Crowley or Constantini, all standing stiffly watching him.

A moment later a seaman came in with a worn and broken-backed book. He put it on the table and went out. Crowley and Doneger and Constantini and Lawrence all looked at the fat, dog-eared book, lying alone on the table. Lawrence stood up and went over and opened to the index. Under A Pg. 941—Appendectomy.

The first time he read through it, the words were a weird and incomprehensible blur. He looked up once or twice only to see the staring, serious eyes of the three other men scanning his face, as though they somehow could tell from that distance whether or not the words he was reading were of any value to him or not.

Lawrence took off his coat and started slowly to read it from the beginning, once more.

Before operating, try to locate the situation of the appendix. The incision should be over the seat of the disease. In the rare left-sided cases and in median cases, the incision is median . . .

The words began to group themselves in his mind into English sentences, capable of being understood by a man who could read and write.

In an acute case in a man I separate the muscular fibres. Battle's incision at the outer edge of the rectus muscle is preferred by many surgeons . . .

In a biology course in college he had dissected the earthworm, the frog, and white rat—but all dead, beyond the reach of pain, unmoved by clumsiness or error.

If there be infection, surround the region involved with packs of plain gauze, each strip being two and a half inches wide, fifteen inches long, and four layers in thickness. Pass a ligature through the meso appendix as shown in Fig. 691, *A, tie the ligature and . . .*

Fig. 691, A, was very simple and if flesh and muscle and organ were anything like the diagram, it was conceivable that a deft, though unpracticed man might be able to manage . . .

"William," Lawrence said. "Are you sure?"

Doneger sighed. "I'm sure."

"Crowley," Lawrence said. "Go to the galley and get a pot of boiling water."

"Yes, sir," Crowley said, and went out softly, already making a hospital out of the room.

Lawrence went back to the close print of the book. He read and reread, studied the diagrams until he felt he could draw them with his eyes closed.

He stood up and unlocked the medical chest. He threw open the doors and stared at the rows of bottles, the serried bandages, the fateful gleaming instruments. Behind him he heard the soft child's voice of Constantini,

rough with the accent of the streets of New York, soft with compassion and
fear.

"It ain't hardly nothing, William. A cousin of mine had this and he was
operated on and three days later he slept with the nurse." Constantini had a
cousin for all eventualities of discussion, naval and civilian. "Everybody ought
to have his appendix out. They don't do you no good. None at all. If I had the
time I'd have 'em out myself. . . ."

Lawrence stared at the bottles, the bandages, the steel instruments. He
made his eyes go slowly and calmly from one thing to another in the chest,
taking a deliberate inventory. The thing is, he thought, not to hurry. After all,
men have done more difficult things than this. The instruments are there, the
one can of ether, the bandage, the scalpel, the needles, the catgut, the clamps,
the sponges, the alcohol, sulfanilamide. And the Navy had given him a course
in First Aid. How to stop bleeding. How to avoid gangrene. How to set a broken leg.

"You hardly feel it," Constantini was saying in his deep melodious
boy's voice. "You take a little nap. You wake up. Appendix absent. You feel a little stiff for a day or two, you get a good rest, the other guys stand your watches,
you read the magazines and drink hot soup. You get to England, you get three
weeks sick leave, you'll have the time of your life. The English girls're crazy
about American sailors. I got a cousin in the merchant marine and he says that
an American in London is like a king, far as the girls're concerned. They can't
do enough for them . . ."

Why, Lawrence thought with a remote and bitter detachment, did this
have to happen the first time we lost a convoy? In a convoy the boy could be
transferred to one of the cruisers accompanying them and there a first-rate
naval surgeon in a shining, brilliantly equipped operating room would do the
job as a matter of simple routine in ten minutes.

Crowley came in with the pot of hot water and Lawrence put the
scalpel, the needles and the clamps into it.

"Anything I can do," Constantini said, as Lawrence watched the steel
gleaming dully as it sank among the bubbles of the boiling water. "Anything at
all."

Lawrence nodded. "There'll be plenty for you to do. Clear that table
and get a sheet out of the locker and spread it over it." Constantini listened eagerly and nodded. "Wash you hands first."

While Crowley and Constantini scrubbed their hands and the strong
smell of the soap pricked his nostrils, Lawrence re-read, slowly, the entire de-
scription of the operation.

Even after he had finished and after the gentle watery sound of scrubbing behind him had long ceased, he sat with his head in his hands, staring at the page before him.

He stood up. Well, that was that . . .

He turned briskly and without words he and Constantini and Crowley lifted Doneger onto the white-covered table. He washed and scrubbed his hands with alcohol. Gently, he shaved the slight downy fuzz from the boy's belly. Then he washed it with alcohol.

Crowley behaved wonderfully. He was a little, impassive Irishman, to whom all things seemed to come as a matter of course, promotions, overwork, murders, drownings, wars. Lawrence was glad it was Crowley who had silently volunteered for this job.

Constantini, too, handled Doneger with soft hands, lifting him gently and securely, making no unnecessary move. Together they bound Doneger to the table with linen bandage, so that the roll of the ship would not throw him off the table.

Lawrence noticed that the ship had swung around and was heading directly into the wind and was much steadier now. He would remember to thank Captain Linsey later.

He took the ether cone and stood at Doneger's shoulder. Doneger and Constantini and seven or eight of the other boys had had their heads shaven when they were last in the States. They had done it as a kind of joke, after Lawrence had complained at inspection that they were letting their hair grow too long. All seven of them had marched solemnly back onto the SS *Rascoe* from their shore leaves and had with one gesture swept their hats off their heads as they reported in. Lawrence had stared at the seven shining plates, scarred with the incredibly numerous battles of childhood, and had lowered his eyes to keep from laughing and had said, "Very good."

They had saluted and swept out and he had heard them roaring with laughter on the deck . . .

Doneger's head, now with a slight baby fuzz standing up all over it, lay flatly, in the shadows, on the table in the small cabin as the old plates on the SS *Rascoe* creaked and wailed under the attack of the sea. . . .

"All right, William," Lawrence said softly. "Are you ready now?"

"I'm ready, sir." Doneger spoke in a whisper and smiled up at him.

Lawrence put the cone gently over the boy's face and said, "Breathe deeply." He poured the ether in and the smell, sweet and deadly leaked into the cabin, making it strange and deathly suddenly. "Count," Lawrence said. "Keep counting."

"One, two, three," Doneger said clearly. "Four, five, six, seven, eight . . ." The young voice began to blur and thicken. "Nine, ten, eleven, twelve, thir—thir . . ." The voice mumbled heavily and wearily through the cone. The long chubby body on the table relaxed for the first time and Crowley gently straightened the legs out. The voice died away completely and the noise of the creaking plates of the old ship was the only sound to be heard.

Lawrence lifted the ether cone. Doneger's face was calm and showed no trace of pain. He gave the cone to Constantini. "If I tell you to," he said, "put this over his face. In case he moves . . ."

"Yes, sir," Constantini said, and moved quickly to Doneger's head.

Lawrence went to the pot of boiling water, and with a forceps took out the instruments he had put in there to sterilize. Crowley had arranged a clean towel on the bunk and Lawrence put the instruments there in a neat and shining row, remembering how dentists who had filled his teeth had done the same thing.

He picked up the scalpel and arranged the lamp so that its full glare fell on the bare stomach of the sleeping boy.

The skin was very pink, and there was a firm small layer of fat under it. Doneger was very young and his belly still had a round little babyswell. He was breathing softly and the muscles trembled rhythmically and gently in the harsh light of the single lamp.

How smooth, how subtle, how complex, Lawrence thought, how close to death. How vulnerable to knife and powder. How irrevocably naked to damage. He closed his eyes for a moment, unable to look any more at the smooth childish skin. With his eyes closed and the moaning and creaking of the tumbling ship in his ears, it all seemed dreamlike and impossible. He, Peter Gifford Lawrence, gently reared, nursed and fed and tended all his years by mother and aunt and teacher and doctor, every boyhood scratch mercurochromed and overbandaged, soft-blanketed sleeper in neat, well-ventilated rooms, student at Harvard where he had taken notes on Plato and Geoffrey Chaucer, on the architecture of the Renaissance and the metrics of John Milton, Peter Gifford Lawrence, gentleman, formal guest at pleasant dinners, polite talker to old ladies at Lenox garden parties, dealer in books and fine prints, now standing scalpel in hand in the cramped, peeling First-Officer's quarters of a wheezing freighter groaning and heaving in a Middle Atlantic gale, with four miles of black sea water and countless drowned sailors under the keel, the prey of deadly vessels that struck unseen and mortal in the turn of a man's head . . .

Battle's incision at the outer edge of the rectus muscle is preferred by many surgeons . . . After opening the peritoneum examine very gently to detect the situation of the . . . This divides the mucous membrane, submucous tissue and muscular coat . . .

He opened his eyes and looked up. Constantini was staring at him. In the soft girlish eyes, besides the worry for his friend's agony, there was deep trust, deep confidence that this kindly, efficient, understanding, courageous man, this officer who had been designated by great authority to guide his wartime fate, would, this time and all times, do well what had to be done. There was no doubt in the soft steady eyes of Salvatore Constantini.

Lawrence bent his head and firmly made the necessary incision . . .

When the operation was over and Doneger had been gently lifted into the extra bunk and Constantini had silently taken the watch at his side, Lawrence opened the door and stepped out onto the deck. The black wind flung bitter spray into his face and he had to half-shut his eyes against it. But he stood there, holding onto the rail, peering sightlessly into the roaring darkness, hardly thinking, hardly feeling, rolling crazily and aimlessly with the roll of the ship.

He stood there drunkenly for a long time, then suddenly turned and went into his room. Doneger was lying there, steady and still, the ether still in control. Constantini sat quietly at his side, never taking his eyes off the pale, exhausted face.

Lawrence lay down in all his clothes and slept immediately.

When he awoke, he opened his eyes slowly and came up deeply from the well of sleep, as though he had slept for weeks on end. Slowly he became aware of Constantini sitting across the room from him, still looking steadfastly at Doneger, as though he hadn't moved all night.

Lawrence opened his eyes wide.

"Good morning, Lieutenant." Constantini smiled shyly at him. His eyes were sunken and he rubbed them like a sleepy infant.

"Morning, Salvatore." Lawrence sat up suddenly and looked at Doneger, remembering in a rush that across from him lay a man whom he had operated upon the night before. Doneger was awake, and drowsily smiled, his face creased by a kind of remote pain.

"Hello, Lieutenant," Doneger whispered.

Lawrence jumped out of his bunk. "How are you?"

"Fine," Doneger whispered. "First class. Thanks."

Lawrence peered at him closely. There were wrinkles of pain in the boy's smooth face, but there was a little color in the cheeks and something in the eyes that seemed to announce that death had once and for all passed by.

Lawrence looked at Constantini. "You get any sleep last night?"

"Not much, sir. I'm pleased to watch William."

"Get below and get some sleep. Someone else'll watch William."

"Yes, sir." Constantini looked shyly at him and then turned to Doneger. "My God," he whispered, as Lawrence poured some water to wash, "will you have a picnic with those English girls . . ."

And he touched his friend's forehead lightly and chuckled as he went out and deep, deep, from the depths of his eighteen years and recovery from death, Doneger chuckled softly in return.

Later in the day, Lawrence started forward toward the bow gun, where the men were assembled for the interrupted examination in gunnery. The sun was shining and the ocean was a sharp, wintry blue, with the whitecaps in the distance looking like the bobbing sails of a regatta with a million entries. He had left Doneger smiling and sipping tea and the bright wind felt festive and alive against his freshly shaven face. He saw the cluster of blue uniforms and the ruddy faces of the gun crew around the gun and heard Constantini's voice, melodious and terribly earnest, chanting in final review before his arrival. Lawrence smiled to himself and was proud of the Navy and the red-faced earnest boys, and the gun and the SS *Rascoe* and himself, abroad, dependable and unafraid, on the wide ocean.

"Tention!" Benson called as he approached, and the boys stiffened rigidly, their faces stern and set, their hands tight at their sides. Lawrence looked sternly at them, carrying out his share of the military drama.

He looked at them and felt once more with the old amusement and pity how old he was at the age of thrity-five, confronted by and responsible for these large, determined, valuable, fearless children.

"At ease," he said.

The tight little knot relaxed and the men shuffled about, making themselves comfortable. They kept their eyes on Lawrence, seriously. Constantini's lips mumbled inaudibly as he ran over the list of questions he might be asked to answer.

"We'll go right into it," Lawrence said. "Harris . . ." he started with the boy nearest him. "What're the duties of the first loader?"

"To receive the shell from the second loader," Harris said. "And to load the gun."

"Levine." Lawrence spoke to the next man. "Duties of the second loader?"

"To pass shells to the first loader," Levine said carefully. "To arrange shells on deck in rear of gun in probable arc of train."

"Constantini . . ." Lawrence went down the line. He saw Constantini's face tense almost painfully with anticipation. "What are the duties of the third loader?"

Constantini's lips started to move. Then he licked them uneasily. He took in a deep breath, looked suddenly, blankly and despairingly at Lawrence. Lawrence glanced at him and saw that all knowledge had fled from his head, like an actor on opening night, with four weeks of rehearsals behind him, who is stricken dumb by the overpowering desire to do well.

A deep red flush surged up over Constantini's collar and stained his cheeks, his ears. He licked his lips in misery, looked straight ahead, hopelessly . . .

Lawrence looked away, called the next man, Moran, went on with the questioning.

Moran answered the question briskly.

One by one, Lawrence went down the line of men. Each man snapped out his answer, their voices ringing clear and triumphant in the bright wind. Once more it was Constantini's turn.

Lawrence looked surreptitiously at him. He was next in line and he was standing as stiff as though all the admirals of all the fleets of the world were passing him in review. His jaws were clenched and the muscles stood out in them like rope. His eyes stared ahead of him like a man watching the execution of his father, wild, hopeless, full of guilt.

Lawrence knew in his heart that no matter what question he put to Constantini, no answer would come from the mourning brain, no word pass those locked, despairing lips. For a moment Lawrence thought of passing him up and going on to the next man. But then, to the shame of Constantini's ignorance and defection would be added the ignominy of official pity.

"Constantini," Lawrence said as crisply as he could, hoping to shock him out of his trancelike trauma. He carefully sought out the simplest, most transparent, easily answered question in the whole book. "Constantini," he said, slowly and clearly and loudly, "what is the purpose of shrapnel?"

Constantini did not move. The tongue froze between the lips, the eyes stared without hope across the Atlantic Ocean, while no answer came to show this good man, this Boston Lieutenant who had done a brave and noble thing to save his friend's life that he, Salvatore Constantini, loved and admired him and would be grateful to him for the rest of his life. The blush settled like a permanent blight on his cheeks, but no answer came from the rockbound brain. The deep, ordinary thanks that a man could give by the crisp performance of his duty could not be given. William lived and Salvatore failed the man who had saved him.

Suddenly the tears started from his eyes and rolled down his rigid cheeks.

Lawrence looked at the weeping boy, staring blindly out to sea, among the men who kindly stared out to sea with him. Lawrence saw the bitter tears and almost put out his hand to comfort the boy, but held back just in time, since comfort now, before his ten friends, would be agony later.

Lawrence glanced once more at him and tried to call the next man's name and ask him the purpose of shrapnel, but the name stuck in his throat and he turned his back on the men and wept and felt the tears cold on his cheeks without surprise.

Mountain Fighting

From *Brave Men*

BY ERNIE PYLE

WHEN A JAPANESE sniper's bullet ended Ernie Pyle's life on Okinawa in 1945 near the end of World War Two, America lost its most beloved war correspondent of that time.

Ernie Pyle's World War Two dispatches were written with the deepest respect for the kind of battlefield detail and specific GI-Joe portraits thirsted for by Hometown USA.

This selection from Pyle's classic *Brave Men* is an account of the war as it was fought in Italy long before D-Day and the invasion of Europe.

"Mountain Fighting" formed the basis of a still-famous World War Two film, "The Story of GI Joe," starring Robert Mitchum.

★   ★   ★   ★   ★

The war in Italy was tough. The land and the weather were both against us. It rained and it rained. Vehicles bogged down and temporary bridges washed out. The country was shockingly beautiful, and just as shockingly hard to capture from the enemy. The hills rose to high ridges of almost solid rock. We couldn't go around them through the flat peaceful valleys, because the Germans were up there looking down upon us, and they would have let us have it. So we had to go up and over. A mere platoon of Germans, well dug in on a high, rock-spined hill, could hold out for a long time against tremendous onslaughts.

I know the folks back home were disappointed and puzzled by the slow progress in Italy. They wondered why we moved northward so imperceptibly. They were impatient for us to get to Rome. Well, I can say this—our

286

troops were just as impatient for Rome. But on all sides I heard: "It never was this bad in Tunisia." "We ran into a new brand of Krauts over here." "If it would only stop raining." "Every day we don't advance is one day longer before we get home."

Our troops were living in almost inconceivable misery. The fertile black valleys were knee-deep in mud. Thousands of the men had not been dry for weeks. Other thousands lay at night in the high mountains with the temperature below freezing and the thin snow sifting over them. They dug into the stones and slept in little chasms and behind rocks and in half-caves. The lived like men of prehistoric times, and a club would have become them more than a machine gun. How they survived the dreadful winter at all was beyond us who had the opportunity of drier beds in the warmer valleys.

That the northward path was a tedious one was not the fault of our troops, nor of their direction either. It was the weather and the terrain and the weather again. If there had been no German fighting troops in Italy, if there had been merely German engineers to blow the bridges in the passes, if never a shot had been fired at all, our northward march would still have been slow. The country was so difficult that we formed a great deal of cavalry for use in the mountains. Each division had hundreds of horses and mules to carry supplies beyond the point where vehicles could go no farther. On beyond the mules' ability, mere men—American men—took it on their backs.

On my way to Italy, I flew across the Mediterranean in a cargo plane weighted down with more than a thousand pounds beyond the normal load. The cabin was filled with big pasteboard boxes which had been given priority above all other freight. In the boxes were packboards, hundreds of them, with which husky men would pack 100, even 150, pounds of food and ammunition, on their backs, to comrades high in those miserable mountains.

But we could take consolation from many things. The air was almost wholly ours. All day long Spitfires patrolled above our fighting troops like a half dozen policemen running up and down the street watching for bandits.

What's more, our artillery prevailed—and how! We were prodigal with ammunition against those rocky crags, and well we might be, for a $50 shell could often save ten lives in country like that. Little by little, the fiendish rain of explosives upon the hillsides softened the Germans. They always were impressed by and afraid of our artillery, and we had concentrations of it there that were demoralizing.

And lastly, no matter how cold the mountains, or how wet the snow, or how sticky the mud, it was just as miserable for the German soldier as for the American.

Our men were going to get to Rome all right. There was no question about that. But the way was cruel. No one who had not seen that mud, those dark skies, those forbidding ridges and ghostlike clouds that unveiled and then quickly hid the enemy, had the right to be impatient with the progress along the road to Rome.

The mountain fighting went on week after dreary week. For a while I hung around with one of the mule-pack outfits. There was an average of one mule-packing outfit for every infantry battalion in the mountains. Some were run by Americans, some by Italian soldiers.

The pack outfit I was with supplied a battalion that was fighting on a bald, rocky ridge nearly four thousand feet high. That battalion fought constantly for ten days and nights, and when the men finally came down less than a third of them were left.

All through those terrible days every ounce of their supplies had to go up to them on the backs of mules and men. Mules took it the first third of the way. Men took it the last bitter two-thirds, because the trail was too steep even for mules.

The mule skinners of my outfit were Italian soldiers. The human packers were mostly American soldiers. The Italian mule skinners were from Sardinia. They belonged to a mountain artillery regiment, and thus were experienced in climbing and in handling mules. They were bivouacked in an olive grove alongside a highway at the foot of the mountain. They made no trips in the daytime, except in emergencies, because most of the trail was exposed to artillery fire. Supplies were brought into the olive grove by truck during the day, and stacked under trees. Just before dusk they would start loading the stuff onto mules. The Americans who actually managed the supply chain liked to get the mules loaded by dark, because if there was any shelling the Italians instantly disappeared and could never be found.

There were 155 skinners in this outfit and usually about eighty mules were used each night. Every mule had a man to lead it. About ten extra men went along to help get mules up if they fell, to repack any loads that came loose, and to unpack at the top. They could be up and back in less than three hours. Usually a skinner made just one trip a night, but sometimes in an emergency he made two.

On an average night the supplies would run something like this—85 cans of water, 100 cases of K ration, 10 cases of D ration, 10 miles of telephone wire, 25 cases of grenades and rifle and machine-gun ammunition, about 100 rounds of heavy mortar shells, 1 radio, 2 telephones, and 4 cases of first-aid packets and sulfa drugs. In addition, the packers would cram their pockets with cigarettes for the boys on top; also cans of Sterno, so they could heat some coffee once in a while.

Also, during that period, they took up more than five hundred of the heavy combat suits we were issuing to the troops to help keep them warm. They carried up cellophane gas capes for some of the men to use as sleeping bags, and they took extra socks for them too.

Mail was their most tragic cargo. Every night they would take up sacks of mail, and every night they'd bring a large portion of it back down—the recipients would have been killed or wounded the day their letters came.

On the long man-killing climb above the end of the mule trail they used anywhere from twenty to three hundred men a night. They rang in cooks, truck drivers, clerks, and anybody else they could lay their hands on. A lot of stuff was packed up by the fighting soldiers themselves. On a big night, when they were building up supplies for an attack, another battalion which was in reserve sent three hundred first-line combat troops to do the packing. The mule packs would leave the olive grove in bunches of twenty, starting just after dark. American soldiers were posted within shouting distance of each other all along the trail, to keep the Italians from getting lost in the dark.

Those guides—everybody who thought he was having a tough time in this war should know about them. They were men who had fought all through a long and bitter battle at the top of the mountain. For more than a week they had been far up there, perched behind rocks in the rain and cold, eating cold K rations, sleeping without blankets, scourged constantly with artillery and mortar shells, fighting and ducking and growing more and more weary, seeing their comrades wounded one by one and taken down the mountain.

Finally sickness and exhaustion overtook many of those who were left, so they were sent back down the mountain under their own power to report to the medics there and then go to a rest camp. It took most of them the better part of a day to get two-thirds of the way down, so sore were their feet and so weary their muscles.

And then—when actually in sight of their haven of rest and peace—they were stopped and pressed into guide service, because there just wasn't anybody else to do it. So there they stayed on the mountainside, for at least three additional days and nights that I know of, just lying miserably alongside the trail, shouting in the darkness to guide the mules.

They had no blankets to keep them warm, no beds but the rocks. And they did it without complaining. The human spirit is an astounding thing.

In this war I have known a lot of officers who were loved and re-spected by the soldiers under them. But never have I crossed the trail of any man as beloved as Captain Henry T. Waskow, of Belton, Texas.

Captain Waskow was a company commander in the Thirty-sixth Divi-sion. He had led his company since long before it left the States. He was very young, only in his middle twenties, but he carried in him a sincerity and a gen-tleness that made people want to be guided by him.

"After my father, he came next," a sergeant told me.

"He always looked after us," a soldier said. "He'd go to bat for us every time."

"I've never knowed him to do anything unfair," another said.

I was at the foot of the mule trail the night they brought Captain Waskow down. The moon was nearly full, and you could see far up the trail, and even partway across the valley below.

They slid him down from the mule, and stood him on his feet for a moment. In the half-light he might have been merely a sick man standing there leaning on the others. Then they laid him on the ground in the shadow of the low stone wall beside the road. We left him there beside the road, that first one, and we all went back into the cowshed and sat on water cans or lay on the straw, waiting for the next batch of mules.

Somebody said the dead soldier had been dead for four days, and then nobody said anything more about it. We talked soldier talk for an hour or more; the dead man lay all alone, outside in the shadow of the wall.

Then a soldier came into the cowshed and said there were some more bodies outside. We went out into the road. Four mules stood there in the moonlight, in the road where the trail came down off the mountain. The sol-diers who led them stood there waiting.

"This one is Captain Waskow," one of them said quietly.

Two men unlashed his body from the mule and lifted it off and laid it in the shadow beside the stone wall. Other men took the other bodies off. Fi-nally, there were five lying end to end in a long row. You don't cover up dead men in the combat zones. They just lie there in the shadows until somebody comes after them.

The unburdened mules moved off to their olive grove. The men in the road seemed reluctant to leave. They stood around, and gradually I could sense them moving, one by one, close to Captain Waskow's body. Not so much to look, I think, as to say something in finality to him, and to themselves I stood close by and I could hear.

One soldier came and looked down, and he said out loud, "God damn it!"

That's all he said, and then he walked away.

Another one came, and he said, "God damn it to hell anyway!" He looked down for a few last moments and then turned and left.

Another man came. I think he was an officer. It was hard to tell officers from men in the dim light, for everybody was bearded and grimy. The man looked down into the dead captain's face and then spoke directly to him, as though he were alive, "I'm sorry, old man."

Then a soldier came and stood beside the officer and bent over, and he too spoke to his dead captain, not in a whisper but awfully tenderly, and he said, "I sure am sorry, sir."

Then the first man squatted down, and he reached down and took the captain's hand, and he sat there for a full five minutes holding the dead hand in his own and looking intently into a dead face. And he never uttered a sound all the time he sat there.

Finally he put the hand down. He reached over and gently straightened the points of the captain's shirt collar, and then he sort of rearranged the tattered edges of the uniform around the wound, and then he got up and walked away down the road in the moonlight, all alone.

The rest of us went back into the cowshed, leaving the five dead men lying in a line, end to end, in the shadow of the low stone wall. We lay down on the straw in the cowshed, and pretty soon we were all asleep.

The Red Badge of Courage

BY STEPHEN CRANE

THIS EXCERPT FROM Stephen Crane's masterpiece is taken from the climatic portions of the Civil War novel, during which Crane's protagonist—identified throughout the story as "the youth"—faces the ultimate horrors of combat.

Published in 1895, *The Red Badge of Courage* brought to the general public of that time the most wrenching battlefield images since the photographs of Matthew Brady that had been taken and exhibited during the war. Brady's photographs and his own research, talent and imagination were the creative impetus that led Crane (1871–1900) to produce his stirring portrait of courage under fire. For despite the book's realism, Crane had never actually witnessed a battle. The popular writer Ambrose Bierce said of Crane, "This young man has the power to feel. He knows nothing of war, yet he is drenched in blood. Most beginners who deal with this subject spatter themselves with ink."

Crane's success with *The Red Badge of Courage* led to his later experiences as a war correspondent. A shipwreck he survived off Cuba inspired his famous story "The Open Boat," but resulted in long-term health problems that contributed to his early demise from consumption in 1900.

Reading *The Red Badge of Courage* today leaves me with the feeling that time has not diminished the novel's impact a bit. It remains to this day an American classic.

★   ★   ★   ★   ★

The youth stared at the land in front of him. Its foliage now seemed to veil powers and horrors. He was unaware of the machinery of orders that started the charge, although from the corners of his eyes he saw an officer, who looked like a boy a-horseback, come galloping, waving his hat. Suddenly he felt a straining and heaving among the men. The line fell slowly forward like a toppling wall, and, with a convulsive gasp that was intended for a cheer, the regiment began its journey. The youth was pushed and jostled for a moment before he understood the movement at all, but directly he lunged ahead and began to run.

He fixed his eye upon a distant and prominent clump of trees where he had concluded the enemy were to be met, and he ran toward it as toward a goal. He had believed throughout that it was a mere question of getting over an unpleasant matter as quickly as possible, and he ran desperately, as if pursued for a murder. His face was drawn hard and tight with the stress of his endeavor. His eyes were fixed in a lurid glare. And with his soiled and disordered dress, his red and inflamed features surmounted by the dingy rag with its spot of blood, his wildly swinging rifle and banging accoutrements, he looked to be an insane soldier.

As the regiment swung from its position out into a cleared space the woods and thickets before it awakened. Yellow flames leaped toward it from many directions. The forest made a tremendous objection.

The line lurched straight for a moment. Then the right wing swung forward; it in turn was surpassed by the left. Afterward the center careered to the front until the regiment was a wedge-shaped mass, but an instant later the opposition of the bushes, trees, and uneven places on the ground split the command and scattered it into detached clusters.

The youth, light-footed, was unconsciously in advance. His eyes still kept note of the clump of trees. From all places near it the clannish yell of the enemy could be heard. The little flames of rifles leaped from it. The song of the bullets was in the air and shells snarled among the tree-tops. One tumbled directly into the middle of a hurrying group and exploded in crimson fury. There was an instant's spectacle of a man, almost over it, throwing up his hands to shield his eyes.

Other men, punched by bullets, fell in grotesque agonies. The regiment left a coherent trail of bodies.

They had passed into a clearer atmosphere. There was an effect like a revelation in the new appearance of the landscape. Some men working madly at a battery were plain to them, and the opposing infantry's lines were defined by the gray walls and fringes of smoke.

It seemed to the youth that he saw everything. Each blade of the green grass was bold and clear. He thought that he was aware of every change in the thin, transparent vapor that floated idly in sheets. The brown or gray trunks of the trees showed each roughness of their surfaces. And the men of the regiment, with their starting eyes and sweating faces, running madly, or falling, as if thrown headlong, to queer, heaped-up corpses—all were comprehended. His mind took a mechanical but firm impression, so that afterward everything was pictured and explained to him, save why he himself was there.

But there was a frenzy made from this furious rush. The men, pitching forward insanely, had burst into cheerings, moblike and barbaric, but tuned in strange keys that can arouse the dullard and the stoic. It made a mad enthusiasm that, it seemed, would be incapable of checking itself before granite and brass. There was the delirium that encounters despair and death, and is heedless and blind to the odds. It is a temporary but sublime absence of selfishness. And because it was of this order was the reason, perhaps, why the youth wondered, afterward, what reasons he could have had for being there.

Presently the straining pace ate up the energies of the men. As if by agreement, the leaders began to slacken their speed. The volleys directed against them had had a seeming windlike effect. The regiment snorted and blew. Among some stolid trees it began to falter and hesitate. The men, staring intently, began to wait for some of the distant walls of smoke to move and disclose to them the scene. Since much of their strength and their breath had vanished, they returned to caution. They were become men again.

The youth had a vague belief that he had run miles, and he thought, in a way, that he was now in some new and unknown land.

The moment the regiment ceased its advance the protesting splutter of musketry became a steadier roar. Long and accurate fringes of smoke spread out. From the top of a small hill came level belchings of yellow flame that caused an inhuman whistling in the air.

The men, halted, had opportunity to see some of their comrades dropping with moans and shrieks. A few lay under foot, still or wailing. And now for an instant the men stood, their rifles slack in their hands, and watched the regiment dwindle. They appeared dazed and stupid. This spectacle seemed to paralyze them, overcome them with a fatal fascination. They stared woodenly at the sights, and, lowering their eyes, looked from face to face. It was a strange pause, and a strange silence.

Then, above the sounds of the outside commotion, arose the roar of the lieutenant. He strode suddenly forth, his infantile features black with rage.

"Come on, yeh fools!" he bellowed. "Come on! Yeh can't stay here. Yeh must come on." He said more, but much of it could not be understood.

He started rapidly forward, with his head turned toward the men. "Come on," he was shouting. The men stared with blank and yokel-like eyes at him. He was obliged to halt and retrace his steps. He stood then with his back to the enemy and delivered gigantic curses into the faces of the men. His body vibrated from the weight and force of his imprecations. And he could string oaths with the facility of a maiden who strings beads.

The friend of the youth aroused. Lurching suddenly forward and dropping to his knees, he fired an angry shot at the persistent woods. This action awakened the men. They huddled no more like sheep. The seemed suddenly to bethink them of their weapons, and at once commenced firing. Belabored by their officers, they began to move forward. The regiment, involved like a cart involved in mud and muddle, started unevenly with many jolts and jerks. The men stopped now every few paces to fire and load, and in this manner moved slowly on from trees to trees.

The flaming opposition in their front grew with their advance until it seemed that all forward ways were barred by the thin leaping tongues, and off to the right an ominous demonstration could sometimes be dimly discerned. The smoke lately generated was in confusing clouds that made it difficult for the regiment to proceed with intelligence. As he passed through each curling mass the youth wondered what would confront him on the farther side.

The command went painfully forward until an open space interposed between them and the lurid lines. Here, crouching and cowering behind some trees, the men clung with desperation, as if threatened by a wave. They looked wild-eyed, and as if amazed at this furious disturbance they had stirred. In the storm there was an ironical expression of their importance. The faces of the men, too, showed a lack of a certain feeling of responsibility for being there. It was as if they had been driven. It was the dominant animal failing to remember in the supreme moments the forceful causes of various superficial qualities. The whole affair seemed incomprehensible to many of them.

As they halted thus the lieutenant again began to bellow profanely. Regardless of the vindictive threats of the bullets, he went about coaxing, berating, and bedamning. His lips, that were habitually in a soft and childlike curve, were now writhed into unholy contortions. He swore by all possible deities.

Once he grabbed the youth by the arm. "Come on, yeh lunkhead!" he roared. "Come on! We'll all git killed if we stay here. We've on'y got t' go across that lot. An' then"—the remainder of his idea disappeared in a blue haze of curses.

The youth stretched forth his arm. "Cross there?" His mouth was puckered in doubt and awe.

"Certainly. Jest 'cross th' lot! We can't stay here," screamed the lieutenant. He poked his face close to the youth and waved his bandaged hand.

"Come on!" Presently he grappled with him as if for a wrestling bout. It was as if he planned to drag the youth by the ear on to the assault.

The private felt a sudden unspeakable indignation against his officer. He wrenched fiercely and shook him off.

"Come on yerself, then," he yelled. There was a bitter challenge in his voice.

They galloped together down the regimental front. The friend scrambled after them. In front of the colors the three men began to bawl: "Come on! come on!" They danced and gyrated like tortured savages.

The flag, obedient to these appeals, bended its glittering form and swept toward them. The men wavered in indecision for a moment, and then with a long, wailful cry the dilapidated regiment surged forward and began its new journey.

Over the field went the scurrying mass. It was a handful of men splattered into the faces of the enemy. Toward it instantly sprang the yellow tongues. A vast quantity of blue smoke hung before them. A mighty banging made ears valueless.

The youth ran like a madman to reach the woods before a bullet could discover him. He ducked his head low, like a football player. In his haste his eyes almost closed, and the scene was a wild blur. Pulsating saliva stood at the corners of his mouth.

Within him, as he hurled himself forward, was born a love, a despairing fondness for this flag which was near him. It was a creation of beauty and invulnerability. It was a goddess, radiant, that bended its form with an imperious gesture to him. It was a woman, red and white, hating and loving, that called him with the voice of his hopes. Because no harm could come to it he endowed it with power. He kept near, as if it could be a saver of lives, and an imploring cry went from his mind.

In the mad scramble he was aware that the color sergeant flinched suddenly, as if struck by a bludgeon. He faltered, and then became motionless, save for his quivering knees.

He made a spring and a clutch at the pole. At the same instant his friend grabbed it from the other side. They jerked at it, stout and furious, but the color sergeant was dead, and the corpse would not relinquish its trust. For a moment there was a grim encounter. The dead man, swinging with bended back, seemed to be obstinately tugging, in ludicrous and awful ways, for the possession of the flag.

It was past in an instant of time. They wrenched the flag furiously from the dead man, and, as they turned again, the corpse swayed forward with bowed head. One arm swung high, and the curved hand fell with heavy protest on the friend's unheeding shoulder.

When the woods again began to pour forth the dark-hued masses of the enemy the youth felt serene self-confidence. He smiled briefly when he saw men dodge and duck at the long screechings of shells that were thrown in giant hand-fuls over them. He stood, erect and tranquil, watching the attack begin against a part of the line that made a blue curve along the side of an adjacent hill. His vision being unmolested by smoke from the rifles of his companions, he had opportunities to see parts of the hard fight. It was a relief to perceive at last from whence came some of these noises which had been roared into his ears.

Off a short way he saw two regiments fighting a little separate battle with two other regiments. It was in a cleared space, wearing a set-apart look. They were blazing as if upon a wager, giving and taking tremendous blows. The firings were incredibly fierce and rapid. These intent regiments apparently were oblivious of all larger purposes of war, and were slugging each other as if at a matched game.

In another direction he saw a magnificent brigade going with the evident intention of driving the enemy from a wood. They passed in out of sight and presently there was a most awe-inspiring racket in the wood. The noise was unspeakable. Having stirred this prodigious uproar, and, apparently, finding it too prodigious, the brigade, after a little time, came marching airily out again with its fine formation in nowise disturbed. There were no traces of speed in its movements. The brigade was jaunty and seemed to point a proud thumb at the yelling wood.

On a slope to the left there was a long row of guns, gruff and maddened, denouncing the enemy, who, down through the woods, were forming for another attack in the pitiless monotony of conflicts. The round red discharges from the guns made a crimson flare and a high, thick smoke. Occasional glimpses could be caught of groups of the toiling artillerymen. In the rear of this row of guns stood a house, calm and white, amid bursting shells. A congregation of horses, tied to a long railing, were tugging frenziedly at their bridles. Men were running hither and thither.

The detached battle between the four regiments lasted for some time. There chanced to be no interference, and they settled their dispute by themselves. They struck savagely and powerfully at each other for a period of minutes, and then the lighter-hued regiments faltered and drew back, leaving the dark-blue lines shouting. The youth could see the two flags shaking with laughter amid the smoke remnants.

Presently there was a stillness, pregnant with meaning. The blue lines shifted and changed a trifle and stared expectantly at the silent woods and fields before them. The hush was solemn and churchlike, save for a distant battery that, evidently unable to remain quiet, sent a faint rolling thunder over the ground. It irritated, like the noises of unimpressed boys. The men imagined that it would prevent their perched ears from hearing the first words of the new battle.

Of a sudden the guns on the slope roared out a message of warning. A spluttering sound had begun in the woods. It swelled with amazing speed to a profound clamor that involved the earth in noises. The splitting crashes swept along the lines until an interminable roar was developed. To those in the midst of it it became a din fitted to the universe. It was the whirring and thumping of gigantic machinery, complications among the smaller stars. The youth's ears were filled up. They were incapable of hearing more.

On an incline over which a road wound he saw wild and desperate rushes of men perpetually backward and forward in riotous surges. These parts of the opposing armies were two long waves that pitched upon each other madly at dictated points. To and fro they swelled. Sometimes, one side by its yells and cheers would proclaim decisive blows, but a moment later the other side would be all yells and cheers. Once the youth saw a spray of light forms go in houndlike leaps toward the waving blue lines. There was much howling, and presently it went away with a vast mouthful of prisoners. Again, he saw a blue wave dash with such thunderous force against a gray obstruction that it seemed to clear the earth of it and leave nothing but trampled sod. And always in their swift and deadly rushes to and fro the men screamed and yelled like maniacs.

Particular pieces of fence or secure positions behind collections of trees were wrangled over, as gold thrones or pearl bedsteads. There were desperate lunges at these chosen spots seemingly every instant, and most of them were bandied like light toys between the contending forces. The youth could not tell from the battle flags flying like crimson foam in many directions which color of cloth was winning.

His emaciated regiment bustled forth with undiminished fierceness when its time came. When assaulted again by bullets, the men burst out in a barbaric cry of rage and pain. They bent their heads in aims of intent hatred behind the projected hammers of their guns. Their ramrods clanged loud with fury as their eager arms pounded the cartridges into the rifle barrels. The front of the regiment was a smoke-wall penetrated by the flashing points of yellow and red.

Wallowing in the fight, they were in an astonishingly short time resmudged. They surpassed in stain and dirt all their previous appearances. Moving to and fro with strained exertion, jabbering the while, they were, with their swaying bodies, black faces, and glowing eyes, like strange and ugly fiends jigging heavily in the smoke.

The lieutenant, returning from a tour after a bandage, produced from a hidden receptacle of his mind new and portentous oaths suited to the emergency. Strings of expletives he swung lashlike over the backs of his men, and it was evident that his previous efforts had in nowise impaired his resources.

The youth, still the bearer of the colors, did not feel his idleness. He was deeply absorbed as a spectator. The crash and swing of the great drama made him lean forward, intent-eyed, his face working in small contortions. Sometimes he prattled, words coming unconsciously from him in grotesque exclamations. He did not know that he breathed; that the flag hung silently over him, so absorbed was he.

A formidable line of the enemy came within dangerous range. They could be seen plainly—tall, gaunt men with excited faces running with long strides toward a wandering fence.

At sight of this danger the men suddenly ceased their cursing monotone. There was an instant of strained silence before they threw up their rifles and fired a plumping volley at the foes. There had been no order given; the men, upon recognizing the menace, had immediately let drive their flock of bullets without waiting for word of command.

But the enemy were quick to gain the protection of the wandering line of fence. They slid down behind it with remarkable celerity, and from this position they began briskly to slice up the blue men.

These latter braced their energies for a great struggle. Often, white clinched teeth shone from the dusky faces. Many heads surged to and fro, floating upon a pale sea of smoke. Those behind the fence frequently shouted and yelped in taunts and gibelike cries, but the regiment maintained a stressed silence. Perhaps, at this new assault the men recalled the fact that they had been named mud diggers, and it made their situation thrice bitter. They were breathlessly intent upon keeping the ground and thrusting away the rejoicing body of the enemy. They fought swiftly and with a despairing savageness denoted in their expressions.

The youth had resolved not to budge whatever should happen. Some arrows of scorn that had buried themselves in his heart had generated strange and unspeakable hatred. It was clear to him that his final and absolute revenge was to be achieved by his dead body lying, torn and gluttering, upon the field.

This was to be a poignant retaliation upon the officer who had said "mule dri-vers," and later "mud diggers," for in all the wild graspings of his mind for a unit responsible for his sufferings and commotions he always seized upon the man who had dubbed him wrongly. And it was his idea, vaguely formulated, that his corpse would be for those eyes a great and salt reproach.

The regiment bled extravagantly. Grunting bundles of blue began to drop. The orderly sergeant of the youth's company was shot through the cheeks. Its supports being injured, his jaw hung afar down, disclosing in the wide cavern of his mouth a pulsing mass of blood and teeth. And with it all he made attempts to cry out. In his endeavor there was a dreadful earnestness, as if he conceived that one great shriek would make him well.

The youth saw him presently go rearward. His strength seemed in no-wise impaired. He ran swiftly, casting wild glances for succor.

Others fell down about the feet of their companions. Some of the wounded crawled out and away, but many lay still, their bodies twisted into impossible shapes.

The youth looked once for his friend. He saw a vehement young man, powder-smeared and frowzled, whom he knew to be him. The lieutenant, also, was unscathed in his position at the rear. He had continued to curse, but it was now with the air of a man who was using his last box of oaths.

For the fire of the regiment had begun to wane and drip. The robust voice, that had come strangely from the thin ranks, was growing rapidly weak.

The colonel came running along back of the line. There were other officers following him. "We must charge'm!" they shouted. "We must charge'm!" they cried with resentful voices, as if anticipating a rebellion against this play by the men.

The youth, upon hearing the shout, began to study the distance be-tween him and the enemy. He made vague calculations. He saw that to be firm soldiers they must go forward. It would be death to stay in the present place, and with all the circumstances to go backward would exalt too many others. Their hope was to push the galling foes away from the fence.

He expected that his companions, weary and stiffened, would have to be driven to this assault, but as he turned toward them he perceived with a cer-tain surprise that they were giving quick and unqualified expressions of assent. There was an ominous, clanging overture to the charge when the shafts of the bayonets rattled upon the rifle barrels. At the yelled words of command the soldiers sprang forward in eager leaps. There was new and unexpected force in the movement of the regiment. A knowledge of its faded and jaded condition made the charge appear like a paroxysm, a display of the strength that comes before a final feebleness. The men scampered in insane fever of haste, racing as if to achieve a sudden success before an exhilarating fluid should leave them. It was a blind and despairing rush by the collection of men in dusty and tattered blue, over a green sward and under a sapphire sky, toward a fence, dimly outlined in smoke, from behind which spluttered the fierce rifles of enemies.

The youth kept the bright colors to the front. He was waving his free arm in furious circles, the while shrieking mad calls and appeals, urging on those that did not need to be urged, for it seemed that the mob of blue men hurling themselves on the dangerous group of rifles were again grown suddenly wild with an enthusiasm of unselfishness. From the many firings starting toward them, it looked as if they would merely succeed in making a great sprinkling of corpses on the grass between their former position and the fence. But they were in a state of frenzy, perhaps because of forgotten vanities, and it made an exhibition of sublime recklessness. There was no obvious questioning, nor figurings, nor diagrams. There was, apparently, no considered loopholes. It appeared that the swift wings of their desires would have shattered against the iron gates of the impossible.

He himself felt the daring spirit of a savage religion-mad. He was capable of profound sacrifices, a tremendous death. He had no time for dissections, but he knew that he thought of the bullets only as things that could prevent him from reaching the place of his endeavor. There were subtle flashings of joy within him that thus should be his mind.

He strained all his strength. His eyesight was shaken and dazzled by the tension of thought and muscle. He did not see anything excepting the mist of smoke gashed by the little knives of fire, but he knew that in it lay the aged fence of a vanished farmer protecting the snuggled bodies of the gray men.

As he ran a thought of the shock of contact gleamed in his mind. He expected a great concussion when the two bodies of troops crashed together. This became a part of his wild battle madness. He could feel the onward swing of the regiment about him and he conceived of a thunderous, crushing blow that would prostrate the resistance and spread consternation and amazement for miles. The flying regiment was going to have a catapultian effect. This dream made him run faster among his comrades, who were giving vent to hoarse and frantic cheers.

But presently he could see that many of the men in gray did intend to abide the blow. The smoke, rolling, disclosed men who ran, faces still turned. These grew to a crowd, who retired stubbornly. Individuals wheeled frequently to send a bullet at the blue wave.

But at one part of the line there was a grim and obdurate group that made no movement. They were settled firmly down behind posts and rails. A flag, ruffled and fierce, waved over them and their rifles dinned fiercely.

The blue whirl of men got very near, until it seemed that in truth there would be a close and frightful scuffle. There was an expressed disdain in the opposition of the little group, that changed the meaning of the cheers of the men in blue. They became yells of wrath, directed, personal. The cries of the two parties were now in sound an interchange of scathing insults.

They in blue showed their teeth; their eyes shone all white. They launched themselves as at the throats of those who stood resisting. The space between dwindled to an insignificant distance.

The youth had centered the gaze of his soul upon that other flag. Its possession would be high pride. It would express bloody minglings, near blows. He had a gigantic hatred for those who made great difficulties and complications. They caused it to be as a craved treasure of mythology, hung amid tasks and contrivances of danger.

He plunged like a mad horse at it. He was resolved it should not escape if wild blows and darings of blows could seize it. His own emblem, quivering and aflare, was winging toward the other. It seemed there would shortly be an encounter of strange beaks and claws, as of eagles.

The swirling body of blue men came to s sudden halt at close and disastrous range and roared a swift volley. The group in gray was split and broken by this fire, but its riddled body still fought. The men in blue yelled again and rushed in upon it.

The youth, in his leapings, saw, as through a mist, a picture of four or five men stretched upon the ground or writhing upon their knees with bowed heads as if they had been stricken by bolts from the sky. Tottering among them was the rival color bearer, whom the youth saw had been bitten vitally by the bullets of the last formidable volley. He perceived this man fighting a last struggle, the struggle of one whose legs are grasped by demons. It was a ghastly battle. Over his face was the bleach of death, but set upon it were the dark and hard lines of desperate purpose. With this terrible grin of resolution he hugged his precious flag to him and was stumbling and staggering in his design to go the way that led to safety for it.

But his wounds always made it seem that his feet were retarded, held, and he fought a grim fight, as with invisible ghouls fastened greedily upon his limbs. Those in advance of the scampering blue men, howling cheers, leaped at the fence. The despair of the lost was in his eyes as he glanced back at them.

The youth's friend went over the obstruction in a tumbling heap and sprang at the flag as a panther at prey. He pulled at it and, wrenching it free, swung up its red brilliancy with a mad cry of exultation even as the color bearer, gasping, lurched over in a final throe and, stiffening convulsively, turned his dead face to the ground. There was much blood upon the grass blades.

At the place of success there began more wild clamorings of cheers. The men gesticulated and bellowed in an ecstasy. When they spoke it was as if they considered their listener to be a mile away. What hats and caps were left to them they often slung high in the air.

At one part of the line four men had been swooped upon, and they now sat as prisoners. Some blue men were about them in an eager and curious circle. The soldiers had trapped strange birds, and there was an examination. A flurry of fast questions was in the air.

One of the prisoners was nursing a superficial wound in the foot. He cuddled it, baby-wise, but he looked up from it often to curse with an astonishing utter abandon straight at the noses of his captors. He consigned them to red regions; he called upon the pestilential wrath of strange gods. And with it all he was singularly free from recognition of the finer points of the conduct of prisoners of war. It was as if a clumsy clod had trod upon his toe and he conceived it to be his privilege, his duty, to use deep, resentful oaths.

Another, who was a boy in years, took his plight with great calmness and apparent good nature. He conversed with the men in blue, studying their faces with his bright and keen eyes. They spoke of battles and conditions. There was an acute interest in all their faces during this exchange of viewpoints. It seemed a great satisfaction to hear voices from where all had been darkness and speculation.

The third captive sat with a morose countenance. He preserved a stoical and cold attitude. To all advances he made one reply without variation, "Ah, go t' hell!"

The last of the four was always silent and, for the most part, kept his face turned in unmolested directions. From the views the youth received he seemed to be in a state of absolute dejection. Shame was upon him, and with it profound regret that he was, perhaps, no more to be counted in the ranks of his fellows. The youth could detect no expression that would allow him to believe that the other was giving a thought to his narrowed future, the pictured dungeons, perhaps, and starvations and brutalities, liable to the imagination. All to be seen was shame for captivity and regret for the right to antagonize.

After the men had celebrated sufficiently they settled down behind the old rail fence, on the opposite side to the one from which their foes had been driven. A few shot perfunctorily at distant marks.

There was some long grass. The youth nestled in it and rested, making a convenient rail support the flag. His friend, jubilant and glorified, holding his treasure with vanity, came to him there. They sat side by side and congratulated each other.

The roarings that had stretched in a long line of sound across the face of the forest began to grow intermittent and weaker. The stentorian speeches of the artillery continued in some distant encounter, but the crashes of the musketry had almost ceased. The youth and his friend of a sudden looked up, feeling a deadened form of distress at the waning of these noises, which had become a part of life. They could see changes going on among the troops. There were marchings this way and that way. A battery wheeled leisurely. On the crest of a small hill was the thick gleam of many departing muskets.

The youth arose. "Well, what now, I wonder?" he said. By his tone he seemed to be preparing to resent some new monstrosity in the way of dins and smashes. He shaded his eyes with his grimy hand and gazed over the field.

His friend also arose and stared. "I bet we're goin' t' git along out of this an' back over th' river." said he.

"Well, I swan!" said the youth.

They waited, watching. Within a little while the regiment received orders to retrace its way. The men got up grunting from the grass, regretting the soft repose. They jerked their stiffened legs, and stretched their arms over their heads. One man swore as he rubbed his eyes. They all groaned "O Lord!" They had as many objections to this change as they would have had to a proposal for a new battle.

They trampled slowly back over the field across which they had run in a mad scamper.

The regiment marched until it had joined its fellows. The reformed brigade, in column, aimed through a wood at the road. Directly they were in a mass of dust-covered troops, and were trudging along in a way parallel to the enemy's lines as these had been defined by the previous turmoil.

They passed within view of a stolid white house, and saw in front of it groups of their comrades lying in wait behind a neat breastwork. A row of guns were booming at a distant enemy. Shells thrown in reply were raising clouds of dust and splinters. Horsemen dashed along the line of intrenchments.

At this point of its march the division curved from the field and went winding off in the direction of the river. When the significance of this movement had impressed itself upon the youth he turned his head and looked over his shoulder toward the trampled and *débris*-strewed ground. He breathed a breath of new satisfaction. He finally nudged his friend. "Well, it's all over," he said to him.

His friend gazed backward. "B'Gawd, it is," he assented. They mused. For a time the youth was obliged to reflect in a puzzled and uncertain way. His mind was undergoing a subtle change. It took moments for it to cast off its battleful ways and resume its accustomed course of thought. Gradually his brain emerged from the clogged clouds, and at last he was enabled to more closely comprehend himself and circumstance.

He understood then that the existence of shot and counter-shot was in the past. He had dwelt in a land of strange, squalling upheavals and had come forth. He had been where there was red of blood and black of passion, and he was escaped. His first thoughts were given to rejoicings at this fact.

Later he began to study his deeds, his failures, and his achievements. Thus, fresh from scenes where many of his usual machines of reflection had been idle, from where he had proceeded sheeplike, he struggled to marshal all his acts.

At last they marched before him clearly. From this present viewpoint he was enabled to look upon them in spectator fashion and to criticize them with some correctness, for his new condition had already defeated certain sympathies.

Regarding his procession of memory he felt gleeful and unregretting, for in it his public deed were paraded in great and shining prominence. Those performances which had been witnessed by his fellows marched now in wide purple and gold, having various deflections. They went gayly with music. It was pleasure to watch these things. He spent delightful minutes viewing the gilded images of memory.

He saw that he was good. He recalled with a thrill of joy the respectful comments of his fellow upon his conduct.

Nevertheless, the ghost of his flight from the first engagement appeared to him and danced. There were small shoutings in his brain about these matters. For a moment he blushed, and the light of his soul flickered with shame.

A specter of reproach came to him. There loomed the dogging memory of the tattered soldier—he who, gored by bullets and faint for blood, had fretted concerning an imagined wound in another; he who had loaned his last of strength and intellect for the tall soldier; he who, blind with weariness and pain, had been deserted in the field.

For an instant a wretched chill of sweat was upon him at the thought that he might be detected in the thing. As he stood persistently before his vision, he gave vent to a cry of sharp irritation and agony.

His friend turned. "What's the matter, Henry?" he demanded. The youth's reply was an outburst of crimson oaths.

As he marched along the little branch-hung roadway among his prattling companions this vision of cruelty brooded over him. It clung near him always and darkened his view of these deeds in purple and gold. Whichever way his thoughts turned they were followed by the somber phantom of the desertion in the fields. He looked stealthily at his companions, feeling sure that they must discern in his face evidences of this pursuit. But they were plodding in ragged array, discussing with quick tongues the accomplishments of the late battle.

"Oh, if a man should come up an' ask me, I'd say we got a dum good lickin'."

"Lickin'—in yer eye! We ain't licked, sonny. We're going down here aways, swing aroun', an' come in behint 'em."

"Oh, hush, with your comin' in behint 'em. I've seen all 'a that I wanta. Don't tell me about comin' in behint—"

"Bill Smithers, he ses he'd rather been in ten hundred battles than been in that heluva hospital. He ses they got shootin' in th' nighttime, an' shells dropped plum among 'em in th' hospital. He ses sech hollerin' he never see."

"Hasbrouck? He's th' best off'cer in this here reg'ment. He's a whale."

"Didn't I tell yeh we'd come aroun' in behint 'em? Didn't I tell yeh so? We—"

"Oh, shet yer mouth!"

For a time this pursuing recollection of the tattered man took all elation from the youth's veins. He saw his vivid error, and he was afraid that it would stand before him all his life. He took no share in the chatter of his comrades, nor did he look at them or know them, save when he felt sudden suspicion that they were seeing his thoughts and scrutinizing each detail of the scene with the tattered soldier.

Yet gradually he mustered force to put the sin at a distance. And at last his eyes seemed to open to some new ways. He found that he could look back upon the brass and bombast of his earlier gospels and see them truly. He was gleeful when he discovered that he now despised them.

With the conviction came a store of assurance. He felt a quiet manhood, non-assertive but of sturdy and strong blood. He knew that he would no more quail before his guides wherever they should point. He had been to touch the great death, and found that, after all, it was but the great death. He was a man.

So it came to pass that as he trudged from the place of blood and wrath his soul changed. He came from hot plowshares to prospects of clover tranquilly, and it was as if hot plowshares were not. Scars faded as flowers.

It rained. The procession of weary soldiers became a bedraggled train, despondent and muttering, marching with churning effort in a trough of liquid brown mud under a low, wretched sky. Yet the youth smiled, for he saw that the world was a world for him, though many discovered it to be made of oaths and walking sticks. He had rid himself of the red sickness of battle. The sultry nightmare was in the past. He had been an animal blistered and sweating in the heat and pain of war. He turned now with a lover's thirst to images of tranquil skies, fresh meadows, cool brooks—an existence of soft and eternal peace.

Over the river a golden ray of sun came through the hosts of leaden rain clouds.

The Perfect Deadfall

From Ambush

BY S. L. A. MARSHALL [BRIG. GEN., USAR, RET.]

T HE LATE S. L. A. MARSHALL was an army historian of such depth and literary productivity that choosing any particular one of his battle-field reports as being "the best" is a somewhat daunting task. In books such as *Battle at Best, Night Drop, The River and the Gauntlet, The Fields of Bamboo* and *Ambush,* Marshall's prose captures small-unit action in vivid detail—from exact weapons and ammo down to the field names of the radios. As I mentioned in the introduction to this book, Marshall was literally sometimes on the scene of the action, interviewing the troops, within hours of the final shots. And, as I also tried to point out, Marshall was the master of de-picting battle as unbridled chaos and confusion, where chance, sheer luck, and timing dictated who lived, who died, who was victorious, and who was forced to retreat.

"The Perfect Deadfall" is from *Ambush,* which, like *The Fields of Bam-boo,* is a classic account of the fighting in Vietnam, the actual combat as it took place in the bush—not on maps in headquarters. Here is the story of a relativ-ity simple patrol that goes wrong. Three infantry squads set out on a walk through the jungle on a mission they expect to complete by 1500 (3 P.M.) and be back in their armored personnel carriers to return to base.

As you will see, things did not work out that way.

★　★　★　★　★

As the newly arrived ADC of the First Infantry Division, Brig. Gen. Bernie Rogers reckoned that all things were coming his way—at least for one day.

The weather on 11 December, 1966, although clear-skied and sunny, was refreshingly cool, a rare thing in any season for the flat, semijungle-grown countryside a short chopper ride from Saigon. There had been a drenching rain during the night and the land fairly sparkled.

So did Rogers' upcoming morning appointment. At 1100, he was to be at Thuc Duc where Second Battalion of the 16th Infantry was in the process of sealing off a suspected village. Playing ringside spectator at a possible flight, however, was not the purpose at hand.

A specialist 4, formerly of the battalion, who had just extended for six months, was to be awarded to combat decorations, and Rogers was to do the pinning.

An extremely intense soldier, with a scholarly bent that had won him honors at Oxford as well as USMA, slightly on the formal side and inclined to blast when he had good reason to feel provoked, Rogers relished the thought of the ceremony. It was a chance to meet men of the division on intimate terms. The soldier to be honored would fly with him. He was now Rogers' driver.

At 1045 the command Huey took off from Phouc Vinh, under the hand of Rogers' pilot, Lt. Marvin Schendler. The aircraft's commander was Capt. Cary Williams. All three were wearing headsets.

Just two minutes after takeoff they heard over the net, "There's a patrol contact near Soui Da." Rogers knew nothing of a patrol being out that morning and Soui Da was as yet little more than a name to him.

"Head for Soui Da," he said to the pilot.

He expected very little to come of it. The word "contact" is hardly more than an ambiguity. It could mean as small a thing as one rifle being fired at a fleeting figure in the bush. But then, one never knows, and it is better to be sure.

So there was no real feeling of urgency as they changed direction toward Soui Da, and Rogers' aide, Lt. Christopher Needels, set about changing communications arrangements within the ship. Needels left his own radio on the division net, a second set monitored First Battalion of the 16th, and the third tuned in on the First Battalion.

The first transmission received told Rogers that the First's commander, Lt. Col. Rufe Lazell, along with his operations officer, were en route to the hot spot by Huey.

Next, Rogers heard Lazell say to his S-3, "It looks to me as if the artillery is getting in too close."

A break followed. Rogers sensed only that it was no small thing. The chopper still had about 20 minutes' flying time to Soui Da.

When the next transmission came, Rogers' ship was almost over coordinate 363–622, the reported scene of the fight. But a mistake had been made and he had been given another coordinate, the numbers of the hit patrol's last checkpoint. So having peradventure flown to nearly the right spot, he went on looking for the wrong spot. It is easily done when one is flying over bush.

The words coming over his earphones were being said by the brigade commander, Col. Micky Marks, to the headquarters at base camp: "All contact with the platoon has been lost."

Rogers now knew that he would be heading into a storm, if he could but find it. He guessed that the platoon had been zapped by its own artillery. He could not have been more wrong.

The patrol, a platoon of three squads out of Charley Company, left the base camp at Soui Da at 0830 aboard APC's (armored personnel carriers).

For the next 20 minutes the tracked column rolled north along Highway No. 13, unloading six kilometers farther along, just short of a blown bridge.

The young commander of 2/C/1/16, Lt. Ben Starr, gave a pitch to the artillery forward observer, Lt. Alfred G. Carter, as they rode along.

Carter was from the Bravo Battery, Second Battalion, 33rd Artillery, based at Soui Da. He was meeting Starr for the first time and telling him straight that he didn't know much about patrolling.

Neither did Starr, but a rifle lieutenant is always loath to admit it to a gunner. "This will be a fairly simple one," he told Carter. "We'll stay on one azimuth most of the time and do a lot of cloverleafing. About 1500, we're due back on the highway, so that the tracks can pick us up."

Carter wondered to himself why, if it was possible to be certain of maintaining such a schedule, it was still necessary for the patrol to move out at all. Here was a tenable doubt. The patrol, presumably, was on an S & D mission. So the prime consideration had to be its own security, which called for care rather than speed. Yet it had to keep an eye on the clock.

The tracks slowed, then went into firing position along the road as they ground to a halt. Starr's men scrambled out. Nearby were two ox carts, the oxen dead from gunshots and aboard each vehicle the sprawled body of a Vietcong, one cold, the other about to expire.

"It looks as if another patrol came this way," Carter remarked.

Starr deployed his people in a circle, then drew the squad leaders to the center to tell them how things would be. The First Squad would lead out, followed by the Second Squad, Third bringing up the rear. A one-man point would stay ahead of the main body about 50 meters. Flankers would be used, two men on either side, about 20 meters out from the column. "We will march approximately northwest," Starr said, "and we will not use any trail."

They were not heavy-laden. The riflemen bore three hundred rounds apiece for their M-16's. There were four hundred rounds for each of the M-60 machine guns. Each man carried four frag grenades, and every other man toted two smoke grenades, besides which there were three claymore mines with each squad.

Exactly at 0915, they jumped off into the sea of elephant grass west of the road, and within about 10 minutes they entered upon the forest, a very light tropical forest, with little of the impedimenta that is to be found in jungle. Thereafter, they did little or none of what they had promised themselves. They got on one trail and stayed on it. They did not cloverleaf, or drop a stay-behind party to see if they were being followed. But it was a most pleasant morning, the air was refreshing, and although it would be wrong to say that they enjoyed the outing, they were under no particular stress.

The forest was sopping wet. Its damp cooled their clothing. But it also fouled communications, or at least Carter attributed the trouble with his radio to that cause. And he needed that radio. It had been arranged that two of the guns in Soui Da would step out fires in front of them, occasional rounds, dropped about three hundred meters to their fore, with the object of breaking up any VC ambush. To regulate the fires at all, Carter had to raise his aerial, which required the halting of the column now and then.

But the noise from the breaking shells was not all. The flankers out in the bush kept yelling back and forth to make certain they were maintaining contact, and no one tried to stop them. So although they were somewhat less tumultuous than a circus parade, altogether they proceeded as if hunting leopards with a brass band.

The forest floor was flat and decently level, although there were a few ditches to be waded, and occasional patches of bamboo forced them to make small detours. There were many footprints on the trail, the marks of bare feet, and also of sandals. They had to be fresh; the trail had been dust the day before. Vietnamese had walked the trail this morning. By 1000, the platoon had marched about twelve hundred meters, which is fast going in any Vietnam forest. Having fired about 60 rounds during the 45 minutes that the patrol was advancing, the guns had broken off.

Carter said, "We have to stop now for a few minutes."

"What's wrong?" Starr asked.

"We're moving beyond the traverse of the guns," the artilleryman explained. "We're walking perpendicular to their line of fire. We had figured that this was just about the limit—where the platoon would turn around. If we're to have fire, the battery will have to be relaid."

Starr did not argue with him. But more than several minutes passed before, over the radio, Carter got the green light from the battery. Meantime the flankers had come in and had been replaced. Up front of the column, a soldier named Hardison, playing second scout, talked things over with the point man, Private First Class Wagner.

"I ain't heard one suspicious sound," said Hardison.

"And we probably won't," said Wagner.

The march resumed. Again the men heard the shells exploding forward of them. But once more there was an interruption.

Starr called a halt. It was not really a fallout for rest, just a pause for a head count. The lieutenant wanted to be sure that all hands were present. They were.

While they tarried, Starr and Carter conferred briefly. The young gunner from Scranton felt uneasy. There was nothing he could put a finger on; it was just that things were too deadly quiet. "Don't you think we've gone far enough?" he asked Starr.

Starr considered, then replied, "No, we've got about another seven hundred meters to go before we turn about."

According to the assigned mission, that was true enough. But it was all too pat. That another patrol had gone the same route the day before and wheeled about at the same point more than trebled the danger from now on. Of that fact, Starr was completely unaware.

The men fretted through the halt for quite another reason. The wide spot in the trail swarmed with king-sized ants, an inch or more long, with a sting like a hornet's. In a trice, they were in every man's clothing. The platoon fought back, swatting, fuming, cursing, and raising a great racket. It was a relief when the order came to resume the march.

They went on for another 20 minutes. Carter, midway in the column with Starr, was silent and brooding. He had been measuring things out as they walked and he thought the platoon had gone the full distance.

The head of the column was already debouching into the open, a natural clearing, about 45 meters across by 60 meters long, and shaped like a great keyhole, flaring angularly at one end, smoothly rounded at the other. Part of it was like meadow, the rest covered with waist-high elephant grass. The flat surface was speckled here and there with slender saplings, several large logs, and at least three tall ant hills. It looked innocently inviting.

Starr did not know that the column point had arrived at a clearing. His map showed none. So no word went forward to avoid the clearing for safety's sake and to swing around it within the tree line. No one on the point thought to hold up within the trees and raise a main question. Being in motion, the point so continued. Automatic, if hardly sensible.

By the time Starr and Carter emerged into the open, the lead files in the column were two-thirds of the way across and stepping out briskly. That they had moved far better than they had scanned became apparent in that instant.

In the lead was Pfc. Hawatha Hardison, a burly twenty-year-old Negro from Winston-Salem. He stopped dead in his tracks and stared, not believing what he saw.

Standing 10 feet away, directly in front of him, and unseen until that moment, were three uniformed figures, stock still and with their backs turned. They were togged in green pants and brown shirts, wore camouflaged pith helmets, and carried rifles at shoulder. So dressed, they had blended into the background.

Getting that sweet picture in one flash, Hardison's mind had room for one thought only: "We sneaked up on them and we've got them." In the nature of things, that would have been impossible. Yet Hardison and his mates had never heard that the Victcong put out human lures, wittingly risking their lives to suck innocents into an ambush. It is a concept in any case too diabolical for ready acceptance by Western minds.

Before Hardison could manually react, the three figures darted away rightward toward the tree line at the founded end of the clearing. It was a hot sprint. Still, Sgt. Ray Dickerson had time to shoulder his M-79 and fire three rounds while they were in sight. The explosions came just as they hit the trees and Dickerson thought he saw two of them stagger and fall. Maybe. Inevitably, the front half of the column, giving chase, became spread out broadside to the dense forest growth on the far side of the clearing, the precise effect for which the three stooges had risked their lives. The name of the game was Follow Me. Hardison had his own technical term for this random and spontaneous deployment: "We went at once into an overmatch formation."

Starr and Carter were six paces into the clearing when Dickerson fired. Neither said a word to the other. Busy with his own thoughts, Carter was not at once jolted into action by the M-79 rounds and later could not remember that he had heard them. Starr left him instantly and ran forward about 30 meters. Before he could flop down, automatic fire broke out from the far tree line directly against the platoon front. The hidden positions could not have been more than 20 to 25 meters from the uneven line of skirmishers. By now Carter was on radio to Bravo Battery: "We're in it, so stand by." The question was where to fire.

Where he lay, Hardison was being buzzed by bullets from his front, and he thought, from his left. It wasn't healthy. He decided to swing as far over as possible to the right, toward the point where the three VC had hit the tree line. He squirmed on his belly in that direction; and six or seven other riflemen followed him. It seemed, at first, like a fair hunch. Although that corner was not exactly quiet, to Hardison's anxious ear it sounded as if the bullet fire "was more thinned out there."

Private First Class Eugene Hicks, a twenty-year-old Negro from Forrest City, Arkansas, had been bringing along the M-60 machine gun in the second half of the column. A good soldier, on the quiet side, Hicks rushed the gun forward into the clearing on hearing the firing. It wasn't given to him to stay long, which was his good luck.

Sergeant Dickerson saw him and yelled, "Take that gun and get back to the trail opening! We're drawing fire from the rear."

Hicks might have let that go, but there came a reenforcing yell from Starr: "Get on the rear with that machine gun!" Hicks started to move. However, Dickerson, reacting compulsively to Starr's order, ran over and grabbed the M-60 from Hicks, then legged it for the trail mouth, with Hicks following along.

Dickerson flopped down as he came to the tree line and opened fire down trail. There were only 20 bullets in the M-60 (of which fact Dickerson was unaware) and within seconds the gun sputtered out. The sergeant wasn't given time to determine what had happened; a bullet hit him and he slumped over.

Hicks' ammo bearer had dropped his load 15 meters back along the trail. Being there on the spot, before Hicks could stop him, he picked up the gun and carried it back to the ammunition deposit. Hicks simply followed along. No one was present to give him orders, and besides, he was not the assertive type. Dickerson crawled along after them just to be near someone. No one was offering first aid and he wasn't asking for it.

The other machine gun was somewhere forward. Hicks didn't know just where; in his less than one-half minute on the open fire field he'd had little chance to see anything. What his ears told him was that the forward gun wasn't firing. He took that as a bad sign. Muffled by the forest, as if far off, he heard cries of "Medic, medic."

Seldom has a soldier had reason to feel lonelier than Hicks at this time. He did not know the platoon. He had joined it 30 days before. On his first morning, he had been hard wounded while on patrol. There followed 29 days in hospital. He had returned the prior evening, a stranger, and a stranger he stayed. It shouldn't happen to a dog.

They now were drawing continuous fire from all around the clearing, in heavy volume and without a single break. Except for that growing rattle, the silence of surprise still hung heavily over the place. All the riflemen had gone flat, and for these minutes only, the depth of the elephant grass gave them a little hold on life. The enemy, too, showed signs of being plagued by nerves; most of the bullet fire was going high.

Hugging his radio in the center of the clearing, Carter heard Starr sing out above the rising whine of the metal, "Where's the goddamn artillery?"

"On the way, sir!" Carter yelled back.

And it was truly on the way; he had just called for it and had less than 30 seconds to wait for the first round.

Starr was on the PRC-25 (lightweight infantry field radio) again. This time he was begging higher command for mortar fire. Carter could hear him yelling, "You got to give me the 81's right now!"

But he was wasting time and breath. Back came the answer, "We can't help you. You're out of range."

Seconds later, he was pleading for gunships (rocket-armed helicopters). The anguish in his voice startled Carter. A minute before, artilleryman Carter had supposed that the infantry platoon would be getting the upper hand in short order. Now he sensed that the situation was becoming fully desperate, or at least he knew Starr thought so.

Starr was putting it over the radio to his company commander, Captain Crain:

"We must have help. There's more than a company against us. We're already hurting and we can't withdraw."

But Starr's estimate was pure guess, reckoned from the sound and fury of the enemy fire. So far, he personally had seen not one VC. Nor had Carter. It does not necessarily follow that there was no visible enemy movement. The grass still stood high and their heads were low; they had to be.

Carter asked himself, "What does it mean?" Continuous VC fire at almost measurable intervals would blaze higher from quadrant to quadrant, as if there were suddenly five or six automatic weapons working where one had been before. The movement was clockwise. Every half-minute or so the fusillade would swing to a different quarter. Carter thought he had it figured out: There must be fixed positions all around the clearing. The VC were clustering their weapons and swinging their killer groups from one fire bunker to another. Now if he could catch them during movement in the open—.

Carter had already made two adjustments. The first shells had landed far off. Now he had them coming where he felt they might check the rotary movement of the VC firers, provided he could lay the rounds on thick.

This was his message to the guns: "Give us continuous fire, not just a shell now and then."

A more pitiful request in the circumstances is beyond imagination. The 105-mm. battery had only three tubes firing in support. There was never any chance that artillery used in such weak numbers could influence the outcome, irrespective of how accurately the fire was adjusted.

And the last chance for adjustment died with Carter's words. In that split second, as the FO quit speaking, a bullet shot his radio's cord away. An earlier bullet had already shattered the microphone and Carter had put on a spare; at the same time another enemy slug snubbed the PRC-25 aerial one foot above his head. With that, Carter was dead as a communicator and could only witness the results. The friendly shells kept falling along the flanks of the clearing; there was no change in the volume of enemy fire except that it steadily built upward. In these moments Carter lost his belief in the magic of artillery.

In these moments also Hardison was lying near one other member of the platoon whom he did not know. Between them was an ant hill about three feet high and looking as if it were made of concrete loosely poured into a weathered conical form. Both riflemen, firing, were using the base of the ant hill for protection, nothing in sight looking better.

There was an explosion, and quite suddenly, the ant hill was gone. Hardison was blown into a spin, and coming to rest, bruised but otherwise unhurt, said, "It looks like Charlie is using mortars, or was it a grenade?"

No answer was returned. His unknown friend, his body badly battered, was dead.

Hicks, low man on the totem pole, at the tail end of the formation, and well out of the fuss and fury, or so he thought, was under fire from both sides. Bullets were kicking up the dirt and clipping the leaves from the vines on his left and right. He guessed that there were two or three VC both ways from him, not more than 15 to 20 meters off, and he decided that their shooting was much too personal. Not wishing to make an issue of it, he got as close as possible to earth and said a few prayers.

Prayers were not for Hardison, he not being the praying type. He noticed that no yelling was rising from the American side, except for the cry, "Medic! Medic!" which rose close at hand, but he could hear it only faintly, almost as an echo at greater distance. His rifle jammed. Beating the M-16 on the ground, Hardison yelled, "Goddamnn that weapon!" The impact, rather than the profanity, partly broke the block, but the rifle would no longer fire full automatic.

Another bullet smashed through the center of Carter's radio, and metal fragments from the instrument slashed him through the shoulder and left arm. Still, he felt no pain, and although he bled profusely, for the moment he did not notice it. He was too busy harkening to the voice of Starr and trying to catch a glimpse of him.

The infantry platoon leader was not more than 10 meters from Carter and directly to his left. He was scrabbling around in the buffalo grass, feeling for M-79 rounds, and finding a few of them. One of the thump gunners had died next to him from a bullet through the heart, and Starr had picked up the launcher. At top voice, he was calling out, "Squad leaders and machine gunners, hear me! Keep firing! But wait till you see targets. I'll tell you when to move."

It was a gallant effort and no less futile. The fight was then about 10 minutes along. Already the small plot where Starr and Carter were sprawled had been bracketed by mortar rounds. Carter reflected idly that there were no targets to be seen, and he wondered dully if anyone save himself was listening to Starr.

Then he heard Starr shout, "Bring the artillery closer!" Carter thought to himself, "Dear God, if I only could," and sensibly held back from singing out to Starr that he no longer had any control over the guns. "It's better that he not know," he thought to himself.

It was forbearance wasted. As he glanced toward the direction of the voice, he saw Starr rise to his knees with just the top of his head showing. In that split second, a bullet swarm hit him in the face and Carter knew from the motion as the body was lifted and thrown back that Starr was dead.

The artillery was not slowing down the VC attack one bit. The few who ultimately survived could all feel it was so. At his roost where the platoon had entered the clearing, Hicks could hear many enemy voices. But it was not the usual taunting chatter and laughter. It was steady and rhythmic: They were chanting directions to one another as they moved from bunker to bunker within the tree line. Hardison followed the beat, also. The VC were deploying more people around the clearing and the fire intensified in anever-widening circle.

The ammo bearer, Private First Class Flagg, later killed, lay motionless within arm's length of Hicks. He became hysterical, and repeated over and over, "I know the sound. It's Chinese assault weapons." The litany jangled Hicks' nerves till, sickening of it, he snapped, "You shut your big mouth. Who doesn't know the sound?" The man quieted for only a few seconds.

Starr's RTO, Specialist 4 White, was already dead from a bullet burst. The forward machine-gun crew had been given no chance to open fire; as they went into position behind a fallen tree, about one rod ahead of Starr, that spot was fairly swarming with bullets.

One of the rifleman scouts, Private First Class Welch, tried to warn them. Having flattened, Welch rose on his haunches and yelled, "Get away from that spot. They're coming over. They're all around us!"

It was too late for them and for Welch. He was cut down by bullets before he could flatten and the same enemy machine gun, traversing, scythed the crew and wrecked the M-60.

Of that, very early in the game, had come the elimination of the platoon aid man, Specialist 4 Harrison. Cries arose from the forward ground, "Medic, medic! Doc, come help us!" There was never a more willing aide man and it was given to Hardison to see him die. Harrison rose from the grass a few feet from Hardison and started running toward the log, made not more than a few strides, and pitched over, dead from a bullet burst.

Carter's RTO, Private First Class Strong, was also down, although not yet unconscious. There were multiple wounds in his head, both shoulders, back, and both arms, some caused by bullets and others from the propelled fragments of the PRC-25. He lay there, eyes open but not speaking, and Carter also maintained silence.

From forward in the clearing, an unidentified rifleman came running toward Strong and Carter. His right sleeve streamed blood. "We're all that's left," he shouted. "Everybody's dead." Then he flopped down between the two of them. Neither said a word. They made no protest that the fight was still going; possibly they could not think on it. The unknown picked up the M-16 that Carter had dropped, relieved Strong of his Colt .45, and started firing them alternately. He did not bother to aim. Blood pulsing from his head, Strong turned slowly to stare at the newcomer as if not understanding. He was still saying nothing. This bizarre scene endured not more than two minutes. The stranger suddenly slumped over and died; his was not quite the last fire from the American side.

Carter, gradually dulling to all sensation from pain and loss of blood as his wounds took over, looked that way to see why the firing had stopped and noted for the first time, without shock or any reaction, that another wounded American was stretched out just beyond the diehard rifleman.

Flagg, and ammo bearer next to Hicks, had ceased muttering about Chinese assault weapons. A bullet had drilled him through the head. The fire seemed to slow a little. Hicks looked about for the first time. Two other U.S. dead lay face down within less than body length to his left. He had no idea how and when they had been killed, nor could he sense how the fight was going in the clearing.

Hardison, from his position in center of the bulge at the extreme right of the clearing, knew more about that. He had wormed his way to another ant hill and intended to use it as a buffer till the finish, if given a chance. Five other riflemen still lived on that far flank, although none was firing. Hardison reckoned this was all that was left of the platoon. But he had no desire to go to them; he preferred the ant hill.

One of them, Private First Class Haskell, in his last moment of panic, arouse shouting, "They're coming on!" and started on a dead run for the mouth of the trail. As he dashed past Hardison, he reached down, grabbed his M-16, and sped on. He almost made it to Hicks before he was cut down by a machine-gun blast.

It "scared the hell" out of Hardison, not so much the snatching of his last weapon as the wild expression on Haskell's face when he passed. One of the riflemen Haskell had quitted rose halfway as if to follow him. Before he could straighten, a bullet swarm hit him around the head and shoulders and toppled him. Hardison crawled over belly down, grabbed his rifle, an M-16, and wiggled back to the ant hill.

Snuggled behind it, Hardison checked the magazine. There were 10 bullets. Somehow he had lost his own extra magazines as the fight opened. Still seeing no human targets, he took deliberate aim, firing nine rounds toward ground level of the tree line on the far side of the clearing.

Then he held fire. Almost instantly, the clearing was silent, or at least free of lethal noises. Hardison heard men moaning and a few feeble cries of "Medic, medic." There was no one to respond; not one American on the field had been given first aid.

The loud silence did not exactly awe Hardison; a phlegmatic Negro, surly by nature, uncommunicative except with himself, he knew what it meant, and continued to hug ground. There no longer remained on American armed and in condition to fight.

He grunted, then checked to make sure that the last bullet was still there. It was. He had his moment of bitter satisfaction that he had hoarded it.

Hicks heard the roar and rattle cease in these same moments and wondered what was happening. Not more than 45 meters from Hardison, he was still unaware that the platoon had died, never really having been in the fight. Even a little distance may make a vast difference.

Carter knew that something had changed. The noise was gone. Physically, mentally, he was too weak to interpret what it meant. He was not resigned to death. He was not even thinking about it. To think at all had become an intolerable strain. He lay motionless.

During these minutes, General Rogers and his party in the Huey had at last made their fix. They were bucketing back and forth above the clearing and viewing it as if from an upper-gallery seat. Of the enemy, they saw nothing. They saw the forms of the Americans, sprawled in the grass, motionless, apparently lifeless. The Huey orbited over the curved end of the clearing, flying just above the trees. Rogers tried to count bodies. The Huey lifted again. Then Rogers could see "a few of the kids down below beckoning to me with their arms."

Over the radio, he heard the battalion commander (who was also somewhere aloft) say, "I've got Charley Company on the road in APC's coming fast to relieve the platoon." It stunned Rogers. Relieve the platoon? It was already too late. Via the road? Rogers knew that the bridge was out a mile or so short of the forest. He had seen it while circling. Someone had blundered.

"I want to go down," he said to the pilot.

"If we do," Williams answered, "we'll never get up again."

"Let's try that area at the squared-off end of the clearing," Rogers suggested.

"We have too much gas and the radio console is too heavy," Williams replied.

Rogers pointed out a second area, still farther removed from the heat. The Huey made a couple of low passes, then lofted again and continued the circling. "There were too many trees," Williams explained.

And although Rogers could see it, he still fumed. He was no expert on Hueys and it wasn't his job to run rescue missions. He knew the rage of total frustration.

Moments later, Hardison regretted that he hadn't kept all 10 bullets. Five enemy soldiers, uniformed in khaki and conical hats, entered upon the clearing at his end; the central figure was carrying a machine gun. It was Hardison's first sight of any enemy figure or weapon. As the five men advanced, the VC gunner dusted the foreground with his weapon, blasting in short bursts. They walked straight toward Hardison, on the way spraying bullets into the three riflemen who still lived, as well as the dead men.

Hardison kept wiggling around the ant hill, hoping (not praying) that by some fluke he would stay out of sight.

Fate was on his side, intervening in the strangest possible way. Suddenly, there was a smell of chemical in the air. Hardison got it faintly, and his eyes smarted. A slight wind carried it in Carter's direction, and he coughed heavily; it came to him that the enemy must be gassing the area to finish the fight, and that was still his impression days later. But Hardison had seen the thing happen. One of the dead riflemen near him had been carrying a gas grenade hitched to his belt. In blasting him, the gunner had put a hole through the container. The VC party turned and headed back toward the tree line to escape the drifting gas. Hardison lived on. All other Americans in the semicircular end of the clearing were now dead.

Several minutes passed. Carter heard men chattering Vietnamese very excitedly. They seemed right at hand. Whether this was another mop-up group or marked the return of the executioners who had worried Hardison, there is no way of knowing. Carter summoned such little strength as remained to him, slid on his belly five feet, turned the third American face down, then did the same for Strong. Both men seemed to be in a dying condition. Carter whispered to Strong, "The one chance is to play dead," but doubted that Strong heard him. He then pulled himself back to his old position by the radio and went limp, face down.

The enemy party (not being able to look, Carter did not know its number) was policing the battlefield and picking up weapons. In that moment, as the VC walked toward them, the third American, suddenly regaining consciousness began to babble. It was Carter's most agonizing time. "If you want to live," he whispered, "keep quiet!" Either the man heard, or he relapsed again.

Now the enemy soldiers stood directly over them, staying there for possibly two minutes. (Carter later estimated that it must have been 10 minutes, but that couldn't have been true.) The VC continued to chatter, and as if by this time weary of the play, they neither prodded Carter and the others to test whether they were living, or picked up the radio, or bothered to collect the four weapons lying about.

One of them fired one shot from his AK-47, possibly at a target stirring elsewhere in the clearing. Carter heard the shooting but could not explain it to himself. Shortly after, the VC party took off in another direction.

They were walking toward Hardison's ant hill, and he saw them coming. His problem had meanwhile doubled. From elsewhere in the clearing, Private First Class Ladd had crawled to him, a seemingly dying man not wishing to die alone. Ladd had been shot twice through the neck and three times through the right arm with bullets. He lay there shaking, but otherwise under fair control.

"Here they come straight our way to get us," Hardison said.

Paying not attention, Ladd pleaded with him, "Won't you bandage my arm?"

"You keep down," Hardison advised, "and if you want to live you better shut up."

The enemy party got to within 10 or so meters of them. At that moment two belated 105-mm. shells landed in the clearing and exploded safely some distance beyond the ant hill, behind Hardison, but directly along the line that the VC were taking. With that, the Congs shied off and hustled back to the tree line.

The guns had continued for five minutes after the Americans had ceased action. By now there were several command Hueys and other choppers orbiting overhead. Someone up there became aware of the folly of it, which was not the battery's fault. The guns were ordered to cease.

The wounded third man with Carter (being a new FO, the lieutenant did not know the name of any of the riflemen, and no other living person witness the act) was conscious again and moving. Carter saw him crawl off in the direction that Starr had fallen and let him go, wondering dully what was on his mind. He soon saw and understood. The third man was on his knees, testing Starr's radio to see whether it would work, so that Carter could get going again. It was no go. Starr's radio had been clouted by a mortar round and there was too little of it left even to cannibalize. The third man seemed not to understand that the fight was all over and that nothing remained except to get away, if possible.

Hardison and Ladd understood it well enough. Slowly, painfully, they crawled on hands and knees through the buffalo grass to join Hicks at the trail mouth, looking for the road out. When Ladd faltered, Hardison pulled him along by the good arm.

While they so labored, an air strike came in; a few VC still wandered around the clearing. The strike missed the clearing by at least two hundred meters, the stuff being dropped about that distance leftward or west of the platoon's position, whereas the main VC positions were obviously to the north of it. A little later, after that first pass, one of the machine-gun crewmen near Hicks heaved green smoke out into the center of the clearing. As the green plume started to rise, the few VC in the clearing took to their heels. The show had ended. For the enemy, it was time to break off action. He went with not one Parthian shot following him out.

Well, that is not quite true. General Rogers' Huey had kept flying round and round the wood line. Repeatedly, it had drawn fire from below. But there are always two strong door gunners on a command ship, and this pair continued paying back in good measure.

About the time that Rogers saw the green smoke, he heard over the net: "The 196th [Brigade] is sending over its choppers to lift Charley Company at the blown bridge."

Rogers said, "To hell with that!" He was watching another chopper settle down on the exact spot he had earlier suggested as the place to put down. That had been 20 minutes earlier—possibly a life-sparing interval for Rogers. As it happened, Captain French of the First Aviation Brigade had pre-empted such honor as attends the first man to dare fully. French and crew were already carrying wounded to their Huey.

"If he can do it, why can't we?" Rogers asked.

Again, he was given a stall.

And for Rogers, that was the last straw.

He exploded: "Now, goddamn it, you go down there!"

Nothing came back. Within seconds, they had made ground without incident.

Rogers started to walk. Both door gunners went with him.

The first body Rogers saw was that of a Negro soldier. His head had been blown away. French had already flown off with his first load of wounded.

Hicks wondered to himself why neither of the machine guns had really tried to engage. The one gun near him was still whole; it hadn't fired a single round, after Dickerson had dropped.

The fact was that the early wounding of Sergeant Dickerson on this same ground had stunned and stopped the crew. He had been hit by fire from the rear, a weapon somewhere down the trail. More bullets came from that direction, and before the gun could be turned around, more fire came from the front. Caught between Scylla and Charybdis, the crew wondered whether to fire forward or rearward, and in the end did neither. Had Dickerson stayed whole, the score might have been different.

Dickerson called to Hicks now, gasping the words one at a time, "I'm-drinking-my-own-blood. I-can't-stand-it. You-must-give-me-water."

Hicks stripped Dickerson's jacket off and looked the sergeant over. He'd been shot through the front of the neck.

Hicks had no canteen. Dickerson's own canteen was lying a few feet away. There was a bullet through it, but the jug remained half full. Hicks lifted it to the sergeant's mouth and Dickerson drank on.

Sergeant Dickerson died some hours later in the hospital.

By the time he made it to the shade, Hardison's further work was already cut out for him. He and Hicks (who had greeted him with a "Man, am I glad to see you!") were the only men remaining whole-bodied on this sorely stricken field. They had not yet counted the casualties, but Hardison said to Hicks, "There's nobody out there that didn't get it." Together, the two Negroes set to it, stripping the wrappers from bandage packages before they stepped out to determine who needed help first.

One medic from French's ship had asked to stay behind. He at once joined Hicks and Hardison and directed their work in helping the wounded. There were but a few of them among the windrows of dead.

Rogers had already given instructions. He and the gunners would stay aground, lightening the command ship so that it would carry out more of the graver cases that might still be saved. There were, by count, 18 dead and 10 wounded, six of whom would die later in the hospital or while being evacuated.

Save for Hicks and Hardison, who had only opened bandages, not one move had been made toward clearing casualties or weapons prior to the appearance of the people from the two Hueys. The platoon had been clean spent. To restore it even slightly, to get only a few men moving, there had to be some transfusion of energy, example, and direction from the outside. With troops broken in battle, it is ever so.

Rogers picked up weapons as he walked. So did his jeep driver, Spec. 4 Gerald Todd, the soldier and driver whose medals didn't get pinned that day. Todd walked ahead of Rogers, toting an M-16 at the ready as in bayonet drill. Came a burst of automatic fire. It was a wounded Cong having his last fling, as was terminated by Todd's fire or some other's.

Hardison and Hicks came walking from out the trees to meet Rogers. They saluted, then shook hands. None of the three could remember later what was said at that moment. But it was broken off quickly, when Hardison, that wholly cantankerous soldier, said to Rogers, "I gotta give some more shots to the wounded." Possibly he was embarrassed by the somewhat high rank of the company.

In his walk, Rogers counted 21 still forms, whether those of the dead or living he did not stop to determine. He came at last to Lieutenant Carter, a still-grounded Carter.

Rogers knelt and introduced himself.

His first question was, "How was the artillery?"

Carter said slowly, "It couldn't have been better."

Rogers knew that gunners cannot speak any other language.

"Then what happened?" he asked.

"General," Carter murmured, "there's only one answer: They were waiting just for us."

The door gunners lifted Carter and carried him to the command Huey. He asked that Strong be brought with him and he followed on the next portage. Several other of the gravely wounded were bundled aboard.

"I think you better go along with them," Rogers told Hardison. "You look like you've had a rough time."

The chopper carried them to the hospital at Soui Da, then turned about to continue the shuttle.

Hicks stayed on with the general. It was something that touched his pride. The newest man in the unit, he couldn't give up. So it was that he became the last able-bodied man to leave the battlefield, following Rogers into the chopper when he called it a day. The bodies of three KIA's were left behind, to be recovered when Charley Company at last got up there and swept the area.

The regimental sergeant major had come with the Huey on that last flight to the clearing. On the way out, Rogers said to him, "How many people were there in that platoon, Sergeant Major?"

"Just thirty," said the sergeant major, "counting Hicks and Hardison."

"An appropriate number," said Rogers. Talking ceased.

It was the mark of the scholarly gentleman. As intellectuals, printers, writers, and a few other folk know, "30" means "It is finished."

On the Road to Freedom:
"Paul Revere's Ride"
and "Concord Hymn"

THIS IS SUPPOSED to be a book of stories, right?

Well, sometimes verse is the most effective way to tell a great story.

Henry Wadsworth Longfellow knew that when he composed "Paul Revere's Ride" to immortalize the night of April 18, 1775, when America's earliest patriots spread the rallying cry of freedom, the call to stand and fight. And Ralph Waldo Emerson knew the power of verse when he sat down to write "Concord Hymn" for a service on July 4, 1837, dedicating the Battle of Concord Monument to commemorate the skirmish that became a war—the shots "heard round the world" when they were fired on the day following Paul Revere's Ride.

The sites of all this, in and around Boston, Concord, and Lexington, Massachusetts, have been maintained with the respect and dignity they deserve. If possible, you really ought to stop by.

★   ★   ★   ★   ★

PAUL REVERE'S RIDE

Listen, my children, and you shall hear
Of the midnight ride of Paul Revere,
On the eighteenth of April, in Seventy-five;
Hardly a man is now alive
Who remembers that famous day and year.

He said to his friend, "If the British march
By land or sea from the town tonight,
Hang a lantern aloft in the belfry arch
Of the North Church tower as a signal light,—

One, if by land, and two, if by sea;
And I on the opposite shore will be,
Ready to ride and spread the alarm
Through every Middlesex village and farm,
For the country folk to be up and to arm."

Then he said, "Good night!" and with muffled oar
Silently rowed to the Charlestown shore,
Just as the moon rose over the bay,
Where swinging wide at her moorings lay
The Somerset, British man-of-war;
A phantom ship, with each mast and spar
Across the moon like a prison bar;
And a huge black hulk, that was magnified
By its own reflection in the tide.

Meanwhile, his friend through alley and street
Wanders and watches, with eager ears,
Till in the silence around him he hears
The muster of men at the barrack door,
The sound of arms, and the tramp of feet,
And the measured tread of the grenadiers,
Marching down to their boats on the shore.

Then he climbed the tower of the Old North Church,
By the wooden stairs, with stealthy tread,
To the belfry-chamber overhead,
And startled the pigeons from their perch
On the sombre rafters, that round him made
Masses and moving shapes of shade,—
By the trembling ladder, steep and tall,
To the highest window in the wall,
Where he paused to listen and look down

A moment on the roofs of the town
And the moonlight flowing over all.
Beneath, in the churchyard, lay the dead,
In their night-encampment on the hill,
Wrapped in silence so deep and still

That he could hear, like a sentinel's tread,
The watchful night-wind, as it went
Creeping along from tent to tent,
And seeming to whisper, "All is well!"
A moment only he feels the spell
Of the place and the hour, and the secret dread
Of the lonely belfry and the dead;
For suddenly all his thoughts are bent
On a shadowy something far away,
Where the river widens to meet the bay,—
A line of black that bends and floats
On the rising tide, like a bridge of boats.

Meanwhile, impatient to mount and ride,
Booted and spurred, with a heavy stride
On the opposite shore walked Paul Revere.
Now he patted his horse's side,
Now gazed at the landscape far and near,
Then, impetuous, stamped the earth,
And turned and tightened his saddle girth;
But mostly he watched with eager search
The belfry's tower of the Old North Church,
As it rose above the graves on the hill,
Lonely and spectral and sombre and still.
And low! as he looks, on the belfry height
A glimmer, and then a gleam of light!
He springs to the saddle, the bridle he turns,
But lingers and gazes, till full on his sight
A second lamp in the belfry burns.

A hurry of hoofs in a village street,
A shape in the moonlight, a bulk in the dark,
And beneath, from the pebbles, in passing, a spark
Struck out by a steed flying fearless and fleet;
That was all! And yet, through the gloom and the light,
The fate of a nation was riding that night;
And the spark struck out by that steed, in his flight,
Kindled the land into flame with its heat.
He has left the village and mounted the steep,

And beneath him, tranquil and broad and deep,
Is the Mystic, meeting the ocean tides;
And under the alders that skirt its edge,
Now soft on the sand, now loud on the ledge,
Is heard the tramp of his steed as he rides.

It was twelve by the village clock,
When he crossed the bridge into Medford town.
He heard the crowing of the cock,
And the barking of the farmer's dog,
And he felt the damp of the river fog,
That rises after the sun goes down.

It was one by the village clock,
When he galloped into Lexington
He saw the gilded weathercock
Swim in the moonlight as he passed,
And the meeting-house windows, blank and bare,
Gaze at him with a spectral glare,
As if they already stood aghast
At the bloody work they would look upon.
It was two by the village clock,
When he came to the bridge in Concord town.
He heard the bleating of the flock,
And the twitter of birds among the trees,
And felt the breath of the morning breeze
Blowing over the meadows brown.
And one was safe and asleep in his bed
Who at the bridge would be the first to fall,
Who that day would be Lying dead,
Pierced by a British musket ball.

You know the rest. In books you have read,
How the British Regulars fired and fled,—
How the farmers gave them ball for ball,
From behind each fence and farmyard wall,
Chasing the redcoats down the lane,
Then crossing the fields to emerge again
Under the trees at the turn of the road,

And only pausing to fire and load.
So through the night rode Paul Revere;
And so through the night went his cry of alarm
To every Middlesex village and farm,—
A cry of defiance, and not of fear,
A voice in the darkness, a knock at the door,
And a word that shall echo for evermore!
For, borne on the night-wind of the Past,
Through all our history, to the last,
In the hour of darkness and peril and need,
The people will waken and listen to hear
The hurrying hoof-beats of that steed,
And the midnight message of Paul Revere.

—Henry Wadsworth Longfellow

★   ★   ★   ★   ★

CONCORD HYMN

By the rude bridge that arched the flood,
   Their flag to April's breeze unfurled,
Here once the embattled farmers stood
   And fired the shot heard round the world.

The foe long since in silence slept;
   Alike the conqueror silent sleeps;
And Time the ruined bridge has swept
   Down the dark stream which seaward creeps.

On this green bank, by this soft stream,
   We set to-day a votive stone;
That memory may their deed redeem,
   When, like our sires, our sons are gone.

Spirit, that made those heroes dare
   To die and leave their children free,
Bid Time and Nature gently spare
   The shaft we raise to them and thee.

—Ralph Waldo Emerson

About the Editor

Lamar Underwood is a former editor in chief of *Sports Afield* and *Outdoor Life* and is presently editorial director of the Outdoor Magazine Group of Harris Publications in New York.

Lamar edited *The Bass Almanac,* published by Nick Lyons and Doubleday in 1978, and is the author of the novel *On Dangerous Ground,* published by Doubleday in 1989 and later in paperback by Berkeley. Lamar's novel draws considerably on his experiences as a magazine editor in New York, and his outdoor experiences in Alaska, where he was graduated from Fairbanks High School in 1954, when Alaska was still a territory. Son of a career Army officer stationed in Alaska during the Korean War, Lamar has maintained his affection for the Alaska outdoors, visiting there every chance he gets.

Currently, Lamar and The Lyons Press are busy completing work on *The Greatest Submarine Stories Ever Told,* to be published in the fall of 2005.

Permissions Acknowledgments

Bert Stiles, "The Leipzig Mission" from *Serenade to the Big Bird*. Copyright © 1947 by Elizabeth Neal Huddleston Stiles, renewed © 1973. Reprinted with the permission of W. W. Norton & Company, Inc.

Thomas Wolfe, "Chickamauga" from *The Hills Beyond*. Copyright ©1935, 1936, 1937, 1939, 1941 by Maxwell Perkins as Executor, renewed 1969 by Paul Gitlin, C.T.A., Administrator of the Estate of Thomas Wolfe. Reprinted with the permission of HarperCollins Publishers, Inc.